BRIAN TURNER'S
favourite British recipes

Also by Brian Turner

A Yorkshire Lad: My Life with Recipes

BRIAN TURNER'S
favourite British recipes

CLASSIC DISHES from YORKSHIRE PUDDING to SPOTTED DICK

Photographs by William Shaw

headline

DEDICATION

To my mum and dad, sadly no longer with us,
and to Louis Virot, my first mentor

Photographs © **William Shaw 2003**, except for title page © **Trevor Leighton**

First published in **2003** by **HEADLINE BOOK PUBLISHING**

10 9 8 7 6 5 4 3

Cataloguing in Publication Data is available from the British Library

ISBN 0 7553 1092 6

Edited by **Susan Fleming**
Designed by **designsection**
Art direction by **Lisa Pettibone**
Home economy by **Annabel Ford**
Styling by **Roisin Nield**
Reprographics by **Spectrum Colour**, Ipswich
Printed and bound in France by **Imprimerie Pollina**, L93620

HEADLINE BOOK PUBLISHING
A division of Hodder Headline
338 Euston Road
London NW1 3BH
www.headline.co.uk
www.hodderheadline.com

Contents

Introduction

Although my basic training was in French cooking, and most years of my long career as well, I'm an Englishman born and proud of it. I grew up on classic British – Yorkshire – food. My mother cooked for us at home, mostly long-cooked stews and baked vegetables, and my father ran a transport café nearby. I used to help at the café, along with my brothers and sister, and could say that I was a head chef at the tender age of twelve! I'm still a dab hand at breakfasts, my speciality then. And my first professional job, at the age of eighteen, couldn't have been more British, as it was at that bastion of Englishness, Simpson's in the Strand. There I learned the vagaries of the catering trade, and eventually was allowed to carve the roasts in front of the customers, the ultimate accolade for a mere whippersnapper from the kitchen.

So I am not unfamiliar with British food, and in fact when at home, I tend to cook things which are much more British in feel than French. But of course the history of cooking in this country has been as hybrid as the language: the Vikings influenced us, as did the French after 1066, and then later, when what seemed like all the French chefs decamped to London in the nineteenth century. It would appear that there have always been two strands of British cooking and eating: one for the rich in the cities who could absorb foreign influences (because they could afford it), and one for the poor in the north and west, who made do with what they could grow, pick, kill or poach (and the latter is not in the culinary sense). The differential between these strands is now far smaller than it was, because of modern communications and our burgeoning interest in food – although, sadly, some people will always eat less well than others. However different these traditions are, though, both are characteristically British, and both are reflected in this book, which will demonstrate, I hope, that you don't need to have money to eat well.

It's been a revelation researching the background of English, Scottish, Welsh and Irish cooking. I don't think I had quite appreciated how rich our agricultural heritage was, or how lucky we have always been to have such a wealth of indigenous produce. This ranges from the fish and seafood caught along our long coastlines, to the magnificent animals reared on the rich pastures, and the vegetables and fruit – some native, lots introduced – grown in our fields. Home cooking, in any country in the world, is always produce- and season-led. Although we may have lost sight of this slightly these days, because of the advent of the supermarket culture, there is still an inherent knowledge and awareness of what is best when. Nothing could be more delicious than the first English asparagus or broad bean, or the first Scottish raspberry.

I have tried to celebrate the magnificence of what was and is British food in the recipes following. No-one has ever agreed as to the 'original' recipe for something in particular, and of course basics differ from country to country and from county to county, for British cooking is very regional indeed. (As are French and Italian cooking, but somehow we're much simpler here.) All of the recipes are easy (well, most), and all are based on what could be an original way of doing things, but often with a slightly modern or peculiarly Turner twist. I'm quite proud of them, and have thoroughly enjoyed the months of reading, inventing, testing and tasting.

Lastly, this is not a chef's book, although written by a chef, and may not always be appreciated by my fellow professionals. My work with Beefeater and Tesco has made me turn to ideas that are less 'cheffy' in nature and more domestic. And *Ready Steady Cook* has honed me in the fine art of cooking food that people want to cook as well as eat – something many chefs have lost sight of. (Incidentally, why that programme is criticised so much by the profession, I cannot understand. Its premise is the same as the chefs' most revered annual competition, 'Chef of the Year'.) And most chefs wouldn't dare to admit, as I happily do, that their favourite foods to eat at home are basically very simple. I'm a great fan of Welsh rarebit…

Chunky Tomato Soup (see page 22)

The words 'soups' and 'starters' signify 'first course of the meal' to us now, but the concept of 'courses' as we know them today is actually fairly recent. At one time dishes in a formal meal were served buffet style, all laid out on the table at the same time. (In fact, we've come full circle now, doing it again in Chinese restaurants, in tapas bars and at Greek mezze tables.) The intention was (and is) to visually impress – and at very grand meals, a groaning table would have been a spectacle indeed. However, there were many drawbacks to this '*service à la française*'. Diners would have to concentrate on

Soups

the dishes in front of them only, or assert themselves and ask fellow guests or servants to pass them something they wanted from elsewhere (difficult if they were shy). And often, of course, the food would be cold by the time it was eaten, particularly soups. It was not until the nineteenth century that the Russian pattern of eating, '*service à la russe*', was introduced and adopted. Foods were carved and plated at the sideboard, served to each diner in a set pattern, and our familiar 'course' system was born.

Soup became and still is a classic starter course, and indeed it can often serve as a complete meal in itself, as a lunch with bread, for instance. In the very earliest times in Britain, soup would have been just that, possibly the only meal the less well off would have all day. 'Pottage' was the early soup, a potful of water in which vegetables, pulses or grains and flavourings – and occasionally some meat, if you were lucky – would be boiled all together. Often the liquid and contents would be poured over bread to serve and this 'sop', as it was known, is probably the origin of the word 'soup' (from the French '*souper*', to taste, as is 'pottage', an anglicisation of '*potage*').

The soups here represent a variety of types. The Scotch broth is perhaps the nearest to the original pottage (and the Scottish porridge is a direct descendant of the medieval grain pottage). The others reveal how tastes gradually changed as new ingredients became available (the tomato and Jerusalem artichoke, for instance), and new influences were introduced (those of the immigrant French and, much later, those returning from India). Fish soup-stews are found all over Europe – think of the French bouillabaisse and garbure, for instance, and there are examples in Britain, from the north of Scotland to Wales to the south of Ireland.

Green Pea and Ham Soup

SERVES 8

The traditional English pea soup was made with dried peas, and its greeny-brown colour was so similar to the dense smog that dominated London in the winter (until as late as the 1960s), that the smog became known as a 'pea-souper'. In *Bleak House*, Dickens referred to the fog as the 'London Particular', and the name has been used for both fog and soup ever since.

There are so many versions of pea soup that to say one is the definitive classical recipe is practically impossible. Soup made from tinned peas is my least favourite but, if made from dried, fresh or a mixture, can work well. The following, however, is the one I like best. It will always remind me of the time Bob Holness came on *Ready Steady Cook*, and I made him some pea soup. This allowed the lovable Fern Britton to utter these immortal lines, 'Can I have a "P" please, Bob?'

85g (3 oz) unsalted butter

1 large onion, peeled and finely diced

900g (2 lb) frozen peas

1 small bunch fresh mint, tied together

85g (3 oz) plain flour

300ml (10 fl oz) double cream

salt and freshly ground black pepper

Ham stock

1 ham hock, about 900g (2 lb) in weight

3.4 litres (6 pints) water

2 carrots, trimmed

2 onions, peeled

1 head celery, washed

12 black peppercorns

1 bay leaf

1 To start the stock, soak the hock for 12 hours in enough cold water to cover.

2 Drain off the soaking water, and cover the ham hock with the measured cold water. Bring to the boil and skim off any scum, then add the carrots, onions and celery, all whole. Leave to simmer gently for about 20 minutes, then add the peppercorns and bay leaf. Gently simmer for a further 1½–2 hours until the ham is cooked through. Watch it carefully: you don't want the liquid to reduce too much. Strain off the stock for the soup – you will need 1.7 litres (3 pints). Put the ham to one side and discard the vegetables and flavourings.

3 Melt the butter in a heavy-bottomed pan, add the finely diced onion and half the frozen peas. Add the mint, and put the lid on the pan. Leave to gently stew for 3–5 minutes. At this point add the flour, and stir in carefully, possibly taking the pan off the heat to stop it sticking. Return the pan to the heat, and cook the pea roux for 2 minutes. Do not let it colour.

4 Slowly add the measured hot ham stock to the roux, beating well with a wooden spoon after each addition to get rid of any lumps of flour. When the stock is all added, make sure that the bottom of the pan is clear of everything. Leave to simmer for 20 minutes.

5 Meanwhile, blanch the remaining peas in boiling water for just 2 minutes. Plunge into a bowl of iced water, which will retain the bright green colour.

6 At the same time it is a good idea to take the skin from the ham hock, to take the meat from the bone and to carefully cut the latter into fine dice. Mix this ham with half of the blanched peas and keep to one side.

7 The soup is now cooked so take out the bunch of mint and put the remaining blanched peas (not those with the ham) into the soup. Liquidise the soup, and then I like to push it through a fine sieve or chinois (conical strainer).

8 When all is through, re-boil the soup gently, adding the double cream, and season as necessary. Put the reserved peas and ham into the soup, and serve immediately.

- It's not always easy to buy ham hocks these days, except from good butchers. You could use gammon instead (or bacon rinds tied up in muslin, for flavour). Use some boiled ham with peas in the soup at the end.
- A pea soup is not traditionally served with ham in it, but this addition makes for a much more 'gutsy' dish.
- This soup is often served with toasted bread triangles, but I prefer it with croûtons, i.e. fried bread dice.
- Pea soup is great chilled with perhaps extra cream and chopped mint. The French serve stewed lettuce and baby onions with their pea soup.

Cock-a-Leekie

SERVES 4–6   Cock-a-leekie is as much associated in people's minds with Scotland as haggis is, and why the Scots should use prunes always puzzled me. But in fact the soup made from chicken, leeks and prunes is a variant on a dish that occurs elsewhere in Britain, in Wales and Lancashire particularly. The dish from Lancashire is known as Hindle Wakes, probably deriving from 'Hen de la Wake', referring to the holiday Wakes Week in the cotton areas of the country; this is a boiled chicken stuffed with prunes and coated with a bright yellow lemon sauce. It was thought to have been introduced by weavers coming in from Belgium in the fourteenth century, and the dried fruit is a familiar addition to many medieval dishes throughout Europe.

Whatever its history, it is a good family soup-meal, similar to a pot-au-feu. You can use a tough old boiling fowl if you like, probably traditional, and once a capon would have been ideal. Beef stock was usually used to cook the chicken in; I've added the beef to give just a further Scottish taste dimension.

450g (1 lb) topside of beef

1.2 litres (2 pints) chicken stock

900g (2 lb) leeks

1 sprig each fresh parsley and thyme

1 small chicken, approx. 900g (2 lb) in weight

12 large prunes, soaked if necessary

salt and freshly ground black pepper

1 Put the beef into a large pot and add the chicken stock. Bring to the boil and allow to simmer for 20 minutes. Skim off any scum that comes to the top.

2 Meanwhile, trim and wash the leeks, discarding the coarsest of the dark green leaves. Slice the leeks finely.

3 Add the parsley and thyme to the pot along with half of the sliced leeks, and leave to simmer for an hour.

4 Take the meat out and put into a clean pot. Strain the stock over the meat to remove the leeks and herbs. Put the chicken into the pot and make sure it is covered with stock; if not, top up with water. Simmer until the chicken is nearly cooked, about 40 minutes. Test by piercing one of its thighs with a roasting fork: the juices should run slightly pink.

5 Add the prunes and the rest of the leeks, and simmer for a further 20 minutes. Check for seasoning.

6 Take the beef and chicken out of the liquid. Take the chicken meat from the bone, and remove and discard the skin. Chop the meat into large chunks. Slice the beef thinly.

7 Divide the beef, chicken, leeks, prunes and hot stock between warmed bowls, and serve immediately.

■ Once, making something like this would have been the way of life, putting a slow-cooking stew or soup on in the morning, and getting on with everything else – feeding the chickens, hoeing the vegetables, washing the clothes – in the meanwhile. You could still do that today, if you just have the right attitude – think about it in advance, and with a few glances at the pot every now and again, you can get on with the ironing, or read a book or watch television. In fact it's really therapeutic…

■ Prunes can come pre-soaked, in which case all you need to do is add them to the soup (they will be identified as such on the packet). But traditionally dried prunes will need soaking, in plenty of water to cover at least for a couple of hours, and preferably overnight.

Cullen Skink

SERVES 4 'Cullen skink' means a soup-stew which comes from Cullen, a village on the coast of the Moray Firth in Scotland. It is typical coastal fare – dishes like this are traditional throughout Europe – but the difference lies in the smoked fish used. Scotland was the centre of fish smoking, and the fish once used would have been an Arbroath smokie or a Finnan haddock (from the Aberdeenshire village of Findon).

Nick Nairn, Paul Rankin and myself were being taught to drive off-road in the latest brand-new Range Rover, in a programme for the BBC. Our pay-back was that in front of the cameras we would cook a Scottish-type menu, devised by the aforesaid Mr Nairn. He took us through the method for Cullen Skink, and this is a slightly sophisticated variant of his, and the original, using hard-boiled egg and potato to thicken and to add flavour, colour and goodness.

675g (1½ lb) natural, rather than dyed, smoked haddock

25g (1 oz) unsalted butter

300ml (10 fl oz) fish stock or water

salt and freshly ground white pepper

2 hard-boiled eggs, shelled

115g (4 oz) cooked mashed potato

850ml (1½ pints) milk

300ml (10 fl oz) single cream

1 tbsp chopped fresh chives or parsley

1 Preheat the oven to 180°C/350°F/Gas 4.

2 Make sure all the pin bones are taken out of the fish. Use pliers or tweezers.

3 Butter a suitable ovenproof dish, and lay the cut smoked haddock in it, along with the stock or water. Season, put into the preheated oven, and bake for 10 minutes.

4 Take out of the oven and drain, keeping the liquid. Take the flesh off the skin. Discard the skin.

5 Put half the fish in a bowl with the shelled hard-boiled eggs and the mashed potato. Purée this together using a wooden spoon or a pestle. Mix the milk into this, then the cream and strained fish-cooking stock, stirring all well together.

6 Pour into a pan and bring to the boil. If necessary, strain.

7 Add the rest of the flaked fish and the chives or parsley to the soup, check the seasoning and serve hot.

Oxtail Soup

SERVES 4

People categorise oxtail as offal, but it is actually an appendage rather than an internal organ, and has a concentrated meaty flavour and texture no organ meat has. We think of oxtail soup and stew as being quintessentially English, but some claim that the inspiration was French: Huguenots fleeing persecution in the seventeenth century settled in East London and had to make their daubes and stews from the cheapest meat available (the tails of the cattle used by the East End tanners). The fame of the soup spread thereafter throughout the country.

675g (1½ lb) meaty oxtail

salt and freshly ground black pepper

25g (1 oz) plain flour

55g (2 oz) beef dripping (or lard)

2 medium onions, peeled and finely chopped

1 large carrot, peeled and finely chopped

4 celery stalks, finely chopped

1 tbsp tomato paste

1.7 litres (3 pints) water or stock

25g (1 oz) unsalted butter

1 tbsp chopped fresh parsley

1 Get the butcher to cut the oxtail between the bones and through the cartilage. Dry off the meat, then season and coat lightly in flour.

2 Heat the dripping until quite hot in a large saucepan, then colour all sides of the oxtail in the fat. Add half the onion and all of the carrot and celery to the oxtail, and colour lightly. Stir in the tomato paste and fry gently for a few minutes. Add the water or stock and bring up to the boil. Cover and simmer for up to 3 hours when the meat is ready to drop off the bones.

3 Take the oxtail out and pick off the meat. Trim off the fat, then throw the bones and fat away, keeping the meat separate. Strain off the liquor and put into the fridge overnight. The next day remove the fat that has set on top and throw this away as well. (This may all seem time-consuming and over-laborious, but I assure you it's well worth it.)

4 Melt the butter in a clean saucepan, add the remaining chopped onion, and sweat until softened. Add the diced oxtail meat and then the strained, de-fatted stock. Bring to the boil, and reduce to taste. Check the seasoning, and serve sprinkled with the chopped parsley.

Jerusalem Artichoke Soup

SERVES 4

What I love about this soup is its silky smooth texture and subtle flavour. It is also known as Palestine soup, presumably because of the vegetable used, Jerusalem artichokes. These were introduced to Europe by French explorers of Canada in the sixteenth century, and were known first as the 'potatoes of Canada'. The name 'Jerusalem' actually comes from a corruption of the Italian word '*girasole*', sunflower, as the vegetable plant is a member of the same family (*Helianthus*). The 'artichoke' bit is just as odd: the Jerusalem artichoke is a tuber, but it does have leaf and stalk growth of up to 3 metres high, as does the globe artichoke. Some say, too, that the flavour of the two artichokes is similar, but I cannot see it.

Try and buy large Jerusalem artichokes, as they will be easier to peel (they are very knobbly). If you don't want to be too sophisticated, just wash the tubers and cook them unpeeled, then sieve; the colour will be different, but the flavour will be just as good.

450g (1 lb) Jerusalem artichokes

salt and freshly ground black pepper

juice of 1 lemon

1 small onion, peeled and finely chopped

1 garlic clove, peeled and crushed

55g (2 oz) celery, chopped

55g (2 oz) unsalted butter

115g (4 oz) smoked bacon rinds, or 2 thick rashers smoked bacon

1.2 litres (2 pints) chicken or vegetable stock

300ml (10 fl oz) double cream

2 egg yolks

1 Choose artichokes that are not too knobbly wherever possible. Peel them: I like to use a small knife or potato peeler. Slice finely and, if not using straightaway, keep in cold water with some salt and the lemon juice to stop them from discolouring. Mix the drained sliced artichokes with the onion, garlic and celery.

2 Melt the butter in a saucepan, and add the vegetables and bacon rinds (perhaps tied together with string for ease of removal) or bacon. Sweat carefully over a low heat with a lid on the pan, not allowing anything to colour.

3 Add the stock, bring up to the boil, and simmer until the vegetables are cooked, about 15–20 minutes.

4 Take out the bacon rinds or bacon. Put the mixture through a liquidiser and then pass through a fine chinois or sieve, which makes for a creamy, velvety soup. Put back into a clean pan and add half the double cream. Bring to the boil, and season with salt and pepper.

5 Mix the egg yolks and the remaining double cream in a bowl. Pour some of the hot soup on to this mixture, stirring all the time. Put back into the pan and heat gently, but do not boil. Check the seasoning, and serve immediately.

■ Croûtons and parsley are good garnishes. Another thing I like to do is roast or grill some almonds and then add two-thirds of them along with the vegetables (at stage 2). This adds flavour, then you sprinkle the remainder over the top of the soup when serving to add texture.

■ If you've ever wondered what to do with the rinds you cut off bacon, well, use them for flavour as here. Freeze them each time you cut them off your breakfast rasher, and you will soon have enough to use.

■ In stage 5 I tell you to pour some of the hot soup into the cold cream. Always do it this way round, hot into cold. If cold went into hot, the cold would curdle (i.e. the proteins would set), whereas the hot going into the cold just makes the cold a little warmer…

■ To bring this soup bang up to date, you could froth it up at the last minute with one of those new-fangled hand blenders to make a cappuccino-style first course. We did this in 1975 at the Capital Hotel, so eat your heart out, Gordon Ramsay!

Mulligatawny Soup

I first encountered this soup when I worked at Simpson's in the Strand (my first job, at the tender age of eighteen). It was popular, along with the infamous Brown Windsor soup, with gentlemen of a certain age who had presumably served in India at some time, and learned to love the heat and pepperiness of the cuisine. For the soup and its name are both relics of the Raj, the word 'mulligatawny' coming from two Tamil words meaning 'pepper' and 'water', the nearest thing to soup in India. It was originally a vegetarian sauce apparently, but the British adapted it to include all manner of flavourings and garnishes: the basic pepper water could be served with side bowls of cooked rice, lime wedges, grated coconut, crispy bacon pieces, sliced chillies and hard-boiled eggs.

This version here is a little posher, but lacks the extras!

55g (2 oz) unsalted butter

2 chicken thighs

1 apple, peeled, cored and finely diced

2 small onions, peeled and finely chopped

4 tomatoes, seeded and diced

1 tbsp Madras curry powder

1.2 litres (2 pints) lamb stock

1 tbsp mango chutney, chopped

4 tbsp cooked basmati rice

salt and freshly ground black pepper

1 Melt the butter in a saucepan, add the chicken thighs, allow them to colour lightly, then turn down the heat.

2 Add the diced apple and chopped onion to the pan, then the tomato dice. Do not allow the vegetables to colour. Sprinkle the curry powder over and fry carefully to release its flavour. Do not let it burn.

3 Now add the stock and bring up to the boil, lower the heat and simmer for about 40 minutes.

4 Take the chicken out of the soup, and remove and discard the bones and skin. Cut the meat into dice and put back into the soup along with the chopped mango chutney. Add the rice, warm through briefly, and check for seasoning. Serve hot.

- The soup in Simpson's was passed through a sieve, even the mango chutney, so that all you got in the pepper water was chicken and rice.
- You could make the soup with coconut milk instead of stock – or half and half – and grind your own spices such as cumin and coriander for curry powder, but you must have some heat – preferably chilli powder or a fresh chilli or two.
- Some versions of the recipe use scrag end of lamb instead of the chicken.
- It's often easier to put the rice straight into the cups or bowls, then pour the soup on top.

Scotch Broth

Also known as barley broth, this soup is simple, but very satisfying, its only necessities being some lamb, barley and vegetables. Barley has become very fashionable nowadays, and many rated restaurants serve barley risottos or pilaffs, but it was a staple in Scotland from very early times, as indeed it was throughout much of the northern hemisphere. It has a good flavour and texture, and here it thickens the broth.

Apparently the famous and acerbic English writer, Dr Johnson, was not too fond of Scotland despite the Gaelic origins of his companion, James Boswell, but did actually approve of Scotch broth!

675g (1½ lb) scrag end or shoulder of lamb, cut into large pieces

55g (2 oz) good pearl barley

1.7 litres (3 pints) cold water

1 bouquet garni (parsley, thyme, bay leaf, black peppercorns)

1 medium onion, peeled and finely diced

2 leeks, cleaned and finely diced

2 carrots, trimmed and finely diced

4 celery stalks, finely diced

1 small white turnip, scrubbed and finely diced

85g (3 oz) shredded cabbage

salt and freshly ground black pepper

1 tbsp chopped fresh parsley

1 Trim the lamb of excess fat.

2 Put the barley into a large saucepan and add the water, then the lamb. Bring up to the boil and put in the bouquet garni. Cover with a lid, but use a wooden spoon to make sure the lid doesn't close properly, and simmer for about 1½ hours, taking off the scum regularly. (If you don't use a spoon, it'll boil over and make an awful mess on the top of your stove.) Stir occasionally as well to make sure the barley doesn't stick.

3 Add the onion, leek, carrot, celery and turnip to the pan, and simmer for about 10 minutes. Take out the meat and dice it.

4 Put the meat back into the pan with the shredded cabbage. Cook for 5–10 minutes more. Check the seasoning, add the parsley and serve.

Cream of Mushroom Soup

SERVES 4

Mushroom soups appear in most cuisines, and on the Continent they would probably be made with wild mushrooms. Here in Britain, however, we seem to have always been a little timid about most fungi, apart from cultivated ones. We took to cultivating them quite early, though, in the mid-eighteenth century, following the example of the French. Around Paris, mushrooms were cultivated in disused quarries; in England, stone mines near Bath were utilised. (In fact, the slightly larger button mushrooms on sale today are still called Paris mushrooms in the trade.)

Field mushrooms have the most intense flavour for a soup, but because of the dark gills, the colour is not good. Use button mushrooms instead, and serve with croûtons if you like.

55g (2 oz) unsalted butter

1 medium onion, peeled and finely chopped

1 medium leek, cleaned and finely chopped

450g (1 lb) button mushrooms, wiped and finely sliced

1 bouquet garni (thyme, parsley, in a leek leaf)

850ml (1½ pints) chicken or vegetable stock, or both

salt and freshly ground black pepper

300ml (10 fl oz) double cream

Garnish

25g (1 oz) unsalted butter

115g (4 oz) button mushrooms, finely diced

1 tbsp chopped fresh parsley

1 Melt the butter in a large pan, and sweat the onion and leek – do not colour – for 5 minutes. Add the mushrooms to the pan, and sweat for another 5 minutes, but still do not colour.

2 Add the bouquet garni, stock and some seasoning, bring to the boil and simmer for 30 minutes. Remove any scum that appears during the cooking.

3 Meanwhile, for the garnish, melt the butter, add the mushrooms and sauté gently. Do not colour them. Season, add the parsley and put to one side.

4 Remove the bouquet garni and liquidise the soup. Put into a clean pan, bring back to the boil, then add the double cream and seasoning to taste.

5 Add the mushroom and parsley mixture, and serve.

Chunky Tomato Soup

SERVES 4

Soup is one of the most traditional of dishes on the British culinary scene, and local 'pot' vegetables were used in the beginning, perhaps with a little grain or, when they were lucky, some meat. When tomatoes gradually came to be accepted, some two centuries or so after they had been introduced from the New World, they were pounded to make soups or acid sauces or ketchups (see page 201). Apparently it wasn't until the twentieth century that we were brave enough to eat these scarlet imports raw!

55g (2 oz) unsalted butter

115g (4 oz) each of carrots, peeled onion and celery, finely chopped

2 garlic cloves, peeled and finely chopped

675g (1½ lb) tomatoes, roughly chopped

basil stalks (see right)

a handful of parsley stalks

1 tbsp chopped fresh thyme

a pinch of unrefined caster sugar

salt and freshly ground black pepper

1.2 litres (2 pints) chicken stock

150ml (5 fl oz) single cream

Garnish

10 tomatoes, skinned and seeded (use skins and seeds in the soup, so do this first)

a splash of olive oil

a bunch of fresh basil, chopped (use the stalks in the soup)

1 garlic clove, peeled and chopped

1 Melt the butter in a large pan, and sweat the finely chopped carrot, onion and celery together. Do not colour. After 3 minutes, add the garlic, the skins and seeds of the garnish tomatoes, and the chopped tomatoes, along with the basil stalks, parsley stalks, thyme, sugar and some salt and pepper to taste. Stew gently for about 10 minutes.

2 When almost all of the liquid has disappeared, add the chicken stock, and cook gently for a further 20 minutes. Pass the soup and vegetables through a sieve.

3 Put back into a clean pan and bring back to the boil. Add the cream and check the seasoning.

4 Chop the skinned garnish tomatoes into neat dice. Warm them in the splash of oil with the basil and garlic. Pour into the soup and serve, with a swirl of cream if desired, as in the photograph on page 8.

Chicken Noodle Soup

SERVES 8

We are famous in this country for making broths or stocks. They were the basis of early pottages, and still add savour to soups and sauces today. The French went one step further, clarifying broths to make consommé, and our clear British soups are probably a borrowing from across the Channel. Almost anything can be used to make a consommé – meat, fish, mushrooms or tomatoes – but the most common is chicken. The classic British clear soup is chicken noodle soup, and the addition of the noodles is probably yet another borrowing, from the Jewish tradition – the *lokshen* (vermicelli) added to the chicken soup known colloquially as 'Jewish penicillin'.

450g (1 lb) raw chicken leg meat,
  off the bone
115g (4 oz) each of prepared carrot, leek,
  onion and celery, chopped
4 tomatoes, chopped
4 egg whites
salt

10 black peppercorns
2.4 litres (4 pints) good chicken stock
85g (3 oz) thin noodles or vermicelli
1 tbsp chopped fresh parsley
2 cold poached chicken breasts,
  skinned and finely diced

1 Chop the chicken leg meat up roughly, and mix with the chopped vegetables. Put all through a coarse mincer. Add the tomatoes.

2 Put this mixture into a heavy-bottomed pan, then mix in the egg whites, some salt and the peppercorns. Add 300ml (10 fl oz) of the cold stock, and mix together. Add the rest of the stock and mix well with a large wooden spoon.

3 Put on to a gentle heat and slowly bring up to the boil, stirring regularly. The proteins in the egg white and chicken will set like a 'cake' on the bottom of the pan. As this cake cooks, it will start to rise in one piece, lifting all the sediment in the stock with it to the top. It's at this moment that care must be taken. As the liquid starts to boil, move the pan to the side, half on and half off the heat, and lower the heat. Try to ensure that the crust is broken on one side only, with the liquid gently simmering through this break. You want to keep it ticking over.

4 At this stage, leave the stock to cook for about 2 hours, uncovered. Taste will tell you when this is ready. It should be lipsmackingly savoury.

5 Carefully strain the majority of the liquid through a folded piece of muslin. Strain the last bit separately, as it might contain some debris which could spoil the bulk of the stock. Degrease the resultant stock using kitchen paper.

6 When you want to serve the soup, season the clarified stock and bring it back to a gentle boil. At the same time, cook the noodles or vermicelli in separate boiling salted water until just cooked. Strain and rinse under cold gently running water.

7 Add the noodles or vermicelli to the stock, along with the parsley and diced chicken. Warm through briefly, then serve.

■ The first secret of a good consommé is the strength of the original stock. If you've got a good strong food processor or mincer, you could put the chicken legs, bones and all, through it, and use that as the clarifying agent, along with the egg whites, for a much more intense flavour. (This works well with fish too, but not, obviously, with the red meats.)

■ Some people like long noodles, some like short, but it's really down to you. As it's a soup, short pieces are probably better – simply break the noodles or vermicelli in your hands before cooking them. I do so in separate boiling water to get rid of the starch which might spoil the clarity of the consommé.

Glamorgan Sausages (see page 36)

'White meats' – the collective name for milk, milk products such as cheese, and eggs – were the food of the poor in medieval times. Unable to afford much red meat, the products of the precious family cow and chickens would have provided important protein in the diet. The eggs would have been cooked very simply: 'roasted', 'poached' and served with collops of bacon (the early form of today's bacon and eggs), or mixed into a grain porridge. The rich would have used eggs in much more sophisticated ways – in pies, custards, and puddings both savoury and sweet. Later people ate buttered or

Eggs, Cheese and Savouries

scrambled eggs, or boiled them in their shells. It surprised me to learn how long it was before the 'foaming' and 'raising' qualities of egg whites were recognised – not until about the late seventeenth century. Thereafter, eggs were used much more widely, particularly in sweet puddings and cakes (see Chapters Seven and Eight).

When I was young, after the war, we had a few chickens in the back garden (as did many a family then), and I used to hate going to collect the eggs, as the hens would peck me! However, I enjoyed eating what I collected (and the chickens themselves occasionally).

Centuries ago the cheese eaten by the poor would have been hard, and local, for not until transport and communications improved did different varieties of cheese become familiar elsewhere in the country. Today, of course, cheese is available in all forms and from all over the world. There's actually been a revolution in Britain: once we only had nine hard cheeses, but now small producers are bringing out some wonderful varieties – fresh, soft and hard – available locally or from farmers' markets. It seems so bizarre, when one of our greatest leaders, Winston Churchill, criticised the French by saying we could never trust a nation that would produce a cheese for every day of the year...

Mrs Beeton wrote that cheese 'is only fit for sedentary people, as an after-dinner stimulant, and in very small quantity'. Which is why the category 'savouries' is here, as many are made with cheese. The savoury is, like afternoon tea, uniquely British and seems to have appeared at some time in the nineteenth century.

Baked Eggs

SERVES 4
I've given you two versions of baked eggs here. The first is the equivalent of '*oeufs sur le plat*', but I'm sure we have been preparing eggs like this for far longer than the French… (It's also known as 'shirred' eggs, which suggests 'scrambling' to me.) The second is slightly posher, more like an egg pudding or unrisen soufflé.

Version One

55g (2 oz) unsalted butter   **8 eggs**
salt and freshly ground black pepper

1 Preheat the oven to 200°C/400°F/Gas 6.
2 Melt a quarter of the butter in each of four flat, eared heatproof dishes of 6cm (2½ in) in diameter. Do not let it colour. Season the dish.
3 Break two eggs per person, one each into separate cups, then carefully pour into the seasoned dishes.
4 Heat on the top of the stove, turning the dishes round to get an even heat, and then put into the preheated oven to set to the desired degree, about 3–4 minutes.

Version Two

55g (2 oz) unsalted butter

8 fresh eggs

150ml (5 fl oz) single cream

2 tbsp chopped fresh parsley

salt and freshly ground black pepper

1　Preheat the oven to 200°C/400°F/Gas 6.

2　Melt the butter and put into an ovenproof pie dish, swirling well to coat all sides.

3　Beat the eggs, cream and parsley together, and season with salt and pepper.

4　Pour the eggs into the pie dish and put into a bain-marie of warm water. Bake in the preheated oven until set, about 8–10 minutes. Spoon out and serve.

■ Both make good snacks, and of course you could tart them up as a starter, lining the dishes with cooked mushrooms, tomatoes, spinach or smoked haddock. I first encountered the idea when I worked in Switzerland; baked eggs were served for breakfast, but on top of slices of cooked ham. (In the kitchen, we cooked this for ourselves in a huge frying pan: sliced sausage then sliced ham with twelve eggs broken on top. We'd eat from the pan.)

■ Use bacon fat instead of butter in both recipes for extra flavour.

Cheesed Eggs

SERVES 4

This is very reminiscent of school days to me, when the only thing they could do properly was a cheese sauce (and no-one can go too far wrong with hard-boiled eggs). Something as simple as this would once have tasted particularly good because of the quality of the eggs, but you can come near if you use the best fresh, free-range and organic eggs you can find. A good Montgomery Cheddar cheese would be delicious.

8 fresh eggs
150ml (5 fl oz) cheese sauce, made with
  single cream (see page 138)
25g (1 oz) unsalted butter

salt and freshly ground black pepper
115g (4 oz) Cheddar, grated
2 egg yolks

1 Boil the eggs for 10 minutes then rest them for 30 minutes in cold water, shell and then slice (a machine for this is perfect).

2 Meanwhile, preheat the oven to 200°C/400°F/Gas 6, and make the cheese sauce.

3 Butter an ovenproof dish well and then season it. Arrange the eggs carefully in the bottom of the dish and season again. Sprinkle with 25g (1 oz) of the grated cheese.

4 Beat the egg yolks into the warm cheese sauce, and pour over the eggs. Sprinkle with the rest of the cheese. Season with pepper and bake in the preheated oven for 10 minutes. Brown the cheesy top under a preheated grill, then serve with lots of bread.

- The French have a similar dish to this, called *oeufs à la chimay*. The cooked yolks are pounded with mushroom duxelles, and stuffed into the white, then coated with the cheese (sorry, Mornay) sauce.
- This very grown-up dish is on the children's menu at the Brian Turner Restaurant at the Crowne Plaza NEC Hotel in Birmingham.

Scotch Eggs

MAKES 6 These sausagemeat-wrapped eggs, served for breakfast or as a snack in Scotland, stood alone, I thought, with no obviously similar dishes existing in other cuisines. Some sources have suggested, however, that there is an association with the Indian Moghul 'kofta', which consists of pounded spiced meat wrapped round savoury fillings, sometimes eggs. How the idea came to Scotland, no-one seems to know, but it could be something to do with men returning from service in India during the days of the Raj.

6 hard-boiled eggs (8–10 minutes)

55g (2 oz) plain flour

salt and freshly ground black pepper

350g (12 oz) sausagemeat

115g (4 oz) boiled ham, very finely chopped

2 eggs, beaten

115g (4 oz) fresh white breadcrumbs

vegetable oil for deep-frying

1 Shell the eggs and dry in a clean cloth. Season the flour with salt and pepper. Dip the eggs in this and shake off the excess.

2 Mix the sausagemeat and ham together, and split this mixture into six even parts. Flatten out in your hands to make a meat coating for each egg. Cover each egg with a portion of this mixture, pressing well at the joins to seal.

3 Dip the coated eggs into the seasoned flour again, and shake off the excess. Dip into the beaten egg and finally into the breadcrumbs to coat completely.

4 Re-shape at this stage, and put into the fridge for 10 minutes.

5 Deep-fry in moderately hot fat for about 10 minutes, turning as they cook. Take out, drain well and serve hot or cold.

■ Try making the recipe with hard-boiled quails' eggs. Very fiddly, but great for a canapé.

■ Many recipes use only sausagemeat, but the addition of ham as well is occasionally found. Try Parma ham, an interesting substitute for boiled ham. And of course you could spice things up by adding some chopped fresh herbs or spices, such as chilli or cayenne, to the mixture.

Omelette Arnold Bennett

SERVES 1

Arnold Bennett based his 1930 novel, *Imperial Palace*, on the Savoy Hotel, where he often ate, and his fictional chef, Roho, on Jean-Baptiste Virlogeux, the then *chef de cuisine*. In return, Virlogeux invented this classic marriage of smoked haddock, eggs and cheese. We made it during my time at the Capital Hotel, and when Egon Ronay once accused us of not changing the menu often enough, I quoted a sad but true story. A Norwegian customer had had this omelette twice on the trot, he liked it so much, and when he went home, he asked his wife to recreate the dish for him. The result was so unlike our original that he brought her straight back on a plane to London. However, we'd changed the menu that very day, so to satisfy his – and her – needs we had to change it back again and make the dish for him!

3 eggs

salt and freshly ground black pepper

15g (½ oz) unsalted butter

85g (3 oz) cooked smoked haddock

3 tbsp double cream

40g (1½ oz) Gruyère cheese, grated

1 Break the eggs into a bowl and beat, then season.

2 Melt the butter in your omelette pan, then add the eggs. Stir regularly until the eggs set. Keep lifting the sides up to make sure the eggs don't stick.

3 When the eggs are cooked enough, but still a little wet, add the smoked haddock. Put the pan under the preheated grill to set the rest of the eggs.

4 In the meantime make the creamy cheese sauce. Reduce the double cream until it begins to thicken, and take off the heat. Season and stir in 25g (1 oz) of the cheese.

5 Turn the omelette over on to a plate. Using the back of a spoon, spread the sauce over the top. Sprinkle with the remaining cheese and put under the preheated grill to brown. Serve immediately.

All-day Breakfast Bap

SERVES 8 The English breakfast is famous the world over, with its egg, bacon, sausage, fried tomato, fried mushroom and fried bread – cholesterol on a plate! Done well, though, it is delicious, but I have played around with the basic idea here to come up with something completely different. The egg, bacon, sausage, tomato and mushroom are served together in a bun, rather like a burger, with lots of different seasonings to taste. I've even added some cheese. It tastes wonderful, at any time of the day!

8 bread buns

Filling

450g (1 lb) Cumberland or
  Lincolnshire sausages
salt and freshly ground black pepper
6 slices best-quality back bacon
vegetable oil
8 button mushrooms

25g (1 oz) butter
3 hard-boiled eggs, shelled and
  roughly chopped
5 sun-blush tomatoes, cut into fine strips
a handful of fresh parsley, finely chopped
1 tbsp tomato ketchup, bought or
  home-made (see page 201)
1 tbsp brown sauce
55g (2 oz) Cheddar, grated (optional)

1 Remove the outer skin from the sausages, and put the meat in a bowl. Season with salt and pepper, gently mix together, and place to one side.

2 Discard the rinds, and cut the bacon rashers into lardons. Fry in a hot pan in 1 tbsp of the oil until golden brown. Drain and cool.

3 Remove the stalks from the mushrooms and cut them and the caps into quarters. Gently fry in the butter and another tbsp of oil. Season and cook until just done. Cool.

4 Incorporate all the ingredients into the sausagemeat and mix well together.

5 Shape the mixture into eight equal-sized patties and store in the fridge for half an hour or so before cooking.

6 To cook, heat a couple of tbsp of oil in a frying pan, to a moderate–high temperature. Add the patties, in batches if necessary, and seal both sides. Cook through well, for about 4–6 minutes each side.

7 Meanwhile, warm the buns through in a low oven, and butter them if you like (I don't). Serve a hot breakfast patty in each bun.

Cheese Pudding

SERVES 4

Very few people make things like this now, but once they would have been a major part of the diet – the protein of the cheese and eggs bulked out with bread. The first version here is a classic Welsh dish, but similar puddings were once known to be popular in East Anglia. If the first is like a savoury bread and butter pudding (something my father used to love – he would have had onions with it), the second is like a savoury queen of puddings.

Version One

6 slices stale bread

55g (2 oz) unsalted butter

salt and freshly ground black pepper

225g (8 oz) mature Cheddar, grated

1 tsp French mustard

freshly grated nutmeg and cayenne pepper

300ml (10 fl oz) milk

300ml (10 fl oz) single cream

2 eggs

1 Preheat the oven to 180°C/350°F/Gas 4.

2 Toast the bread on one side only. Use a little of the butter to grease an ovenproof pie dish, then season it. Take the crusts off the bread, and butter the untoasted side of the bread. Cut each slice into three rectangular pieces each.

3 Place a layer of buttered toast, toasted side down, into the greased pie dish. Mix the cheese with the mustard and some salt, nutmeg and cayenne, and sprinkle over the bread. Lay on more toast, buttered side up, and sprinkle with more cheese. Continue until everything has been used up, finishing with a layer of cheese.

4 Warm the milk and cream together. Beat the eggs to a froth, then strain into the milk. Mix well and pour over the bread.

5 Bake in the preheated oven for 30–40 minutes. Serve hot.

Version Two

115g (4 oz) unsalted butter
salt and freshly ground black pepper
300ml (10 fl oz) single cream
150ml (5 fl oz) milk

115g (4 oz) fresh breadcrumbs
1 tsp English mustard
225g (8 oz) mature Cheddar, grated
3 eggs

1 Use some of the butter to grease a pie dish of about 850ml (1½ pint) capacity. Season with black pepper.

2 Bring the cream and milk to the boil, then add 55g (2 oz) of the butter. Season the breadcrumbs and mix with the mustard in a bowl, then pour in the hot cream mixture. Cover and leave to stand for 20 minutes.

3 Meanwhile, preheat the oven to 200°C/400°F/Gas 6.

4 Stir the grated cheese into the breadcrumb mixture. Beat the eggs well until frothy and strain into the mixture. Stir together well.

5 Pour the cheese mixture into the pie dish, and bake in the preheated oven for 20 minutes. Serve immediately.

■ Version Two is best with ordinary bread, but you could ring the changes in the first one by using more exciting examples – an olive oil one such as ciabatta or focaccia, or even some of the flavoured breads like sun-dried tomato…

Glamorgan Sausages

SERVES 4

Made from cheese, leeks or onions and breadcrumbs, this is more a savoury, meat-free rissole than a sausage, and it can be cooked in either shape. It is attributed to South Wales, where of course there has always been a strong cheese-cooking tradition (think of *Welsh Rarebit*, see page 38), but similar mixtures exist elsewhere. As a cheese lover, I like these very much, but especially since Franco Taruschio (then of the Walnut Tree in Abergavenny) cooked some superb examples at Turner's one St David's Day. And he's an Italian!

140g (5 oz) Caerphilly cheese

175g (6 oz) fresh white breadcrumbs

55g (2 oz) young leeks or spring onions, finely chopped

1 tbsp chopped fresh chives

½ tsp dried thyme

a pinch of dry English mustard powder

salt and freshly ground black pepper

2 egg yolks

1 egg, beaten

lard for frying

1 Preheat the oven to 200°C/400°F/Gas 6.

2 Grate the cheese and mix in a bowl with 115g (4 oz) of the breadcrumbs. Add the chopped leek or spring onion, chives, thyme, mustard, salt and pepper and egg yolks, and mix well together.

3 Divide the mix into eight, and roll each piece into a sausage shape. Dip the sausages into the beaten egg, and then coat with the remaining breadcrumbs.

4 Fry the sausages in a little lard, until they become golden brown on the outside. Finish them in the preheated oven for 3–4 minutes.

- If I were going to serve these as a main course, I would accompany them with a rustic, spicy tomato sauce.
- You could also make the mixture into tiny patties and cook to serve as canapés or an *amuse-gueule*.
- As it stands, this is a great dish for vegetarians, but you could cater for meat-eaters too by adding a dice of smoked bacon, ham or cooked sausage to the basic mixture.

Scotch Woodcock

SERVES 4

This classic after-dinner savoury, the most popular in Victorian times apparently, is basically fancy scrambled eggs on toast. I believe it still appears on the menus of many gentlemen's clubs. The only thing I can see to ally the game bird with the savoury is that both are served on toast. The name of the recipe may also be a snide reference to the parsimony of the Scots (Yorkshiremen stripped of their generosity, as an old joke has it), who might serve scrambled eggs instead of woodcock, the most expensive of the game birds.

4 eggs

4 egg yolks

300ml (10 fl oz) single cream

salt and freshly ground black pepper

55g (2 oz) unsalted butter

4 slices sliced bread

12 anchovy fillets

1 tbsp capers, rinsed

4 fresh parsley leaves

1 Beat the eggs, egg yolks and cream together, then season with salt and pepper. Use 25g (1 oz) of the butter to scramble this mixture.

2 Toast the bread, then butter the slices. Use a round cutter to cut out a large circle from each slice of bread.

3 Load the toast circles with the scrambled eggs. Criss-cross with the anchovy fillets and sprinkle with the capers. Garnish with parsley, and serve immediately.

- Many recipes advocate mashing the anchovy with the butter and spreading it on the toast before topping with the scrambled egg. Or you could use some minced ham mixed with mustard and butter. It's the spiciness you want.

- Don't waste the remnants of buttered toast – eat them!

Angels on Horseback

SERVES 4

Who would have thought this favourite Victorian savoury could be successful, but the sea tang of the oyster with the saltiness of the bacon makes for a perfect marriage. Although a good and tasty mouthful at the end of a meal, the angels (and indeed devils) could also be served as a canapé, a starter or a light lunch. (Incidentally, a scallop cooked in the same way is called an 'archangel'.)

12 rashers streaky bacon

12 large oysters, shelled and cleaned

½ lemon

freshly ground black pepper

a little lard or olive oil, if necessary

4 slices thick white or brown bread

25g (1 oz) unsalted butter

4 sprigs fresh parsley or dill

1 Take the rashers of bacon and stretch out using the back of a large knife so that they are thinner and more elongated than before. Lay out on a chopping board.

2 Meanwhile, take the cleaned oysters, squeeze over the lemon juice and sprinkle on some black pepper.

3 Wrap each oyster with a rasher of bacon and then secure three per person on a wooden skewer (which has been soaked in water if they are to be grilled). Grill until the bacon crisps and the oysters are just cooked. An alternative is to fry them in lard or oil until just cooked.

4 Toast the bread, butter the slices, and cut into your preferred shape. Lay an oyster skewer on each piece of toast and garnish with a sprig of parsley or dill. Serve immediately.

Thinning the bacon rashers by stretching them with the back of a knife will ensure they crisp up quickly.

Devils on Horseback

SERVES 4

We have 'angels' and 'devils' because of colour, I presume – the white of the oysters and the black of the prunes. But why 'horseback', I cannot fathom. Whatever the reason for the name, devils on horseback are almost as delicious as angels, the sweetness of the prunes a good contrast with the salty bacon.

12 large prunes

55g (2 oz) unsalted butter

12 rashers streaky bacon

a little lard or olive oil, if necessary

4 slices thick white or brown bread

4 sprigs fresh parsley or dill

1 Stone the prunes, then fry in a frying pan in half the butter. Drain.
2 Stretch the bacon rashers as in the previous recipe, then wrap them round the stoned prunes.
3 Skewer, cook and serve in exactly the same way as the angels on horseback.

Angels (foreground) and devils on horseback can be served as a canapé, a starter, a light lunch or as a tasty end to a meal.

Salad of Scallops with Bacon (see page 64)

For an island nation, we seem to have had a chequered relationship with foods from the sea. From the very earliest days, fish and shellfish had been a hugely important part of the diet of the British: piles of shells have been found in prehistoric sites from the Orkneys to the Channel Islands. By medieval times, fish was as important as bread in the diet, but for a very different reason. The Roman Catholic Church had decreed that three days of each week must be meat free; and during Lent eggs and dairy foods were forbidden as well. This meant that for virtually half the year fish was the only permitted

Fish and Shellfish

3

protein (although barnacle geese, puffins and beavers were, curiously, classified as fish). For most people living away from the coasts, this fish had to be preserved in some way – dried, salted, smoked or pickled – and this would undoubtedly have proved a little monotonous after a while. It is probably because of this need to preserve the huge catches of fish that there are so many smoked, pickled and potted fish dishes in the British canon. It may also explain why fish was for so long liked *less* than meat: eating fish was mandatory, while meat was special, for high days and holidays.

As the power of the Church diminished, fish did not need to be eaten so often. Ironically, though, transportation began to improve and fresh fish could at last be enjoyed more widely. With the arrival of faster ships, then the railways, salmon from Scotland, for instance, could be brought down to London fresh rather than smoked. Fish became cheaper as a result and soon became the food of the poor: it was nutritious and didn't require much cooking (many homes did not have any means of cooking food). Stalls selling shellfish – oysters, whelks, cockles – sprang up all over the country. Eels became a favourite dish to buy in London, and salmon was so common that London apprentices were said to have complained at having to eat it several times a week. Fried fish was sold too, often with a potato accompaniment, and this was the forerunner of our very British fish and chips.

Turning full circle, fish and shellfish have recently been looked on as luxury foods, principally due to their scarcity because of pollution and over-fishing. However, things seem to be looking up again, and Rick Stein has almost single-handedly been responsible for reintroducing us to the joys of fish cooking at home. I urge you to buy, cook and enjoy.

Herrings in Mustard and Oatmeal

SERVES 4

Herrings used to be a major part of the economy of the east coast of Britain, particularly East Anglia, but sadly they have been over-fished and stocks are in decline. Great Yarmouth in Norfolk was the centre for 'red herrings', whole fish that were brined and then cold smoked so they turned from pale to dark red. I went to a herring fair there once, and I cooked the following recipe on the sand dunes!

Herrings in Scotland are often served with a mustard sauce (a reflection of the Scandinavian influence) or are fried in oatmeal (*the* Scottish grain). Here I've combined the two ideas, but I've used Dijon mustard, as I think English is too strong (although, interestingly, English mustard is as Norfolk based as the red herrings above). Herrings are best in the spring, summer and autumn.

4 herrings

25g (1 oz) plain flour

salt and freshly ground black pepper

2 eggs, beaten

1 tbsp Dijon mustard

225g (8 oz) fine oatmeal

4 rashers bacon

1 tbsp vegetable oil or 55g (2 oz) lard

25g (1 oz) unsalted butter

1 Make sure the herrings are scaled. Take off the fins and the head of each, then cut down each side of the backbone and pull the backbone out so that the fish is split to look like a kipper. Remove the guts and clean well.

2 Put the flour, seasoned with salt and pepper, the beaten eggs mixed with the mustard, and the oatmeal in three separate flattish plates.

3 Rinse and pat the double fillets dry, then coat them with flour on both sides. Shake off any excess. Dip in the eggs and finally into the fine oatmeal.

4 Fry the bacon in the oil and butter in a frying pan until crisp, and the fat has rendered. Remove from the pan and keep warm.

5 Fry the herrings in the fat remaining in the pan until crisp and golden brown on each side. Cook very gently or the oatmeal will fall off. Drain and serve with a bacon rasher over each double fillet.

Mackerel with Gooseberries and Potatoes

SERVES 4

The French and the English disagree as to who invented the magical marriage of oily mackerel and tart gooseberry. Some say it came in at the time of the Norman Conquest, others that it was a natural combination of May's fat, fresh fish (particularly in Cornwall) and the ripening fruit. No less an expert than M. Escoffier himself, however, suggests that it is English in his recipe for '*Maquereau à l'anglaise*', poached fish served with a purée of green gooseberries. That's enough proof for me…

4 mackerel

1 tbsp vegetable oil

25g (1 oz) unsalted butter

salt and freshly ground black pepper

Gooseberries and potatoes

25g (1 oz) unsalted butter

55g (2 oz) unrefined caster sugar

25g (1 oz) chopped fresh root ginger

450g (1 lb) gooseberries, trimmed

450g (1 lb) new potatoes, cooked and warm

1 tbsp chopped fresh parsley

1   Melt the butter in a pan, add the sugar and then the ginger and gooseberries. Cover with a lid and cook slowly for 5 minutes. Take the lid off and cook gently until all the liquid has evaporated.

2   Meanwhile, fillet the mackerel, then take out the pin bones from each fillet. Cut on each side of where the pin bones are, down to the skin but not through it. Then with your knife and thumb, get hold of the piece of flesh and pull away in one fell swoop taking the bones away (much easier than pulling out individual pin bones using tweezers). Slash the fillets across the skin side at the head end to help even cooking.

3   Heat the oil and butter in a frying pan. Cook the fillets in this until golden brown, about 3–4 minutes, then take out, drain and season.

4   When the gooseberries are cooked, add the new potatoes, heat through briefly, and check the seasoning. Add the chopped parsley, then arrange on hot serving plates. Criss-cross the mackerel fillets over the top and serve.

Jubilee Salmon

SERVES 4

Salmon has always been caught in Britain, primarily in Scottish waters, and there are references to 'kippered salmon' in documents from as early as the mid-fifteenth century. Sadly, there are fewer fish now in the wild, due to pollution and over-fishing. Farmed fish can never be quite the same, although the quality is generally good. If you do come across a wild salmon in the early summer, all you need do is simply poach it; it doesn't need much else doing to it.

I cooked this dish for the actress Liza Goddard when she came on Anglia TV's programme, *Brian Turner's All-Star Cooking*, during the Queen's Jubilee year. Liza was on tour in a play in which she actually played the Queen, and the salmon and asparagus combination was chosen because the Queen had apparently eaten that to celebrate her Silver Jubilee.

4 x 175g (6 oz) salmon steaks, trimmed and pin-boned

25g (1 oz) unsalted butter

2 shallots, peeled and finely diced

salt and freshly ground black pepper

12 asparagus spears, trimmed

150ml (5 fl oz) white wine

150ml (5 fl oz) fish stock

4 plum tomatoes, seeded and diced

Herb hollandaise

175g (6 oz) clarified butter (see opposite)

3 egg yolks, lightly beaten

1 tbsp white wine vinegar

2 tbsp lightly chopped fresh tarragon

2 tbsp snipped fresh chives

1 Preheat the oven to 180°C/350°F/Gas 4.

2 Lay the steaks skin side down on the work surface, and make an incision through to the skin from back to belly rather than head to tail. Take care not to cut through the skin. Open up the steak so that the skin is folded in on itself in the middle at the back. You should end up with a rough 'heart shape'.

3 Grease an ovenproof baking dish with butter, and sprinkle in the finely diced shallot. Add the salmon steaks, and season. Arrange the asparagus spears around them. Add the wine and fish stock, cover with foil and put into the preheated oven for 10 minutes only, no more.

4 Remove from the oven and take out the salmon. Keep this warm. Take out the asparagus spears and trim off the tips. Chop the remainder of the spears finely, and keep both these dice and the tips warm.

5 Meanwhile, dribble a little clarified butter (from the hollandaise ingredients) into a small pan, add the tomatoes and warm through. Season. At the same time, reduce the salmon cooking liquor by two-thirds in another small pan.

6 To make the hollandaise, over a gentle heat, whisk the egg yolks and vinegar in a round-sided pan to a frothy consistency. Do not overcook. Remove from the heat regularly so that the eggs do not overheat and scramble.

7 Take off the heat and, still whisking continuously, slowly drizzle in the remainder of the clarified butter. (If at any time this starts to curdle, add a tsp of cold water to bring it back.) Add the reduced cooking liquor, some seasoning, the chopped herbs and diced asparagus.

8 Arrange the salmon steaks in the middle of individual warm plates and then spoon over the herb hollandaise. Put a tsp or so of tomato dice on the top, and garnish each steak with three asparagus tips. Serve immediately.

■ To make clarified butter, put a block of butter in a pan and warm very gently over or beside heat until the milk solids sink to the bottom. Very slowly pour off the clarified golden liquid into another container, leaving the milky residue behind. Clarified butter keeps for ages and you can cook at high temperature with it as it now lacks the solids which burn. (Ghee, the fat used in Indian cooking, is a clarified butter.)

Trout with Almonds

I think this recipe is probably a French import, but I remember that 90 per cent of the fish courses I served at banquets during my college days and immediately after – in the early 1960s – were '*truite amandine*' or '*truite grenobloise*' (like *meunière*, with capers and lemon segments). The former we took to our hearts, and indeed a good trout needs nothing more than a quick frying in butter, and then the added texture and flavour of some toasted almonds.

4 x 280g (10 oz) trout, scaled, gutted
  and fins removed
25g (1 oz) plain flour
salt and freshly ground black pepper

115g (4 oz) unsalted butter
115g (4 oz) split almonds
juice of 2 lemons
2 tbsp chopped fresh parsley

1 See that the trout are well cleaned, then wash inside and outside and pat dry.
2 Put the flour on a plate, season it, and then dust each fish on both sides, shaking off the excess.
3 Heat half the butter in a frying pan that is large enough to hold at least two fish at a time. Lay the fish carefully in the pan, and cook to golden brown on one side then turn over, turn the heat down, and cook through for 8–10 minutes.
4 Meanwhile, toast the almonds to a light golden brown in a dry frying pan (watch them), then throw them into the pan with the trout for the last 4 minutes. Take out the trout and place on a hot platter.
5 Add the remaining butter to the cooking pan, and let it colour to a golden brown. Taking the pan off the heat, add the lemon juice and parsley. Bring to the boil, and spoon over the fish to serve.

■ I'm sure you already know this, but the correct etiquette when serving trout is to place it on the plate, belly away from the diner (ladies might be offended). I'm not convinced of this, seeing that the heads, eyes and tails are still there, but this is probably why, although it's harder work, fillets of trout are usually served in top restaurants.

Jellied Eels

Eels, those amazing fish that are born in salt water and travel for some three years back to their fresh home waters in Britain, were once very much more abundant than they are now. They were so prolific, along with mussels and oysters, that they became a popular food with the poor of the East End of London, thus the continuing association of eels with Cockneys! Once street stalls and shops selling pie and mash, eel and mash and jellied eels flourished, but sadly these seem now to be diminishing in number. A shame, because eel is delicious, whether baked, poached, grilled or indeed smoked (the latter one of life's joys).

I went eel fishing once in the Fens when filming the Anglia TV series, *Out to Lunch*. We weren't quite blindfolded, as we were in cars, but our guide took us there and back by the most circuitous route so that we couldn't retrace our steps to where his nets were...

675g (1½ lb) fresh eel

2 bay leaves

4 fresh parsley stalks

1 onion, peeled and chopped

6 black peppercorns

salt

150ml (5 fl oz) white wine

300ml (10 fl oz) white wine vinegar

2 tbsp chopped fresh parsley

(lots of parsley is essential)

1 Get the fishmonger to kill, bleed, gut and skin the eel to order, then cut it into 5cm (2 in) lengths.

2 Preheat the oven to 140°C/275°F/Gas 1.

3 Lay the eel pieces in a flat deep pot vertically, then add the bay leaves, parsley stalks, onion, peppercorns and a pinch of salt. Pour in the wine and vinegar, and top up with water to cover well.

4 Put a lid on the pot and put into the preheated oven for 2–3 hours, depending on the thickness of the fish.

5 When the eel is cooked, carefully remove the stock and herbs. Strain the juices, discarding the herbs, then add the chopped parsley. Spoon this back over the eel, and leave to cool overnight, when the juices will set to the characteristic jelly (from the dissolved eel bones).

Grilled Dover Sole

SERVES 4
There are various types of sole, but Dover is the very best.

Sole were once filleted at the table for you in old-fashioned restaurants, and in my capacity as Chairman of the Academy of Culinary Arts, I have been helping to bring back some of those old skills we seem to have lost. In this I am very grateful for the work done by Silvano Giraldin, restaurant manager of the Gavroche, and Sergio Rebecchi of Chez Nico, who have been passing on their vast knowledge to a new generation of chefs and waiters.

4 x 450g (1 lb) whole Dover sole
55g (2 oz) plain flour
salt and freshly ground black pepper
55g (2 oz) unsalted butter, melted
2 lemons, halved

Parsley butter
115g (4 oz) unsalted butter
juice of ½ lemon
1 tbsp chopped fresh parsley

1 Make the parsley butter first. Mix the butter with the lemon juice and parsley, and some salt and pepper. Roll up in dampened greaseproof paper to a sausage shape and put in the freezer until needed. Preheat the grill.

2 To clean the soles, remove the black skin first. Dip the tail into boiling water then, using the back of a knife, scrape from the tail end towards the body to loosen a piece of the skin. Hold the fish down and grip the skin piece in a cloth. Pull firmly and all will come away. Turn the fish over and carefully remove the scales from the white-skinned side. Remove the head by chopping it off (optional), then cut the side fins away using scissors. Wash and dry well.

3 Season the flour with some salt and pepper, and dip the sole, skinned side only, into it. Shake off the excess flour and place on a grilling sheet, floured side up. Brush with melted butter, and grill on one side for about 5–6 minutes. If necessary, turn over, but test for doneness first. Do this by pushing your finger on to the backbone: if the meat gives sufficiently for you to feel bone, the sole is ready.

4 Take the parsley butter from the freezer and, using a warm knife, cut into thin slices. Lay two slices on each sole and allow to melt naturally. Serve with half a lemon and new potatoes.

- You probably don't need to know this, but lemon soles, although fine fish, are not true soles – because they are 'left-handed'. True soles like Dovers are dextral or right-handed, because they have both eyes on the right-hand side of their heads. Now you know.
- In restaurants sole are grilled on salamanders, a bottom heat like a barbecue, rather than a top heat. This marks the fish with grid marks, and if you would like to recreate this at home, heat a metal skewer over a flame. Mark the fish before you cook, to scorch the flour.
- You can concoct different savoury butters to accompany grilled fish. Use anchovies, oysters, garlic or tarragon, for instance.

Fish and Shellfish   **53**

Whitebait

SERVES 4

Whitebait, the fry of herrings and sprats, are said to be so called because they are 'white' and were used as bait to catch larger fish. They once shoaled so prolifically on the coasts and estuaries of Essex and Kent that fisheries grew up around them. They were caught in the Thames as well, and wealthy Londoners used to travel downriver for whitebait dinners at Greenwich. Whitebait used to be a big seller at Simpson's in the Strand, and I think they make a very tasty mid-table nibble for people to share.

The whitebait fishery in Britain is discouraged now because of the effect on mature fish stocks, but frozen fish are brought in from abroad. Let the fish defrost and drain well in a colander before cooking.

450g (1 lb) whitebait

150ml (5 fl oz) milk

85g (3 oz) plain flour

1 tsp cayenne pepper

salt

vegetable oil for deep-frying

1 lemon, quartered

1 Simply put the whitebait into the milk and stir round. Handling carefully, drop them into the flour mixed with the cayenne pepper and salt to taste. Shake off any excess.

2 Heat the oil to 190°C/375°F. Drop the tiny fish into the oil in the fryer, not too many at a time. Fry until golden brown, then strain and drain on kitchen paper.

3 Sprinkle with salt and lemon juice, and serve immediately.

- Don't overcook them: it's very easy to let them frazzle. And don't even *think* of coating them in breadcrumbs: the flour will give you the right texture.
- If you don't like the 'devilled' flavour here, simply leave out the cayenne pepper.

Yorkshire Fishcakes

SERVES 4

There are two different types of fishcake in Yorkshire. One is the traditional one with mashed potato, fish and parsley, which is breadcrumbed or battered then fried. This is known as a 'parsley cake'. What I call a real Yorkshire fishcake is two slices of potato with a piece of fish in the middle. Whenever I travel to Yorkshire by car to work, I call in at Norman's Mermaid fish and chip shop in Morley, my home town, to get a piece of fish, a fishcake or two and a bag of chips.

When I was asked by Tetley to present a high tea at a catering competition, we cooked these fishcakes, followed by custard tarts. All the other chefs there were laughing at our simple menu, but the queue outside our back door for a sample was the largest – and Tetley won as well!

16 x 3mm (⅛ in) potato slices	*Salt and vinegar batter*
450g (1 lb) fish fillet (cod or haddock)	**175g (6 oz) plain flour**
plain flour for dusting	**2 tbsp salt**
vegetable oil for deep-frying	**125ml (4 fl oz) water**
** (lard or dripping in the north)**	**150ml (5 fl oz) malt vinegar**

1 To make the batter, put the flour and salt in a bowl, and make a well in the centre. Add the water and vinegar and whisk until smooth. Leave to rest.

2 Using a 6cm (2½ in) ring, cut the potato slices into even sizes. Cut the fish into thin 55g (2 oz) pieces of a similar size. Dust lightly with flour.

3 Sandwich the pieces of fish between two pieces of potato. Dip the cakes into flour and shake off the excess, then dip into the batter to cover well.

4 Heat the oil in a flat-bottomed pan to about 190°C/375°F. Carefully drop a fishcake into the hot fat and let it settle to the bottom. Add another couple of fishcakes if there is room. They will rise to the top when hot enough, about 5 minutes. Turn over, then cook for another 5 minutes until brown.

5 Take out and drain well on kitchen paper. They're better left for 5 minutes as they are too hot to eat straightaway, and they do need to drain very well. Serve hot with *Tomato Ketchup* and some *Pease Pudding* if you like (see pages 201 and 136), although I prefer just salt and vinegar.

Fish Pie

In medieval times, mixtures of fish would have been topped with pastry, both to seal in the flavour, and to serve as a carbohydrate accompaniment. Although pastry can of course still be used, we now commonly use the words 'fish pie' to mean fish topped with mashed potato. Comfort food par excellence, but you'll find a few variations here…

225g (8 oz) each of fillets of haddock, white fish, smoked haddock and salmon, skinned
55g (2 oz) unsalted butter
salt and freshly ground black pepper
24 small button onions, peeled
16 small button mushrooms, halved
juice of 1 lemon
75ml (2½ fl oz) dry sherry

Sauce
40g (1½ oz) unsalted butter
40g (1½ oz) plain flour
300ml (10 fl oz) milk
300ml (10 fl oz) double cream
3 tbsp finely chopped spring onion
1 tbsp chopped fresh parsley
a dash of Tabasco sauce

Topping
675g (1½ lb) potatoes
55g (2 oz) unsalted butter
1 tbsp vegetable oil
55g (2 oz) clarified butter (see page 49)

To skin fish fillets: use a sharp knife to make a nick between flesh and skin at the tail end. Either persuade skin from flesh with the blade, or simply pull once you can get proper purchase!

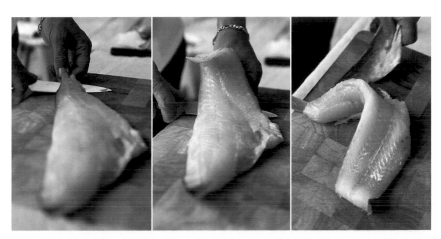

1 Cut the fish into evenly sized 2.5cm (1 in) pieces or cubes.

2 Use the butter to grease a large pie dish, and season it with salt and pepper. Preheat the oven to 200°C/400°F/Gas 6.

3 Put the button onions and mushrooms in a saucepan with 150ml (5 fl oz) water. Add the lemon juice, sherry and some salt and pepper. Cover with greaseproof paper, and leave the vegetables over a gentle heat, covered with the lid, so that they steam and cook, about 15 minutes. Strain off the liquid and cool both liquid and vegetables.

4 To make the sauce, melt the butter in a medium pan, add the flour and stir together to make a blond roux. In another pan, bring the milk, cream and the vegetable cooking liquor to the boil together. Slowly add the hot liquid to the roux, stirring, to make a white sauce. Leave to cook for 5 minutes, then add the spring onion, parsley, Tabasco and some salt and pepper if necessary. Put to one side, and cover with clingfilm to prevent a skin forming.

5 Mix the fish with the onions and mushrooms, then pile into the pie dish and season with salt and pepper.

6 For the topping, peel, wash and dry the potatoes and cut into thin slices. Pan-fry the potatoes in the butter and oil to colour nicely. Drain.

7 Pour the sauce over the fish and tap the pie dish to let the air escape. Carefully place the coloured potatoes over the fish in two layers to make a crust, the top layer being nicely presented. It should look like a hotpot topping.

8 Bake in the preheated oven for 25–30 minutes, brushing with the melted clarified butter every now and again during cooking. Serve hot, straight from the oven.

■ Or follow all the stages of the recipe, but simply cover the fish and its sauce with mashed potato. It needn't be plain mash: horseradish mash, mustard mash or even bubble and squeak mash would look and taste good.

Mussels with Cider

SERVES 8

We think of mussels as being French (*moules marinières*) or Belgian (*moules et frites*), but of course mussels are found all around the coastlines of Britain, and have been eaten here for centuries. Musselburgh in Scotland was actually named for the famous nearby mussel beds, and there are several soup-stews in traditional Scottish cooking. (Mussels are now farmed in Scotland and Ireland, on ropes.) Mussels feature in Welsh and Irish cooking as well – think of Molly Malone plying her live 'cockles and mussels' through the Dublin streets.

Instead of the French wine, I have used our English cider here, along with apples, and the flavours are good.

2.25 litres (4 pints) mussels

2 shallots, peeled and chopped

2 apples, cored and finely diced

300ml (10 fl oz) dry cider

2 tbsp chopped fresh parsley

150ml (5 fl oz) double cream

juice of ½ lemon

25g (1 oz) unsalted butter

salt and freshly ground black pepper

1 Clean the mussels well, removing the beards, and discard any that are cracked, or remain open after you tap them sharply against the edge of the sink. Put into a large heavy-bottomed pan.

2 Add the chopped shallot, the apple dice, cider and half the chopped parsley. Cover with a lid. Cook over a fierce heat until all the mussels have opened, about 6–7 minutes.

3 Lift the mussels out, using a spider sieve, into a colander over a bowl. Strain the cooking liquor into a clean bowl and allow to stand for 5 minutes to allow any sand to sink to the bottom. Discard the vegetables.

4 Carefully strain the liquor into a clean pan, taking care not to disturb any sand at the bottom. Add any liquor from below the mussels as well.

5 Add the cream and lemon juice to the liquor, and boil to reduce by half. Add the butter and remaining parsley, and check the seasoning.

6 Meanwhile, discard any mussels that remain closed. (If in doubt, throw 'em out, they're really quite cheap.) Divide them between eight soup plates, pour the sauce over and serve immediately.

Dressed Crab

SERVES 4

I love crab, and still remember the crab paste we used to have in Yorkshire as kids (once a speciality of Scarborough, I believe). I've been fortunate enough to have worked in three British crab areas. In Cromer, Norfolk, where the crabs are very small but sweet, I met Richard David who catches them at sea and sells them on the High Street. I've also cooked and tasted crab in Whitby, further north, where they are bigger – and indeed they seem to get bigger the further north you go, particularly in Scotland. However, perhaps to gainsay that, I've caught and eaten crab in Guernsey (where they're called 'shankers'), and there they are quite massive.

Most crabs are dressed in their shells, but I think there is complication enough already in getting all the meat out without worrying about keeping the shells whole. I just serve the white and dark meat separately in bowls, and use the shells for quite a different purpose (see opposite).

1 x 1.8kg (4 lb) live male crab

4.5 litres (7½ pints) water

175g (6 oz) salt

To dress the crab

juice of 1 lemon

Tabasco sauce to taste

Worcestershire sauce to taste

55g (2 oz) fresh white breadcrumbs

salt and freshly ground black pepper

4 hard-boiled eggs, shelled

2 tbsp chopped fresh parsley

1 small onion, peeled and finely chopped

1 Bring the salted water up to the boil, plunge in the crab, bring back to the boil and simmer for 25 minutes. Then take off the heat and allow the crab to cool in the liquor. Take out, drain, and put into the fridge. Alternatively, you can buy a fresh cooked crab from a reputable fishmonger.

2 Twist off the legs and claws, and break each joint so that it is easier to remove the meat. Using a small hammer to tap and crack open the pieces, and a skewer, push all the pieces of white meat out into a bowl. The claws

contain the nicest, sweetest and moistest meat, but this needs careful checking for any bones.

3 Next take the body in one hand, then, using a kitchen knife, insert and twist to remove the central case of the body that held the legs and claws. Pull this free then remove the ring of 'dead men's fingers' and throw away. This will reveal the brown crabmeat. Using a spoon remove this from the shell and put into another bowl.

4 Break the brown meat up, adding the lemon juice, Tabasco and Worcestershire sauces to taste, and enough breadcrumbs to form a paste which is not too soft. Season to taste with salt and pepper.

5 Pass the boiled eggs through a sieve, add the parsley and onion, and mix well together.

6 Put the brown meat into a shallow bowl with the egg mixture scattered around the edge to decorate.

7 Serve the white meat in a separate bowl, perhaps with a lemon mayonnaise, brown bread and butter, and even a tomato salad for perfection.

■ You may think I have forgotten to season the white meat. But I don't think it needs it. Try it and see.

■ Don't waste your time keeping the shells for presentation. Break them up with the claws, using a hammer, and put them in a pot with fish stock, garlic, tomatoes and other vegetable flavourings to make a strong stock. Take the shells out and put some rice in. Pound the shells, and return to the pan until the rice is cooked. Press everything through a fine sieve, squeezing to get as much flavour out as possible. Add double cream and brandy to taste, and you will have a wonderful crab soup.

Lobster with Dill, Tomato and Mustard

SERVES 4 Lobsters have always been highly rated and highly priced, and those of Scotland are said to be the best in Britain, growing sweet in the cold waters of the north. But I have eaten lobsters much further south, in the Channel Islands, and in Alderney, so legend has it, the lobster population flourished and grew fat on the bodies of slave labourers thrown into the sea around the island during the German occupation in the 1940s...

This recipe is similar to a Scottish one, and to many that became popular in Victorian times in gentlemen's clubs. It's my 'almost Thermidor'. A lobster per person is a large main course, but I think if you're pampering yourself, you don't want half measures. However, as a first course, two lobsters between four would be sufficient.

4 x 450g (1 lb) live lobsters
  (approx. weight)
55g (2 oz) unsalted butter
1 shallot, peeled and chopped
150ml (5 fl oz) fish stock
150ml (5 fl oz) white wine
300ml (10 fl oz) double cream

4 tbsp crème fraîche
1 tbsp Dijon mustard
salt and freshly ground black pepper
2 tbsp chopped fresh dill
4 tomatoes, finely diced
2 egg yolks
55g (2 oz) Parmesan, freshly grated

1 Cook the lobsters by plunging in boiling water and boiling for 4 minutes, then take out and leave to cool.

2 Split the carcass in half lengthways. Take out the body meat carefully and put to one side. Break off the claws, and separate into the three different joints, removing the cartilage from the middle of the pincer. Gently tap the joints with the back of a large knife and take out the meat. Keep separate. Discard the intestinal tract from the body then cut the body meat into nice-sized pieces.

3 Preheat the oven to 160°C/325°F/Gas 3. Wash and clean four of the half shells, and put them in the oven to warm through.

4 Meanwhile, melt half the butter in a pan, and sweat off the shallot, not allowing it to colour. Add the fish stock and white wine and reduce by two-thirds. Add the double cream, boil and reduce by half until thickened. Remove from the heat, add the crème fraîche and mustard, mix in and season.

5 Heat the sauce gently then add the lobster meat except for the claws. Heat through gently but well. Dab the claw meat with the remaining butter and heat for a few minutes in the low oven.

6 Add the chopped dill and tomato dice to the sauce, then beat in the egg yolks. Pour this mixture evenly into the four warm half lobster shells.

7 Lay the meat from a claw on top of each mounded half lobster, sprinkle with the Parmesan, colour under the preheated grill and serve.

- If there are eggs in the tail of a female, or a greenish sac in the head (the tomalley), make sure you use these in the sauce.
- Break up the spare half shells, put into a small but tall saucepan, and add some unsalted butter. Leave to stew slowly on the side of the stove. The butter will turn red and taste incredibly of lobster. Strain. You can chill this flavoured butter, or freeze it, to use in sauces.

Salad of Scallops with Bacon

SERVES 4

The combination of scallops and bacon crops up in Scottish, English and Manx cooking, one of those wonderful anomalies of flavour balance, which is similar to oysters and bacon (see page 42) and the Welsh trout cooked with bacon. I've taken it a little into the present time by presenting it in a salad.

Scallops are one of our most delicious shellfish, native to the cold waters of western Scotland and around the Isle of Man (where there has apparently been a scallop fishery for some 3,000 years). Giant or king scallops are the largest, the queens or queenies being much smaller (and, if used instead, you will need six to seven – or even more – instead of three per person).

12 large scallops in the shell

5 tbsp olive oil

salt and freshly ground black pepper

6 rashers smoked back bacon

6 spring onions, chopped

1 tbsp grain mustard

2 tbsp white wine vinegar

2 tbsp groundnut oil

1 tbsp each of chopped fresh parsley,
   chives and chervil

To serve

mixed salad leaves (more or less, depending
   on whether for a starter or main course)

1 Trim the scallops, using the white muscle meat only for this dish.

2 Heat 1 tbsp of the olive oil in a solid flat-bottomed frying pan, and sear the

Cut into the side of the shell using a sharp knife. Twist the blade to prise the shell open. Detach the large white muscle from the shell. Take off the skirt (the frill round the muscle), and discard the little black sac.

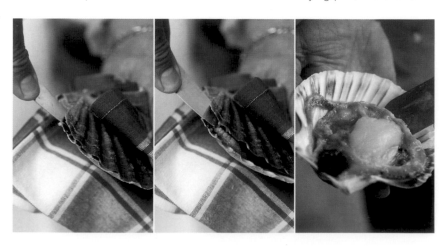

scallops until golden brown, a minute or two only. Turn over just to sear, season and then take out and keep warm.

3   Meanwhile, trim the bacon and cut into thin strips. Sauté and colour these in the frying pan that the scallops were cooked in. Add the chopped spring onion, and sauté until coloured, and then put both bacon and onion into a large bowl.

4   Mix the mustard and vinegar well in a bowl or jar, then add the remaining olive oil, the groundnut oil, herbs and some seasoning. Take some of the dressing and toss with the salad leaves then lay these in the middle of four plates.

5   Add the remaining dressing to the bacon and onion. Balance the three scallops per person on each mound of salad leaves, and then spoon the bacon, onion and dressing over and around.

Potted Shrimps

SERVES 4

Shrimp teas were traditional in the north of England, and potted shrimps became a popular feature of afternoon tea in the late eighteenth century. The shrimp industry in Britain centres on the dangerous shifting sands and shallow waters of Morecambe Bay in Lancashire, where tractors now carry the nets instead of horses. Brown cold-water shrimps, found along many coasts in northern Europe, are very small (which makes them difficult to shell), but taste wonderful. The shelled shrimps widely available now come mostly from Holland, and I urge you to buy those you can shell yourself. The shells will make a fantastic stock. Or, if you can't be bothered with shelling, simply blend the fish, shells and all, to make a great paste for spreading on toast.

Fish or meat has been preserved in butter like this since at least the sixteenth century.

140g (5 oz) clarified butter (see page 49)
350g (12 oz) peeled cooked brown shrimps
a pinch of ground mace

1 tsp anchovy essence
a pinch of cayenne pepper
lemon juice (optional)

1 Preheat the oven to 150°C/300°F/Gas 2.
2 Melt the clarified butter, then take out just less than half and put to one side. Add the brown shrimps to the bulk of the butter in the pan, and season with the mace, anchovy essence and cayenne pepper. You must taste at this stage and if you are unhappy with the balance, add the lemon juice.
3 Now lift the shrimps out using a slotted spoon, and divide between four ramekins or nice oven-to-table dishes.
4 Pour the seasoned butter equally over the shrimps and put the ramekins into a bain-marie (a roasting tray) with warm water. Put this into the preheated oven and cook for 30 minutes. Remove the ramekins from the oven and the tray, and tap the ramekins gently on a carefully folded cloth to get rid of any air bubbles in the mix.
5 Melt the remaining clarified butter and pour gently over the top of the mixture, then leave to cool and set.

Kedgeree

SERVES 4

Although thought of as a quintessentially English dish, kedgeree originated in India during the days of the Raj (as did *Mulligatawny Soup*, see page 18). The original '*khichri*' was a vegetarian combination of rice and lentils. It was thought to be the British Army in India who adapted it to be a rice-only breakfast dish, and who added bits of dried or salted fish. Smoked haddock is the most common fish used now (salmon too), and it's on the menu as such at our Foxtrot Oscar restaurants, very popular with old colonials and old public schoolboys – and, much to my surprise, we sell a lot to young people as well.

550g (1¼ lb) smoked haddock fillet

600ml (1 pint) fish stock

1 bay leaf

juice of 1 lemon

salt and freshly ground black pepper

25g (1 oz) unsalted butter

1 onion, peeled and finely chopped

225g (8 oz) long-grain rice

1 tsp curry powder

a pinch of cayenne pepper

a pinch of freshly grated nutmeg

a pinch of saffron strands (optional)

4 hard-boiled eggs, shelled

1 tbsp chopped fresh coriander

1 Preheat the oven to 180°C/350°F/Gas 4.

2 Make sure the haddock fillet is skinned and boned totally. Put into a large ovenproof dish. Bring the fish stock to the boil, and pour over the fish. Add the bay leaf and lemon juice, and season well. Cook covered in the preheated oven for 5 minutes until just cooked. Strain off the stock.

3 Meanwhile, melt the butter in a saucepan, add the onion and sweat without colouring for a few minutes until soft. Add the rice and stir, then cook until the rice is completely coated with butter. Add the spices.

4 Pour in the strained fish stock topped up with enough water to make twice the volume of the rice. Cover with buttered greaseproof paper and cook in the preheated oven as above for 18 minutes.

5 Take out of the oven, leave to sit for 2 minutes, and then stir with a fork.

6 Cut the eggs into big chunks, add half to the rice and stir in. Check the seasoning of the rice, then pour into a warmed serving bowl. Flake the smoked haddock over the top, sprinkle with the rest of the eggs and coriander, and serve.

Prawn Cocktail

SERVES 4

No-one seems to be quite sure where and when the infamous prawn cocktail originated, but it appeared on restaurant menus in Britain throughout the 1960s, and can still be found today. It may be an American idea. A combination of shredded lettuce, prawns and, usually, a bottled mayo-based sauce, it has been much maligned, but in actual fact when made correctly, can be wonderful. Marco Pierre White even included it on his Mirabelle menu!

350g (12 oz) shelled prawns

1 little gem lettuce

1 tbsp Dijon mustard

1 tbsp white wine vinegar

4 tbsp olive oil

salt and freshly ground black pepper

2 tbsp finely chopped cucumber

Sauce

6 tbsp mayonnaise

2 tbsp *Tomato Ketchup* (see page 201)

1 tbsp double cream

1 tsp each of brandy and
   creamed horseradish

juice of ½ lemon

4 drops Tabasco sauce

To garnish

2 tomatoes, seeded and finely diced

1 shallot, peeled and finely chopped

1 tbsp chopped fresh chives

1 Put the prawns into a bowl. Finely shred the lettuce.

2 Make a vinaigrette with the mustard, vinegar and oil. Season with salt and pepper.

3 Make the sauce by mixing the mayonnaise with the ketchup and cream, then stir in the brandy, horseradish, lemon juice and Tabasco. Check the seasoning.

4 Mix the prawns with 1 tbsp of the sauce and 1 tbsp of the vinaigrette.

5 Mix the shredded lettuce with the cucumber, add the remaining vinaigrette and season.

6 Put the lettuce into four glasses, with the prawns on top. Cover lightly with the rest of the sauce.

7 Mix the tomatoes, shallot and chives, sprinkle over the sauce and serve.

Roast Loin of Pork with Crackling (see page 97)

In the very earliest of times, meat and offal would have been cooked beside or on the fire. Once metal cooking pots were invented, meat could be boiled or stewed in water. Most meat eaten was actually 'game' – even cattle, pigs, sheep and goats were animals of the wild until they were domesticated. Cows, sheep and goats could be milked, so had a dual purpose, while pigs, because they could forage for themselves and be fed on scraps, were perhaps most commonly attached to households large and small.

It was not until the seventeenth century that crops were introduced specifically to

Meat and Offal 4

feed animals during winter. Before then animals would have been slaughtered during the autumn. The offal would have been cooked then and there, or preserved by salting, drying or smoking. Nowadays we seem only to use the superior 'organ' meats, such as liver, kidneys and sweetbreads, disliking the lesser offal as 'poverty food' perhaps.

The meat of the slaughtered beasts would have been preserved too, by salting principally, but 'corning' was popular in Ireland. Fresh meat was eaten of course, but until the problem of over-wintering was solved it would have been largely seasonal. The tender cuts would have spit-roasted beside the fire (our current 'roasting' in an enclosed space is actually baking), and tougher cuts would have been boiled, often in a pottage, or wrapped in a cloth or a suet casing as a pudding. Once ovens developed, other meat-cooking techniques could evolve, such as braising and baking in or under pastry. Britain was once famous for its meat pies, and we have quite a few still – steak and kidney, veal and ham, the Scottish mutton pie, and Cornish pasties.

Why Britain became so renowned for its roast meats is not easily explained. But, despite increasing French culinary influences throughout the centuries, the love of roast meats, plainly served and sauced, did not diminish. Some say it was because the quality of the meat was so good. In France, animals were worked until old, then slaughtered; the flesh would be tougher and riper, so needed fancy flavourings and longer, more complicated cooking to render it palatable. In Britain, animals were reared specifically for the table, so therefore could be roasted much more successfully.

Why the British still love meat so much is just as unclear, but 'meat and two veg' is almost mandatory, at least for Sunday lunch.

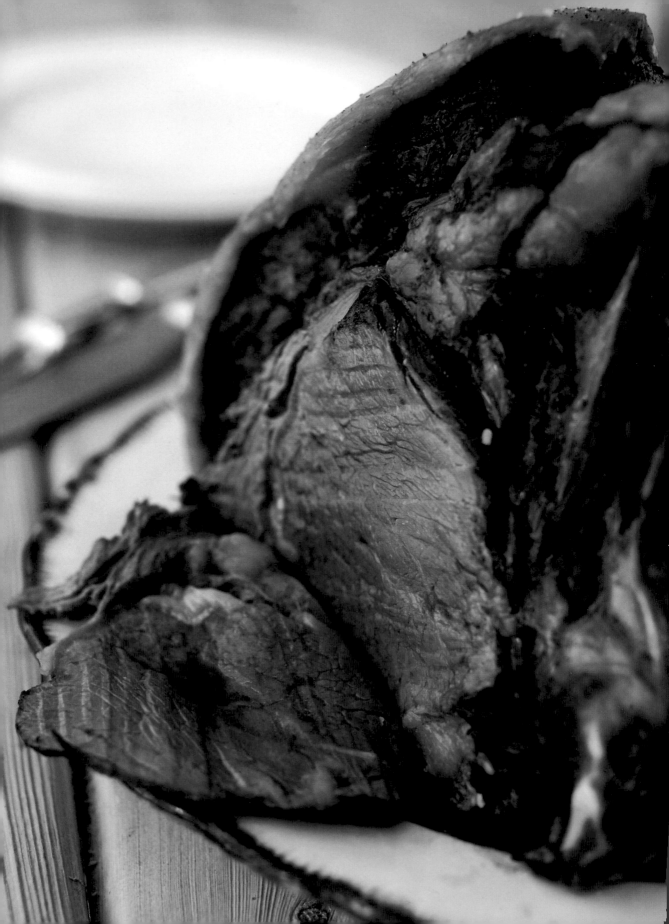

Roast Beef and Yorkshire Pudding

SERVES 8–10 Whatever the reason for the undeniable quality of our beef, Britain wouldn't be so great without its roast beef and Yorkshire pudding. I remember we cooked 25-pound sirloins on the bone at Simpson's in the Strand, and then we took them into the dining room to be carved in front of the guests.

Batter puddings are traditional all over the British Isles, and Yorkshire pudding is the most famous, originally cooked in the tray of dripping under the meat as it turned on the spit. Why it became so associated with Yorkshire, I don't know. Perhaps it was because of the renowned meanness of my fellow countrymen: the pudding was served first, before the meat, in order to fill people up so that they would then eat less meat! To me its main purpose is to soak up the meat juices and the gravy.

1 x 4.5kg (10 lb) rib of beef (5 ribs)
salt and freshly ground black pepper

Yorkshire pudding
1 large cup plain flour
a pinch of salt
1 large cup eggs
1 large cup milk and water mixed
1 tbsp malt vinegar

1 For the Yorkshire pudding batter, sift the flour and salt into a large bowl. Add the eggs and beat well with half the liquid until all the lumps have disappeared. Add the rest of the liquid and the vinegar, and allow to stand.

2 Meanwhile, preheat the oven to 220°C/425°F/Gas 7.

3 Prepare the meat by cutting down the backbone towards the rib bones with the knife angled towards the backbone. Take a chopper and then break the backbones near the bottom of the cut (this is called chining). Lift up the fat from the back and take out the rubbery sinew. Tie the beef with string.

4 Put the joint into a roasting tray and season well. Roast in the preheated oven for 30 minutes and then reduce the heat to 190°C/375°F/Gas 5 for a further 1½ hours. This will give you blood-red beef in the middle. The way to check this is by using a meat thermometer to test to 55°C/130°F or, as I prefer, by plunging a metal skewer through the middle of the beef, holding it

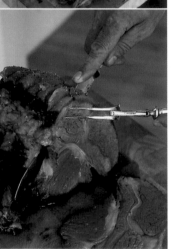

there for 10 seconds and then running it either across the wrist or under the bottom lip. If the skewer is cold the meat is not ready; if warm, it's medium; and if hot, then the meat is well done.

5 When cooked, put the meat in a warm place to rest for 20–30 minutes before carving and serving. Meanwhile, increase the oven temperature again to 200°C/400°F/Gas 6.

6 Heat some of the excess dripping from the roast in a suitably sized ovenproof pan or roasting tray. Whisk up the Yorkshire pudding batter, then pour into the tray and immediately place in the oven. Close the door quickly, and bake for 25 minutes. Turn the pan round and cook on for another 10 minutes.

7 Meanwhile, carve and portion the beef on to hot plates, and make a gravy using the juices left in the roasting tray (see the *Roast Chicken* recipe on page 108). As soon as the Yorkshire pudding is ready, serve with mustard and *Horseradish Sauce* (see page 216), or indeed some horseradish mustard.

- The bigger the joint, the better the meat, and it should always be cooked on the bone. The meat should have a good covering of fat, be dark red in colour (which shows it has been hung properly), and have a good marbling of fat throughout.

- Sprinkling some English mustard powder over the top of the meat halfway through its cooking gives a nice heat.

- This Yorkshire pudding recipe works not by weight, but by volume. Use any size of cup, but measure each ingredient with the same cup. I'm not sure why the vinegar is there, but that's what my gran did. It seems to work, so why change it?

- Yorkshire pudding is very versatile. It can be eaten by itself, with onions and gravy, or can be used in a sweet context as well – not surprising, as the batter is virtually the same as that for popovers and pancakes. In Yorkshire we eat it with sugar and jam, and that's *after* the pudding and the meat!

1 Preheat the oven to 180°C/350°F/Gas 4.

2 Heat the dripping in a casserole, add the beef and kidney and colour on all sides. Add the onion and mushroom strips, and cook for 2 minutes. Sprinkle with the plain flour, take off the heat and mix the stock, wine and Worcestershire sauce in well. Season with salt and pepper, then put into the preheated oven, and cook for 1 hour. Remove the casserole from the oven and allow to cool.

3 To make the pastry, put the self-raising flour, baking powder and salt into a bowl and mix. Rub in the suet, then add enough iced water to bind to a fairly soft, pliable dough. Leave to rest for about 20 minutes.

4 Butter a 1.2 litre (2 pint) pudding basin well, and have ready a steamer large enough to hold it, or a large saucepan with a stand in it on which the bowl can sit. Cut a circle of greaseproof paper, larger than the circumference of the top of the bowl. Make a couple of pleats in this, and grease the pleated side.

5 Divide the pastry into three-quarters and one-quarter. Take the larger piece and roll it out to a circle to line the basin, with 1cm (½ in) extra hanging over the edge. Gently line the pudding basin.

6 Mix the herbs into the meat mixture, and pour this mixture into the bowl. Wet the lip of the pastry with water, then roll the remaining pastry out to cover the top. Place on top of the basin, and press down well to seal.

7 Put the greaseproof paper, pleated and greased side down, over the pudding. This pleat allows the pudding to expand. Tie the paper on round the top of the basin, under the lip, with string, and make a handle as well, so that you can lift it in and out easily.

8 Put the pudding in the top of the steamer over boiling water or on the stand in the saucepan, with enough boiling water to come halfway up the pudding. Cover, bring to the boil and cook for 2 hours. Check the water level occasionally.

9 Serve the pudding from the bowl. Slice the top off, lift it off, and spoon out the meat and juices. Serve each person a bit of the top and some of the juicy pastry from the sides.

Beef Olives

SERVES 4

The idea of olives – a flavourful filling encased in a thin slice of meat, and braised – has been around for a long time in Britain. Apparently the veal version was a seventeenth-century variant on the much older beef or mutton olives, which were once called 'allowes' (possibly how the name 'olives' evolved). The idea is not uniquely British, though: think of the French *paupiettes* and the Italian *involtini* or *bocconcini*.

This was one of the first dishes I learned to cook at college, useful because it embodies all of the basic principles of stewing and braising. I've adapted it, though, principally in the sauce: incorporating the braised sieved vegetables into the sauce gives extra flavour, thickness and richness. So serve with separately cooked vegetables, but if you wanted to be more sophisticated, you could do a dice of carrots and add them to the sauce at the last minute to cook and heat through.

4 x 175g (6 oz) slices topside beef

25g (1 oz) unsalted butter

55g (2 oz) fresh breadcrumbs

½ tsp chopped fresh thyme

1 tsp chopped fresh parsley

1 tbsp chopped cooked bacon

1 egg

salt and freshly ground black pepper

55g (2 oz) beef dripping

1 onion, peeled and finely chopped

1 carrot, peeled and finely chopped

1 garlic clove, peeled and crushed

1 tbsp tomato purée

150ml (5 fl oz) red wine

850ml (1½ pints) brown meat stock

1 Tap the slices of topside out evenly between two layers of plastic or clingfilm to make them thinner. Be careful not to tear them.

2 Melt the butter, then add the breadcrumbs, herbs and bacon. Stir in the egg and some salt and pepper, and mix together well. Smear equal parts of this stuffing on to each tapped-out piece of meat, season again and roll up into a cylinder shape. Tie with thin string to hold together, to look like a mini Swiss roll.

3 Meanwhile, preheat the oven to 160°C/325°F/Gas 3.

4 Heat the dripping in a casserole, and seal and colour the olives. Remove from the casserole. Add the chopped vegetables to the hot fat and colour lightly, followed by the garlic and then the tomato purée. Stir in the red wine and boil to reduce by half.

5 Lay the olives in the casserole, and add the brown stock. Stir, then bring to the boil. Cover with greaseproof paper and a lid, then put into the preheated oven and cook for 1–1½ hours.

6 Remove the olives from the sauce and keep warm. Reduce the sauce a little over a high heat, then push through a sieve. Check the seasoning and consistency. Remove the string carefully from the olives, then pour the sauce over them and serve. Delicious with mashed potato.

■ Instead of bacon, you could use Parma ham in the filling or, to be really outrageous, you could use haggis by itself.

Beef Wellington

SERVES 4

I have been unable to discover the origins of this dish, but it was named for the first Duke of Wellington, who defeated Napoleon at Waterloo in 1815. He was no gourmet, it's said, but the pastry-encased fillet, glazed and shiny brown, looks rather like the leather boot that also came to be associated with him. It is most similar in concept, actually, to the Russian dish, *coulibiac*, in that a prime piece of protein is encased in several layers before being baked or roasted.

675g (1½ lb) beef fillet, a piece cut from
   the centre of the fillet
1 tbsp vegetable oil
salt and freshly ground black pepper
25g (1 oz) unsalted butter
1 shallot, peeled and chopped
55g (2 oz) cooked ham, diced

350g (12 oz) button mushrooms, minced
115g (4 oz) meat pâté or terrine
1 tbsp chopped fresh parsley
6 large, about 25cm (10 in), pancakes
   (see note opposite)
2 eggs, beaten with a little water
450g (1 lb) puff pastry

1 Tie the fillet with butcher's string to keep a nice round shape.

2 Heat the oil in a frying pan. Seal the beef fillet and colour well on all sides. Leave to cool, then remove the strings and season with salt and pepper.

3 Meanwhile, melt the butter and sweat the shallot without colouring. Add the ham and minced button mushrooms and cook, stirring regularly, until all the liquor has evaporated and the mushrooms are quite dry. Season and leave to cool (this is now what is called a duxelles).

4 Mix the pâté and parsley with the mushrooms. Smear half of this mixture evenly over the top of the beef fillet.

5 Lay the pancakes out to make a 'sheet' of pancakes, side by side and overlapping. Lift the fillet carefully on to the centre of the pancake sheet, upside down so that the 'bare' side is uppermost. Smear the exposed side with the remaining mushroom mixture so that it is now completely covered with the duxelles. Brush the edges of the pancakes with the egg wash and carefully fold these over to completely seal the beef in the pancakes.

6 Roll out the pastry to about 3mm (⅛ in) thick. Trim the pastry into an even oblong just enough to fold over the beef. Brush the edges of the puff pastry

with the egg wash. Lay the pancake-covered beef in the centre, and fold the edges of the pastry in and over to make a neat parcel. Turn over so that the joins are underneath. Reshape if necessary, and cut a cylindrical hole in the top to allow the steam to escape. Egg wash and decorate if wanted, then leave to rest for 30 minutes.

7 Preheat the oven to 200°C/400°F/Gas 6.

8 Egg wash the pastry again, then bake the Wellington in the preheated oven for 25 minutes. Turn the oven down to 160°C/325°F/Gas 3 and cook for another 10–15 minutes until the pastry is brown and the meat inside is nicely rare. Cover with foil if the pastry is getting too brown.

9 Leave to rest for about 15 minutes, just like any other roast meat. One of the best ways to test whether the meat is done is to stick a skewer in the middle, count to ten, and then run the skewer along your bottom lip. You'll feel a variance in temperature, the middle part being the coolest. You should feel hot, hot, cool, cool, hot, hot.

10 When slicing, take off the end bits first, as they will be well done. Serve with a Madeira sauce (see page 219).

- The pancakes and pâté/duxelles layers here are vital to prevent the juices of the fillet running into the pastry.
- You could use brioche pastry instead of puff, but that is considerably more complicated as you have to make it from scratch.
- Other ingredients could be used to encase the fillet inside the pastry, such as sun-dried tomato paste or olive paste, or spinach, but then it would no longer strictly be a Wellington.
- Everyone has a pancake recipe, but if you don't, use the Yorkshire pudding recipe on page 73 to make thin pancakes.

Cornish Pasties

MAKES 12

Variations of this idea – ingredients wrapped in pastry to make individual pies – occur all over Europe, but perhaps the nearest to the most famous one, that of Cornwall, are the Forfar Bridie, from the east of Scotland, and the Lancashire Foot. There are all sorts of legends surrounding the quintessential pasty: it is real only if it is dropped down a Cornish tin mine and the pastry doesn't break; that it is unlucky to take a pasty aboard a ship. In Cornwall, the pasty is occasionally called Tiddy Oggy (a local name for potato).

The basic recipe can also be varied in a number of ways. You could use any meat as a filling, and you could use vegetables alone (common when money for the costly meat was scarce). Whatever and however, the pasty is the ultimate portable food, as handy now for a picnic as it once was for the miner to take into the bowels of the earth or the farmer into the field.

Shortcrust pastry
450g (1 lb) plain flour
a pinch of salt
225g (8 oz) lard
55g (2 oz) butter
approx. 150ml (5 fl oz) water
2 eggs, beaten with a little water
  for egg wash

Filling
450g (1 lb) topside beef
1 medium onion
225g (8 oz) potatoes
55g (2 oz) carrots
55g (2 oz) turnip
salt and freshly ground black pepper
1 tbsp chopped parsley
Worcestershire sauce
Tabasco sauce

1 To make the pastry, sift the flour and salt into a bowl. Chop the lard and butter straight from the fridge into small cubes, then rub into the flour until like breadcrumbs. Add enough water to make the ingredients come together to a dough, then clingfilm and rest for 30 minutes.

2 Preheat the oven to 200°C/400°F/Gas 6.

3 To make the filling, trim the meat of all fat and gristle, cut into small dice then put into a bowl. Peel and finely chop the onion. Peel and cut the

potatoes, carrots and turnip into 1cm (½ in) dice, and add to the bowl along with the onion. Mix well, then season with salt and pepper, and add the parsley and a splash each of the sauces.

4 Cut the pastry into four pieces and roll each of them out thinly. Cut into circles of 15cm (6 in) in diameter. Brush the edges of each pastry circle with egg wash, then pile a quarter of the filling into the middle of each. Spread in a line across the centre of the pastry. Fold the pastry over and up to make a seal on top of the filling. Using your thumb and forefinger, crimp the edges in a wavy fashion. Brush with egg wash and make a hole in the top for the steam to escape.

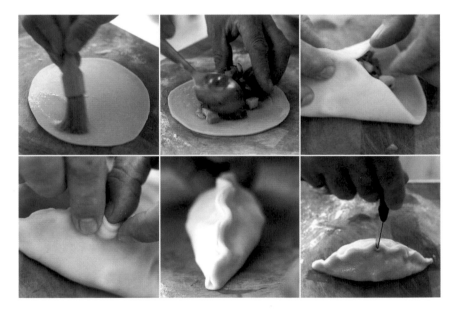

5 Bake in the preheated oven for 30 minutes, then reduce the oven temperature to 180°C/350°F/Gas 4 and continue to cook for a further 20 minutes. Serve hot or cold.

■ You could use rough puff or hot water crust pastry (see page 92) instead of the shortcrust.

Irish Stew

SERVES 4

The combination of lamb, onions and potatoes is common throughout Europe, but the most famous version is that from Ireland, where potatoes were such a staple, and sheep thrived on the lush grazing. Hogget or mutton was probably used at first, and some say that kid was common as well.

The version here is unusual because of the cabbage, but that's how we used to do it at The Savoy Hotel, plating the lamb chops with a separate braised cabbage 'ball', the whole potatoes and the sauce, flavoured and thickened by the potato and cabbage (and sometimes enriched with cream). The celery leaves were the final touch.

900g (2 lb) large potatoes

3 large onions

½ white cabbage

8 large middle neck lamb chops

salt and freshly ground black pepper

600ml (1 pint) white stock (made from unroasted bones or vegetables)

1 bouquet garni (bay leaf, parsley, thyme etc.)

1 tbsp chopped celery leaves

1 Peel the potatoes and trim into twelve even-sized pieces. Put to one side in water and keep the trimmings.

2 Peel and thinly slice the onions, and lay in the bottom of a large, deep, heatproof stewing pan. Shred the cabbage and place on top of the onion. Put the chops on top. Slice the potato trimmings and scatter over the chops. Season with salt and pepper.

3 Cover the vegetables and meat with the stock and add the bouquet garni. Bring up to the boil, cover with a lid and cook slowly for 1–1½ hours on top of the stove.

4 Put in the trimmed potatoes, and gently simmer for another 20–30 minutes until the potatoes and the chops are cooked. Take out the chops and whole potatoes, put into a serving dish and keep warm.

5 Remove the bouquet garni and purée the liquor in a food processor. Check for seasoning and consistency.

6 Pour the sauce over the meat, sprinkle with the chopped celery leaves and serve.

Pot-roasted Shoulder of Lamb

SERVES 6–8

It is said that until the nineteenth century, sheep were valued more for their wool than their meat. Older sheep would have been slaughtered once past their best fleece days, and probably salted for winter eating. Lambs would have been an occasional treat, whereas now of course it is mutton that is rare.

A piece of sheep – or indeed a whole one – would traditionally have been roasted in front of the fire. Here I'm pot-roasting a boned shoulder, a good way of dealing with and dissolving the fat and cartilage of the cut (once very underrated, now becoming popular again, thank goodness). The meat is rolled round garlic (not very British, I admit) and rosemary, and then served with some traditional accompaniments. They say that these 'tracklements' should be made of foods the animals themselves might have eaten, thus the rosemary here, and sheep might very well have eaten wild mint and redcurrants as well.

I have in my mind that if you tie the lamb correctly, with the remaining bone at the right angle, the lamb looks rather like a duck, which some wag of a parson at some time called Parson's Duck…

1 x 2kg (4½ lb) shoulder of lamb

1 bunch fresh rosemary, leaves separated from the stalks (keep the latter)

2 garlic cloves, peeled and crushed

salt and freshly ground black pepper

1 tbsp olive oil

2 onions, peeled and roughly chopped

1 celery stalk, roughly chopped

1 large carrot, roughly chopped

25g (1 oz) unsalted butter

150ml (5 fl oz) white wine

300ml (10 fl oz) meat stock

1 Preheat the oven to 180°C/350°F/Gas 4.

2 There are three bones in shoulder of lamb, and we want to take out two of them. If unhappy, get your butcher to do it, but it's really quite easy and because you can't go too far wrong, it's good boning practice for you! Remove the shoulder blade and the 'upper arm' bone from the flesh side by carefully following the bones round. Open up from the centre to create a two-flap pocket.

3 Chop the rosemary leaves, then mix with the crushed garlic and some salt and pepper, and smear into the inner side of the lamb. Roll the lamb up like a Swiss roll, so that it looks like the body of a duck. Tie the shoulder with string to help keep the shape.

4 Heat the oil in a large frying pan, and sear and colour the outside of the lamb until golden brown.

5 Put the vegetables in the bottom of an ovenproof casserole or roasting tray big enough for the lamb. It should have a tight-fitting lid (if not, foil will have to be used). Put the lamb on top of the vegetables and season it. Put in the butter, the white wine and the stalks from the rosemary.

6 Cover with the lid and cook in the preheated moderate oven for 1½ hours. Turn the heat down to 120°C/250°F/Gas ½, and cook for a further hour. The lamb should be well cooked and ready to melt in the mouth (rather like the Greek *kleftiko*).

7 Take the dish out of the oven and allow the lamb to stand for 10 minutes.

8 Meanwhile, pour off the excess fat from the cooking dish, then add the meat stock. Boil together to reduce by about a third, then skim off the fat, strain and serve hot with the meat.

Lancashire Hotpot

SERVES 4

Slow-cooked dishes such as this only evolved properly once people had ovens. As these were few and far between domestically at first, many hotpots were taken to the local baker or cookshop to be cooked (similar dishes in France bear the adjective '*boulangère*' because of this). At home, a hotpot would be cooked in the baking oven as it cooled after the high heat of baking day.

Speaking as a Yorkshireman, I don't know why Lancashire has the kudos of inventing hotpot. However, it's a fantastic dish, traditionally made with neck end chops. I prefer to use chump chops from the other end, as there's less bone, more meat, and they eat well. So could we call this a Yorkshire hotpot?

4 x 225g (8 oz) lamb chump chops
  on the bone
55g (2 oz) beef dripping
450g (1 lb) large onions, peeled and
  finely sliced
900g (2 lb) even-sized potatoes

85g (3 oz) unsalted butter, melted
salt and freshly ground black pepper
4 lambs' kidneys, cored and sliced
600ml (1 pint) lamb or chicken stock
1 tbsp chopped fresh chives

1 Preheat the oven to 200°C/400°F/Gas 6.

2 Trim the chops. Heat the dripping in a large frying pan, and colour the chops well on each side. Put to one side. Add the onion to the pan and colour quickly. Pour out into a dish and leave to cool.

3 Peel the potatoes and, if you can be bothered, cut and trim them to a cylindrical shape. (This is what chefs would do, and it looks very impressive.) Then slice into even slices of about 3mm (⅛ in) thick.

4 Put a third of the melted butter into the bottom of a large casserole dish. Place a layer of potatoes on top of the butter (keep the best shapes for later) and season. Sprinkle with half the onions, then place the chops on top. Season again. Mix the kidneys with the rest of the onions, then sprinkle over the meat. Pat flat.

5 Carefully arrange the rest of the potatoes overlapping each other to cover the top of the meat and onions. Pour the stock over to come just two-thirds of the way up. Season with salt and pepper, then brush the potato layer carefully with most of the remaining melted butter.

6 Cover the pot with a lid and put into the preheated oven for half an hour. Reduce the oven temperature to 180°C/350°F/Gas 4 and cook for a further 1½ hours.

7 Remove the lid, brush the potatoes again with melted butter and cook on until the potatoes are brown. Remove the casserole from the oven and leave to rest for a few minutes. Sprinkle the potato topping with chopped chives and serve.

■ If you like, you could leave out the kidneys and substitute mushrooms as in a steak and kidney pudding or pie.

Mutton Pies

MAKES 4

Large and small pies made with mutton or lamb have been popular since the Middle Ages. At first, like so many meat dishes of the time, they would have been quite sweet, mixed with dried fruit, sugar and sweet spices; later they became more savoury. There are lots of such pies in the north of England (perhaps *the* pie centre of the country) and in Scotland. North of the border they use minced, spiced mutton; in places like Northumberland the meat is chunkier, as here. But both are made with a hot water crust pastry, as is the famous British pork pie.

Apparently mutton pies were admired by Dr Johnson (he also liked Scotch broth), and were served at Balmoral and Buckingham Palace receptions by Queen Victoria and King George V. Fine fare indeed.

25g (1 oz) unsalted butter

1 red onion, peeled and finely chopped

1 tsp chopped fresh rosemary

115g (4 oz) mushrooms, finely chopped

a little vegetable oil

450g (1 lb) shoulder of lamb, off the bone,
  trimmed and cut into 5mm (¼ in) pieces

300ml (10 fl oz) lamb stock

salt and freshly ground black pepper

1 tsp freshly grated nutmeg

1 tsp fécule (potato flour) or cornflour,
  slaked in 1 tbsp lamb stock

Hot water crust pastry

350g (12 oz) plain flour

a pinch of salt

150ml (5 fl oz) water

115g (4 oz) white lard

1 egg yolk

1 egg, mixed with a little water, to glaze

1 Make the filling first. Melt the butter and sweat the finely chopped onion and rosemary without colouring for a few minutes. Add the mushrooms and cook for 3 minutes.

2 Put the meat in a frying pan, and pan-fry in the oil to colour on all sides. Add to the onion mixture along with half the lamb stock and season with salt, pepper and nutmeg. Cover and cook for 30 minutes on top of the stove, then allow to cool.

3 Meanwhile, preheat the oven to 190°C/375°F/Gas 5.

4 To start the pastry, sift the flour and salt into a bowl.

5 Bring the water up to boiling in a medium pan, take off the heat, add the lard and allow it to melt. Add the flour and beat well to amalgamate, then knead until smooth. Stir in the egg yolk and keep warm. Try to work quickly.

6 To use, roll out and cut into rounds to fit patty tins or muffin moulds of about 10cm (4 in) in diameter. Keep the leftover pastry covered and warm; you need it for the lids.

7 Spoon the cold filling into the pie cases. Roll out the rest of the pastry and cut out the correct lid shapes. Moisten the edges of the pie cases and put the lids on top, pressing to make a seal. Make a hole in the middle, and brush the tops with mixed egg and water to glaze. Bake in the preheated oven for 45 minutes, until the pastry is crisp and golden.

8 Mix the slaked fécule or cornflour with the remaining lamb stock. Bring to the boil gently, stirring, until thickened (this is what chefs call a 'thickened stock').

9 When the pies come out of the oven, re-cut the hole in the top, and carefully pour some thickened stock into each pie. Serve hot or cold.

■ Pies such as this are very portable, good for picnics. You could make them in smaller moulds if you liked.

■ Note that I haven't asked you to use the pastry in the traditional way, persuading it up around the sides of a jam jar or similar to get the shape. Very hands on and complicated!

Shepherd's Pie

SERVES 4 There are always leftovers from a roast joint, and they can be re-used in a number of ways. Although it's simple, I think shepherd's pie, using lamb, is one of the best – but cottage pie, its beef equivalent, is good too. The recipe is said to have been the creation of shepherds' wives in Cumbria and the Lake District (where the lamb is so good nowadays), who needed to make tough leftover mutton more palatable. Cutting it up small or pounding it would have helped, as would the gravy, but we of course now have the mincer and processor to help us.

Always make plenty of a shepherd's pie, because it's something people always want seconds of. It's more than greed, it's actually psychological!

25g (1 oz) beef dripping or lard

1 large onion, peeled and finely chopped

1 carrot, peeled and diced

450g (1 lb) cooked lamb, minced

1 tsp tomato purée

1–2 garlic cloves, peeled and crushed
  (optional)

15g (½ oz) plain flour

300ml (10 fl oz) meat stock

a dash of Worcestershire sauce

1 tbsp chopped fresh parsley

salt and freshly ground black pepper

Potato topping

450g (1 lb) potatoes

2 tbsp double cream

115g (4 oz) unsalted butter

a pinch of freshly grated nutmeg

1 Melt the dripping in a pan and add the onion and carrot (you could have chopped them together in a processor). Cook until soft but not coloured.

2 Add the minced lamb and fry for 2 minutes, then add the tomato purée, garlic if using it, and flour, and mix well. Add the stock and bring to the boil, then simmer for 10–15 minutes until the stew thickens but does not stick to the pan. Stir in the Worcestershire sauce, parsley and some salt and pepper, and remove from the heat. Put into a pie dish of about 850ml (1 ½ pints) and leave to cool.

3 Peel the potatoes then cut them into even pieces and put into cold salted water. Bring to the boil and cook until tender, then drain and return to the pan. Put back on the heat to dry out, carefully stirring all the time.

4 Put the double cream and 85g (3 oz) of the butter into a clean pan and bring to the boil. Pass the potatoes through a potato 'ricer' into the cream mixture. Stir well, season with salt and pepper and add some nutmeg. Allow to cool.

5 Preheat the oven to 180°C/350°F/Gas 4.

6 Put the potato into a piping bag with a 2cm (¾ in) plain nozzle and pipe on to the meat mixture in the pie dish. Put the pie dish into the preheated oven for 10 minutes: this sets the potato topping.

7 Melt the remaining butter and carefully brush over the top of the pie. Put back in the oven for a further 20 minutes or until golden brown. Serve immediately.

- This is essentially a leftover recipe, but you can make it with fresh lamb (or beef). Buy mince, and cook it with the vegetables for longer than above.
- You don't have to use a piping bag for the potato. Spoon it on evenly, and level with a palette knife dipped in olive oil or melted butter, then scroll to make a pattern.
- When we were very good as kids, my mum used to add some grated cheese to the potatoes and then sprinkle some more on top before baking.
- You can leave out the garlic if you like – a modern addition – or you can add something like fried mushrooms or sun-dried tomatoes.

Roast Loin of Pork with Crackling

SERVES 6–8

Wild pigs – or wild boars as they are more commonly known – once ran free in British forests and were hunted by royalty. But pigs, easy to tame, have been domesticated for thousands of years, and in the Middle Ages, most country people, rich and poor, would have kept at least one pig. This would forage in woodlands, accept scraps and household waste, and generally cause little trouble – and then in the autumn it would provide fresh meat for roasting, and sausages, hams, bacon, black puddings and salted joints for the winter. The pig was probably the most useful animal for, as the saying goes, you could eat everything but the squeak.

Unlike other animals, the pig is sold with its skin on, and it is this which crisps up on roasting, to make crackling. The hoary question is whether to leave the crackling on or not during cooking. If you are marinating the meat, you must obviously take the skin off, but it cooks well on the joint. If you take it off, you can roast it separately between two trays to keep it flat. In Mexico, they sell large strips of crackling that look like prawn crackers, but we of course have our own pork scratchings…

1 x 1.8kg (4 lb) loin of pork

fine salt and 1 tbsp coarse sea salt

1 onion, peeled and sliced

150ml (5 fl oz) dry cider

600ml (1 pint) meat stock

1 small bunch fresh sage

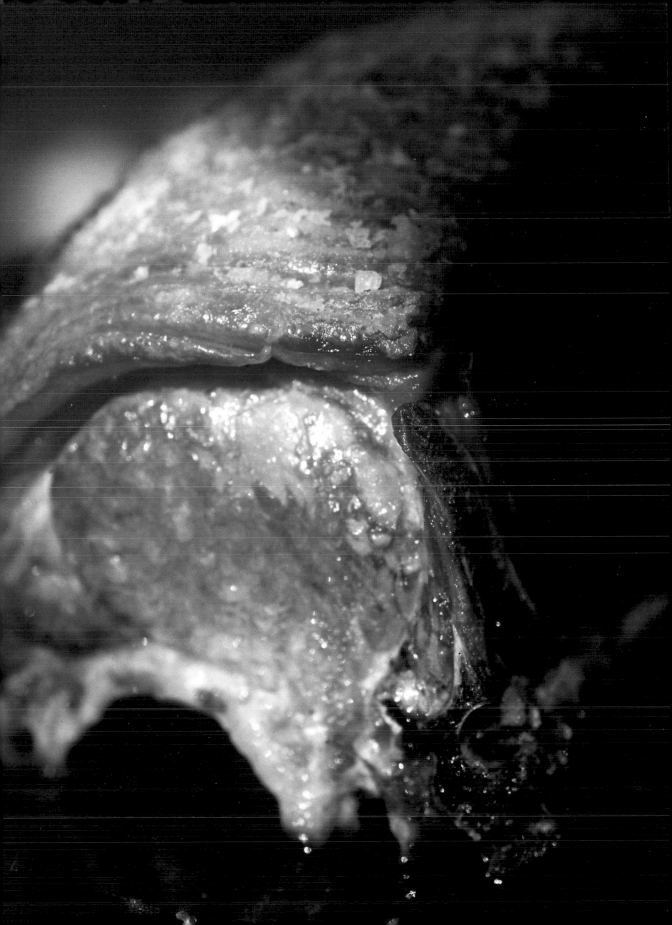

1 Preheat the oven to 220°C/425°F/Gas 7.

2 Wipe the loin with a dry cloth. Using a sharp knife, e.g. a Stanley knife, carefully score the rind of the pork from the back to the belly. Score quite deeply through the rind into the fat, but not into the meat. Score 5mm (¼ in) apart and across the length of the joint. Rub the skin with fine salt.

3 Put the meat on a metal trivet in a roasting tray and then into the hot oven for 25 minutes. Turn the oven down to 190°C/375°F/Gas 5 and cook for another 55 minutes approximately. About 10 minutes before the end of cooking, sprinkle the crackling with the sea salt.

4 When cooked take the pork out of the oven, and leave to rest in a warm dry place. Do not pinch all of the crackling!

5 Add the sliced onion to the fat in the tray and fry to colour slightly. Carefully pour off the excess fat (keep to use as dripping for roast potatoes etc.).

6 Add the cider to the onions, and boil to reduce by half, then pour all of this into a saucepan. Add the stock and sage, bring to the boil and reduce until the desired strength of flavour is achieved. Skim off any scum, and strain.

7 To serve, take off the crackling by cutting from the back down to the belly. Put this to one side. Take the meat off the bone by cutting down the backbone to the ribs and then over the ribs to release the meat. Cut from the side with a longish knife. Serve slices of the meat with strips of crackling, the hot gravy and some *Apple Sauce* (see page 214).

■ Gloucester Old Spot is an old breed with black spots on its skin, said to have been caused by apples falling on them in the orchards where they traditionally foraged. The meat is dense and full of pork flavour.

■ Chop off the backbone using a large knife. Keep the ribs, smear them with a honey/soy glaze and reheat to make great spare ribs.

Roast Ham

SERVES 12–16 Means of preserving hams – the cured legs of pig – vary all over the world. In Italy and Spain, they salt-cure and then 'air-dry' the legs to make Parma and serrano hams respectively. In Britain, though, most hams are for cooking: they are soaked in brines of varying flavours, then hung to mature and dry, sometimes smoked, before being boiled and perhaps roasted or baked thereafter.

I'm telling you how to cook a whole piece of gammon here, which is huge, so before embarking on the recipe, make sure you have a pot and oven big enough to hold it. (You can of course use a smaller piece; cut down the proportions and times accordingly.) It's an ideal dish for a party, for family gatherings, or for that Christmas week when cold turkey begins to pall.

1 x 4.5–5.4kg (10–12 lb) gammon
1 onion, peeled and chopped
2 carrots, chopped
2 leeks, chopped
2 apples, chopped (no need to core)
2 bay leaves
a handful of parsley stalks
12 cloves

12 black peppercorns
600ml (1 pint) cider vinegar

Glaze
1 pineapple
175g (6 oz) unrefined demerara sugar
4 tbsp Dijon mustard

1 Soak the ham overnight in cold water to cover (it might be wise to ask your butcher, when buying, how long he thinks you might need to soak).

2 Put the ham into a large pot, and add the chopped vegetables, apples and the herbs and spices. Pour in the vinegar and cover with cold water. Bring slowly up to the boil and then turn down to a simmer. Skim off the scum. Put on a lid, propping it slightly open with a wooden spoon to prevent boiling over, and allow to simmer gently for approximately 3–4 hours.

3 To test if done, either stick a large roasting fork in (if cooked it will come out easily), or if using a whole gammon (much preferred), a small bone that sticks out at the knuckle end will be easy to release when wiggled.

4 When cooked, leave the ham in the stock for 20 minutes to rest. If serving hot and boiled, drain well and serve.

5 But if roasting, drain, then remove the skin first of all. This will easily pull off from the body end, not the knuckle end. Then trim off the excess fat using a sharp knife, trying all the time to retain the shape of the leg.

6 Preheat the oven to 200°C/400°F/Gas 6.

7 To make the glaze, peel the pineapple and put the chopped flesh through the processor. Drain the flesh well, keeping the juice for the sauce. Mix the pineapple pulp with the sugar.

8 Brush the mustard over the fat of the ham, then carefully press the pineapple mixture over the ham. Score the sugar carefully in parallel lines one way and then at an angle to make diamonds of white lines.

9 Put into the preheated oven for about 20 minutes until the sugar caramelises. Take the ham out, leave to stand for 10 minutes, and then carve.

■ Check the stock. If it's not too salty, keep it for soups (great in the pea soup on page 10), or a parsley sauce which would be perfect with the ham, whether boiled or roasted (see page 110). Otherwise the *Cumberland Sauce* on page 218 would be good with it when served cold, as would the *Piccalilli* (see page 204).

■ You will have plenty of ham left over for sandwiches, cold meats, or for putting into mixtures.

Calf's Liver with Sage, Caper and Sherry Sauce

SERVES 4

We once ate very much more offal than we do now. Liver, as one of the more reasonable *looking* of the various 'off-falls', has always been popular, and has usually been fried with onions or with bacon. It can be stewed too, and one such dish made with ox liver, sage and a sliced potato topping is known as Yorkshireman's Goose…

For this dish I've used calf's liver, but you could substitute lamb's livers if you can find them. I've also used sage, as the Yorkshiremen did above, but have added some capers and sherry for extra flavour. Neither is native to Britain, but both have been appreciated for many centuries, sherry especially. It was Sir Francis Drake who introduced Jerez 'sack' to England when he appropriated several thousand barrels from Cadiz while 'singeing the King of Spain's beard'. The name 'Jerez' was gradually anglicised to 'sherry' (the 'sack' was dropped), and in the succeeding centuries, the popularity of the drink grew. Adventurers from all over Britain went to Jerez to make their fortunes, and many of the names of the great sherry houses – Harvey's, Croft's etc. – reflect this still.

4 x 1cm (½ in) thick slices calf's liver, about 140–175g (5–6 oz) total weight

2 tbsp olive oil

salt and freshly ground black pepper

55g (2 oz) butter

2 shallots, peeled and finely chopped

2 tbsp midget capers (they're tiny and expensive!)

150ml (5 fl oz) dry sherry

1 splash sherry vinegar (or lemon juice)

1 tbsp chopped fresh sage

150ml (5 fl oz) veal stock

1 tsp fécule (potato flour) or cornflour, slaked in 1 tbsp water

1 Trim the liver well, cutting out any large tubes. The butcher should have removed the filmy skin.

2 Heat the olive oil in a frying pan until very hot. Lay the liver slices in carefully, but do not over-fill the pan. Cook in two batches if necessary. When golden brown, turn over, cook quickly and take out. Put to one side, season and keep warm.

3 Throw away excess oil from the pan and melt half of the butter in it. Add the shallots and capers, and sauté to soften, but do not colour. Add the dry sherry and reduce by half. Add the sherry vinegar, sage, stock and the slaked fécule or cornflour. Bring up to the boil, stirring until it thickens, then add the remaining butter. Shake in until melted.

4 Reheat the liver quickly, serve on warm plates and pour the sauce over.

- I think the thickness of liver to be fried is very important, with each slice no thicker than specified overleaf, but it's up to you.
- Good served with buttery mashed potato or *pommes lyonnaise*, sautéed potatoes and onions.

Mustard-devilled Calf's Kidneys

SERVES 4

Lamb's kidneys, still encased in their own suet, were once grilled whole and served, split open, on toast – a favourite breakfast for Edwardian gentlemen. Those same worthies also liked them at the other end of the day, devilled on toast, as a savoury after dinner. I'm using calf's kidney here, but lamb's kidneys can be substituted.

You either love kidneys or hate them, and I'm of the former persuasion. I associate them with José, who opened up at Turner's for fourteen years, and put our stockpots on (he's now retired to Spain). When veal, pork or lamb loins came in, José would take the kidneys off, divest them of their fat, and grill them with garlic. Served on good toast, they were my best start to the day ever.

2 whole calf's kidneys in their fat

a splash of olive oil

25g (1 oz) butter

2 shallots, peeled and finely chopped

150ml (5 fl oz) dry white wine

150ml (5 fl oz) double cream

3 tbsp grain mustard

1 tbsp chopped fresh chervil

salt and freshly ground black pepper

Tabasco sauce

1 Preheat the oven to 220°C/425°F/Gas 7.

2 Trim the excess fat from the kidneys using a knife, but try to retain the original shape. Sear and colour the kidneys on all sides in a little oil in a hot frying pan. Put into the preheated hot oven, and roast for 15 minutes. Take out and leave to rest.

3 Meanwhile, melt the butter and sauté the shallots, but do not let them colour. Add the wine and boil to reduce by two-thirds. Add the cream and bring to the boil. Boil to reduce by a third. Take off the heat and stir in the mustard and chervil. Check for seasoning and consistency.

4 Thinly slice the kidneys and arrange on a hot plate to fill the plate. Collect all the juices from the kidneys and pour into the sauce. Add Tabasco to taste (careful, it's hot), then warm the sauce through again.

5 Spoon the sauce over the kidneys and serve immediately.

Game Pie (see page 121)

At one time, all the meat eaten by the British was 'game' – elk, deer, wild ox, wild pig and birds of every description. As we domesticated cattle, pigs and sheep, so we did the same with birds such as geese, ducks and chickens. The Romans were probably a major influence, for they introduced and intensively reared birds such as peacocks, pheasants and guinea fowl (as well as rabbits, dormice and snails).

For centuries, because of the difficulty of keeping the 'great meat' animals (cattle, sheep and pigs) over the winter, poultry birds and game birds and animals would have

Poultry and Game   5

provided a major source of fresh meat. Nothing was omitted, and many birds we wouldn't dream of eating now were enjoyed: swan, bustard, stork, blackbirds, finches, larks… (I once met a Paris chef who specialised in game of this nature when I was at The Capital. The chef himself was in his eighties, and his kitchen 'boys' must have been in their sixties. They wore aprons that looked as if they hadn't been taken off since the day they started!) Rabbit and hare were eaten by rich and poor alike – when game laws did not bar the latter from hunting – but venison was always for the aristocracy alone.

Almost every household, however poor, would have had a few hens but they were too valuable as egg-layers to eat. Only when old, scrawny and beyond egg-laying might they be consigned to the poor man's cooking pot (and, as we know, the stock from an older chicken is much more flavourful). The rich, however, would have relished poultry much more often: roasting chickens, geese, ducks and pigeons on the spit, cooking them in pottages and pies, and potting them in butter.

Because poultry and game were so readily available on the whole, they were less well thought of in culinary terms than red meat (as was fish). However, curiously, a roasted bird was often considered a food for celebrations – the goose at harvest festival, and originally at Christmas, before the interloper turkey became the norm. I remember chicken – often tasting of the fishmeal in its diet – being a very special treat for Sunday lunch. Nowadays chicken is so common that we are tending to ignore it again. Rabbit too, once the most available of wild meats (and therefore the least appreciated), is making a comeback in popularity.

Seasonality is one of the joys of British food and game is perhaps the prime example.

Roast Chicken with Bread Sauce

SERVES 4

As with all other meats, 'roast' chicken would once have been cooked on a spit in front of a fire, instead of in an oven. A young cockerel would normally have been used, as hens were far too valuable as egg-layers. Nowadays, we can get chickens aplenty, but when cooking them as simply as this, do try and buy the very best you can, preferably corn-fed and free-range.

Bread sauce is perhaps the oldest British sauce, dating from medieval times. The Scots claim it as a northern invention, but it appears all over the islands, and is good with most roast birds, domesticated or wild.

1 x 1.6kg (3½ lb) free-range roasting
  chicken, cleaned weight
salt and freshly ground black pepper
25g (1 oz) lard
55g (2 oz) unsalted butter

Bread sauce
300ml (10 fl oz) milk
150ml (5 fl oz) double cream
1 onion, peeled and stuck with 6 cloves
1 bay leaf
approx. 75g (2¾ oz) fresh white breadcrumbs
25g (1 oz) unsalted butter

1 Preheat the oven to 200°C/400°F/Gas 6.
2 Take out the wishbone, and truss the chicken back to its original shape. Lay it on its side and crush the backbone to allow the chicken to sit on its side and not to spring back to shape. Season the chicken.
3 Heat the lard in a heatproof and ovenproof dish, then add the butter and the chicken lying on one side to start to colour. If the breast touches the fat as well, put a little piece of potato under it to protect it.
4 Roast in the preheated oven for 20 minutes, then turn the chicken on to its other side and cook in the same way, making sure that the legs in both instances are touching the fat, for 20 more minutes.
5 Turn the bird over on to its back and baste with lard and butter. Turn the oven down to 180°C/350°F/Gas 4 and roast until ready. To test after 10 minutes, pierce the thickest part of the thigh: if the juices run clear, the bird is cooked. If not, roast for a little longer.
6 Leave to rest for 10 minutes in a warm place before carving.

7 Meanwhile, make the bread sauce. Bring the milk and cream up to the boil with the onion, cloves and bay leaf. Leave to sit for 10 minutes then add the breadcrumbs. Stir until smooth, then take out the onion. Add the butter and some salt and pepper. Cover with clingfilm or buttered paper.

8 To carve the chicken, first take off the strings. Turn it on to its side and cut the skin between the leg and the breast. Now pull the leg away using a carving knife, pulling away from the neck. This will release the meat. (It will also expose the little hidden nugget of meat, the cook's treat, the oyster. Eat it and don't tell anyone.) Put the leg on a chopping board and chop to separate the thigh from the drumstick. Turn the bird over and repeat.

9 Stand the bird on its back and carve down one side of the breastbone, bringing the knife down between the wing and neck joints. Do the same on the other side. Cut each breast in two.

10 Serve the thigh with the smaller piece of breast, and the drumstick with the other. Offer the bread sauce and gravy if you like (see below) separately. (And some roast potatoes, cooked chipolatas and bacon rolls would make for the full monty!)

■ Stages 3–4 may seem complicated, but this is the best way to cook any fleshy bird. As legs are always tougher than breasts, they take longer to cook. By placing the legs directly on the heated dish, in the hot fat – and protecting the breast from that same exposure – both should be cooked at about the same time.

■ To make a gravy with the pan juices, thinly slice half an onion and throw into the roasting pan. Fry quickly so that the onion absorbs the juices, then carefully pour away the excess fat (this can be used again). I now like to add a drop of wine, but this isn't classically British. Add some chicken stock, bring to the boil and reduce. Strain into a clean pan, skim off any excess fat, and check for seasoning. Many British gravies have some flour in them to form a sauce-like gravy, but my take on gravy, particularly with chicken, is that it should be thin.

Poached Chicken with Parsley Sauce

SERVES 4 Poaching or boiling would once have been the commonest method of cooking chicken (usually a tough old hen past her best laying days), and there was the added bonus of a delicious stock with which to make a soup. Here I've used the stock to make a wonderful sauce, full of the flavour of the chicken, and thickened with lots of butter and parsley. The sauce is an echo of the traditional green herb sauce of medieval times, in which parsley played a major part.

1 x 1.6kg (3½ lb) free-range chicken,
  cleaned weight

1 lemon, halved

2 onions, peeled and chopped

1 leek, cleaned and chopped

2 celery stalks, chopped

1 bay leaf

6 cloves

salt and freshly ground black pepper

Parsley sauce

600ml (1 pint) reduced chicken stock
  (see method)

300ml (10 fl oz) double cream

115g (4 oz) cold unsalted butter, diced

3 tbsp chopped fresh parsley

1 Remove the wishbone from the chicken. Trim and tie the chicken to its proper shape. Rub the outside of the chicken with the fresh lemon to keep the skin white.

2 Put the chicken into a large pot and add the chopped onion, leek and celery, the bay leaf, cloves and a little salt and pepper. Cover with water and bring up to the boil. Pull to one side, and clean off any scum that arises.

3 Cover with a lid for the first half-hour, simmering slowly, then bring to the boil. Remove the lid, and slowly cook for a further hour, skimming occasionally. To check if the bird is cooked, push a skewer into the thickest part of the thigh: if the juices run clear or a little pinkish, then the bird is cooked. If the juices are at all red, then the bird needs a bit longer.

4 When the chicken is cooked, remove from the stock and keep in a warm place. Use a clean tea towel, dipped in the stock and squeezed out, to cover the bird and keep it from drying out.

5 Strain the stock into a clean pan (or two) and boil to reduce by about half – or until the stock has a good, round, concentrated flavour.

6 Put 600ml (1 pint) of this stock into a separate pan, and the cream into the original stock pan. Reduce the cream until it thickens, and then add the stock. Reduce again until you have a sauce-like consistency.

7 Check for seasoning, then add the butter and swirl the pan to melt the butter dice. Add the chopped parsley.

8 Carve the bird into two drumsticks, two thighs, two wing pieces and then the breast in half. Arrange the pieces in a dish and pour the sauce over and around.

■ At stage 5, using two pans means that the stock reduces more quickly, so the chicken doesn't hang around too long.

■ At stage 7, the professional chef in me would always strain the sauce through a fine sieve to make it absolutely smooth before adding the parsley. However, if you can't be bothered, I can understand…

Roast Goose Stuffed with Apple and Fig

SERVES 6

Goose was the celebratory bird in Olde England before the turkey was known, and it still serves that role in much of Europe. Although geese were valued, they had rather a hard time of it. If caught eating someone's corn in Wales, they could be executed (a good excuse to eat goose?). They were force-fattened in much the same way as *foie gras* ducks and geese are in France today. They were plucked regularly throughout the year to supply quills and down (which rendered them rather tough), and then they could be marched off to London (with tarred feet like turkeys) to feed the capital's multitudes.

Geese are traditionally best in September, when they were fattened on stubble and eaten on Michaelmas Day, the 29th.

1 x 7.25kg (16 lb) goose
salt and freshly ground black pepper

Stuffing
10 slices dried bread, broken into pieces
2 Cox's apples, grated
4 ripe figs, pulped with a fork
1 onion, peeled and finely chopped
1 tbsp chopped fresh sage
1 small egg
2 tbsp cider
2 tbsp Calvados
unsalted butter

Glaze
2 tbsp runny honey
1 tbsp Calvados
juice of ½ lemon

1 Preheat the oven to 220°C/425°F/Gas 7.

2 To prepare the goose, take out the wishbone and then remove the excess fat from the cavity end.

3 For the stuffing, mix all the ingredients together except for the butter, and season well with salt and pepper.

4 Use a quarter of this stuffing to stuff the neck end of the goose, and put the rest separately in an ovenproof dish greased with butter.

5 Before roasting the goose, prick all over the breast and neck end to allow the excess fat to be released. Put the bird in a roasting tray on a rack and roast in the preheated oven for 30 minutes. Turn the oven down to 180°C/350°F/Gas 4 and cook for a further 2 hours.

6 Take the bird out and pour the fat from the tray (keep to use for cooking roast potatoes etc.). Put the goose back into the same temperature oven, along with the dish of stuffing, which needs to roast for an hour. Cook the goose for a further 30 minutes on its breast, not on the rack, then turn it on to its back.

7 Mix together the honey, Calvados and lemon juice for the glaze, and brush over the breast of the bird. Cook for a final 30 minutes, basting regularly with the glaze.

8 Remove the goose from the oven, and leave to rest for 20 minutes before carving.

■ A tart sauce or stuffing is normal with goose: apple in the autumn (the fig here is an interesting but not untraditional addition) and, in spring, sorrel would be good.

Braised Duck with Peas

SERVES 4

Ducks from Aylesbury were becoming popular in the London markets of the eighteenth century, and in many cookery books thereafter (although some say it's a Roman or Elizabethan idea) they were boiled with turnips. I remember at The Savoy we used to cook our duck with turnips too, along with olives and cream. However, peas are traditional with ducklings as well – possibly because they are in season at about the same time of year – and that too became a popular braising combination. Lettuce was often added, which is a French touch, and indeed some old cookbooks describe the dish as '*à la française*', in the French fashion.

Some recipes add cream to the peas and then purée them for a sauce, but I don't think this is necessary. The simple step of braising them and the lettuce in with the duck gives amazing flavour.

2 x 1.1kg (2½ lb) ducks, with giblets
600ml (1 pint) duck or chicken stock
85g (3 oz) butter
225g (8 oz) bacon in the piece, cut into
   stubby strips (lardons) of about
    5 x 5mm x 2.5cm (¼ x ¼ x 1 in)
salt and freshly ground black pepper

175g (6 oz) small button onions
   (12 plus), peeled
1 round lettuce, shredded at the last minute
450g (1 lb) frozen peas
1 tbsp each of chopped fresh sage, mint
   and parsley

1 Take the giblets out of the ducks. Put the giblets into the stock and leave to gently simmer for 30 minutes.

2 Preheat the oven to 160°C/325°F/Gas 3.

3 Melt 25g (1 oz) of the butter in a casserole dish large enough to hold both ducks. Add the bacon lardons and button onions, and gently colour on all sides. When nicely coloured, take out and keep on one side.

4 Prick the ducks all over with a fork, and rub with a little salt. Colour all over in the same dish as the lardons and onions, then take out of the dish. Drain off all the fat and put the ducks back in the dish.

5 Strain the stock into the dish along with the ducks, bring to the boil and cover with the lid. Put into the preheated oven and cook for 1½ hours.

1 Preheat the oven to 200°C/400°F/Gas 6.

2 Sprinkle the pigeons with half the oil and roast in the preheated oven for 10 minutes. Remove from the oven, and cut the legs and backbone away from the breasts, leaving what is called the 'crown' of the pigeons.

3 Put the shallots and remaining oil into a casserole and place the pigeon breasts on top. Put the legs into the casserole as well, and add the nutmeg, parsley, garlic, bay leaf, tomatoes (which you have squeezed in your hands first) and Madeira. Season well and add the chicken stock. Bring to the boil, put the lid on and put into the same temperature oven for 15 minutes.

4 Take out of the oven. Remove the breasts and keep them warm while you reduce the sauce by half on the stove top.

5 Melt 25g (1 oz) of the butter in a clean pan and cook the mushrooms until golden brown.

6 Strain the stock, pushing down to extract the last drops of flavour from the vegetables, herbs and pigeon legs. Add the stock to the mushrooms along with the rest of the butter. Shake this into the sauce so that it starts to thicken.

7 Carve the breasts from the bones and put into a serving dish. Add any blood or juices to the sauce. Check the seasoning and pour over the breasts, three per person.

- Pigeons can be shot all year round, but are best between August and October (when fat from all the summer crop-stealing). Young birds have pink legs: the legs darken as the birds age. Or buy from a reliable butcher or game dealer.

- Pigeon legs are very difficult to cook and eat as they are so small, so this is a good way of using them, to get flavour into the sauce.

- This would be an ideal way of cooking pigeon for a game pie. Just put some pastry on the top and put into the oven to get crisp, brown and hot.

Game Pie

Game was once the most plentiful fresh meat available in Britain, until royal laws were passed and it became an offence for the ordinary man to snare a rabbit or game bird for the family pot. Because the birds obtained (whether legally or by poaching) were often older, they would be encased in suet and steamed for hours as a pudding, or braised first and then covered with a pastry crust as a pie.

Pigeon pie is a speciality of Yorkshire, where young pigeons are cooked with chunks of steak, bacon and hard-boiled eggs under pastry. I've added partridges here as well – in fact you could substitute virtually anything, pheasant or rabbit for instance – and the quails' eggs are a nice modern Turner touch.

225g (8 oz) puff pastry

1 egg yolk, mixed with a little water, to glaze

Filling

55g (2 oz) butter

4 smoked bacon rashers, chopped into 5mm (¼ in) wide strips

2 shallots, peeled and chopped

4 pigeon breasts

4 partridge breasts

salt and freshly ground black pepper

2 tbsp chopped fresh parsley

8 quails' eggs, hard-boiled and shelled

1 tsp Worcestershire sauce

150ml (5 fl oz) chicken stock

1 Melt half the butter in a frying pan and cook the bacon for 2 minutes to colour. Add the finely chopped shallot, cook for a few minutes to soften, then remove both from the pan using a slotted spoon. Put to one side.

2 Melt the remaining butter in the same pan to mix with the bacon fat. Remove the skin from the pigeon and partridge breasts, then seal and colour the flesh in the hot fat. Season and leave to cool.

3 Put a third of the bacon mixture in the bottom of a 1.2 litre (2 pint) pie dish. Lay the pigeon breasts on top and season again. Sprinkle with half of the remaining bacon mixture and half the parsley. Lay the quails' eggs on top along with the partridge breasts, then season. Sprinkle with the remaining bacon mixture and parsley.

4 Mix the Worcestershire sauce with the stock, and pour gently over the ingredients in the pie dish.

5 Preheat the oven to 220°C/425°F/Gas 7.

6 Roll out the puff pastry and cut to make a strip that will fit around the edges of the pie dish, and a large piece to fit the top. Dampen the edges of the dish and lay a thin strip of puff pastry around. Seal to the dish. Dampen the edges of the pastry shape and arrange on top of the strip around the pie dish edges. Crimp the edges to seal. Brush all over the pastry with egg wash, and decorate with a fork. Cut a hole in the centre for the steam to escape.

7 Bake in the preheated oven for 20 minutes, and then reduce the temperature to 180°C/350°F/Gas 4. Cook for a further 40 minutes or so, covering the pastry with foil if getting too brown. Serve hot.

■ Breasts of game birds are now available from supermarkets, but if you buy or acquire the birds whole, cut the breasts off to use in the pie, and use the skins and carcasses to make a wonderful game stock.

Venison Stew

SERVES 4

For centuries, the peasants had to stand back when wild deer raided their kitchen gardens, for they were not allowed to kill them. Deer and venison have always been the prerogative of the aristocracy, and the only taste others might have had would be of 'umbles' (offal) pie. Poachers were hung, drawn, quartered, executed and, later, transported. Luckily venison is now farmed, and we can enjoy its gamey flavour without looking over our shoulders...

This is a classic meat stew recipe. You could do exactly the same with beef, lamb or pork, altering the vegetables, and the jelly flavouring.

675g (1 ½ lb) venison (shoulder or haunch)

2 tbsp olive oil

2 garlic cloves, peeled and crushed

450g (1 lb) tomatoes

2 large carrots, trimmed and finely diced

300ml (10 fl oz) red wine

1 bunch mixed herbs (parsley, sage, thyme), tied together

salt and freshly ground black pepper

a little brown stock (made from roasted bones), to moisten if needed

2 tbsp redcurrant jelly

12 small cooked new potatoes

12 pre-cooked chestnuts

1 Preheat the oven to 160°C/325°F/Gas 3.

2 Cut the venison into large dice of 2.5cm (1 in) square.

3 Heat the oil in a casserole dish and colour the meat on all sides. Add the garlic, tomatoes and carrots, and cook for 5 minutes. Add the wine, herbs and seasoning, cover with a lid and cook in the preheated oven for up to 2 hours, until the meat is tender. Add a little stock if needed.

4 Lift the meat out of the dish and put to one side. Discard the herbs.

5 Add the redcurrant jelly to the juices and vegetables, then liquidise.

6 Put this sauce back on the stove, add the cooked new potatoes and chestnuts, and bring back to the boil. Add the meat and reheat gently.

7 Serve with mashed potato. Some *Apple and Rowan Jelly* (see page 210) would be a good accompaniment.

Rabbit with Mustard

SERVES 6

Like pigeons, rabbits were bred — in special *leporaria* — by the Romans when they came to Britain. Rabbits are actually native to Iberia, and after being introduced to various other parts of the Roman Empire, became a pest as well as a good source of fresh meat. The people of the Balearic Islands had to call for help from the Emperor when they were overrun — and remember what happened more recently in Australia. If we're not careful, according to present-day farmers, and despite myxomatosis, there's a great danger that rabbits will once again become a pest.

Rabbit would once have been the most common game animal, available to rich and poor alike. Although it is not now so popular (probably because of the pet connection, I wasn't allowed to use rabbit on *This Morning* in case children were watching), there are still a good number of recipes in the British tradition. Most of these, as in France and elsewhere in Europe, flavour the generally mild meat with strong spices such as the mustard here, which adds moisture at the same time.

2 small wild rabbits, skinned

600ml (1 pint) chicken stock

150ml (5 fl oz) white wine

3 tbsp Dijon mustard

salt and freshly ground black pepper

1 tbsp olive oil

1 carrot

1 onion

2 celery stalks

½ tsp freshly grated nutmeg

150ml (5 fl oz) double cream

1 tbsp grain mustard

2 tbsp lemon juice

2 tbsp chopped fresh parsley

1 Preheat the oven to 200°C/400°F/Gas 6.

2 Cut the rabbits into pieces: four back legs and four shoulders (the front legs). Trim the saddles, removing the belly, and cut each saddle in half to give four pieces in all.

3 Chop the rest of the carcass and put into a pan with the belly pieces, the chicken stock and white wine. Boil to reduce this stock by half.

4 Meanwhile, mix the Dijon mustard with some salt and pepper and the olive oil. Smear this over the rabbit pieces.

5 Prepare the vegetables and chop into fine dice. Put these in the bottom of a casserole, then lay the rabbit pieces on top. Sprinkle the grated nutmeg over, cover and cook in the preheated oven for 20 minutes.

6 Turn the rabbit pieces over and strain the stock into the casserole. Put back into the oven for a further 20 minutes or until cooked. Take out the pieces of rabbit, place in a clean pan and keep warm.

7 Add the cream to the stock left in the casserole and bring up to the boil. Strain into the clean pan with the rabbit, add the grain mustard and lemon juice, and bring back to the boil.

8 Check the seasoning, add the parsley and serve.

- I had the most fantastic rabbit dish recently in Menorca. The rabbit pieces – legs and saddle – were marinated in oil and garlic, and then barbecued.
- Wild rabbits have much more flavour, but less meat, than hutch-bred rabbits. And remember that rabbits have lots of small bones, so do be careful.

Braised Leeks (see page 142)

Vegetables were once a major part of the diet of the poor, who could not afford to eat meat. The native root vegetables such as turnips, parsnips and carrots would be boiled in pottage (probably *over*boiled), with onions and perhaps alongside some grain (or meat if they were lucky). Broad beans and peas would be dried rather than eaten fresh, and it is 'peasant' pulse and protein combinations that have survived, such as beans and bacon and pork and pease pudding. Vegetable cooking was actually rather boring.

Vegetables 6

After the great transatlantic explorations of the sixteenth century, unknown vegetables were introduced to Europe, among them potatoes, tomatoes, maize (sweetcorn), green beans, peppers and pumpkin. None was accepted very enthusiastically at first, either here or on the Continent, although Ireland, too wet for successful grain cultivation, was quick to adopt the potato, by about 1650. (This disastrous reliance on one crop alone led to the starvation and mass emigration of the populace in the 1840s after potato blight struck.) Gardeners in France, Italy and the Low Countries were also developing new types of vegetable, and as these were introduced to Britain, so vegetables – among them celery, broccoli, Brussels sprouts and artichokes – started to become more popular and more fashionable (at least with the recipe-writing and recipe-reading classes).

It was only at this time that vegetables were defined as a separate category of food, plants grown especially to be eaten. We are fond of vegetables now, and grow them for pleasure, not for necessity. We also cook and treat vegetables properly. Chefs like Paul Gaylor have actually made a speciality of cooking vegetables in an exciting way, and we now have farmers' markets, to which growers bring their produce, often organic, always very fresh.

We are enjoined to eat lots of vegetables for health, and the 'five a day' campaign – eating five portions of fruit and vegetables every day – is a very easy target, especially for children. If we can get children to eat healthy foods as early as possible, and to enjoy them, we will, hopefully, have prevented the tide of obesity that has been worrying us so much lately.

Asparagus

SERVE ABOUT
6 THICK STEMS
PER PORTION

The Romans were apparently very fond of asparagus, and perhaps, like so many other foodstuffs, they were responsible for its introduction to Britain. It has always been a vegetable for the rich rather than the poor, as an asparagus bed takes up so much garden space – and only produces a result for less than two months per year.

Asparagus is imported from many countries throughout the world, but I have to say I really do prefer the English spears that arrive in late May, early June – thin (sprue) or fatter, and always green.

1 Using a potato peeler or the back of a strong knife, scrape the lower two-thirds of the stem. Always peel from the tip end to the base and try to get uniformity in look. Much of the flavour and goodness is in the skin, so you only want to remove the outer tough layer. Lay the stems side by side with the tips all levelled up, and cut the lower parts of the stems off so that each stem is the same length. Tie carefully into bundles.

2 One way to cook the asparagus is to stand them upright in an asparagus basket in boiling water up to three-quarters of the height of the asparagus stems with the top section, the tips, steaming. When cooked the stems will just have a little 'give' about 5cm (2 in) down from the top of the tip or, when the tip of a knife is inserted, they feel only just tender. (It is not essential to stand asparagus stems upright to cook, however. You can plunge the untied spears into boiling salted water in a large wide pan.)

3 When they are cooked, plunge into iced water to stop the cooking and then reheat in boiling water before draining and serving.

4 To serve, put the stems on to a plate, with an upturned fork under the stem end side. This means that they are not covered with sauce and can be picked up without dirtying the hands.

5 Serve with a hollandaise sauce (see page 48), or a melted butter sauce (add 225g/8 oz pieces of cold butter to 1 tbsp cold water and the juice of ½ lemon; whisk over heat to make an emulsion).

Potato Salad

SERVES 4 I don't expect this is very traditionally British – is it an American import? – but it has become part of our repertoire and, sadly, is often very badly done. But a good potato salad is a joy, perfect on a buffet or at a barbecue, and deserves much more respect. I give you a couple of ideas below. Both are great with ham, beef or any cold meat.

Version One

450g (1 lb) waxy potatoes, washed

1 onion, peeled and finely chopped

150ml (5 fl oz) mayonnaise

salt and freshly ground black pepper

chopped fresh chives

1 Cook the potatoes in boiling water in their skins. When tender, drain them and leave to cool.

2 Skin the potatoes and cut them into 5mm (¼ in) dice. Mix with the onion, mayonnaise and salt and pepper to taste. Add the chopped chives.

Version Two

450g (1 lb) new potatoes, washed

150ml (5 fl oz) chicken stock

2 tbsp white wine vinegar

2 tbsp olive oil

1 tbsp Dijon mustard

salt and freshly ground black pepper

1 tbsp mayonnaise

1 bunch spring onions, the whites and a bit of the green, finely chopped

1 Cook the new potatoes in boiling water in their skins. When tender, drain them and remove the skins if you like (but I don't).

2 Meanwhile, bring the chicken stock to the boil with the vinegar and oil. Take off the heat and stir in the mustard.

3 Immediately slice the potatoes into the hot liquor. Leave to marinate and cool, during which time the potatoes will absorb most of the liquid.

4 Season with salt and pepper, then stir in the mayonnaise and spring onion. Serve lukewarm.

Champ

Champ is the Irish equivalent of mashed potatoes, but it includes greenery such as young leeks or kale, peas, nettles, salad or spring onions, which have been poached in milk or buttermilk. It is very similar to two other Irish dishes, boxty (see page 137) and colcannon, both of which are traditional at Hallowe'en. Colcannon often contains favours: a wedding ring for marriage, a sixpence for wealth, and a thimble and button for spinsterhood and bachelorhood respectively…

900g (2 lb) floury potatoes

salt and freshly ground black pepper

150ml (5 fl oz) buttermilk

150ml (5 fl oz) double cream

225g (8 oz) spring onions (or young leeks), finely chopped

115g (4 oz) unsalted butter

1 Wash, peel and cut the potatoes into large pieces. Cover with water, add salt and bring to the boil. Cook until tender, then strain off and return to the pan over a gentle heat to dry out. Do not colour.

2 Bring the buttermilk and double cream to the boil in a large clean pan. Add the spring onions to the milk-cream mixture, and simmer for 5 minutes. Drain off the spring onions, keeping the cream mixture.

3 Add the spring onions to the potato and mash finely. Add half the butter to the milk mixture, then beat into the potato. Season well.

4 Pour the potatoes into a serving dish and make a well in the middle. Melt the rest of the butter, pour into the well and serve immediately.

■ Today people always seem to want to make things more sophisticated – turning a mixture like this into little moulds, or encasing it in breadcrumbs. Let it be. The good old-fashioned way has always got to be the best.

Baked Beans

A mixture of salted bacon and soaked dried beans was a dish for the poor from very early times. The Pilgrim Fathers took the idea (and the basic ingredients) to America in 1620, where the dish was adopted, adapted and developed into the famous Boston baked beans. And thereafter it was returned to us, in the form of beans canned in a tomato sauce. Such is culinary history!

450g (1 lb) dried white beans (haricots blancs)

5 garlic cloves, peeled

2 large onions, peeled and quartered

2 large carrots, trimmed and quartered

1 x 280g (10 oz) tin peeled plum tomatoes

6 medium tomatoes, skinned and seeded

salt and freshly ground black pepper

1 Soak the beans in plenty of cold water to cover for 3 hours (unless it says different on the packet).

2 Drain and put into a saucepan. Cover with water again, bring to the boil and cook for 30 minutes.

3 Put 4 of the garlic cloves, the onions and carrots into the pot, and cook for a further hour.

4 Preheat the oven to 200°C/400°F/Gas 6.

5 Strain off the cooking liquid, and pick out and discard the vegetables and garlic.

6 Chop the tinned tomatoes, fresh tomatoes and remaining garlic clove together. Mix with the drained beans and season well. Put into an ovenproof dish with a lid.

7 Bring up to heat, put the lid on, then cook in the preheated oven for 30 minutes. Give one final check to the seasoning and serve.

■ Pick through the beans for grit, stones etc., but it shouldn't be necessary these days. They shouldn't need soaking for too long either.

■ Add bacon if you like, cut into strips and sautéed first.

Bubble and Squeak

SERVES 4–6   When I was a child, we always had plenty of cooked potato and cabbage left over after a meal so that we could make bubble and squeak, a classic dish for leftovers. Here, though, I describe how you might do it from scratch. Serve with cold meat, *Piccalilli* (see page 204) and/or brown sauce – and my dad used to serve it with runny fried eggs on top in his café. My own personal favourite accompaniment is black pudding…

The name 'bubble and squeak' is said to come from the noise the dish makes as it cooks, and it was originally a way of utilising leftover meat, made with meat and cabbage only. The potato addition and the gradual loss of the meat made it more like the Irish colcannon.

675g (1½ lb) medium baking potatoes, scrubbed
55g (2 oz) bacon or duck fat

450g (1 lb) Savoy cabbage, cored, finely shredded and cooked until tender
salt and freshly ground black pepper

1 Preheat the oven to 180°C/350°F/Gas 4, and bake the potatoes until tender, about an hour. Take out and leave to cool.

2 Melt the fat in an ovenproof frying pan and add the potato flesh scraped out from the potato skins. Leave until it starts to colour. Crush with a fork, but leave some lumps in.

3 Add the cooked cabbage, season with salt and pepper, and fry well. Keep moving in the pan.

4 When the bottom is coloured, put the pan in the preheated oven for 15 minutes.

■ You can add other ingredients to the basic mix if you like – onions, carrots or peas, say – and you could use mashed instead of baked potato if you had that left over, or sliced cooked Brussels sprouts instead of the cabbage.

■ You could shape the mixture into little cakes before frying, but why bother? It's the taste that counts – and the choice of fat is *vital*.

■ A tendency these days is to undercook cauliflower for this dish. But, although you don't want it to be a mush or purée, it should be soft enough to be able to spoon out easily (soft enough for your grandma to eat without her teeth!).

■ Another way of cooking the cauli would be to gouge out the centre stalk, leaving the vegetable whole with a hole in the middle. Cook it for a little longer to ensure the inside parts are cooked.

■ Much as I hate to admit it, in my tests the acidity and crumbliness of Lancashire cheese worked better than a Yorkshire Wensleydale. (But if you can't get either, a Cheddar will do fine.)

Brussels Sprouts with Chestnuts

SERVES 4

Brussels sprouts were developed in the Low Countries in the Middle Ages, but did not become popular in Britain until the mid-nineteenth century (and are still not particularly popular in some quarters…). Chestnuts too have been with us for ever, although the French and the Italians have always appreciated them rather more in a culinary sense. The combination of the two is fairly recent, I imagine, created probably because both are in season at the same time.

Although now traditional with our Christmas turkey, the vegetable mixture is so good it deserves to be used more often – delicious with roast pork or poultry, for instance.

225g (8 oz) chestnuts

350g (12 oz) Brussels sprouts

salt and freshly ground black pepper

55g (2 oz) unsalted butter

1 Make a cross with a small sharp knife in the bottom of each chestnut and cook in the preheated oven for 20 minutes or until the shells start to split. Cool a little until you can handle them, then peel.

2 Meanwhile, prepare the Brussels. Trim off the outside leaves and put a cross in the stalk of each. Plunge into boiling salted water and cook until just done. Refresh and drain.

3 Cut the peeled chestnuts and the cooked sprouts in half. Fry in the butter to heat through and brown a little, then season and serve.

■ You could cook the dish in an interesting alternative way. Shred the sprouts before cooking. Stir-fry in butter, add some chopped garlic to taste and the cooked, peeled and crumbled chestnuts. Season and serve.

■ The best chestnuts are those cooked in a special container over an open fire. To test whether a chestnut is ready, shell one, dip it in salt and eat. You'll soon know. (And be sure to buy more chestnuts than you need if, like me, you are obliged to carry on testing to see whether they are ready…)

Laverbread with Bacon

Laver is an edible seaweed which is found on coastlines mainly in the west of Britain, in Wales, Scotland and Ireland (known as 'sloke' in the last two countries). It is gathered, washed and boiled for several hours until it is like a dark-green spinach purée. This is when it is known as 'laverbread' in Wales, where laver is most commonly eaten still. It is served on toast, dressed as a salad, or mixed with oatmeal to make laver cakes, which are fried in bacon fat. I have taken the basic cake idea a little further here. Apparently laver was once mixed with orange juice to make a sauce for roast lamb and mutton.

Laver is known as *nori* in Japan, where it is cultivated. It is mainly available in dried sheets, and in this form has become very much more fashionable than poor old laver, as a wrapping for sushi and similar foods.

225g (8 oz) cooked laver
350g (12 oz) plain mashed cooked potato
25g (1 oz) unsalted butter, melted
salt and freshly ground black pepper
freshly grated nutmeg

4 rashers streaky bacon
225g (8 oz) oatmeal
55g (2 oz) lard
8 rashers smoked back bacon

1 Mix the laver and mashed potato together. Stir in the butter and season with salt, pepper and nutmeg. Leave to stand for a few minutes.
2 Cook the streaky bacon until crisp in a hot pan, and then chop into small dice. Mix into the laver mixture along with half of the oatmeal.
3 Mould into four balls of about 115g (4 oz) each. Roll in the remaining oatmeal and flatten into cakes to look like fishcakes.
4 Fry in the hot lard until golden brown, then turn over and cook through. Meanwhile, cook the smoked bacon.
5 Serve the laver cakes with the rashers of bacon over them.

Braised Leeks

SERVES 4

Leeks have been valued since the time of the ancients. The Emperor Nero apparently ate them in an attempt to improve his singing voice! Everyone grew leeks at one time, as they were a pot (pottage) vegetable, and many towns are actually named after the 'leac-tun', or leek enclosure (such as Leighton). Leeks went into a decline in a fashionable sense, but in the furthest parts of Britain, in Ireland, Scotland and Wales – especially the latter, where it's the national symbol – it survived in many classic recipes. The Welsh make leek pies and braise them, the Scots use in them in *Cock-a-Leekie* (see page 12), and the Irish use them in *Champ* (see page 130).

Most traditional leek recipes have them boiled or braised in butter. I have refined the braising idea a little, which gives good flavour. The leeks are good with any roast meats, particularly lamb and duck.

900g (2 lb) young leeks

salt and freshly ground black pepper

unsalted butter

1 onion, peeled

1 carrot, trimmed

2 celery stalks, trimmed

1 tbsp fresh thyme leaves

300ml (10 fl oz) chicken or vegetable stock

1 tsp fécule (potato flour) or cornflour, slaked in 1 tbsp water

1 Preheat the oven to 180°C/350°F/Gas 4.

2 Trim the leeks of their roots and cut away the dark green tops in a pointed 'v' shape. Wash well, turning them upside down under running water.

3 Plunge the leeks into boiling salted water and cook for 5 minutes, then run under cold water to refresh.

4 Butter a suitably sized ovenproof dish. Chop the vegetables into small dice and put into the dish, along with the thyme.

5 Squeeze excess moisture from each leek. Tap halfway up with a knife and fold in half. Lay on top of the diced vegetables and pour over the stock.

6 Cover with buttered greaseproof paper and cook in the preheated oven for 45 minutes. Take the leeks out of the cooking dish and put into a serving dish. Keep warm.

7 Strain the liquor, discarding the vegetables. Reduce the liquor by one-third and thicken with the slaked fécule or cornflour. Add 25g (1 oz) butter to the sauce, season, then pour over the leeks and serve.

■ You don't have to discard the braising vegetables, although they will have given most of their flavour to the liquor. Simply leave the leeks and veg in the dish (as in the photograph on page 126) and pour the sauce over all.

■ Celery, chicory and other vegetables could be cooked in the same way. You could also sprinkle some grated cheese on the top and brown under the grill at the last moment.

Broad Bean and Bacon Salad

SERVES 4

Before the great explorations of the sixteenth century, we only had the broad bean in Europe, and it would have played a huge part in the diet, being eaten fresh in the summer (pods and all at first, as is becoming popular among fashionable gardeners), then dried for winter use. Dried beans and bacon was a common combination from the very earliest times, and I have brought the idea up to date, using fresh beans instead in a starter salad.

900g (2 lb) broad beans in their pods
salt and freshly ground black pepper
4 rashers back bacon, finely diced
4½ tbsp olive oil
2 tomatoes, skinned and seeded
1 shallot, peeled
½ tsp French mustard

1 tbsp white wine vinegar
1 garlic clove, peeled
1 tbsp chopped mixed fresh parsley, chervil
   and tarragon

To serve
about 55g (2 oz) mixed salad leaves

1 Remove the beans from their pods. Plunge into boiling salted water and simmer for 10 minutes or until tender. Remove, refresh in cold water and drain.

2 If the 'inner' grey skins are tough (more likely in larger and older beans), remove these skins with your thumb and forefinger to reveal the bright green insides, being careful not to crush them.

3 Meanwhile, fry the bacon in ½ tbsp of the olive oil until brown and crisp. Remove from the heat. Cut the tomato flesh into small dice and finely chop the shallot.

4 Mix the shallot with the mustard and then the wine vinegar. Crush the garlic and add to the bacon. Toss and put into a serving bowl with the shallot and mustard mixture.

5 Add the remaining olive oil, and the beans and herbs. Mix and season to taste with salt and pepper. Leave for 30 minutes to marinate and cool.

6 To serve, present on a small bed of mixed leaves, making sure the beans and their dressing coat the leaves. Finish off with a good grinding of black pepper.

Spotted Dick and Custard Sauce (see pages 154 and 220)

Monsieur Misson, a French visitor to England in the 1690s, wrote about the English penchant for puddings. 'Ah, what an excellent thing is an English pudding! To come in pudding-time, is as much as to say, to come in the most lucky moment in the world.' What he was so enthusiastically referring to was mainly the pudding which was made with a mixture of suet or marrow, flour, dried fruits, spices and sugar. This would have been stuffed into an animal gut, and boiled in water, either alone, or with other foods such as meat. These guts were available when the animals were slaughtered, in the

Puddings

autumn, thus his reference to 'pudding-time'. With the invention of the pudding cloth or bag, though, puddings could be made at any time of year. The pudding was the carbohydrate part of a meal, but was not served as a separate course: that came later. Steamed puds, such as spotted dick, Snowdon pudding and jam roly-poly – and indeed Christmas pudding – are current examples of these early puddings.

Gradually the word 'pudding' came to refer to other sweet things, and specifically to sweet things that were served as a separate course at the end of a meal. Many of the other 'sweet things' had as long a heritage as the steamed or boiled pudding. Rice puddings and other grain and milk puddings are an echo of the medieval grain dishes known as 'frumenty', simply using imported ingredients instead of local. Egg custards were popular in the Middle Ages, and they are used in many famous puddings. Bread and butter pudding (now so ubiquitous I didn't think you needed another one here!), apple charlotte and queen of puddings also illustrate another consistent strand in British puddings, the use of bread and breadcrumbs.

But it is perhaps our sweet pies for which we are most famous: our plate pies with one or two layers of pastry, our deep-dish pies, flans, tarts, turnovers and pasties. And there are a host of other fruit puddings with or without pastry, among them apple crumble (well, the crumble topping is *almost* pastry) and the more recent, but famous summer pudding (where bread is used *instead* of pastry). And a final strand represented here is that of the cold creamy puddings such as syllabubs, trifles and fools. They were thought to be less important than other courses in the meal, so all gained rather silly names...

Apple Pie

SERVES 4

This must be the most ancient of British apple puddings, a layer of apple between two layers of pastry. This was a medieval idea (taken by the Pilgrim Fathers to America), and it seems to have survived particularly in the north of England. Elsewhere an apple pie usually has a pastry top only (a pastry *bottom* in France), but plate fruit pies are still made in Yorkshire, Lancashire and further north. This is my father's recipe, which he served in his café, often mixing the apple with blackberries, raspberries or (tinned) cherries. My gran used to serve it with Wensleydale cheese: 'Apple pie without cheese is like a kiss without a squeeze.'

Pastry

225g (8 oz) plain flour

3½ tsp salt

25g (1 oz) unrefined caster sugar, plus
   extra for sprinkling

finely grated zest of 1 orange and 1 lemon

85g (3 oz) cold unsalted butter, diced

85g (3 oz) cold lard, diced

about 3 tbsp cold water to mix

1 egg mixed with a little water for egg wash

Filling

450g (1 lb) cooking apples

55g (2 oz) unrefined caster sugar

55g (2 oz) liquid honey

1 To make the pastry, sift the flour and salt together, then add the sugar and lemon and orange zests. With cold fingertips, carefully rub in the butter and lard until like breadcrumbs. Add only enough water to pull it together to a dough. Wrap in clingfilm and put aside to rest for 30 minutes.

2 Peel and core the apples, and cut them into large chunks. Add the sugar and honey and leave to stand for 20 minutes.

3 Meanwhile, preheat the oven to 200°C/400°F/Gas 6.

4 Use a third of the pastry and roll it out into a round shape to fit your chosen non-stick ovenproof pie plate (they used to be enamel). Start with a ball of pastry, it's easier. Lightly grease the oven plate.

5 Lay the pastry gently on the greased plate and pile in the apple mixture. Brush around the edges with egg wash.

6 Roll out the remaining pastry, again from a ball shape to a round which will fit over the mounded tart. Put in place and pat down to seal roughly. Trim around the outside and firmly 'crimp' the edges. Brush with the remaining egg wash, sprinkle with sugar, and cut a hole in the centre for the steam to escape.

7 Bake in the preheated oven for 15 minutes, then turn the temperature down to 180°C/350°F/Gas 4 and bake for a further 20–25 minutes.

8 When out of the oven, dredge with caster sugar and serve hot, with clotted cream, crème Chantilly, ice-cream (as they did at Simpson's in the Strand) or *Custard Sauce* (see page 220) – or a combination of the whole lot!

■ You can add spices to the basic apple filling. Cloves are traditional, and I remember one particular occasion when I was at college being taught how to make a deep apple pie. Being a smartie pants, I read the recipe very quickly and, without thinking, chopped up a clove of garlic, and included it in my pie. When mine was ready and the tutor was tasting it, I had to think quickly, having already realised my mistake. 'Sorry, sir, I must have forgotten to wash my knife.'

■ Raisins and sultanas can also be added. In fact, there are no end of variations possible.

Bakewell Tart

Another pudding which includes a layer of jam (see *Queen of Puddings*, page 165), Bakewell tart was originally known as Bakewell pudding and still is in parts of Derbyshire today. There are several stories about how it came into existence, but most are apocryphal as it has long been known in its present form – a pastry case with a jam lining and an almond 'cake' topping. This almond mixture is known as 'frangipane' in the business, and I always wondered what the connection between it and the flower, frangipani, was. It seems a trifle tenuous, but the almond mix was supposedly named after an Italian aristocrat, Frangipani, who invented a perfume, probably using red jasmine, or frangipani, for the gloves of Louis XIII...

Pastry

175g (6 oz) plain flour

a pinch of salt

25g (1 oz) unrefined caster sugar

finely grated zest of 1 orange and 1 lemon

55g (2 oz) cold unsalted butter, diced

25g (1 oz) cold lard, diced

about 2 tbsp ice-cold water to mix

Filling

55g (2 oz) raspberry jam

3 eggs

115g (4 oz) unrefined caster sugar

115g (4 oz) unsalted butter, melted

115g (4 oz) ground almonds

**25g (1 oz) icing sugar, mixed with a little
   water to a thin icing**

1 Make the pastry as in the recipe on page 152, adding the finely grated citrus zests, and put it aside to rest for about 20 minutes.

2 Meanwhile, preheat the oven to 180°C/350°F/Gas 4.

3 Roll the pastry out to a round to fit a 25cm (10 in) flan ring, and place in the ring. Cut off any excess pastry, and crimp the edges.

4 Warm the jam and then, if you can be bothered (but it's the correct way), press it through a fine sieve to get rid of the seeds. Spread over the base of the tart.

5 Meanwhile, beat the eggs and sugar together, and then slowly fold in the melted butter and the ground almonds. Pour carefully into the pastry-lined flan ring.

6 Bake in the preheated oven until set, about 35 minutes. Take out and cool.

7 Pour the icing into the centre of the tart and, using a palette knife, spread it as thinly as possible. Leave to set.

Treacle Tart

SERVES 4

Treacle tart must be the quintessential British pudding – a pastry base filled with bread, eggs and sugar. It's made all over Britain, from Scotland (where a huge amount of sugar came in from the West Indies) down to Yorkshire. Sometimes the tart is actually a plate pie (top and bottom pastry); often it is a plate tart, but with interwoven pastry strips decorating the top. Here I have made little individual tarts with only one layer of pastry. Whatever you do, it is an unadulterated sweet delight.

250g (9 oz) *Sweet Pastry* (see page 152)

Filling

25g (1 oz) fine fresh breadcrumbs

275g (9½ oz) golden syrup

1 tbsp dark treacle

juice and finely grated zest of 1 lemon

3 eggs

1 Roll out the sweet pastry and use to line four 10cm (4 in) round, non-stick tart moulds, 2cm (¾ in) deep. Rest in the fridge for half an hour.

2 Meanwhile, preheat the oven to 180°C/350°F/Gas 4.

3 For the filling, mix together the breadcrumbs, syrup, treacle, lemon juice and zest.

4 Beat the eggs, then add to the breadcrumb mixture.

5 Pour the filling into the pastry-lined moulds and bake in the preheated oven for 15–20 minutes. Serve warm with clotted cream.

Lemon Meringue Pie

SERVES 8   Fruit tarts and fruit cheese or curd tarts are long-standing elements of British cooking, but the meringue topping, possibly an American influence – they have 'chiffon' pies – dates from much later. There are several other puds which use a meringue topping – butterscotch tart, Oxford and Cambridge pudding, a Welsh border tart – and, of course, *Queen of Puddings* (see page 165).

Sweet pastry

225g (8 oz) plain flour

a pinch of salt

25g (1 oz) unrefined caster sugar

115g (4 oz) cold unsalted butter

2 egg yolks, beaten

approx. 2 tbsp water

Lemon filling

4 juicy lemons

150ml (5 fl oz) water

55g (2 oz) unsalted butter

85g (3 oz) unrefined caster sugar

25g (1 oz) cornflour, slaked in a little water

3 egg yolks

Meringue topping

3 egg whites

a pinch of salt

115g (4 oz) unrefined caster sugar

icing sugar

1   To make the pastry, sift the flour and salt into a bowl and add the sugar. Chop the cold butter and rub into the flour until the texture resembles breadcrumbs. Add the egg yolks. Mix to a dough, using the water if necessary, and form into a ball. If you have time, chill, wrapped in clingfilm, for about 20 minutes.

2   Roll the pastry dough out to a circle of about 33cm (13 in) to line the base and sides of a 25cm (10 in) flan ring. Place the flan ring on a baking sheet and line with the pastry circle. Neaten the edges, and leave to rest in the fridge for half an hour.

3   Meanwhile, preheat the oven to 180°C/350°F/Gas 4.

4   Fill the pastry casing with a circle of greaseproof paper and fill with beans or rice. Bake in the preheated oven for 15 minutes. Take out of the oven,

remove the beans and paper, and reduce the oven temperature to 140°C/275°F/Gas 1. Bake for 10 more minutes. Remove and turn the oven temperature up to 160°C/325°F/Gas 3.

5 Meanwhile, for the lemon filling, zest two of the lemons into a saucepan. Squeeze all four lemons into the pan and add the water, the butter and sugar, and bring to the boil.

6 Add the slaked cornflour, bring up to the boil again and gently stir until thickened.

7 Beat the egg yolks together, then pour a little sauce on to them. Stir in and then pour back into the pan. Gently heat and stir – do not boil – for 2 minutes. Pour into the flan case.

8 Meanwhile, for the meringue topping, whisk the egg whites to peaks with the salt, then add 25g (1 oz) of sugar at a time, continually whisking, until all the sugar has been whisked in.

9 Spoon the meringue over the pie and use the back of the spoon to make random peaks. Sprinkle with a little icing sugar.

10 Bake the pie in the preheated oven for 25 minutes. Take out, sprinkle with more icing sugar and leave to cool. Eat cold.

- Any citrus fruit will work – oranges, grapefruit, mandarins – but always check for the quantity of juice. I actually worry a little about giving fruit for juice in numbers: at certain times you might need ten fruit to get the same amount of juice as from four juicier ones at a different time.
- If you want to be really posh, you could use a piping bag to put the meringue on.

Spotted Dick

SERVES 4–6 Perhaps the most infamous of British roly-poly puddings – and not just the cause of many a schoolboy snigger: recently an English health service board was forced to rescind its decision to re-christen the pudding 'Spotted Richard' on hospital menus, with a well-known supermarket chain following suit… It is also known as spotted dog (strictly speaking, when the dried fruit is mixed *with* the pastry instead of being encased in it) and plum bolster.

225g (8 oz) plain flour, plus extra
  for sprinkling
15g (½ oz) baking powder
a pinch of salt
115g (4 oz) finely chopped beef suet

150ml (5 fl oz) water
115g (4 oz) currants
55g (2 oz) raisins
finely grated zest of 1 lemon

1 To make the basic suet pastry, sift the flour, baking powder and salt together, then rub in the suet. Add the water and mix to a dough.

2 Roll out to a rectangle 25 x 15cm (10 x 6 in) and 1cm (½ in) thick. Sprinkle with the currants and raisins, leaving a border of 1cm (½ in) round all sides. Press the fruit in and sprinkle with the lemon zest. Paint the borders with water.

3 Turn the two short sides in and seal. Roll up from a long side carefully, to keep all the fruit in. Seal when rolled up.

4 Rinse a clean tea towel in boiling water. Sprinkle with flour and shake off the excess. Lay the roll on top of the cloth, fold the cloth over and fix at the ends with string. Steam the cloth-wrapped roll for 1½ hours. Or you could put the pud on a rack in a roasting tray full of water, then cover it with foil. Bring to

the boil then steam in the oven at 200°C/400°F/Gas 6 for about 2 hours. Top up the water occasionally. Or bake at the above oven temperature, but not in the cloth, brushed with egg wash, for about 1¼ hours.

5 Take out, unwrap while still hot (if necessary), cut into slices and serve with *Custard Sauce* (see page 220) or jam sauce.

Snowdon Pudding

SERVES 6 This Welsh suet pudding is made in the classic way, but with a few characteristic differences. The raisins and marmalade form a light coating around the rest of the pudding mix, and the white cream sauce, poured on at the end, looks like the snow that often lies on the top of Snowdon during winter.

25g (1 oz) unsalted butter

115g (4 oz) raisins

2 tbsp orange marmalade

115g (4 oz) chopped beef suet

175g (6 oz) fresh white breadcrumbs

1 tbsp ground rice

2 tbsp orange marmalade

finely grated zest of 1 orange

finely grated zest of 1 lemon

55g (2 oz) unrefined caster sugar

2 eggs

Sauce

85g (3 oz) unrefined caster sugar

juice of 1 lemon

150ml (5 fl oz) dry white wine

150ml (5 fl oz) double cream

1 Blitz the butter and raisins together in the blender, then push through a sieve. Brush the inside of a 1.2 litre (2 pint) pudding basin with this mixture, and then put the marmalade in the bottom of the pudding basin.

2 Mix all the other pudding ingredients together and put into the basin. Cover with greased greaseproof paper and a pudding cloth and tie tightly. Steam for 1½ hours.

3 Meanwhile, for the cream sauce, boil the sugar, lemon juice and white wine together to reduce by two-thirds. Add the double cream and boil to thicken.

4 To serve, turn the pudding out and pour the sauce over.

Sticky Toffee Pudding

SERVES 8

Dried fruit boiled in a suet pastry base in a cloth would once have been the most traditional British pudding. As ovens became more common, the pastry base became lighter, and here the fruit is mixed with a darkly sweet cake mixture. Francis Coulson and Brian Sack of the Sharrow Bay Hotel in Cumbria were responsible, I think, for reintroducing us to the joys of this pudding.

175g (6 oz) medjool dates
115g (4 oz) dried figs
55g (2 oz) sultanas
150ml (5 fl oz) boiling water
finely grated zest of 2 oranges
115g (4 oz) unsalted butter
175g (6 oz) unrefined demerara sugar
3 eggs, beaten

140g (5 oz) self-raising flour
55g (2 oz) ground almonds
55g (2 oz) pistachio nuts, chopped

Sauce
115g (4 oz) unsalted butter
175g (6 oz) unrefined demerara sugar
150ml (5 fl oz) double cream

1 Grease a baking tray about 20cm (8 in) square, or the same volume, and preheat the oven to 180°C/350°F/Gas 4.

2 Stone the dates and chop them finely with the figs and sultanas. Put them into a bowl and pour the boiling water over. Whisk to a pulp, then add the orange zest.

3 Cream the butter and sugar together, then add the egg. Beat together, then fold in the flour, ground almonds and fruit pulp.

4 Pour the mixture into the prepared baking tray and bake in the preheated oven for 30–40 minutes. To test if cooked, press with your hand: there will be some resistance. Take out when cooked and allow to cool slightly.

5 Cut the cooled cake into shapes. I like round ones, although this means wastage: use a round metal cutter (the leftover bits could possibly be used in one of the other puddings in the book). Squares mean you can use the whole thing!

6 Meanwhile, for the sauce, melt the butter, add the sugar and bring to the boil. Add the double cream and simmer for 5 minutes until lightly thickened.

7 Pour a little sauce over and around the pudding, sprinkle with the chopped pistachios and serve.

Rice Pudding

SERVES 8
A cereal 'pottage', a semi-liquid cooked dish, was everyday fare for rich and poor alike from the Middle Ages all over the country. In the north they would use oats (and 'porridge' is the dish still most similar to the medieval pottage), in the south, rye, barley and wheat. When rice was (expensively) introduced from Italy, it was mixed with milk and sweet spices and baked or boiled. Sometimes eggs were added for a richer result, and in Yorkshire, suet was often included as well. Our present-day rice puddings are not too different from these early originals. Whether they liked the skin then or not, I don't know…

55g (2 oz) Carolina short-grain rice

450ml (15 fl oz) milk

150ml (5 fl oz) double cream

55g (2 oz) unrefined caster sugar

1 vanilla pod

25g (1 oz) unsalted butter

freshly grated nutmeg

1 Put the rice, milk and cream into a thick-bottomed pan and bring to the boil, stirring all the time.

2 Add the sugar, the seeds from the vanilla pod and the pod itself. Simmer until cooked, stirring regularly, about 45–50 minutes. Remove the pod.

3 Add the butter and nutmeg to taste, then pour into a dish and colour the top under the preheated grill until golden brown.

4 Serve with freshly made, whole fruit *Strawberry Jam* (see page 206).

■ For a slightly fancier version, you could add a couple of eggs. When the rice is cooked, butter a pie dish. Beat 2 egg yolks into the rice. Whisk 2 egg whites and then fold them into the rice. Spoon into the pie dish and bake in the preheated oven at 160°C/325°F/Gas 3 for 15–20 minutes. Sprinkle with icing sugar and serve.

Apple and Pineapple Crumble

SERVES 6

Although we have long loved fruit pies using pastry, fruit with a crumble topping – basically sweet pastry ingredients without the water – is very much more recent. Some suggest it did not come into use until after World War Two, perhaps when sugar had stopped being rationed. And of course a crumble is much easier and quicker to make than a pastry! The idea may have come from the Austrian '*streusel*', a cake topping which, because it contains less flour, bakes to a crisper texture than our distinctly crumbly crumble.

25g (1 oz) unsalted butter

350g (12 oz) eating apples

225g (8 oz) fresh peeled pineapple

85g (3 oz) unrefined caster sugar

Crumble topping

115g (4 oz) cold unsalted butter, diced

225g (8 oz) plain flour

115g (4 oz) unrefined demerara sugar

1 Preheat the oven to 180°C/350°F/Gas 4. Butter a pie dish generously.

2 Peel and core the apples and cut into 1cm (½ in) dice. Cut the fresh pineapple to the same size and mix with the apple. Put into the buttered pie dish and pat down. Sprinkle the caster sugar over to form a flat bed.

3 To make the crumble topping, rub the cold butter dice into the flour to form a breadcrumb-like mixture. Stir in the demerara sugar, then sprinkle some of this over the fruit. Pat down firmly, then sprinkle the rest on top.

4 Bake in the preheated oven for 15 minutes. Turn the oven temperature down to 160°C/325°F/Gas 3 and bake until well coloured, about another 25 minutes.

5 Serve with *Custard Sauce* (see page 220) or ice-cream.

■ Apple and blackberry crumble is probably more familiar, but pineapple is a good foil for the apple. (And, although it is not very British, it has actually been enthusiastically grown in English hothouses since the seventeenth century. The pineapples which adorn iron railings and gates from that period are proof of its popularity and familiarity.)

Queen of Puddings

SERVES 6

This old-fashioned pudding combines two major strands of the British pudding tradition. The baked custard is one, and the use of bread is another. The jam is fairly characteristic too, but the meringue was a later, probably foreign addition (and which features in many other traditional sweets, such as *Lemon Meringue Pie*, see page 152).

However, having said all that, I've used cake crumbs here instead of breadcrumbs, which just refines the idea a little. In fact you could use any cake, really, even chocolate, as a good way of using up those last wedges that no-one wants. And, of course, instead of using a lattice meringue as in the photograph opposite you could always simply spread the meringue over the top with a palette knife.

300ml (10 fl oz) milk

300ml (10 fl oz) double cream

1 vanilla pod, split

4 eggs, separated

140g (5 oz) unrefined caster sugar

finely grated zest of 1 lemon

freshly grated nutmeg

55g (2 oz) unsalted butter

115g (4 oz) plain sponge cake crumbs

55g (2 oz) raspberry jam, warmed
  and strained

To decorate

glacé cherries

angelica

icing sugar

1 Put the milk and cream into a suitable saucepan, and scrape in the vanilla seeds. Add the pod and bring the mixture just to the boil.

2 Beat the egg yolks and 55g (2 oz) of the sugar together in a bowl. Pour the cream mixture over the eggs and sugar, then add the lemon zest and nutmeg to taste.

3 Grease a pie dish with the butter, and put the cake crumbs into it. Pour the sauce over and leave for 20 minutes. Remove the vanilla pod.

4 Meanwhile, preheat the oven to 180°C/350°F/Gas 4.

5 Bake the custard in the preheated oven until set, about 30 minutes. Take out and leave to set for 5 minutes, then spread the warmed raspberry jam over.

6 Warm the remaining sugar slightly in the oven, no more than 5 minutes. Take out when it feels just warm to the touch.

7 For the meringue topping, whisk the egg whites to firm, and then whisk in the warmed sugar. Put in a piping bag and pipe lattice style round and over the top.

8 Decorate (like a crown) with cherries and angelica, then dredge with icing sugar and put back in the oven to brown and set the meringue, about 10–15 minutes. Serve warm.

Slit your vanilla pod in half lengthways, and scrape out the seeds from both halves with the blade of a knife. The seeds hold the most intense flavour, but you should always use the pod as well.

Cabinet Pudding

SERVES 6

A relative of many other British custard puddings, this one can be either baked and served hot as here, or made to be served cold. It also varies in title, being known variously as cabinet, diplomat and chancellor's pudding. Why the political connection I don't know, but it's a good rib-sticking winter warmer.

55g (2 oz) unsalted butter

300ml (10 fl oz) milk

150ml (5 fl oz) double cream

1 vanilla pod

2 eggs plus 3 egg yolks

55g (2 oz) unrefined caster sugar

55g (2 oz) muscatel sultanas

25g (1 oz) glacé cherries

25g (1 oz) angelica

175g (6 oz) sponge cake, diced

finely grated zest of 2 lemons

150ml (5 fl oz) brandy

1 Using all the butter grease a medium-sized pie dish (or small moulds).

2 Put the milk and double cream on to a gentle heat. Scrape the vanilla seeds from the pod and put into the milk, along with the pod.

3 Beat the eggs and yolks well together with the sugar.

4 Chop the dried fruits finely, then sprinkle half of them on to the base of the pie dish. Mix the sponge cake with the rest of the fruit and the lemon zest, and pile into the pie dish. Pour the brandy over and leave for 5 minutes.

5 Pour the heated milk over the beaten eggs and sugar, and stir in well. Take the pod out and pour half of the custard over the cake. Leave for 15 minutes.

6 Meanwhile, preheat the oven to 180°C/350°F/Gas 4.

7 Pour the rest of the custard on top of the dish and bake in the preheated oven in a bain-marie of warm water for 20 minutes. Turn the temperature down to 160°C/325°F/Gas 3 and cook for another 20 minutes.

8 Take out of the oven and allow to stand for 5 minutes. Turn out and serve hot, with a jam sauce perhaps. Also good cold with ice-cream.

■ Instead of the sponge cake, you could use soaked sponge fingers, macaroons or ratafia biscuits.

Chocolate and Raspberry Trifle

SERVES 4

One of the most famous cold British desserts, the trifle has changed in nature over the years. Originally it consisted of wine-soaked almond biscuits, covered with custard, then topped with *Syllabub* (see opposite). When I was a child, trifle was made in a posh crystal bowl. The jelly was out of a packet, fruit out of a tin, sponge out of a packet, and custard out of a tin. If you were lucky, it was topped with cream out of a cow. When you put your spoon in, it made a noise that made Gran look askance... This is my version!

175g (6 oz) white chocolate

2 egg yolks

25g (1 oz) unrefined caster sugar

150ml (5 fl oz) milk

85ml (3 fl oz) double cream

2½ tbsp icing sugar

4 x 4cm (1½ in) slices Swiss roll

2 tbsp Kirsch liqueur

225g (8 oz) fresh raspberries

a few sprigs fresh mint

1 Put a 55g (2 oz) piece of the white chocolate in the fridge; this will make it easier to grate later. Break the remainder into small pieces.

2 Cream the egg yolks and sugar together in a large bowl. Whisk for about 2–3 minutes until the mixture is pale, thick, creamy and leaves a trail.

3 Pour the milk and cream into a small, heavy-based saucepan and bring to the boil. Pour on to the egg yolk mixture, whisking all the time. Pour back into the pan and place over a moderate heat. Stir the mixture with a wooden spoon until it starts to thicken and coats the back of the spoon. Add the broken-up pieces of chocolate and stir in until completely incorporated. Remove the pan from the heat and allow to cool slightly. Cover the custard with a little icing sugar and a piece of clingfilm to prevent a skin forming.

4 Place the Swiss roll slices in a large glass bowl and sprinkle with the Kirsch. Scatter with most of the fresh raspberries, reserving a few for decoration. Pour the white chocolate custard over the Swiss roll and leave to set in the fridge, preferably overnight.

5 To serve, decorate the trifle with the reserved raspberries. Take the piece of white chocolate from the fridge and finely grate over the trifle. Finally, dust with a little icing sugar and place the mint sprigs on top.

Syllabub

SERVES 6–8 Syllabub is one of the great British milk puddings. Once it was made with milk squeezed straight from the cow on to a sweetened wine called 'sill' or 'sille' (from Champagne); this created a froth on top, and it was served as a drink. Sometimes the creamy milk was whipped, which led to the separation of curds and wine after sitting. Today it is made with cream and wine along with some spirit, which makes for a thicker mixture with a slight separation.

Incidentally, they say that a syllabub without brandy is like kissing a man without a moustache…

150ml (5 fl oz) white wine

1 tbsp dry sherry

1 tbsp brandy

finely grated zest of 1 lemon

juice of 2 lemons

freshly grated nutmeg

55g (2 oz) unrefined caster sugar

450ml (15 fl oz) double cream

150ml (5 fl oz) single cream

1 Mix the wine, sherry and brandy in a bowl with the lemon zest, and allow to stand for 2 hours.

2 Strain into a bowl, then add the lemon juice, nutmeg to taste and the sugar. Stir to dissolve the sugar.

3 Whip the double cream into peaks, then carefully stir in the single cream and then the wine mixture. Whisk back to stiffness, but do not over-whip.

4 Pour into chilled glasses and allow to stand overnight until a slight separation occurs in the glasses.

- Some syllabubs used to be made with cider, and many whisked raw egg white into it to make it lighter.
- Thinking about what I said above. Have you ever tried milking a cow straight into a glass? I should think it's impossible!

Burnt Cream

There has been constant disagreement as to which came first, the French *crème brûlée* or the English burnt cream. The English version is usually accredited in cookbooks to an original served at Trinity College, Cambridge, dating from about the mid-nineteenth century. But recipes exist from earlier, and in one of 1769, a custard flavoured with orange-flower water is topped with sugar, and caramelised under a salamander. As custards have been part of the British tradition for so long, and sugar became such a passion, I think the British can have a good claim.

1 vanilla pod

600ml (1 pint) double cream

225g (8 oz) unrefined caster sugar

6 egg yolks

1 Preheat the oven to 140°C/275°F/Gas 1 and prepare a bain-marie (a deep roasting tray is fine).

2 Scrape the seeds from the vanilla pod into the cream, add the pod too, then bring up to the boil with 25g (1 oz) of the sugar.

3 Mix the egg yolks in a bowl with 55g (2 oz) of the sugar. Pour the hot cream over, stirring all the time. Put back on to the heat and slowly reheat until the cream starts to thicken.

4 Remove from the heat, and strain into individual ramekin dishes. Put into the bain-marie, pour in enough boiling water to come halfway up the dishes, and bake in the preheated oven for 30 minutes. Take out and cool.

5 Sprinkle the rest of the sugar over the top of each set custard, and put into a tray full of ice. (It may seem a bit of a fiddle, but the ice is really necessary. You don't want the custard to cook any more while the sugar is cooking, and the ice will keep it suitably cool. Brûlées are not meant to be warm…) Put under a well preheated grill until the sugar sizzles, melts and starts to turn colour.

6 Leave the dishes until the sugar sets, then serve very cold.

Brown Bread Ice-cream

SERVES 6–8   Milk- and cream-based ices are thought to have originated in Italy (an influence of the Arabs in Sicily, perhaps?), then spread through France (where they preferred, and still prefer, water ices) to other parts of Europe. Ice-creams were popular in England from the eighteenth century, and the cream base was often mixed with puréed fruit. Brown breadcrumbs were added then as well, another example of the widespread use of bread in British puddings. The ice-cream may seem to be modern in concept, but history has proved otherwise.

3 egg yolks

115g (4 oz) unrefined soft brown sugar

1 vanilla pod

300ml (10 fl oz) single cream

300ml (10 fl oz) double cream

140g (5 oz) brown breadcrumbs

2 tbsp brandy

1 Whisk the egg yolks and sugar together in a bowl to dissolve all the sugar.

2 Meanwhile, scrape the seeds from the vanilla pod and put them and the pod into a saucepan with the single cream. Bring to the boil.

3 Pour over the egg yolks, stir well, and put back into the pan on a gentle heat, stirring all the time. Allow to thicken slightly, then take off the heat. Take out the pod and leave the custard to cool. Cover with clingfilm to prevent a skin forming.

4 Whisk the double cream (not too much) and fold into the cold custard mixture.

5 Preheat the oven to 180°C/350°F/Gas 4.

6 Put the brown breadcrumbs on a tray and toast in the preheated oven for 5 or so minutes. Take out and cool. When the breadcrumbs are cold, mix into the ice-cream mixture with the brandy.

7 Put in a suitable tray, and place in the freezer. When the mixture starts to freeze, stir with a wooden spoon. As the whole tray starts to set, every now and then turn the ice-cream out into a bowl and whisk, then return to the tray and the freezer. Do this until completely set.

Chelsea Buns *(see page 181)*

The earliest breads would have been rather like oatcakes, ground cereal mixed with water or fat, and baked on heat – at first on hearthstones beside the fire. It wasn't until a form of aeration, or leaven, was discovered that lighter breads became possible. The Romans introduced basic forms of enclosed ovens, and many larger establishments would have had their own, but for many centuries thereafter, the poor still continued to bake bread at the hearth, or take their dough to be baked at a communal bakery.

Bread, Cakes and Baking

Plain breads – made from locally available grain – were gradually enriched by flavourings such as spices, and by dried fruits, much as were the pudding mixtures. Bara brith and barm brack are good examples of this, as are teabreads like gingerbread and parkin (both of which can, of course, be found in biscuit form). Small sweet breads were made too, raised by yeast or, later, by chemicals such as baking powder, and baked on the griddle or in an oven. Buns were a further and later development, a cross between an enriched yeast bread and a cake.

At first the dividing line between the two would have been hard to draw. It was only when it was realised that eggs could replace the previous bread yeasts and leavens that cake-making as we know it today properly developed, and cakes are now characterised by their high content of fat and eggs.

Baking seems very *British*, and of course we have two uniquely British institutions – afternoon tea and high tea – at which to enjoy many of its sweet results. High tea is rather more northern, perhaps one reason why the baking tradition has survived so much more successfully in the north of England, Scotland and Wales than it has in the south. There are numerous other theories, many of them quite plausible. And, although the north–south divide is sometimes referred to in disparaging terms, I'm really quite glad that it exists, in that it has ensured the survival of many wonderful breads, cakes and biscuits.

Irish Soda Bread

MAKES 1
ROUND LOAF

Ireland is famous for its simple baking. In the absence of sophisticated raising agents like yeast, and domestic ovens, other means of raising and cooking had to be utilised. At one time buttermilk and other leavens (including sourdough and fermented potato juice) would have raised breads. It was only after the introduction of baking chemicals such as bicarbonate of soda and cream of tartar in the early nineteenth century that the full range of Irish soda breads began to be baked. They are simple to make, but delicious to eat, with butter for breakfast, or as an accompaniment to stews.

Bread such as this would once have been baked on a girdle or griddle or in a frying pan. The bastible, an iron pot with its base in the fire, and hot coals on the lid, was an effective baking oven, still used until very recently in Ireland.

450g (1 lb) flour, half plain white,
  half wholemeal
salt to taste

½ tsp each of bicarbonate of soda and
  cream of tartar (or 1 tsp baking powder)
300ml (10 fl oz) buttermilk

1 Lightly grease a baking tray or cast-iron frying pan, and preheat the oven to 200°C/400°F/Gas 6.

2 Sift the flour, salt to taste, bicarb and cream of tartar into a bowl. Add the buttermilk and mix to a dough. Knead and stretch until smooth.

3 Shape into a round on a floured board, and roll flat, or use your knuckles, to 4cm (1½ in) thick.

4 Put on to the tray or into the frying pan, and cut lightly into quarters (or farls). Bake in the preheated oven for 25 minutes, then turn the oven down to 180°C/350°F/Gas 4, and cook for a further 20 minutes.

5 Take out and wrap in a cloth to keep soft. Eat quickly, as it does not keep well. In Ireland, it is made daily and eaten that day.

Bara Brith

MAKES 1 CAKE The Welsh bara brith, which means 'speckled bread', is very closely aligned to other British fruit loaves – especially the caraway-spiced barm brack of Ireland (the name of which means 'speckled cake'). Both the Welsh and Irish versions were associated with high days and holidays, particularly New Year, inviting comparison with black bun, the Scottish Hogmanay treat, although that is more like a huge 'fly cemetery' cake than a bread.

475g (1 lb 1 oz) plain flour

1 tsp salt

25g (1 oz) unrefined caster sugar

approx. 250ml (9 fl oz) warm milk

25g (1 oz) fresh yeast

1 egg, beaten

½ tsp ground mixed spice

½ tsp ground cinnamon

115g (4 oz) unsalted butter, melted,
    plus extra for greasing

115g (4 oz) currants

55g (2 oz) raisins

1 tbsp treacle

1 tsp caraway seeds

1   Sift 450g (1 lb) of the flour and the salt into a bowl. Make a well in the middle. Mix the sugar and milk together and warm to blood heat, then remove from the heat and crumble in the yeast. Stir to make sure it dissolves. Add to the flour and mix to make a dough. Leave in a warm place to prove until doubled in size, about 40 minutes.

2   Add the egg, spices and melted butter to the dough, then knead and knock back.

3   Cover the dried fruits in the remaining flour, and mix into the dough with the treacle and caraway seeds.

4   Butter a 20cm (8 in) round cake tin and preheat the oven to 180°C/350°F/Gas 4.

5   Split the dough in half, then split one of the halves into two-thirds and one-third pieces. Take the largest half piece, and roll it into a long snake-like shape. Lay this in the cake tin and coil around the inside edge. Do the same with the next largest piece, coiling it inside the first piece. Finally do the same with the smallest piece. Prove in a warm place for about 20 minutes.

6   Bake in the preheated oven for about 1 hour or until golden. Turn out of the tin and cool on a cake rack.

Saffron Bread

MAKES 2
LOAVES

Saffron, the most expensive of spices, consists of the orange-red stigmas of the saffron crocus. These have to be plucked by hand, which is the costly part. Although the spice seems very exotic – it comes mostly now from Spain, India and Iran – the crocuses used to be cultivated in Essex, causing one particular town to affix 'Saffron' to its original name of 'Walden'. Saffron became popular too in the West Country, and saffron cakes – enriched breads really – are still produced there. According to some, the original saffron bread was plain, coloured only by saffron water; the dried fruits were added later.

Eat as an afternoon teabread, sliced with butter. In Cornwall, buns made of this dough were once eaten with clotted cream on Good Friday. However, the best version I have ever had of saffron bread was baked by my friend Clive Davidson at the Champney Inn at Linlithgow, near Edinburgh. He wrapped the dough round black pudding and rolled it up like Chelsea buns.

a pinch of saffron strands

4 tbsp warm water

300ml (10 fl oz) milk

85g (3 oz) unrefined soft brown sugar

55g (2 oz) unsalted butter

25g (1 oz) fresh yeast

450g (1 lb) plain flour

a pinch of salt

½ tsp freshly grated nutmeg

115g (4 oz) lard, plus extra for greasing

1 egg, beaten

225g (8 oz) currants

115g (4 oz) mixed candied peel

1 tsp finely grated lemon peel

1 Put the saffron to soak in the warm water and leave overnight.

2 Warm the milk in a small pan very gently to blood temperature, then add a pinch of the sugar and the butter. Make sure it's the right temperature – that of a baby's bottle – then crumble in the yeast. Stir to dissolve.

3 Mix the flour, the salt, the rest of the sugar and the nutmeg in a bowl. Rub in the lard until the texture resembles breadcrumbs, then make a well in the centre. Pour in the yeast-milk mixture, saffron water and beaten egg, and mix to a dough.

4 Knead until the dough is smooth and elastic in consistency. Put to prove in a warm place, covered lightly (we use clingfilm), until doubled in size, about 1 hour. Meanwhile, use a little of the lard to grease 2 x 450g (1 lb) loaf tins.

5 Knock the dough back, then mix in the dried fruit and peel. Divide between the prepared loaf tins. Prove for a further 30 minutes until risen.

6 Meanwhile, preheat the oven to 200°C/400°F/Gas 6.

7 Bake the loaves in the preheated oven for 40–50 minutes. Remove from the heat, and leave to cool in the tin.

■ You could use a mixture of equal parts of milk and caster sugar to brush over the top of the loaves as they come out of the oven. This gives a good shine.

■ Saffron strands are better to use than powder (which can be adulterated). Don't strain the strands out from the coloured water after soaking, as they give exotic little pools of accentuated colour after baking. And never use turmeric as a cheaper alternative: the colour may be similar but the flavour is unpleasant.

Hot Cross Buns

MAKES 16 British buns are made from a sweet yeast dough enriched with butter and eggs, dried fruit and spices. The basic mixture for both these hot cross buns, *Chelsea Buns* (see page 181) and many other traditional sweet breads, is similar; the difference lies in what happens thereafter!

When I was a lad I worked during the school holidays, with Frank and Theo, in the Glendale bakery, which sold its product to market stalls. Our busiest time of the year was Maundy Thursday, preparing thousands of hot cross buns for Good Friday. We worked all night, moulding them all by hand (not much technology then...). Frank's late auntie was said to haunt the place, which gave me the willies, but my consolation was as many hot buns as I could eat, straight from the oven.

The cross on hot cross buns, traditionally associated with Easter, can be made simply by cutting into the dough, by piping in a dough mixture, by placing on a cross of separately made pastry, or lines of candied peel.

Basic bun dough

450g (1 lb) plain flour

a pinch of salt

approx. 300ml (10 fl oz) milk

115g (4 oz) unsalted butter

55g (2 oz) unrefined caster sugar

20g (¾ oz) fresh yeast

1 large egg, beaten

Filling

55g (2 oz) currants

55g (2 oz) sultanas

¼ tsp ground allspice

¼ tsp freshly grated nutmeg

Topping

55g (2 oz) plain flour

1–2 tbsp water

115g (4 oz) unrefined caster sugar

150ml (5 fl oz) water

1 To make the basic bun dough, sift the flour and salt into a bowl. Make a well in the centre.

2 Very gently warm the milk in a pan, with the butter and sugar, to blood temperature. Take off the heat, make sure it's the right temperature – as for a baby's bottle – then crumble in the yeast. Stir to make sure it dissolves.

3 Add to the well in the flour, along with the beaten egg, and mix to make a dough. Knead well, cover with a cloth, and put in a warm place to prove until doubled in size, usually anything from 20–50 minutes.

4 Knock the dough back and add the dried fruit, allspice and nutmeg. Form into sixteen even-sized balls, and flatten them slightly. Using a sharp knife carefully cut a cross on top of each bun.

5 Mix together the flour and water for the pastry cross. Put into a piping bag, and pipe into the crosses on top of the buns. Place the buns on a greased baking tray, cover and allow to prove until doubled in size, about 30 minutes.

6 Meanwhile, preheat the oven to 220°C/425°F/Gas 7.

7 Bake the buns in the preheated oven for 15–20 minutes. Meanwhile, boil the sugar and water together to make a syrup.

8 Take the buns out of the oven and, while still hot, brush with the syrup to glaze them, giving the buns their characteristic sticky sheen.

■ Perhaps the plainest of British buns is the well-known Sally Lunn from Bath. Apart from endless arguments about the origin of the name (is it the name of the baker herself, or derived from 'soleil et lune'?), the basic dough as here is made up into a sweet bread or buns, occasionally enlivened with lemon zest.

■ You can add different spices and proportions of dried fruit etc. to the basic bun mixture, and you can also add different toppings. I love those buns with rock sugar on top – Bath buns – and at the Glendale we used to make up 'long buns' with an icing sugar mixture topping, and eat them split with slices of very cold butter.

■ It's said in the north of England that if you hang a hot cross bun up in your kitchen it will protect the house from fire for a whole year…

Chelsea Buns

MAKES 16

Made from the same dough as *Hot Cross Buns* (see page 178), Chelsea buns were the speciality of a bakery, The Chelsea Bun House, from the middle of the eighteenth century.

Basic bun dough (see page 178)

Filling and topping
55g (2 oz) unsalted butter, melted
55g (2 oz) unrefined caster sugar

½ tsp ground cinnamon
55g (2 oz) currants
115g (4 oz) sultanas
25g (1 oz) chopped candied peel
2 tbsp icing sugar

1 Make the basic bun dough as described in steps 1–3 of the recipe.

2 Knock the dough back and knead until it is firm, with no air in it. Roll out into a large square about 1cm (½ in) thick.

3 Brush the square with melted butter leaving a 1cm (½ in) margin all around. Sprinkle with the sugar and cinnamon, then the mixed dried fruits and peel, and carefully press these down.

4 Roll up like a Swiss roll and cut into sixteen 2.5cm (1 in) slices. Place these carefully on to a greased, deep-sided baking sheet about 5cm (2 in) apart. Cover with a clean cloth and allow to prove until doubled in size, about 30 minutes.

5 Meanwhile, preheat the oven to 220°C/425°F/Gas 7.

6 Bake the buns in the preheated oven for 15–20 minutes.

7 When taken out, brush immediately with a mixture of icing sugar and enough water to make a single cream consistency. This gives the buns their characteristic white sheen.

The coiled flat circles of fruity dough are placed together in a tin to bake, when they coalesce, creating the characteristic square shape.

Scotch Pancakes

SERVES 8

Pancakes – thin circles of cooked batter – exist all over Europe (think of the French crêpes), and the batter is very similar to that for Yorkshire pudding. In Scotland, though, what they call 'pancake' is actually a drop scone, made from a thicker batter, raised by baking powder, and cooked on a griddle to a fat circle rather like a crumpet or blini (although the last two are both yeast-raised).

Eat freshly made: they are not so good cold and old. Serve them with cream and jam, or maple syrup or golden syrup and butter.

225g (8 oz) plain flour

1 tsp baking powder

½ tsp salt

25g (1 oz) unrefined caster sugar

1 egg, beaten

1 tbsp golden syrup

approx. 150ml (5 fl oz) milk

25g (1 oz) unsalted butter, melted

vegetable oil for greasing

1 Sift the flour, baking powder, salt and sugar together into a bowl, and mix well. Add the beaten egg and golden syrup, along with some milk to make a stiff batter. Add the butter and enough of the rest of the milk to maintain a dropping consistency. Don't be frightened to add a little more milk if you think it needs it.

2 Heat a griddle or frying pan and brush with a little oil.

3 Using a tablespoon, 'drop' an amount on to the griddle and leave to set and colour. Turn over and cook the second side. Each pancake takes about 5 minutes to cook. Store the pancakes inside a tea towel while making the rest.

- A greased metal ring helps to keep the right shape and an even size.
- Although the pancakes are sweet, they go rather well with bacon, but make sure it is a sweet-cure bacon.
- In summer, these pancakes with marinated raspberries and strawberries, topped with clotted cream, make for a real treat.

Scone

MAKES 1
LARGE SCONE

Rather like soda bread (see page 174), a scone mixture would have been raised with buttermilk and cooked on the griddle until the advent of chemical leavens and domestic ovens in the nineteenth century. Varieties of scones are found all over Britain, but the name (pronounced to rhyme with 'gone' in Scotland, 'clone' elsewhere) and the basic concept are claimed as their own by the Scots.

In his café, my dad and his helper, Annie Denton, used to make large scones like this, divided into four farls. They were made to eat then and there, not to be kept.

115g (4 oz) cold butter, diced, plus extra
  for greasing
450g (1 lb) self-raising flour
a pinch of salt

115g (4 oz) unrefined caster sugar
300ml (10 fl oz) milk or buttermilk at room
  temperature, plus extra for brushing

1 Lightly butter a baking tray and preheat the oven to 200°C/400°F/Gas 6.
2 Sift the flour and salt into a bowl, and quickly rub in the cold butter. Make a well in the centre.
3 Dissolve the sugar in the milk or buttermilk and pour into the well. Gradually stir the flour into the liquid and mix to a dough. Do this as cleanly and quickly as you can. (Speed is of the essence when making scones.)
4 Shape into a large round, brush with milk, and cut a cross in the top.
5 Put on to the baking tray and bake in the preheated oven for 10–15 minutes.

■ You can vary scones almost infinitely. The Welsh add 115g (4 oz) extra butter and 225g (8 oz) currants, and I remember Dad used to make date scones. You could also make savoury scones, adding 225g (8 oz) grated Cheddar to the above mixture instead of the sugar.
■ In Yorkshire we used to roll out the mixture and cut small shapes out with a fluted cutter to make individual scones. These would take slightly less time to cook.

Parkin

SERVES
ABOUT 6–8

Gingerbread has been made in Britain for centuries, and parkin is basically the northern form of gingerbread, but made with the local cereal, oats. Like early gingerbreads, some parkins were made as biscuits, cooked until as hard as most gingerbread men, and on the griddle. Others were made into chemically raised soft sponges that could be baked in the oven, sliced and spread with butter. Different parkins are identified by county names, and this one, inevitably from Yorkshire, and one of the most famous, is traditionally eaten on 5 November. Guy Fawkes was a York man born and bred...

225g (8 oz) fine oatmeal

225g (8 oz) plain flour

1 tbsp ground ginger

½ tsp baking powder

115g (4 oz) unsalted butter

115g (4 oz) unrefined demerara sugar

1 egg, beaten

115g (4 oz) black treacle

115g (4 oz) golden syrup

2 tbsp milk (optional)

1 Line a 20cm (8 in) square baking tray with greaseproof paper and preheat the oven to 160°C/325°F/Gas 3.

2 Mix the oatmeal and flour with the ginger and baking powder, then rub in the butter to a crumb consistency. Add the sugar and beaten egg.

3 Warm the treacle and syrup gently to melt, and add to the mixture. Mix to a paste, using the milk if necessary to achieve a slightly sloppy consistency.

4 Pour the mixture into the prepared baking tray and bake for 1 hour plus. Press the top with the back of a spoon: if it springs back into shape immediately, it is cooked. Take out of the oven and leave to cool a little.

5 After 5 minutes cut into squares, and then leave to cool completely before taking out of the tin.

6 Store in an airtight container for about a week before eating. This is quite important, as the characteristics of the cake change. Eat as a cake.

Gingerbread

MAKES 1 LOAF Various types of ginger bread, biscuits and cakes exist through Europe – think of the French *pain d'épices* and the German *Lebküchen* – and this differentiation is actually found in Britain itself. The famous gingerbread from Grasmere is more like a shortbread, while *Parkin* (see page 185), the northern equivalent of gingerbread, can be biscuit-like or cake-like. Ginger nuts and gingerbread men are the most famous perhaps of the biscuit types (the latter often sold as 'fairings' and eaten on Guy Fawkes Night). Most other gingerbreads are either teabread-like in texture, for slicing and buttering, or richly cake-like as here. It is baked in a loaf tin as a teabread, but it is richer and moister, ideal as a pudding.

Serve cold with fresh fruit and ice-cream, or reheat in a little butter and serve as a pudding with a whisky sauce and perhaps some more diced preserved ginger – or some orange slices caramelised in butter, as in the photograph.

115g (4 oz) unsalted butter, plus extra
for greasing
225g (8 oz) plain flour, plus extra
for dusting
115g (4 oz) unrefined caster sugar
2 eggs, beaten

225g (8 oz) black treacle, lightly warmed
55g (2 oz) sultanas, finely chopped
85g (3 oz) preserved ginger, finely chopped
2 tsp ground ginger
2 tbsp double cream
½ tsp bicarbonate of soda

1 Butter and flour well a terrine mould or 900g (2 lb) loaf tin, and preheat the oven to 160°C/325°F/Gas 3.
2 Cream the butter and sugar together, then mix in the eggs, treacle, chopped sultanas and preserved ginger.
3 Sift the flour and ground ginger together, and stir into the mixture.
4 Warm the cream slightly, add the bicarb and stir into the mixture.
5 Pour into the prepared mould or tin and bake in the preheated oven for 1½–2 hours.
6 Leave to cool and 'set' in the tin, and then turn out on to a wire cake rack.

Victoria Sponge

MAKES

1 x 2-LAYER

CAKE

A true sponge is actually fatless – made from eggs, sugar and flour only – and is so light that it could never be used to hold any type of filling other than jam or some cream. The Victoria sponge, a 'creamed' cake, was created later, obviously named after the old Queen, and included butter 'creamed' with the sugar, and baking powder. (It's the butter that makes it rather crumbly.) I used to make these at school with Elsie Bibby, my teacher. We called them 'jam and cream' sponges, but would sometimes use a butter cream too (icing sugar and unsalted butter). A Victoria sandwich sponge cake is good for tea, along with other cakes and biscuits, but must be very fresh.

115g (4 oz) unsalted butter, plus extra
  for greasing
115g (4 oz) plain flour, plus extra
  for dusting
115g (4 oz) unrefined caster sugar
2 eggs, beaten
½ tsp baking powder

Filling and topping
about 4 tbsp jam
icing sugar

1 Butter and flour two 18cm (7 in) sponge tins and preheat the oven to 230°C/450°F/Gas 8.
2 Cream the measured butter and sugar together until soft and white. Gradually add the beaten eggs.
3 Sift the flour and baking powder together and lightly fold into the butter mixture.
4 Divide the mixture between the two tins and bake in the preheated oven for 10–15 minutes. Turn out on to a wire cake rack and cool.
5 Spread one sponge with jam and lay the other on top. Dust with icing sugar and serve.

Genoese Sponge

This is actually one of the original types of sponge, being what we call a 'whisked' cake (when the eggs and sugar are first whisked lengthily to incorporate air). It is sturdier than the basic sponge or Victoria sandwich mixture, and less crumbly – it has less butter, but more egg – so I would say this is the cake to use as a vehicle for something else. It's good as a base for fruit and whipped cream, for instance, or in trifle. When I was at the Capital Hotel, we used to soak genoese sponges in sugar syrup flavoured with a liqueur (Kirsch, cherry brandy, Poire William), and then top the almost liquid sponge with fruit and cream. Very popular it was too.

55g (2 oz) unsalted butter, melted, plus extra for greasing

115g (4 oz) plain flour, plus extra for dusting

4 eggs

115g (4 oz) unrefined caster sugar

1 Butter and flour a 23cm (9 in) sponge tin and preheat the oven to 200°C/400°F/Gas 6.
2 Whisk the eggs and sugar together in a bowl over hot water until light, creamy and doubled in size. Take off the heat and whisk until cold.
3 Sift the flour, then carefully fold into the beaten mixture. Fold the melted butter in gently.
4 Pour into the prepared sponge tin and bake in the preheated oven for 25–35 minutes. To test if cooked, run your hand across the top of the cake: the indentations should disappear almost immediately.
5 Leave to cool in the tin, then turn out on to a wire rack.

■ There are a few danger signs with sponges:
Too dense a crumb: too much flour, oven too low.
Holes in the mixture: flour not sufficiently folded in.
Sponge sinking or cracked uneven crust: tin filled unevenly, oven too hot.

Dundee Cake

MAKES

1 x 23cm
(9 in) CAKE

It is said that this rich and buttery sultana cake came into being through the Dundee marmalade industry. The Keiller family had started their first marmalade factory in 1797, having been inspired by imports of a Portuguese '*marmelo*' or quince paste several generations earlier. They used Seville oranges, which come into season at the end of January. After making the new preserve, the factory might stand unoccupied, so they decided to diversify, and make a cake. They would have established fairly close relationships with Spanish suppliers, so would have access to the almonds and sherry, and two of the cake's defining characteristics, the plump sultanas and candied orange peel, the latter possibly left over from the preserve manufacture. Some Dundee cakes include glacé cherries but, historically, this is a later addition.

225g (8 oz) unsalted butter

225g (8 oz) unrefined caster sugar

4 eggs, beaten

225g (8 oz) plain flour

1 tsp baking powder

85g (3 oz) ground almonds

2 tbsp dry sherry

350g (12 oz) sultanas

115g (4 oz) candied orange peel, chopped

55g (2 oz) blanched whole almonds

1 egg white

1 Grease or line with greaseproof paper a 23cm (9 in) round cake tin, and preheat the oven to 160°C/325°F/Gas 3.

2 Cream the butter and the sugar well together, and slowly beat in the eggs.

3 Sift the flour and baking powder together (keeping back 1 tbsp flour) and add to the mixture along with the ground almonds. Fold in carefully. Add the dry sherry. Mix the sultanas in the remaining 1 tbsp of flour and add to the mix with the orange peel.

4 Spoon into the prepared cake tin, smooth the top and decorate with the blanched almonds.

5 Beat the egg white and brush over the top of the cake. Bake in the preheated oven for 1 hour, then turn the oven down to 140°C/275°F/Gas 1. Bake for another hour plus until cooked through. To test, run a skewer all the way through the cake. If it comes out dry, the cake is ready.

Mince Pies

MAKES ABOUT
A DOZEN
INDIVIDUAL
PIES OR
1 LARGE PIE
TO SERVE 6

Apparently little pies with a filling of *Mincemeat* (see page 205) were associated with Christmas as long ago as the sixteenth century. They were known as 'minced' or 'shred' pies, referring to the actual meat they once contained. I make them now only for Christmas, but my dad served them throughout the year in his café, often making a single large tart.

They say you should eat a mince pie on each one of the twelve days of Christmas, preferably in a different house each time, to ensure twelve happy months in the year to come.

Individual Mince Pies

450g (1 lb) puff pastry
350g (12 oz) *Mincemeat* (see page 205)

milk and unrefined caster sugar to finish

1 Grease a Yorkshire pudding or muffin tray and preheat the oven to 220°C/425°F/Gas 7.
2 Roll out two-thirds of the pastry to 3mm (⅛ in) thick. Cut into small circles big enough to line the tins, both base and sides, usually about 13cm (5 in) in diameter. Fill the pastry-lined tins with mincemeat.
3 Roll out the rest of the pastry to 3mm (⅛ in) thick and cut smaller circles as lids, usually about two-thirds the size of the bases (so about 7.5cm/3 in).
4 Dampen the edges of the bases with water and press the lids on securely. Make two little holes in the middle to allow the steam to escape. Brush with milk and dredge with sugar.
5 Bake in the preheated oven for about 15 minutes. Serve hot with some brandy butter slotted in under the lid.

Large Mincemeat Pie

225g (8 oz) sweet pastry
   (see *Bakewell Tart* on page 150)

225g (8 oz) *Mincemeat* (see page 205)
milk and unrefined caster sugar to finish

1 Grease a 20–25cm (8–10 in) ovenproof plate and preheat the oven to 220°C/425°F/Gas 7.

2 Take half of the pastry and mould it carefully and quickly into a ball. Roll out to a round of 3mm (⅛ in) thick and put on the greased plate. Prick the bottom with a fork, then put in the mincemeat.

3 Roll out the remaining pastry into the same circular shape. Moisten the edges of the pastry round the mincemeat and place the second pastry circle on top. Push down to seal and trim off excess pastry around the plate. Crimp the edges to decorate. Brush with milk and dredge with sugar.

4 Bake in the preheated oven for about 35–40 minutes. Serve hot, again with brandy butter if you like.

■ You could use suet pastry to make a mincemeat roly-poly (see the *Spotted Dick* recipe on page 154). Mincemeat would be good in a cheesecake as well.

■ Sweet or shortcrust pastry would work as well as puff in the small pies. No reason why not.

Sausage Rolls

MAKES
ABOUT 6

Given our British love for sausages and for pastry, it can be no surprise that the two came together. However, despite their continuing appearances on buffet tables, at cocktail and children's parties, and at picnics, I can find no history for them at all. They were a standby in my dad's café, and I remember learning how to make them at grammar school cookery classes, taught by Miss Elsie Bibby every third week.

225g (8 oz) puff pastry

1 garlic clove, peeled and crushed

1 tbsp chopped fresh parsley

450g (1 lb) sausagemeat

salt and freshly ground black pepper

1 egg, beaten with a little water

1 Grease a baking sheet and preheat the oven to 220°C/425°F/Gas 7.

2 Roll out the pastry to a long strip 3mm (⅛ in) thick and 10cm (4 in) wide.

3 Mix the crushed garlic and the parsley with the sausagemeat, and season with salt and pepper. Roll into a sausage shape of about 2.5cm (1 in) in diameter.

4 Lay this sausage on top of the pastry just off centre, closer to the front. Brush the edges of the pastry with water, then fold the pastry over and seal by pushing down carefully.

5 Brush the top with egg wash, then score the top with a fork and brush again with egg wash. Cut the sausage pastry shape into 7.5cm (3 in) lengths.

6 Put on to the greased baking sheet and bake in the preheated oven for about 20 minutes. Serve hot or cold.

- You could make these very much smaller, and serve them as canapés.
- You can vary them in infinite ways. Use shortcrust instead of puff pastry, or indeed filo pastry, which you could deep-fry as you might a spring roll. You can add diced tomato, chilli, cheese, herbs or other spices to the sausagemeat. I've already done that here – my mother would not have countenanced the garlic, for instance… Another idea is to chop up some black pudding with the sausagemeat.

Shortbread

Shortbread biscuits appear all over Britain (in Shrewsbury cakes and the Goosenargh cakes from Lancashire, for instance, both containing caraway seeds), but they are most associated with Scotland. They are 'short' because they contain no liquid, and may be made as 'fingers' or 'petticoat tails'. I've done the latter here, although I haven't cut out a circle from the middle in the traditional way (to prevent broken points to the wedges).

Through John Grant, whose family make Glenfarclas, my favourite whisky, I met James Walker of Aberlour, whose family make the best commercial shortbread. I have encountered him on the odd occasion since, at food exhibitions and the like, and always seem to get a box of shortbread shortly afterwards! Not that I'm complaining…

225g (8 oz) unsalted butter, plus extra
  for greasing
115g (4 oz) unrefined caster sugar,
  plus extra for dredging

225g (8 oz) plain flour
115g (4 oz) rice flour
a pinch of salt

1 Lightly butter a baking sheet and preheat the oven to 160°C/325°F/Gas 3.
2 Cream the measured butter and sugar together until light.
3 Sift the flour, rice flour and salt together, and fold carefully into the butter mixture.
4 Split the mixture in two and shape each half into balls. Flatten each with the hands and put on to the baking sheet. Crimp the edges, then cut across the top, not quite through, into eighths. Prick the centres with a fork.
5 Bake in the preheated oven for 20 minutes, then turn the oven down to 140°C/275°F/Gas 1 and bake for a further 20–30 minutes.
6 Leave to cool. The shortbread will be soft baked at this stage, but as it cools it will crisp up. Dredge with sugar before serving.

■ The secrets of shortbread are: use the best ingredients possible (there are so few) and handle the dough as briefly as possible.

Oatcakes

Oatcakes were made all over the country, particularly in the areas where oats flourished – upland Wales, Yorkshire and northwards, and in Scotland. Most were simple amalgams of oatmeal, fat and water as here, some were raised by baking powder, and a few from Derbyshire, Staffordshire and Yorkshire were raised by yeast, making them more like thin drop scones or pikelets than the crisp biscuits we mostly associate the name with.

Oatcakes such as these are delicious with cheese, or for breakfast, but were once the staple diet of many a Scot. In the eighteenth and nineteenth centuries, a Scottish university mid-term holiday was known as 'Meal Monday', allowing the student time to go home and stock up on oatmeal, the source of his porridge, brose and oatcakes while he was away.

115g (4 oz) fine oatmeal

½ tsp salt

1 tbsp melted lard

4 tbsp hot water

1 Mix the oatmeal and salt in a bowl. Add the fat and water and bind together.
2 Roll out to 3mm (⅛ in) thick, using extra oatmeal dusted on the work surface. Cut into 7.5cm (3 in) diameter circles.
3 Heat a heavy frying pan or griddle and cook the cakes, with no fat, for 2–3 minutes on one side. Turn over then take off the heat. The residual heat of the pan will finish the second side off.
4 Cool thoroughly, then store in an airtight tin.

Mint Sauce and Cumberland Sauce (see pages 215 and 218)

Before refrigeration, a culinary priority was finding a way of preserving ingredients for winter consumption, when fresh produce was unavailable. Meat and fish were salted, dried and smoked from very early on. Many of these techniques were said to have been learned from the invading Vikings although, oddly, we do not seem to have taken to the dried cod and stockfish that they introduced, to such long-lasting effect, in Iberia and the Mediterranean.

The flavours of these preserved meats and fish would have been rather strong, and

Preserves, Sauces and Accompaniments

indeed even fresh meat could probably have been rather high once it was eaten, leading to a generous addition of spices to mask any off tastes. Gluts of vegetables were not mild on the palate either, once preserved in salt and/or vinegar. This enforced familiarity with intensely sharp, salty and spicy flavours may explain why we British have invented and are so keen on all the pickles, ketchups, chutneys and sauces for which we have become renowned. You don't find bottled brown sauce on the Continent, or even the tanginess of mint or horseradish sauces. The famous commercial Worcestershire sauce – believed to be based on a recipe from the East – is another good example of the British penchant for the piquant.

Sweet preserves are a different kettle of fish (so to speak). Gluts of fruit needed to be preserved in much the same way as vegetables, but in a sweet preservative rather than salt or vinegar. Before sugar became more readily available in the eighteenth century, honey would have been used, and sweet quinces, cherries and plums, and sourer gooseberries, crab apples and rosehips, would have been put in containers to be enjoyed through the winter months. Jams, jellies and marmalade are all examples of this early British culinary thrift, as are what we call fruit 'curds', 'butters' and 'cheeses'.

Early British preserves were made to last, preferably throughout the winter, but today we don't need to bother with that. Try some of these simple recipes – it's good fun! – but eat them up quickly, as there are no E numbers here…

Pickled Onions

Pickles have been around in Britain for much longer than ketchups or chutneys, and it was probably the taste for spicy, tangy, vinegary pickles that led to the introduction of the other two. Vegetables (and fruit) have been pickled since very early on, as they needed to be preserved for winter eating. The word 'pickle' comes from the German '*pekel*' which means 'brine', apt since most vegetables to be pickled in vinegar are brined first. This reduces the moisture content of the vegetable, ensuring a crisper texture.

Pickled onions are one of the country's favourite pickles, powerfully good with cold meats and with cheese (the proverbial ploughman's). At home we always had some on the table and ate them with fish and chips (you still see pickled onions, eggs and gherkins in chippies), and with meat pies. I think they're quite addictive...

900g (2 lb) small pickling onions
 (or shallots)
115g (4 oz) salt
850ml (1½ pints) water
450ml (15 fl oz) malt vinegar
450ml (15 fl oz) white malt vinegar

1 x 2.5cm (1 in) piece fresh root ginger,
 squashed
20 black peppercorns
1 tsp ground allspice
2 small fresh red chillies

1 Peel the onions and put them into a bowl.

2 Mix the salt and water together, pour over the onions, and leave to soak for 24 hours.

3 Rinse the onions in fresh water and put them into a sterilised glass jar. Bring the vinegars, ginger, peppercorns, allspice and chillies to the boil together, and pour over the onions.

4 Cool, then cover, and leave in a dark place for four to six weeks before opening and eating.

Tomato Ketchup

**MAKES ABOUT
450ml
(15 fl oz)**

Both tomatoes and the idea of 'ketchup' are fairly new in British culinary terms. The word 'ketchup', which comes from the Chinese name for a fermented fish sauce, did not enter the language until the seventeenth century and tomatoes, although known in Europe in the sixteenth century, did not become familiar (not necessarily *popular*) until well into the late eighteenth century.

Sharp sauces, pickled vegetables and other accompaniments, though, had always been popular, and many gradually acquired the name of 'ketchup', among them mushroom, anchovy, walnut and, eventually, the new-fangled tomato. America was first with its famous, commercially produced tomato 'catsup', and we in Britain have followed enthusiastically, even allying it with our much more traditional fish and chips.

175ml (6 fl oz) red wine vinegar
125g (4 oz) unrefined caster sugar
24 large ripe tomatoes

**a couple of dashes each of Tabasco sauce
and Worcestershire sauce**

1 Bring the red wine vinegar and sugar to the boil together, stirring until the sugar has dissolved.
2 Meanwhile, skin the tomatoes, remove the seeds, then finely chop the flesh.
3 Add the tomato flesh to the vinegar and boil quickly until the tomatoes 'melt' and the sauce becomes smooth.
4 Remove from the heat and add the two seasoning sauces. Stir in and leave to cool.

■ Commercial ketchup is made very differently, but the simplicity of this recipe makes it very special in my book. Because it is so simple, it will not last long.

Fruit Chutney

MAKES ABOUT
1.8kg (4 lb) Like 'ketchup', 'chutney' is an imported word, derived from the
Hindi *'chatni'*, meaning hot or spiced relish, and is a relic of the Raj.
In India, the preserve would have been made with mangoes, limes or
tamarind, but when the sahibs (or, more importantly, the memsahibs)
retired to Britain, they quickly adapted the idea to use native fruit
such as apples, pears, plums, gooseberries and green tomatoes.

just over 450g (1 lb) pears

just over 675g (1½ lb) apples

juice of 1 lemon

225g (8 oz) stoned dates

700ml (1¼ pints) malt vinegar

225g (8 oz) onions, peeled

1 fresh red chilli, seeded

1 tbsp salt

1 tbsp ground ginger

½ tsp dry mustard powder

225g (8 oz) unrefined soft brown sugar

1 Wash, peel and core the pears and apples. Make sure you have 1.1kg
   (2½ lb) in weight.

2 Dice 225g (8 oz) each of the pears and apples, and put to one side in a
   bowl of water acidulated with the lemon juice.

3 Put the rest of the apples and pears, plus the stoned dates, through the mincer.

4 Put into a pan with the vinegar, bring to the boil and simmer for 10 minutes.

5 Finely chop the onions and chilli and add to the pot along with the salt,
   ginger, mustard and sugar.

6 Drain and squeeze excess moisture from the diced pears and apples and
   add to the pan. Simmer for 20 minutes, then allow to cool.

7 Put into sterilised jars, cover with clingfilm and non-corrosive lids, and leave
   for at least 48 hours before eating, and for up to a month or so. As it ages it
   will become less acid.

■ This would go well with curry or cold meats, and I like it in toasted
cheese (see page 38). At Turner's we served a chutney like this with a
sweetbread terrine.

Banana Chutney

MAKES ABOUT
1.8kg (4 lb)

Bananas could very well have been included in the original Indian chutneys, for they are native to south-east Asia. As they did not travel well from their tropical homelands, they did not become common in Europe until the advent of steamships and refrigerated ships at about the end of the nineteenth and the beginning of the twentieth centuries. I still remember my astonishment at the look and taste of my first banana in the early 1950s, when shipments from the Caribbean started again after the war.

225g (8 oz) sultanas

850ml (1½ pints) malt vinegar

350g (12 oz) unrefined soft brown sugar

1 tsp turmeric

1 tsp curry powder

1 tsp salt

½ tsp ground ginger

225g (8 oz) stoned dates

450g (1 lb) onions, peeled

10 medium bananas, peeled

1 Chop the sultanas and then soak them in the vinegar overnight.

2 The next day, add the sugar, turmeric, curry powder, salt and ginger.

3 Finely chop the dates and onions and add to the other ingredients in a heavy-bottomed pot. Cut the bananas up roughly and add to the pot.

4 Bring up to the boil, then simmer gently until cooked, about 30 minutes. Pot in sterilised jars when cool, and you can eat it virtually straightaway.

■ Use as the fruit chutney opposite. It will be slightly sweeter.

Piccalilli

MAKES ABOUT
1.6–1.8kg
(3½–4 lb)

Nobody quite knows where this particular pickle got its name, but it must be related to the word 'pickle'. It probably originated later than other traditional British pickles, because it includes so many spices imported from India. The turmeric is used for both flavour and colour, and it is this and the generous use of the British-grown mustard that distinguishes piccalilli from its other relatives.

Our Sunday high tea table when I was a child would always have a jar of home-made piccalilli to go with the cold meats on offer.

450g (1 lb) small cauliflower florets

225g (8 oz) vegetable marrow or courgette,
  cut into 1cm (½ in) dice

225g (8 oz) small button onions, peeled

450g (1 lb) runner beans, cut into 5mm
  (¼ in) dice

225g (8 oz) cucumber, cut into 5mm
  (¼ in) dice

350g (12 oz) salt

1.2 litres (2 pints) white vinegar plus 1 tbsp

a pinch of curry powder

45g (1½ oz) dry English mustard powder

175g (6 oz) unrefined caster sugar

25g (1 oz) piece fresh root ginger, bruised

6 black peppercorns

1 fresh red chilli

25g (1 oz) plain flour

15g (½ oz) turmeric

1 Prepare the vegetables and spread on a deep tray. Sprinkle with the salt and 1.2 litres (2 pints) water, and leave for 24 hours. Rinse and drain.

2 Put the vegetables into a non-reactive pan with the bulk of the vinegar, the curry powder, mustard and sugar. Put the ginger, peppercorns and chilli in a muslin bag and add as well. Bring up to the boil and simmer for 20 minutes.

3 Blend the flour and turmeric with the remaining tbsp of vinegar, add to the mixture, and bring up to the boil. Cook for 3–5 minutes until thickened.

4 Leave to cool, then pot in sterilised jars. Cover with clingfilm and store in a cool dry place. It can be eaten virtually straight away.

■ Piccalilli does mature, though, and you'll often find it has a softer, rounder flavour if you leave it for at least three to four weeks.

Mincemeat

MAKES ABOUT
900g (2 lb)

In the Middle Ages, we British used to love sweet meat mixtures, and mincemeat is actually very medieval in flavour. It would once have contained meat – beef, lamb or offal – but the only remnant of that now is the beef suet. However, as late as the 1860s, Francatelli, chef to Queen Victoria, gave four recipes for mincemeat in his *A Plain Cookery Book for the Working Classes*. These were all price based: the cheapest, at 9d, was made with tripe. Hard to believe, but true. Could you imagine this today?

115g (4 oz) chopped beef suet

115g (4 oz) each of chopped mixed peel, currants, sultanas and raisins

2 apples, peeled, cored and finely diced

175g (6 oz) unrefined demerara sugar

finely grated zest and juice of 1 lemon

finely grated zest and juice of 1 orange

1 tsp ground mixed spice

½ tsp freshly grated nutmeg

75ml (2½ fl oz) each of rum and brandy

1 Make sure that all the chopped items are very finely chopped.

2 Mix all the ingredients together, then put into a bowl. Cover with clingfilm, pushing it on to the surfaces of the mincemeat – you don't want any air to get to it.

3 Allow to stand for 1 week in the fridge before using. It could last longer, but it's so delicious I don't think it'll get the chance.

■ Use this mincemeat in things like mincemeat roly-poly, mincemeat cheesecake, and *Mince Pies* (see page 193).

Strawberry Jam

MAKES ABOUT
1.3kg (3 lb)

Sweet preserves or jams are common and traditional all over Europe. Before sugar became more readily available, in the eighteenth century, honey would have been used to preserve fruits such as quinces, cherries, plums and raspberries. At one time jams would have been made with gluts of fruits, and they would last, hopefully, until the fruit season came round again. That's not so necessary nowadays, but it's still fun to make jam.

Although strawberries are the most difficult of the lot to turn into a jam – they lack the natural pectin vital for a good set – strawberry jam is somehow the one most revered. Lemon juice is used to supply the pectin, as is redcurrant juice, and this recipe, although very simple, is quite delicious.

1.1kg (2½ lb) strawberries

1.3kg (3 lb) unrefined granulated sugar

150ml (5 fl oz) redcurrant juice

juice of 1 lemon

15g (½ oz) unsalted butter

1 Put the strawberries into a large heavy-bottomed pan and heat gently.
2 As the juice starts to come out, add the sugar and stir until dissolved. Add the two juices.
3 Bring the mixture to the boil and remove any scum. Boil rapidly, testing for setting point every 15 minutes (see opposite). Take the pan off the heat to do this.
4 When setting point has been reached, add the butter. Allow the jam to cool slightly before putting into sterilised jars. Before doing this, give the jam a stir to move the fruit around.
5 Keep for a couple of days before eating, and eat within a couple of weeks.

- Individual jams and jellies have individual setting points, which you can test with a sugar thermometer: dip it in hot water, then sink the bulb end into the jam. If the temperature is around 105°C/220°F, the jam has reached setting point.

- However, it is just as simple to keep several small saucers in the fridge. When you think the jam has reached setting point, take the pan off the heat and put a tsp of jam on the cold saucer. Let it cool for a few seconds – count to ten – then push the surface with your finger. If the surface wrinkles, the jam is ready. If the jam is 'loose', it needs to be boiled for a few minutes more and tested again.

Marmalade

MAKES ABOUT
1.3kg (3 lb)

Marmalade is thought of as very Scottish, but the idea is based on those solid and long-keeping confections popular on the Continent such as the Spanish '*dulce de membrillo*' and the French '*coing*' (in fact quite similar to our own fruit cheeses). The story goes that when Janet Keiller's husband bought some Seville oranges off a ship in their native Dundee at the turn of the eighteenth century, she made a preserve from them. This was based loosely on a recipe for '*marmelo*', a Portuguese quince paste she had encountered previously. She altered the recipe though, making the preserve less solid, in order to fill more jars – she was a thrifty Scot, after all. (And the Keiller marmalade factory, which was founded thereafter, in 1797, was also where the Dundee Cake – see page 191 – is said to have originated.)

Most of Iberia's Seville orange crop in January is destined for the UK and marmalade manufacture. And, in case you didn't know, Dundee marmalade has shredded peel, while Oxford marmalade uses thick-cut peel…

900g (2 lb) oranges

1.4 litres (2½ pints) water

900g (2 lb) unrefined caster sugar

juice of 2 lemons

1 Wash the oranges well and put in a preserving pan with the water. Slowly boil in the water for around 1½–2 hours then take out and cool. Keep the water.

2 Carefully cut off the peel, leaving the pith behind. Mince or shred the peel – I prefer to mince it.

3 Peel the pith from the oranges with a sharp knife and discard. Take out the pips and wrap them in a muslin bag.

4 Cut the peeled oranges into halves and then slice thinly.

5 Put the orange slices into the orange water, then add the minced peel and the muslin bag of pips. Bring to the boil and simmer for 5 minutes.

6 Take off the heat, then add the sugar and lemon juice. Stir until the sugar has dissolved.

7 Put back on to the heat and bring up to the boil quickly. Test for setting after 15 minutes (see page 207).

8 If the marmalade is ready keep the pan off the heat and allow it to cool for 20 minutes. If not ready, put back on to the heat and bring back to the simmer. Check every 2 minutes.

9 When the marmalade has rested, stir and bottle in sterilised jars.

■ Most marmalades are made from Seville oranges, but this one, with less sugar, can be made from ordinary sweet oranges at any time of year.

Apple and Rowan Jelly

MAKES ABOUT 1.3–1.8kg (3–4 lb)

Fruit jellies are wonderful preserves and have long been made by thrifty British housewives. They are a good way of using up gluts of fruit, fruit that is not perfect enough to eat, and a good way of supplying a tart-sweet accompaniment to many other dishes.

You can use redcurrants, quinces, crab apples, blackberries, plums or damsons, rosehips, gooseberries, grapes – and indeed herbs (with green cooking apples as the pectin source).

900g (2 lb) apples
1.3kg (3 lb) rowanberries

unrefined granulated sugar

1 Clean the fruit carefully and drain and dry. Cut the apples up roughly.

2 Put into a big pot with enough water just to cover, bring to the boil and simmer gently for 1 hour.

3 Carefully strain the juice through a jelly bag suspended above a bowl. Do not press, as the resultant juice will become cloudy. Be patient.

4 Measure the juice and put into a clean pot. For every 600ml (1 pint) juice, add 450g (1 lb) sugar.

5 Simmer and stir together until the sugar melts, then simmer gently until the jelly reaches setting point (see page 207). Test regularly.

6 Decant into sterilised jars, cool then cover with clingfilm. The jelly should last well for at least three weeks.

■ The principle is the same for most fruit jellies. So long as you have something with pectin in it (apples, lemons etc.), you should be successful. Try any of the fruits mentioned in the introduction above.

Lemon Curd

MAKES ABOUT
450g (1 lb)

The modern lemon curd is of fairly recent origins – the 1800s – and is a direct descendant of the flavoured curd fillings that had been used in pastry tarts since the Middle Ages. Curd, the lumpy protein and fat part of curdled milk (and the basis of most cheeses), was mixed with eggs and flavoured (the lemon only arrived in the late seventeenth century). Yorkshire boasts several curd tarts of this kind, and the famous Richmond Maids of Honour are basically small curd cakes.

Lemon curd was probably developed as a filling for tarts, although gradually it lost the curds, being made only with sugar, butter and eggs, and only very slowly would its other qualities have emerged – its spreadability on bread or on cake as a filling. You can make fruit curds with a variety of fruit.

My mother used to make lemon curd like this, but she called it 'lemon cheese', a prime example of the confusion there has always been in this area.

225g (8 oz) unrefined cube sugar
4 lemons, washed
115g (4 oz) unsalted butter

2 eggs
2 egg yolks

1 Rub the sugar lumps over three of the lemons to soak up the essential oils from the zest, and put into the top of a double saucepan or a bowl over simmering water.

2 Finely grate the rind of the fourth lemon into the pan, and then add the juice of all the lemons. Add the butter and gently melt these together.

3 Beat the eggs and yolks together lightly. Pour some of the hot mixture into the eggs, stirring continuously, then scrape back into the pan.

4 Heat gently, stirring continuously, until the mixture thickens enough to coat the back of a wooden spoon, about 30 minutes.

5 Leave to cool a little, then pot in small jars. Cover and seal when cold, then store in the fridge for no longer than two to four weeks (if you have the patience – I bet you haven't!).

Sage and Onion Stuffing

SERVES 4–6   A stuffing is hardly a preserve or a sauce, but it is almost as traditional an accompaniment to meats of all sorts as horseradish sauce or piccalilli. Birds and rolled pieces of meat have been stuffed with savoury fillings for centuries. Some of the most classic have got a seasonal nicety about them – the chestnuts with turkey for instance.

2 medium onions, peeled and finely
  chopped
55g (2 oz) pork dripping (lard will do)
1 tbsp chopped fresh sage

115g (4 oz) fresh white breadcrumbs
1 egg, beaten
salt and freshly ground black pepper
25g (1 oz) unsalted butter

1 Preheat the oven to 200°C/400°F/Gas 6.
2 Slowly fry the onion in the lard to soften, but do not colour. Take off the heat and add the sage, breadcrumbs, beaten egg and some salt and pepper.
3 Put in a small buttered ovenproof dish and bake in the preheated oven for 20–30 minutes until well coloured.

■ I am cooking the stuffing separately here, but you can of course stuff it into a bird, but remember to do so at the neck end, not in the cavity.
■ You could cook the stuffing rolled into individual balls, or you could roll it into a sausage inside foil and roast so that it could be sliced.
■ You could add chopped apple or bacon to the basic stuffing, or indeed some chopped dried apricots as in the photograph.

Apple Sauce

It is said that traditional 'tracklements', or accompaniments, for animals should be made from ingredients on which the animals might have fed. Lamb could possibly have eaten wild mint or redcurrants, I suppose, but I find it hard to think of cattle enjoying horseradish! However, pigs being allowed to wander in apple orchards, eating up the windfalls, is a much more likely scenario, and apple sauce remains a wonderful accompaniment to pork, its sharpness cutting the sweetness and fattiness of the pork. (In Italy, the first food of some suckling pigs is windfall persimmons or sharon fruit, and their flesh is pink, tender and very sweet.)

450g (1 lb) cooking apples

75ml (2½ fl oz) dry cider

25g (1 oz) unrefined caster sugar

55g (2 oz) unsalted butter

a twist of freshly ground black pepper

1 Peel and core the apples. Chop them roughly and put into a non-reactive pan with the cider, sugar and butter. Put on a tight-fitting lid and cook slowly to a purée.

2 Season with black pepper, then pass through a sieve or blend in a liquidiser.

3 Reheat gently to serve.

- If you use dessert apples, leave out the sugar. This is meant to be a tart, not sweet, sauce.
- Try chopping some fresh marjoram into the sauce as you serve.

Mint Sauce

SERVES 4–6

In the Middle Ages, they used to love sweet and sour, herbal flavours in sauces, and this may be a relic of those tastes. Or it could be a reflection of the tradition, found all over Europe, of eating young lamb with bitter herbs (at Easter usually). It's the vinegar content of our mint sauce that the French object to, apparently, forgetting that there are many such sharp sauces in their own cuisine. The sweet redcurrant (or rowan) jelly often eaten with lamb as well (see page 210), can counter-balance the sharpness of the other.

We like mint a lot in this country, often putting a bunch in with the new potatoes or peas. In the north of England we actually eat mint sauce with peas, meat pies and a host of other foods. A famous northern chef was eating in Langan's Brasserie recently, and demanded some mint sauce to eat with his fish, chips and mushy peas. Nobody blinked…

3 tbsp chopped fresh mint leaves
1 tbsp unrefined caster sugar
freshly ground black pepper

150ml (5 fl oz) white malt vinegar
   (or white wine vinegar)

1 Mix the mint with the sugar in a bowl, and give it a couple of good turns of the peppermill.
2 Stir in the vinegar and do a taste test. If it is too sharp, add a dash of water. Use within a couple of hours.

Horseradish Sauce

SERVES 6

Horseradish was introduced to Europe from Asia, and to Britain from Germany apparently, where they use it a lot in sauces. Although we think its association with roast beef must be as old as the hills, it seems only to have been around since the beginning of the nineteenth century.

The flavour is incredibly pungent, but is the pain of peeling and grating worth it? The grated stuff in jars is fine, and is easy to find and use along with the other ingredients.

25g (1 oz) freshly grated horseradish
1 tbsp white wine vinegar
150ml (5 fl oz) double cream

salt and freshly ground black pepper
a squeeze of lemon juice

1 Mix the horseradish and vinegar together.

2 Lightly whip the cream, then season it with salt, pepper and lemon juice.

3 Mix the horseradish and cream mixtures together well. Use within a day or so.

Stand well back when you peel and grate fresh horseradish root, as the effect is ten times worse than peeling the strongest onion!

■ Use horseradish or horseradish sauce in various ways. It's particularly good with smoked meats or, perhaps surprisingly, smoked fish. It can also be added to mashed potatoes, and a horseradish mash can be made into a potato cake and fried like bubble and squeak.

Cumberland Sauce

SERVES 8

It was Elizabeth David who suggested that this sauce might have been named after Queen Victoria's uncle, the Duke of Cumberland. As the sauce is very German in feel, and he was the last independent ruler of Hanover, this could be correct. The recipe also first appeared in cookery books during Victoria's reign, and became a vital accompaniment to game dishes. We serve it with ham mostly now, but it's good with any cold meat. At The Capital we served scallop mousse with horseradish and Cumberland sauce.

Oxford sauce is very similar, but uses only the zest of the orange, not the juice.

1 orange

1 shallot, peeled and finely chopped

juice of ½ lemon

150ml (5 fl oz) port

a pinch of cayenne pepper

350g (12 oz) redcurrant jelly

1 Cut the zest from the orange, leaving behind any pith, and then cut it into fine julienne strips. Squeeze the juice from the denuded orange.

2 Put all the ingredients except the jelly into a pan and slowly simmer to reduce to one-third of its original volume. Pour into a bowl.

3 Whisk or liquidise the redcurrant jelly, then pour into the bowl. Mix well.

Wine Sauce

SERVES 4

There's nothing particularly British about this wine sauce, although we have been flavouring sauces with wines for centuries. In the Middle Ages it was verjuice, the juice of unripe grapes (all English grapes were good for, I should think).

This simple and straightforward sauce was taught to me by Eric Scamman, my mentor at The Savoy, and can add flavour and texture to many dishes. Make it with white wine, red wine, sherry, port or Madeira, or even with Cognac.

25g (1 oz) unsalted butter

2 shallots, peeled and finely chopped

300ml (10 fl oz) wine or spirit of choice

150ml (5 fl oz) white wine

600ml (1 pint) veal stock

115g (4 oz) butter, cold and chopped

salt and freshly ground black pepper

1 tsp fécule (potato flour), slaked in 1 tbsp
   white wine

1 Melt the unsalted butter in a pan, add the shallots, and sweat to soften, but do not colour.

2 Add your chosen wine or spirit, plus the white wine. Bring to the boil and reduce to nearly nothing, to what we call a syrup.

3 Add the veal stock to this intensely flavoured syrup, bring to the boil and reduce by one-third.

4 Shake in the chopped cold butter and check the seasoning.

5 Thicken slightly over a gentle heat, using the fécule and white wine.

6 Pass through a fine sieve and serve.

■ As to which sauce to serve with which meats, there are no real rules. A red wine sauce goes with the big red meats, beef and lamb. A white wine sauce is good with pork or chicken. A Madeira sauce is ideal with fillet of beef, or *Beef Wellington* (see page 82), and a port sauce accompanies kidneys, liver and game birds. Cognac is good with kidneys, chicken and beef, and sherry is delicious with offal, chicken and pork.

Custard Sauce

Eggs and milk are basic ingredients in any cuisine, and most countries have several custard dishes. The English name comes from 'crustade', meaning a pastry case, in which custards were originally cooked (and Fullerton's in Morley High Street still sells custard tarts to die for). The sauce evolved from the baked puddings, and has become so indissolubly associated with Britain that the French call it '*crème anglaise*'. An accolade indeed!

This is a rich version, and although it is a little more difficult to make than simply opening a tin or carton, or mixing custard powder with milk (how times have changed!), it's well worth it.

450ml (15 fl oz) milk

300ml (10 fl oz) double cream

1 vanilla pod

6 egg yolks

4 tbsp unrefined caster sugar

1 Put the milk and double cream into a pan. Scrape the vanilla seeds from the pod into the pan, add the pod as well, and bring up to the boil. Pull to one side of the stove, off the heat.

2 Meanwhile, whisk the egg yolks, then add the sugar, and whisk until the sugar has dissolved.

3 Pour the warm milk over the egg yolks and stir well. Put back into the pan and, stirring continuously with a wooden spoon, bring back to heat, but do not boil. (A double boiler might be safer, if you have one.)

4 When the custard thickens sufficiently to coat the back of the wooden spoon, about 4–5 minutes, take off the heat and pour into an old-fashioned custard jug.

- If not using the sauce immediately, put a piece of buttered greaseproof on the top of it to prevent a skin forming. Or use a butter wrapper – waste not, want not!
- To re-use, either hot or cold, mix with some double cream. Even more luxurious!

Index

Acknowledgements

Thanks are due to a number of people, not least all those who have written about British food over the last few decades, and whose expertise was invaluable in my researches. I am hugely grateful to my editor, Susan Fleming, who pulled it all together and made it fun. Thanks also to my agent Laura Morris, to the Headline gang – particularly Heather Holden-Brown, Lorraine Jerram and Bryone Picton – and to those involved in the wonderful photography: William Shaw, Lisa Pettibone, Annabel Ford and Roisin Nield. A special mention too for the team at designsection, who have made the book look great. Finally a big thank you to Jon Jon Lucas, Gerard O'Sullivan and Paul Bates for their help in advising and testing recipes, to Louise Hewitt in the office and, last but not least, to my wife and sons.

PROSPECTING FOR GOLD
From Dogtown to Virginia City, 1852–1864

By
Granville Stuart

Edited by
Paul C. Phillips

University of Nebraska Press
Lincoln and London

Publishers on the Plains

UNP

First Bison Book printing: 1977
Most recent printing indicated by the first digit below:

3   4   5   6   7   8   9   10

Library of Congress Cataloging in Publication Data

Stuart, Granville, 1834–1918.
  Prospecting for gold from Dogtown to Virginia City,
1852–1864.

  Reprint of v. 1 of Forty years on the frontier . . .
published by A. H. Clark Co., Cleveland, which was
issued as no. 2 of Early western journals.
    1.   Montana—Gold discoveries.   2.   Overland journeys
to the Pacific.   3.   Pioneers—Montana—Biography.
Early western journals; no. 2.
F731.S912   11977   978'02'0924[B]   77-7244
ISBN 0–8032–0932–0
ISBN 0–8032–5869–0 pbk.

Edition Note

PROSPECTING FOR GOLD: FROM DOGTOWN TO VIRGINIA CITY, 1852–1864, originally was published as Volume I of Granville Stuart's *Forty Years on the Frontier*, edited by Paul C. Phillips. The second volume, reprinted by the University of Nebraska Press under the title PIONEERING IN MONTANA: THE MAKING OF A STATE, 1864–1887, consists of nine chapters: "First Years of Montana Territory"; "Quartz Mining and Railroads"; "Life and Customs of the Indians"; "Indian Wars of the Northwest"; "Looking for a Cattle Range"; "Life on the Cattle Range"; "The Cattle Business"; "Cattle Rustlers and Vigilantes"; and "End of the Cattle Range." It also includes the index for both volumes.

Contents

Illustrations

Introduction

Granville Stuart had a knowledge of the far western frontier that was intimate and varied. He saw it at its beginning, and he was a part of every development until its end. As a boy in the pioneer agricultural settlements of Iowa, with the gold rush to California, and then through many years as miner, Indian fighter, trader, packer, merchant, and cattle baron, he lived every phase of frontier life. In his experience we see the seamy side of the gold craze in California and we learn something of the back wash from the tide of this great western movement. As a trader and packer he watched the currents that surged over the Immigrant road to the gold fields. Through his vision and luck, combined with that of his companions, the mountains of the Northwest, abandoned by the trapper and fur-trader, became the Mecca of thousands of gold seekers. For many years he lived the life of the gold camps. He saw its beginning in the craze for wealth; he saw its passions, its heartlessness, and crime. He also saw it in its happier moods, its drinking, its dancing, and its sports. Then as a merchant he grappled with the problems of transportation over thousands of miles of wilderness, and of distributing his goods to widely scattered customers. As pioneer conditions in the mining camps began to recede he sought a new frontier. He went into the Great American Desert east of the mountains, and was one of the first of the great cattle men of the Northwest, and as a cattle man he saw the end of the frontier.

Granville Stuart wrote in his journal, the daily experiences of more than forty years. The journals remain now, some in small memoranda books, some in account books, and others in large sized blank books. The day-by-day story of these years is so vast that many large volumes of print would not contain it.

Realizing this fact Mr. Stuart devoted the later years of his life to condensing these journals and making them into a narrative that would tell the outstanding experiences of his life. Not content with this he was busy collecting materials to explain more fully the history of the frontier, and especially the history of Montana. He sought and received sketches from many other pioneers, and he searched letters and other old papers for material. All of this he had drafted into a voluminous manuscript when death stopped his labors. The journals, the manuscript, and the other papers were put into the hands of the editor to prepare for publication.

The task was not a simple one but statement of what was done is due the reader. First the contributions of the other pioneers were excluded. Mr. Stuart had never fitted them into his narrative and the task of doing so after his death looked hopeless. Furthermore the extent of these contributions would make the work too large for publication. Mr. Stuart had been closely associated with Thomas J. Dimsdale and Nathaniel P. Langford, the historians of the "road agents" and the "Vigilantes," and had furnished them material for the writing of their books. In his last years he attempted to write the story again. He was influenced, however, by the writings of his friends to such an extent that his own contribution added little to what had already been published. For this reason the editor excluded that part of his narrative. Other parts of his manuscript had previously been published and that also was excluded. As Mr. Stuart had worked over his manuscript for years but had not finished it there were several sketches describing the same thing. The editor selected what he thought was the best and omitted the others. Finally the editor compared the completed manuscript with the old journals to verify their accuracy.

The history of Granville Stuart and his brother James is essentially a pioneer history. They broke the sod but others reaped the harvest. They gave to the world knowledge of the gold resources of Montana but they themselves panned but little of the precious metal. From their discoveries, however, there sprang up a host of millionaires. They were the first merchants of the gold mining era but others garnered the profits. And finally when Granville Stuart embarked in a business that brought him wealth, conditions beyond his control overwhelmed him with financial ruin. During all these years, however, the Stuart brothers were men of influence and character.

James Stuart was a man of action. He was an aggressive gold seeker, and he managed the mercantile business with daring skill. He was the first sheriff of a Montana county, and a desperate fighter of criminals. He led the Yellowstone expedition of 1863, and was active in the search for a direct route from the East to Montana. He was a man of tremendous energy and of violent impulses. He was a gambler, and a fighter, and a prince of good fellows. He showed marked political ability and was a man to whom the pioneers looked for advice and direction. An early death cut short a career that promised to be brilliant.

Granville Stuart was a dreamer and philosopher. He was a student of books and of nature, and a lover of all creation. He was a seeker after knowledge, and reflective both by nature and habit. He was a lover of music and art, and his pen and ink sketches, though crude, are well done. He had fine powers of observation, and he described sincerely what he saw. He had a talent for literary expression that was often enlivened by touches of bright humor.

Granville Stuart's writings are of real historical importance. He has given us the fullest description of life in Montana before and during the gold rush. He has sketched the last days of the old Hudson's Bay Company in the Northwest. He has given us glimpses of the Catholic Indian Missions when the white men were coming and the church was striving to control its converts. He has given us the best description of the old chief Victor and of the peaceful Indians, and he has presented the pioneer's views of the hostile redskins. The history of the cattle business in the Northwest is his most important contribution. No other leader in this great industry has told the story and probably no one else could tell it as well as he has done. He was with it at its beginning and throughout its whole turbulent life he was at the very center of its activities. He knew how it was financed, how it was organized, and how managed. He knew its personnel, and the plans, and ambitions, and schemes of all its members. He has described the downfall with a candor and breadth of view that carries conviction. His narrative is an important source for every student of the cattle range.

For thirty years after the end of the great cattle ranges Granville Stuart lived a life of varied fortunes. The loss of wealth had been a severe blow but his knowledge and experience on the range gave him hopes of recovering some of it. The memory of thousands of starved and frozen cattle, however, was too much for his sensibilities, and he turned his back on this business for himself. In spite of his feelings he stayed with the stockmen and for several years remained president of the Board of Stock Commissioners of Montana. This position carried heavy responsibility and no pay, but under his direction many stockmen were helped to rebuild their business on a different plan and the dangers from thieves and cattle diseases greatly reduced.

In 1891 Mr. Stuart was appointed state land agent and personally selected some six hundred thousand acres of land which the federal government had given to the state of Montana for school purposes. He had recently married Miss Isabel Allis Brown and the two of them explored every part of the state in search of desirable land. Mrs. Stuart remained his companion and helper during the remainder of his life.

In 1894 Mr. Stuart was appointed envoy extraordinary and minister plenipotentiary to the republics of Uruguay and Paraguay. As there was no direct steamship line to South America he went by way of Europe. During the five years of his mission there he traveled extensively. He went up the Paraguay river to the head of navigation and then across to the headwaters of the Amazon. On another trip he visited the great Parana Falls on the border between Brazil and Argentina. At the end of his mission he traveled around South America, stopping at every port and making many visits to the interior. The journals of his South American residence contain much information about the copper, nitrate, and other resources of that continent.

In 1904 Mr. Stuart was appointed librarian of the Butte (Montana) Public Library and there he began the preparation of his journals and reminiscences for the press. In 1916 he was commissioned by the state to write a history of Montana and was at work on this at the time of his death on October 2, 1918.

At eighty years of age Granville Stuart was a suave and courtly gentleman with an alert and inquiring mind. He regarded with reverence the sterling characteristics of pioneer life but he could laugh at its eccentricities. His retentive mind, broadened by a wealth of experience, and study, and living was engrossed by an intense desire to finish his work so that the new generation could understand the pioneers who had made the West. How well he succeeded is left for the reader to judge.

PAUL C. PHILLIPS

Preface

These reminiscences are written for the purpose of presenting, as best I can, a pen picture of the life of the "Montana Pioneer."

Civilization has moved forward so rapidly that in the short span of my life I have seen the tide of emigration sweep from the Mississippi river to the Pacific coast, and from the Rio Grande to Alaska. I can remember when there was not a single railroad west of the Mississippi, when there was not a telephone or telegraph line in existence, and a tallow dip was our best means of illumination.

The great expanse of country between the Missouri river and the Rocky mountains was put down on our maps and in our geographies as, "The Great American Desert." I crossed that desert when there was not a habitation from the Missouri river until the small Mormon settlement at Salt Lake was reached; nor one from Salt Lake until the Sierra Nevada mountains were crossed. I came to what is now our magnificent state of Montana when it was a trackless wilderness, the only white inhabitants being Jesuit fathers, and a few Indian traders and trappers at the missions and trading posts; when the mountains and valleys were the homes of countless herds of buffalo, elk, deer, moose, antelope, bear, and mountain sheep; when the streams swarmed with fish and beaver and the Indians were rich and respectable. I have watched the frontier push from the Mississippi river to the Rocky mountains, there to join hands with the settlements that had advanced from the Pacific coast; and from the Rio Grande to the Yellowstone, there to greet civilization that moved down from Hudson Bay. I saw in the valley of the Yellowstone the last of the buffalo, the last of the wild free Indians, the last of "The Great West that Was."

Now I see fields of alfalfa and waving grain where were once the bunch grass and the wild sage. Electric trains travel smoothly along o'er what once were trails, and tunnel through the mountains over which I have climbed with much difficulty. Automobiles spin along on splendid highways which but a few short years ago were my hunting trails, difficult to travel even on my sure-footed Indian pony. Where I was wont to cross streams on hastily constructed rafts I now see splendid bridges of steel and concrete. The places where I pitched my tent for a few days hunt or a prospecting trip are now the sites of thriving cities and villages illuminated by electric light. The placer mines have given place to the mines of copper and zinc. On the bank of the Missouri where I sat and sketched the falls, with one eye on my work and the other casting about for the hostile Sioux, is a great city and the largest smelter and copper reduction plant in the world. I have seen the time in Montana when there was not so much as a scrap of printed paper to read. Now every town supports one or more good newspapers; and libraries well stocked with books and periodicals are in every town and hamlet.

I was here to greet the brave men and noble women who left their homes and civilization, crossed the plains, suffering toil and privations and attacks by hostile Indians, to lay the foundation for this magnificent state. I have bidden farewell to many of these same splendid men and women who, after finishing their labors here, have crossed the Great Divide. Now there are but few left of the little band of Montana pioneers.

I leave these recollections written that those who come after may know something of the hardships endured, perils encountered, and obstacles overcome by this warm-hearted, generous, self-sacrificing band of men and women who suffered so much to attain their ideals. No finer type of men and women ever lived on this earth than were these pioneers, all of whom I hope to meet and greet some time, just over on the other side.

I see our work carried forward by the splendid young men and women of Montana and rest in confidence that it will be excellently done. To this younger generation as well as to the pioneers I am indebted for the assistance and financial aid that has enabled me to complete this work.

GRANVILLE STUART

Early Life

I was born in Clarksburg, Virginia, August 27, 1834, of Scotch descent. The Stuarts seem always to have been pioneers. An old memorandum book of my grandfather's, James Stuart, tells of his trading with Indians in Virginia in 1793. My father and mother, Robert Stuart and Nancy Currence Hall Stuart, with their two children, James and Granville, left Virginia in 1837 to try their fortunes in the then frontier state of Illinois.

They loaded their household effects on a steamboat at Wheeling, Virginia, and went down the Ohio river to its mouth and then up the Mississippi to Rock Island. Here they left the steamer and journeyed by wagon to Princeton, Bureau county, Illinois. They arrived in the early summer, having been one month making the journey.

There was a school in Princeton which my brother James attended and, although I was not of school age, I often accompanied him. The school teacher was not particularly desirous of my attendance at school and mother tried to persuade me to remain at home. Although it almost killed me to sit still so long I preferred that to remaining home alone.

My father succeeded in finding an old style compass, and he began surveying land for new settlers who were coming into the country in considerable numbers.

About this time the government purchased the land west of the Mississippi river from the Indians, and

Iowa territory was created and settlers began moving
into that fertile region. In 1838 my parents also moved
across the river and took up a claim, number sixteen,
west of the river, on a stream called, "Wapsanohock" [1]
which means crooked creek in the Musquawkee [2] Indian language (which later in Montana, I found was
the same as Chippeway). The name, as is usual among
Indians, exactly describes that miserable muddy little
creek, which could not have been more crooked.

The bottom land, along this and other small creeks,
was covered with timber of good size; consisting of
walnut, elm, linden, hackberry, oak, hard maple (the
blessed sugar tree) butternut, hickory, and some other
kinds. These strips of timber land, however, were
narrow, from a quarter to half mile wide, while all the
rest of the country was treeless, but covered with good
grass and many wild flowers. The distances between
streams were great, often being from ten to twenty
miles. After the grass became dry in the autumn, fires
of great extent, driven by high winds, became a source
of great danger and serious loss to the settler, who for
this reason usually built his cabin on the edge of the
woods where the fire could be more easily checked.

My father built his one room log cabin in the woods

---

[1] Wapsanohock creek in Cedar and Muscatine counties, Iowa. – ED.

[2] Miss Louise Kellogg, Fox Indian Wars during the French Regime in
Wisconsin State Historical Society Proceedings (1907), p. 142, states that the
Musquawkee are a branch of the Fox Indians. According to her, the Fox
Indians were also called "Mus quak kie" (Mus-quak-ku-uck). The Chip-
pewa and the Fox Indians, although bitter enemies, are both classed as
Algonquins by Frederick W. Hodge, in *Handbook of American Indians*.
(*Bureau of American Ethnology*, Bulletin no. 30, Washington, 1907). The
Potawatomi who were closely related to the Chippewa had one branch known
as Maskotens, meaning "people of the prairie." *Ibid*. These were also
known as "Maskoutechs which may be Musquawkee. They spoke the same
language as the Chippewa. It is possible that the Musquawkee were the
same as the earlier Maskotens. Miss Kellogg, however, does not believe
this. – ED.

a short distance from the creek, on a little run (the Virginia name for a small brook) which took its rise out on the prairie and flowed into the creek. This was pretty safe from the furious prairie fires, but Oh! Oh! the mosquitoes that swarmed there, and almost devoured us in the spring, summer, and fall, until frost came. Some idea of their incredible number may be gathered from the fact that the water in the run (which we had to use) was so full of their larvae, commonly known as "wiggletails," that we could neither drink nor use it until it was strained through a cotton cloth. I think that many of these mosquitoes must have carried the germs of malaria fever for we all had fever and ague, for several years, it being the worst in the autumn.

A few families of Musquawkee Indians lived in bark huts near us; my brother James and I used to play with the little Indian children of about our age and their good mothers would give us all the maple sugar we could eat, and then give us a cake of it to take home to our mother. These were good kind-hearted people although the whites were rapidly settling up their old hunting grounds, and exterminating the game. In about a year after we came, they moved further west and we saw them no more.

One of our neighbors, named Andrew Phillips, had three sons, William, John, and Solomon. One day the Phillips's, my father, James, and I were at the bridge crossing the creek, near where some Indians were camped. William Phillips, who was then about sixteen years old, was wrestling on the bridge with a young Indian of about his own age. Getting a good hold he flung the Indian over his shoulder, off the bridge and into the creek. He swam out in a furious rage, and ran to the camp to get his bow and arrows, saying he would kill young Phillips. The older Indians and women caught and held the young one, and William's father and mine went to explain how it happened, gave them some trifling presents, and the trouble ended. These Indians would listen to reason, and were not viciously inclined.

In the spring of 1840, my parents moved out of the creek botttom into a house on high ground, on the edge of the prairie. There was more or less wind and consequently a few million less mosquitoes. Near by, a small school house was built by the three or four families of the vicinity, and James and I went to school with five other young children.

The first school building I remember was a small cabin. The logs composing it were not even hewed or peeled. The windows – there were none – but in their stead a log was cut out of each side of the cabin, about three feet from the ground, and nearly the full length of the room, and in this space were fastened sheets of greased paper, which let in a somewhat dim and uncertain light, especially on dark cloudy days. The door was at one end of the house, while a large open fireplace occupied the other end, and the floor was simply earth, wet and then beaten down smooth and solid. All the children attending the three months term of school in summer time, were barefooted. The seats, however were triumphs of mechanical genius, being nothing more than rough unplaned slabs, without backs or desks of any kind. It was pretty rough sitting I can tell you. These slab seats were about ten inches wide and had slanting holes bored in them near the ends, into which short pieces of saplings were inserted for legs. They were made so high that the children's feet were from six inches to a foot and a half from the floor.   Of course the trustees were not to blame for the children being too short to fit the benches.   At any rate the effect was to effectually double us up, and we could beat Wellington at Waterloo in wishing that night would come.   For a teacher we had some young woman in the neighborhood whose educational possibilities were embraced in the three R's (reading, ritin, and rithmetic) and who was generally a little shaky on the last R.   This fortunate young woman commanded the large salary of five or six dollars a month and the right to board in turn among the parents of her scholars.

I remember one of my first teachers giving me a reward of merit which was a kind of thumb stall which was put on my left thumb with which I held my book open, and was to keep my thumb from soiling the book. It was made with wings on each side and painted red and yellow to resemble a butterfly.   I thought it very beautiful and kept it for long years afterward, until the house burned down and destroyed it along with my carefully preserved early· school books.   Perhaps this little work of art is responsible for my love for red and yellow colors to this day.

This summer saw the famous political campaign between the Whigs and Democrats.   The Whigs nominated William Henry Harrison for president and the Democrats nominated Martin Van Buren.   Harrison was familiarly called "Old Tippecanoe," because he defeated the Indians in the battle of that name, where the famous Indian chief Tecumseh was killed by Colonel Richard Johnson of Kentucky.   While this campaign was in progress my father was building a frame dwelling house, and had in his employ several carpenters.   Among them was an old chap named Ben Sailor, and I well remember one of his quaint sayings.   There were large numbers of prairie chickens all about there, and in the spring when mating, they had a melodious song or refrain which sounded like "Boo-oo-oo Boo-oo-oo" long drawn out. One morning when the air was full of their music, Ben, who was an ardent Whig, said "There, listen to that, even the birds are saying, 'Tippecanoie-oo and Tyler-too-oo-oo.'" If the Democrats had any rallying cry it escaped my infantile memory.

During all this time we just shook, and shook, and shook, with the ague. We could only eat when the chill was on us, being too sick when the fever was on. I well remember how the cup would rattle against my teeth when I tried to drink and how, while trying to put the food in my mouth I would nearly put it in my ear, and how my spleen (commonly called the "melt" in those days) was swollen and felt hard as a piece of wood just below my ribs. This was known as ague cake. Almost everybody in that thinly settled part of Iowa would have the ague part of the time. Fortunately it was seldom fatal, but I can still see how thin and pale and woe-be-gone everyone looked.

In 1843 my parents moved a few miles to a farm on the bank of Red Cedar river, a lovely stream, about two hundred yards wide, with sandy bottom and water as clear as crystal. Best of all, it contained great numbers of fish, which were a welcome addition to the rather limited variety of our menu; although there was never any lack of enough, such as it was. In the winter of 1843 there was a two months term of school a mile and a half up the river, and on the farther bank at a little village called Moscow. The river was frozen over and brother James had a pair of skates, and we just flew up that lovely river to school. James did the skating and I just squatted down and held to his coat tail. For text books we had Webster's spelling book, with that discouraging frontispiece, a picture of a very lightly clad young man weakening when half way up a high mountain with a little cupola on top of it and on its front gable the word "Fame," in large letters, and a rough looking female ordering him to climb or bust. I attribute my failure to achieve greatness to that picture. The constant contemplation of it so impressed the difficulty of being famous (in that costume) upon my youthful mind that hope died within me. After we had worn our spelling books all to tiny little bits, we began on arithmetic, and each scholar seemed to have a different kind of a one. There were Doboll's, Pike's, Colbert's, and many others whose names as well as their contents have escaped me. Along toward the close of my education we had McGuffey's readers, which I thought were the very "ultima thule" of progress in the way of a reading book. Attending this school was a red-headed boy about ten or eleven years old who was a bright intelligent lad, named Erastus Yeager, who twenty-one years later was hung by the Vigilantes in Montana for being a road agent. In Montana he went by the sobriquet of "Red" and it was not until he was hanged that I learned he was my schoolmate in Iowa.[3]

[3] The road agents were a band of highwaymen who terrorized Montana during 1863. They were after gold dust and did not hesitate to kill in order to get it. Yeager was hanged January 4, 1864, by members of the vigilance committee who had organized to free Montana from the road agents. Before Yeager was hanged he confessed and gave the names of many other road agents. This assisted the committee in exterminating the band during the next two months. For an account of the road agents and vigilance committee in Montana see Thomas J. Dimsdale, *The Vigilantes of Montana* (first edition, Virginia City, 1865, third edition, Helena, 1915) and Nathaniel Pitt Langford, *Vigilante Days and Ways* (2 vols. in 1, New York, 1893). Stuart wrote that after Yeager was cut down "in his pockets were found letters addressed to him in his family name and post-marked from the little

The winter of 1843-4 was one of great severity in
Iowa.   Snow fell to a depth of two feet and laid nearly
all winter with much weather below zero.   The spring
was very late.   The ice in Cedar river did not break
up until April 8, 1844, when we saw many fearful
gorges, the ice piling up in hugh mounds and ridges,
and all pushed far out of the river banks whenever the
shore was low and flat.   The snow was hard-crusted
that winter, and many deer and wild turkeys perished
from the extreme cold and the great difficulty of getting
food.

In the summer of 1844 my father and two other men
went up Red Cedar river with a pair of horses and a
wagon on a hunting trip.   There were but few people
up the river in those days and they found plenty of elk
and deer, where is now the town of Cedar Falls, and
also many bee trees full of wild honey.   They killed
much game and trapped a few beavers.   They dried a
quantity of elk meat and filled a barrel with honey;
then sold their horses and wagon, and made a large
canoe out of a big walnut tree, and floated down the
clear waters of Cedar river, feasting by the way on
game and fish of all kinds which were there in greatest
abundance.   They met a few Indians, but they were
all friendly.   I remember well how we feasted on that
dried elk meat, which was the first we children had
ever eaten.   The honey in the barrel was all candied
and was delicious.

The big walnut canoe was so broad and steady that it
could not be overturned by two men standing on one
edge of it.   Mother let brother James and me use it,
and we soon became expert canoe boys and fearlessly

town of West Liberty, Iowa.   When shown to James and me we knew that
Red was Erastus Yeager.   . ." – ED.

went everywhere in it. We very often paddled it at night for our father, who would place on its bow a tin lamp holding about a quart of lard with a rag wick in its spout which, when lighted, would cast a strong light for several yards in front of the canoe. The water of the river being as clear as glass our father could plainly see every fish as far as the light shone on the water. He used a three prong spear called a gig, with a red cedar shaft about ten feet long. Fish seemed attracted by the light and did not seem alarmed by the canoe. In two or three hours he would spear fifteen or thirty fine large ones of various kinds, with occasionally a gar, which was a fish three or four feet long, not fit to eat but which had a snout over a foot long filled with long sharp teeth. The next morning after a night's fishing my brother James and I had the task of carrying the surplus fish as presents to the neighbors.

About half a mile from our house there was a pretty little lake about seven hundred yards long and four hundred yards wide; along its shores on the west side were pleasant woods with some crabapple and plum thickets. Amid these beautiful surroundings on the shore of the lake the settlers of the vicinity built a small log school house which was rough plastered inside. It had glass windows and a real board floor, but best of all, there was a good swimming hole near by. We scholars just thought that anyone who wanted a better school house than that was too hard to please for any use. In this school house was held a summer school for three months (in 1844) where my three brothers and myself increased our small supply of knowledge.

At this time, 1843 to 1850, there was an abundance of game in the wooded creek bottoms and on the prairies and as my father was a good hunter we always had plenty to eat of squirrels, prairie chickens, wild turkeys, deer, and elk, and after the first year there were corn-meal and vegetables. The scarce articles for the larder were coffee, tea, and sugar, although we had plenty of maple sugar and syrup, pure from the tree, something that one seldom ever gets in this year, 1916.

This was still the era of tallow-dip candles for light-ing and of open fire-place for heating and cooking and the cast-iron skillet and Dutch oven for baking. The first cooking stove I ever saw was in 1845 and it was rather a crude affair, but a great relief from cooking over an open fire, although some of the first to use the new invention had more or less trouble getting used to it. My father-in-law used to tell a story about an old couple who were the first to invest in a cook stove in his neighborhood. They got the stove in St. Louis and brought it up the Mississippi river and home. The neighbors came from near and far to view the stove and it became the center of interest and subject of gossip for the entire neighborhood. Finally the excitement subsided, and little was said or heard of the new stove, when one day someone asked Mr. Jones how he liked the new stove by this time. "Well," the old man answered, "the stove is all right I reckon, but mother and I are getting too old to lift the tarnal thing on and off the fire-place, so we jest cook the old way."

The guns used for hunting in those days were flint-lock rifles brought by the frontiersmen from Virginia and Kentucky. They were full-stocked, that is, the wood of the stock reached to the muzzle of the barrel. They were heavy, weighing from eleven to thirteen pounds, all hand work with small calibres, running from about sixty round bullets to the pound of lead. A cousin of mine bought a four-foot barrel, full stock rifle, carrying one hundred and fifty bullets to the pound of lead, for which he paid six dollars in cash. Money was very scarce in those days, nearly all trading being carried on by barter.

Father had two guns which I well remember, as it was with these guns he taught me to hunt. One was a flint-lock that he used when hunting along streams where there was timber and little wind. If the weather was cold and snow on the ground he could quickly start a fire with his flint-lock by which he would dress the deer he had killed. With the gun he was sure of killing a deer, if it was within one hundred and twenty-five yard distance. The other gun he used while hunting on the prairies or out in the wind. It was a small-bore rifle fired with percussion caps placed on the nipple. The cap would not blow off as did the powder in the pan of the flint-lock.

In our neighborhood was a widow with several children whose husband had been a good hunter. His rifle was a flint-lock half stock, of large calibre for those days, using forty round balls to the pound of lead. A half stock rifle was one in which the wood only extended along the barrel about one-third of the way to the muzzle, and from its end to the muzzle, on the under side of the barrel was a slender piece of iron called a rib, on which was soldered from two to four small pieces of iron or brass tubing called thimbles, in which the ramrod of tough hickory wood was carried. All rifles in those days were muzzle loaders and the Johnson one was the first half stocked gun I ever saw. My father used to borrow it occasionally because its large balls were more fatal to the deer than those of his small calibre rifle. When he was successful the Johnson family always received half of the venison. This rifle was much better finished than most of the guns then in use. It had an oval silver box set in the butt stock on the right side, a few inches forward was a hole in which to carry an extra flint for the lock, and a greased piece of rag to use in keeping the gun from rusting if it got wet. On the inside of this lid Johnson had scratched or roughly engraved three letters, "B," and just below it, "D," and below that, "F." After B he marked the list of bucks killed by him (numbering 16); after D, the list of does (numbering 13); after F the list of fawns (numbering 10). My father, leaving a little space after each of Johnson's list, added those killed by him when he used the gun. How I would like to have that gun now as a souvenir of the ancient days and conditions when life was just unfolding to me.

In the spring of 1849 the news of the discovery of gold in California reached Iowa, and my father at once determined to go to the gold fields. He formed a traveling partnership with three other men and they bought a wagon and four yoke of oxen and about four months' supply of provisions, clothing and ammunition. About the middle of April, 1849, they started on the long dangerous journey across the plains and mountains; eighteen hundred miles through an unknown and uninhabited country, save the settlement of Mormons in Great Salt Lake valley and the roving tribes of Indians who had no fixed abode.

The emigrants, as these gold seekers were called, soon learned that in union there was strength, and united their scattered forces into trains of from ten to fifty wagons, with from forty to two hundred men. The two principal starting places for these trains were, Council Bluffs, Iowa, and St. Joe, Missouri. Emigrants would come from all points, east and south and when there were a sufficient number of wagons to form a train, they would start out.   The Indians rarely ever attacked these large trains but were always lurking around trying to steal their stock and they frequently got away with a few scattered horses or mules.   On the western end of their route the Digger [4] Indians were particularly annoying, as they were constantly stealing cattle and horses.

On Black's fork of Green river the emigrant road forked.   The left hand road went up Black's fork to Fort Bridger,[5] and then on to Salt Lake City.   The right hand road went up Ham's fork about thirty-four miles and then crossed over some high clay ridges, without any timber on them, to Bear river, then down Bear river to Soda springs where it left the river and

[4] This name first applied to a small Shoshone tribe in Utah because they practiced agriculture came to be applied to many tribes who lived on roots. As most of these Indians were of low type the term became one of reproach. Stuart probably referred to the tribes living between the Great Salt Lake and Fort Hall.   They were very degraded, living mostly upon roots and insects.   They seldom built habitations and had little clothing.   They were also often without shelter of any kind and were unable to purchase fire-arms. The French called them *"Digne de pitie"* (worthy of pity).   The Digger Indians are sometimes classed with the Piutes, a more vigorous tribe.   See Thwaites's note in *Early Western Travels* (Cleveland, 1906) vol. xxviii, p. 312.   Father De Smet described them with other tribes in 1841 in a letter to Father Roothaan, General of the Society of Jesus.   *Letters and Sketches* . . . (Philadelphia, 1843) pp. 34-39.   Also in Thwaites, *Early Western Travels*, vol. xxvii, pp. 164-168.   Fremont described the Diggers in 1845 as follows: "They had the usual very large heads, remarkable among the Digger tribe, with matted hair, and were almost entirely naked; looking very poor and miserable, as if their lives had been spent among the rushes where they were. . ." *Report of the Exploring Expedition to the Rocky Mountains in the Year 1842* (Washington, 1845) p. 149. – Ed.

[5] On the site of Fort Bridger was a small trading post in 1834.   In 1843 Jim Bridger acquired it and started a blacksmith and repair shop and a supply station for emigrants on the Oregon trail.   Most travellers either to Oregon or California passed this way for the conveniences of the post. Grace R. Hebard and E. A. Brininstool, *The Bozeman Trail* (2 vols., Cleveland, 1922) vol. i, p. 48; Hiram Chittenden, *History of the American Fur Trade in the Far West* (3 vols., New York, 1902) vol. i, p. 476.

went northwest to old Fort Hall on Snake river, then
down that stream for some thirty-five miles, then west
to the City of Rocks (which was a number of curiously
grouped granite pinnacles, which resembled build-
ings).[6]   At this place the branch roads reunited and
continued on as one until far down the Humboldt river.

This river should not be named Humboldt river for
this reason: In 1847 a party of Mormons found a man
named Peter Ogden, with his wife and children,
camped on Weber river, where now stands the city of
Ogden.   These Mormons were desirous of journeying
further west than the basin of Great Salt lake and Ogden told them of this river.   Following his directions
they found the river.   Ogden's wife's name was Mary
and she was the first white woman to travel down the
river, so out of compliment to her the Mormons always
called it the Mary Ogden river and so it should be
called.[7]   My father's party followed down this river

---

[6] This right hand road was known as the Sublette "Cut Off." While
shorter than the route via Fort Bridger it had no water and no supply
stations and was seldom used. *Ibid.*, vol. i, p. 478.   The old Oregon trail
by Fort Bridger joined the Sublette "Cut Off" near Bear lake.   The trail
by Salt Lake City went around the north end of Great Salt lake and down
the Humboldt joining the trail from Bear river and another from Fort Hall
as described by Stuart. – ED.

[7] Stuart is wrong regarding the date of Ogden's visit to this region.
Ogden became chief trader in charge of the Snake river brigade in 1824 and
left the mountains in 1831.   Lewis and Phillips editors, *The Journal of John
Work* (Early Western Journals no. 1, Cleveland, 1923) pp. 28, 29.   T. C.
Elliott, "Peter Skene Ogden, Fur Trader" in *Oregon Historical Quarterly*, xi,
no. 3, p. 23, thinks that Ogden penetrated this country in 1828.   Traders and
trappers called this river Mary's or Ogden's river for a number of years
before the Mormons migrated to this country.   Thomas J. Farnham, *Travels
in the Great Western Prairies* . . . in Thwaites, *opus citra*, xxviii, p.
113.   This account was written in 1839.   See also Chittenden, *American Fur
Trade*, vol. ii, p. 797.   Ogden was one of the most daring of the Hudson's
Bay Company's fur traders.   Mary, his wife, was an Indian squaw.   Fremont named this river, the Humboldt, on his third expedition apparently not
knowing it was the Mary's river, he had previously hunted.   John Charles
Fremont, *Memoirs of My Life* (Chicago and N. Y., 1887) p. 434. – ED.

some two hundred miles to Big Meadows where an old trapper named Larson had laid out a new route to the mines, which he claimed was the best and shortest road. They took that road, but found it went too far north, crossing the Sierra Nevada mountains near Goose lake and thence down Pit river into the head of Sacramento valley, being quite two hundred miles longer than the southern route by way of Carson river to Hangtown (afterwards Placerville). They reached Sacramento valley without a loss, late in the fall of 1849.

My father mined part of the time, hunted large game, elk, deer and antelope, which he sold at a good price.

In the winter of 1851 he returned home to Iowa via the steamship line to Nicaragua, across that country, and then by Garrison's steamer to New Orleans and up the Mississippi river. He kept a journal all the time but unfortunately our house burned down and with it many other valuable family records were destroyed. I remember well reading his journal which was a perfect pen-picture of the days of forty-nine.

Overland to California

In the spring of 1852, in company with my father, my brother James, and a jovial Irishman named Fayal Thomas Reilly, I started from near the village of West Liberty, Muscatine county, Iowa, on the long adventurous journey to California; overland across the vast uninhabited plains, then known on the maps as the "Great American Desert," but now (in 1916) forming the wealthy states of Nebraska, Kansas, Colorado, and Wyoming. Iowa then was very sparsely settled, and there was not a single railroad west of the Mississippi river, and I had never seen one, and never did until fourteen years later in 1866, at Atchison, Kansas.

Our outfit consisted of two light spring wagons each drawn by four good horses. In the wagon boxes we carried our supply of food and extra clothing. A loose floor of boards was placed across the top of the wagon boxes on which we placed our bedding, and on which we slept at night. The wagons had the usual canvas curtains which buttoned on to each end of the canvas roof. Inside we slept dry and comfortable through the worst storms. The storms along the Platte river were regular cloudbursts, accompanied by such fierce gales of wind as often to blow down the tents, which were used by most of the emigrants, and thoroughly soak their bedding. My father having had that disagreeable experience when he crossed this region in 1849, had so arranged that we slept in our wagons, using no tents, and thus were always dry, though many times we were obliged to picket the wagons to the ground to prevent their blowing over.

My father and brother occupied one wagon, and Reilly and myself the other. We each had a rifle and father had a small five-shooter revolver of twenty-five calibre, using black powder and round balls. I think it was called "Maynard's patent." No one would carry such a pistol nowadays, but revolvers were then just invented. This was the first one I had ever seen and I longed for the day when I could possess one, and bid defiance to whole villages of Indians, little knowing that the Indian with his bow and arrows, was quite beyond the reach of such a puny weapon. Our rifles were hung up in leather loops fastened to the sides of the wagon boxes, always loaded (they were all muzzle loaders) and ready for instant use. Our journey across the state of Iowa was a most disagreeable one. The western half of the state was very thinly inhabited. We had great difficulty in crossing the deep miry sloughs that at that period filled every low place. There being few people, there were still fewer bridges, and when our horses and wagons mired down, which usually happened about twice a day, we were forced to wade in mud and water up to our knees while unloading our wagons and then lift with all of our strength on the wheels to enable our horses to pull them out. Somewhere between Des Moines (then a small village) and Council Bluffs, we came to a Mormon village called Kanesville. These people, mostly Welsh and English, had wintered here in 1851 while on their way to Great Salt lake, and now found it profitable to stay this summer and repair the wagons and shoe the horses of the emigrants, who were passing through in large numbers on their way to California. We remained with them two days waiting our turn to get our horses shod and some small repairs to our wagons.

After many annoyances and much profanity we at last arrived at Council Bluffs on the east bank of the Missouri river. The village consisted of some twelve or fifteen one-story log cabins. We had to cross the river here, and when I saw the ferry boat, a flat scow, large enough to hold one team and wagon, the motive power of which was three men with oars, I looked at the wide swift flowing muddy river and thought we might possibly get across safely, but that the chances were rather poor. The price for crossing was ten dollars for each wagon and horses, which seemed to me exorbitant. However, we got across and from the way those oarsmen had to pull I concluded the price was reasonable enough. On the west side of the river to our astonishment, we found a considerable town of log houses, but every house was dismantled. We afterwards learned this had been the town where the Mormons had waited in 1846-47, until their leaders went on ahead and looked up a future abiding place for them. They called the settlement on the bank of the Missouri, "Far West." This is the site of the present city of Omaha. After crossing the river we traveled for several days across a gently rolling prairie country, till we came to Elk Horn river, a beautiful clear stream about fifty yards wide, with a fine strip of cottonwood timber along its banks. We crossed this river also on a ferry for which we paid five dollars for each team, but as we traveled up it for several miles we saw that if we had camped near the ferry and examined the stream for a few miles we could have forded it and saved our ten dollars.

From Elk river we crossed a prairie country and struck Platte river at Grand island and then traveled up its north bank for over two hundred miles. In this distance we saw only one lone tree which the emigrants had partly destroyed and doubtless not a vestige of it remained by July. In this long distance there was not a willow along this strangest of all rivers, with its yellowish, whitish water, which was usually over a half mile wide and in no place more than three feet deep, flowing with a swift current over a bed of quicksand dangerous to cross. The banks on either side were only from two or three feet high and the adjacent plains were covered with a fine growth of grass. It was while traveling up this stream that we encountered the most terrific storm that I had ever seen. Dark clouds appeared in the sky and distant thunder growled a warning. We lost no time in making ready and it was well we did. We buttoned our canvas covers down closely and tied one end of a stout rope to each wagon wheel and the other end to stakes driven deep into the ground, thus securely fastening the wagons so the wind could not blow them over. We had just finished our preparations when the storm broke. The wind blew a gale. Rain and small hail fell in torrents and we could not hear each other speak for the deafening peals of thunder which were preceded by blinding flashes of lightning. We expected every minute to have a wagon overturned or to be struck with lightning. The storm lasted about two hours, but without any serious damage to us. The tight canvas covers kept us dry and the picket ropes kept the wagons from turning over.

Next morning we passed a train that had set up tents. The tents were blown over and their blankets and provisions were soaked with water and they presented a dismal appearance trying to dry out their things and gather up their tents. The women and children looked particularly uncomfortable, but they greeted us with a cheery "Good-morning" and were all making the best of the situation.

Cholera was raging among the emigrants all along the road and many were dying. We drove as fast as our horses could stand it to get through this dreadful region of death, where we were seldom out of the sight of graves and saw many heartrending scenes. Abandoned wagons were numerous, and their former owners were in graves near by. We met a young woman driving a span of horses to a light wagon and with her were four little children, from two to seven years old. She stopped to talk with us. Her husband had died three days before and she was trying to return to Illinois, where her relatives lived. We gave her some sugar and coffee and did what we could to comfort her, telling her always to camp at night with some other wagons, that she would be meeting every day, for if any Indians saw her camped alone, they might take her horses, plunder her wagon, and abuse her.

One evening we camped near five abandoned wagons. Close by were freshly made graves and by one of the wagons was a large yellow dog, with a bushy tail. He was thin and nearly starved. While we were eating supper he came near us and stood looking longingly at our food. I could not stand that, so I coaxed him to me and divided my supper with him, which he devoured ravenously. He then went back and laid down by one of the graves and there remained all night. In the morning I called him to me and fed him well. He then went back to the same grave and laid down by it again. When we hitched up our horses and got ready to start I called him and we started to go. He followed a few steps, and then turned and went part of the way to the graves, stopped and began howling, Oh! so mournfully. We stopped to see what he would do. He quit howling and turned and came slowly to us, and when we again started he followed us. His pitiful howling was his leave taking of the loved one who lay there in the lonely grave. My eyes filled with tears of sympathy for him and I did my best to make him feel at home with us, little thinking that he was to save my life the next year. After he followed us a short distance I saw that he was too weak to keep up, for we traveled at a fast trot, so I took him up on the footboard of the wagon, where he lay part of the time, all the way to California.

The cholera did not extend above Fort Laramie,[8] and as soon as we struck the mountains we felt safe from it. How I did enjoy gazing upon them, and drinking clear ice-cold water from many lovely little streams. We continued up the North Platte river to the cañon and James and I went some distance from camp to take our first look at a mountain stream. Here the water was roaring and foaming over enormous boulders, with cliffs almost perpendicularly rising from one hundred to three hundred feet above the water, a

---

[8] Fort Laramie was located at the confluence of the Laramie and the North Platte. It was built in 1834 as a fur trading fort and named Fort William for William L. Sublette. Sublette sold it in 1835 to the fur trading firm of Fitzpatrick, Sublette, and Bridger who soon turned it over to the American Fur Company who renamed it Fort John for John B. Sarpy. The name Laramie gradually came into use and finally supplanted its official name. Chittenden, *opus citra*, vol. iii, p. 967.

Some years later Stuart wrote of Fort Laramie . . . "There are wood and water plenty; and, before many trains have passed, the grass is good above the fort. Mail station and post office here, with sutler's store, well stocked with travellers' outfits." *Montana As It Is* (New York, 1865) p. 132. – ED.

wonderful sight for two boys who had always lived in a level prairie country with sluggish muddy creeks.

In the summer of 1907 I traveled along this same strange river, in a luxurious car of the Union Pacific Railroad and saw all that was once a lonely stretch of plains, occupied by highly cultivated farms and fine residences, the owners of which were entirely unconscious that there were few fields bordering the view that did not have several unknown graves in them, where rested the bones of the hardy pioneers who fell by the wayside, when on their way to form a western empire on the shores of the far distant Pacific ocean.

Here we left the river and traveled several miles through red, desolate looking hills, passed Red buttes,[9] and then saw a pond of reddish looking water, where some good men (among the many who had preceded us) had put up a notice not to let horses or cattle drink of that water, as it was poisonous. The water carried so strong a solution of alkali as to make it dangerous to animals who drank it. Not far from the spring we saw two dead oxen and a horse. We took warning and did not stop, but kept on to a point where the water was less alkaline. We could now see Laramie peak, far away to the south, with patches of snow on it. This was our first look at snow in July and a wonderful sight it was. We passed Independence rock,[10] so named by the emi-

---

[9] Red buttes about one hundred fifty miles from Fort Laramie. *Ibid.*, pp. 132-133. – ED.

[10] Independence rock. The name originated long before 1842. Chittenden, *American Fur Trade*, vol. ii, p. 472, thinks it goes back to the Ashley expedition of 1823. Father De Smet described it in 1841, and even then he was not sure of the origin of the name. H. M. Chittenden and A. T. Richardson, *Life, Letters, and Travels of Father Pierre-Jean De Smet, S. J.* (N. Y., 1905, 4 vols.) vol. iv, p. 1348. John Wyeth visited the rock in 1832 and even that early the origin of the name was forgotten. Wyeth, *Oregon, or a Short History of a Long Journey*, edited by Thwaites, *Early Western Travels* (Cleveland, 1905) vol. xxi, p. 53. – ED.

grants of 1842, on their way to Oregon, who camped
near it on July 4.   It is an enormous lump of granite,
which rises about twenty-five feet above the plain of
sand and gravel.   It covers about a half acre and is
worn smooth by glacier action in past ages.   It is a
most remarkable object.   There are hundreds of names
and dates that passers-by have put on it with tar and
paint, and a few cut into the hard rock.   I saw a number bearing the date of 1849, and among them was my
father's name, Robert Stuart, July 29, 1849.

Just above Independence rock we came to a large
creek called "Sweetwater river," which is a branch of
North Platte river.   We forded this stream just below
"The Devil's Gate," where the river runs through a
high ridge between two perpendicular cliffs, one hundred and fifty to two hundred feet high.   What seemed
strange was that the river could have made a bend
around the end of the ridge without passing through it,
and probably did so in ancient geological times, until
an obliging earthquake made a big crack through it,
which the river at once took possession of.   This short-
ened its course a little.   This stream takes its name
from its beautiful clear cold waters having a sweetish
taste, caused by the alkali held in solution in its waters,
not enough, however, to cause any apparent injurious
effects.   In this vicinity we saw a most remarkable
pond, with water that looked white as snow.   On ex-
amination it proved to be not white water, but a bed of
pure white soda, several feet thick, deposited by the
evaporation of the alkali water, which had leaked in
out of the neighboring soil, during a long period of
time.   The Mormon emigrants took large quantities of
this soda to Salt lake and they said it was fully as good
as the commercial article.

We traveled up Sweetwater river three days when we came to Strawberry creek, where the road left the river and ascended a long rocky hill, known as "Rocky Ridge." Not much wood during these three days, but some large sagebrush and plenty of good grass and water. Somewhere in this vicinity was a grassy swamp, where we dug down about eighteen inches and came to a bed of solid clear ice. We dug up enough to put into water-kegs and enjoyed the luxury of ice-water all that hot day, while we traveled through the famous "South pass,"[11] of the Rocky mountains. There are no mountains near on either side, but only low grassy ridges with a slight depression through them where the emigrant road passed, but twenty miles on, more to the north was a range of snow-clad mountains, the highest one known as Fremont's Peak, because Lieutenant Fremont ascended it in 1842, and estimated its height as thirteen thousand feet.[12] The South pass is six thousand feet above sea level.

For several days I was greatly annoyed by frequent bleeding at the nose, which I afterwards ascertained was caused by the increasing altitude. I have never had any trouble with it since, when at much greater altitudes. On the west side of the pass we camped at Pacific springs, called because their waters flow into the Pacific ocean, by way of the Colorado river, which here is known as Green river because in the autumn, its water, where deep, has a beautiful green tint. Good

---

[11] South pass. Probably discovered in 1823 by Thomas Fitzpatrick. This opened the way for the discovery of a central route to the Pacific. Harrison C. Dale, *The Ashley Smith Explorations and the Discovery of a Central Route to the Pacific*, 1822-1829 (Cleveland, 1918) pp. 89, 90. For other claims see *ibid.*, p. 40. Seymour Dunbar, *History of Travel in America* (Indianapolis, 1915, 4 vols.) vol. iv, p. 1216, *note*, states that South pass is located on a map, by Melish about 1820. – ED.

[12] J. C. Fremont, *opus citra*, p. 174. – ED.

water and grass at the springs, no wood, but sagebrush. From Pacific springs we traveled sixteen, miles over a sandy gravelly plain, with thin scattering grass, to Dry Sandy creek. No wood, but small grease wood and sagebrush, water blackish, but drinkable. "Sublette's Cut Off" road turns off to the right here for Soda springs, on Bear river, and Fort Hall on Snake river. We took the left-hand road for Fort Bridger and Great Salt Lake City. From Dry Sandy to Little Sandy creek was fifteen miles, over the same gravelly sandy plain. Here we found good water, but very little grass. Almost no fuel from here to Big Sandy creek, eighteen miles of same kind of prairie. Good water here, but only grass in spots along the creek, fuel scarce all the way from here to the upper ford on Green river. Here was a ferry used during high water, but the stream is fordable in the late summer and autumn.

At Green river we found plenty of grass and wood. We went down this stream seven miles, to the lower ford and ferry, where we found some Mormons, who were ferrymen and traders. We then traveled across gravelly bench lands sixteen miles to Black's fork of Green river. All along here we had fine grass, plenty of wood, and good water. We journeyed up Black's fork crossing and recrossing the river, traveling over sagebrush valleys and rolling grassy hills to Smith's fork. This is a small branch of Black's fork coming in from the south. The road was good, but there was very little grass. No wood here, the hills are of hard clay, bad land formation from Ham's fork all the way to Fort Bridger, with many eroded buttes, scattered about often resembling ancient castles and old ruins. Fort Bridger like Fort Laramie was not a military fort but a trading post. There was a stockade with cabins inside, built solely to trade with Indians, who were numerous through here, but were not hostile. We camped a few miles below the fort on the creek where we found plenty of grass and wood enough for our use. We did not lay over at Fort Bridger as we intended to stop at Salt Lake.

We traveled six miles across grassy hills to Muddy creek and on over to Sulphur creek. There were several fine springs of good water along the road, but wood was very scarce. Quaking Aspen hill between Muddy creek and Sulphur creek is the eastern rim of the Great Basin of Great Salt lake. All streams in this great basin run into the lake which has no outlet. Bear river is the first river we strike after entering the basin. It is a fine large stream of clear cold water. Here was a good camping place, plenty of wood, water, and grass. Bear river is easily forded excepting during the months of May and June, when the water is high and the ford becomes dangerous.

From Bear river to Red fork of Weber river, nineteen miles, is mostly through the wonderful "Echo cañon," which is bordered by the lofty pinnacles and cliffs of deep red sandstone forming some grand scenery. In this cañon, two miles below the cavern called "Cache cave," were good water and grass, but little wood. Here my brother James and I killed a deer. We had done scarcely any hunting and had seen little game. The emigrant trains were so numerous at that time that the wild game had all been driven away from the road and this was the first deer we had seen on the trip. At Spring branch, five miles below, the road leaves the river and strikes a little valley to the left. Here we saw a fine spring of clear cold water, to which we hastened to get a drink, which we as hastily spit out, for it was as salt as strong brine. It was the first salt spring we had seen, but we found several others between there and Salt Lake City.

Our next stop was at Beauchemin fork, nine miles. The road followed down Beauchemin fork to Big Cañon creek fourteen miles. In the first eight miles of this journey the road crossed Beauchemin fork thirteen times and was very dangerous in time of high water. At Cañon creek the road left Beauchemin fork and ascended Big mountain by way of a very steep ravine, to Big Cañon creek, where there was good water, wood, and grass. High mountain ridges all around. Then by way of Emigrant creek to Great Salt Lake city, ten miles. Our horses were greatly in need of rest so we stayed with the "Latter Day Saints," as the Mormons called themselves, for several weeks and were very kindly treated by them. In fact, I here got into better society than I have been in since, for I lived a month with one of the "Twelve Apostles" and his family. It was "Apostle John Taylor," a pleasant old gentleman, who succeeded Brigham Young, as head of the Mormon Church. He wore a snuff colored suit, and a rather rusty old plug hat. He owned a whole block and had an adobe house on each of the three corners, in which lived his three wives, each in her own house. I had the honor of living with the Apostle and wife no. 1, in house on fourth corner. She was a most amiable woman, a good cook, and a good housekeeper. She kept everything nice and clean, but the confounded bed bugs ran us out of the beds in the house, and we all slept out in the yard. Luckily it never rained. Mrs. Taylor felt greatly mortified about the bed bugs and said that she just couldn't keep them out, although she fought them all the time, and when one day, I pulled a piece of bark off a fir pole on a near by fence and found innumerable bed bugs under it, I knew why Mrs. Taylor could not keep them out of the house. The entire valley swarmed with them.[13]

When we camped on Weber river, where is now the city of Ogden, the sagebrush, just after sundown, swarmed with skunks, and I felt certain that Great Salt lake could beat the world for bed bugs and skunks. At this place I was stricken with a severe attack of mountain fever which laid me on my back in the wagon until we reached the Sierra Nevada mountains.

We had traveled one thousand miles since leaving Council Bluffs on the Missouri river, and the entire distance was uninhabited, except by a few Indian traders at Fort Laramie on North Platte, who live mostly like the Indians on wild meat straight – a few ferrymen on Green river and a few traders at Fort Bridger. We saw only a few Indians (Pawnees) on the trip, and they were friendly to the emigrants. We saw only a few straggling buffalo, as the great herds had passed on their annual migration north, while we were on the Platte river.

From Salt lake we took the emigrant road to Goose creek, up which we traveled something like seventy-five miles, then crossed over a divide into Thousand Spring valley. Most of the springs were hot. We passed over to the north fork of the Humboldt river. Here the emigrant road forks. One road follows down the river several hundred miles to its sink, and crosses

---

13 Mr. Stuart wrote of Great Salt Lake city in 1865, "Feed for stock can be purchased here and so can any articles that the traveller may require, but the price will make his hair stand straight on 'end.' There is no camping place within two miles of the city and it is best either to stop near the mouth of 'Emigration cañon' or to cross to 'The other side of Jordan.'" *Montana As It Is*, p. 136.

a desert, distance of thirty miles, to Carson river. This was the southern route.[14]   We took the other route and left the Humboldt river above its sink, going west across a desert forty-five miles wide, to Truckee river. Half way across this forty-five miles of sandy desert there was a very large boiling spring around which passing emigrants had left some surplus water barrels. These the departing emigrants would fill with hot water and leave to cool for those who were coming behind. In this way there was nearly always cool water in the barrels, awaiting the thirsty emigrant.

We started across the desert about four o'clock in the afternoon and reached the spring about midnight, where we rested an hour and watered our horses with the cooled water. We then filled everything with the hot water and started on, reaching Truckee river shortly after noon the next day. This river takes its source at Lake Tahoe and is a beautiful clear cool mountain stream flowing over a pebbly bottom, certainly a most refreshing sight to us coming from the heat, sand, and dust of the desert. It was full of magnificent trout, weighing from one to two pounds. We lost no time getting out fishhooks and lines, and during our stay here (two days) we feasted on trout.

We crossed the Sierra Nevada mountains by way of Beckwith pass, so named because old Jim Beckwith was living there and claimed to have discovered the pass. We found him living up in the valley leading to his pass. Many of the emigrants reaching his place were nearly starved. His nature was a hospitable and generous one and he supplied their pressing necessities,

14 *Ibid.*, pp. 137-139. Here Mr. Stuart gives the itinerary for this southern route but not for the road his party followed. The details in his account of the trip from Fort Laramie to this place are the same as in the earlier book. – ED.

often without money, they agreeing to pay him later, which I regret to say a number of them failed to do. This so impoverished him that he was compelled to give up his place in the pass and resume a roving life, which he had long been accustomed to. The next place I heard of him was at Napa valley, California. Later he returned to Montana and resumed his old life among the Crows.[15]

After we crossed the Sierra Nevadas we came into American valley and halted at a wayside hostelry called the "American Ranch," which was the first ranch that I had seen. Here to our dismay, we learned that we had reached the end of the wagon road, as that part between there and Bidwell's bar on Feather river, a distance of fifty miles had not been constructed yet. A trifling detail that the robust liars on the Humboldt river (who were boosting for this route over the

[15] Beckwith should be spelled Beckwourth. For Beckwourth's account of this pass see *Life and Adventures of James P. Beckwourth*, edited by Charles G. Leland. (London, 1891) pp. 423-431, or edited by T. D. Bonner (New York, 1856) pp. 514-520. Stuart's manuscript here contains long accounts of Beckwourth taken from his *Life and Adventures* which the editor omits. Stuart's description of the last of Beckwourth's adventures is not contained in the Beckwourth book and is as follows: "In 1876 he was back on the Big Horn river in Montana with Captain John W. Smith, post-trader at Fort C. F. Smith. Beckwith had regained some of his former influence among the Crows. As soon as the troops came to the fort, Smith sent him to the river to bring up a large party of Crows that was camped there for the purpose of trading with them. Beckwith who was gettting old, was mounted on a spirited cavalry horse and seeing a small herd of buffalo he determined to kill one. His companions tried to persuade him not to attempt to run buffalo on such a horse, but he would not listen to them and started in pursuit. He soon was in the midst of the buffalo herd. His frightened horse became unmanageable, plunging and rearing among the running buffalo, and the old man was thrown and seriously injured. Some Indian women picked him up and placing him on a travois started with him for camp, but he died before reaching it. He was buried on the Big Horn in the hunting grounds of his adopted people." This story was apparently told Mr. Stuart by Tom H. Irvine one time sheriff of Custer county, Montana. – Ed.

Sierra) neglected to tell when telling us this route was the nearest and best one to the Sacramento valley. We remained a few days at the "Ranch" eating three meals a day at one dollar a meal. The food was good, and I gained rapidly in strength. As the road from American valley into Sacramento valley had not been built, being only a pack trail for the greater part of the distance, we found ourselves bottled up, unable to go further into California with our wagons. We were obliged to sell them for a mere trifle; my recollection is that we got only twenty-five dollars for each of the spring wagons, which if we could have taken them on to Sacramento valley would have been worth two hundred dollars apiece. Our eight fine horses and harness we subsequently sold for sixteen hundred dollars. Getting some old saddles we took the pack-horse or rather mule trail for the Sacramento valley. This trail ran along across mountain ridges, often quite steep, and I can never forget how I suffered the next day, being still weak, and entirely unused to riding on horseback. It was all I could do to keep from falling off when going down the steep hills.

The first night out we staid at Balsein's ranch, on the divide between the middle and north forks of the Feather river. The food was excellent, but I was unable to eat and I was so exhausted I could scarcely stand up. The second day the road was much better, and we reached Bidwell's bar on Feather river. We crossed on a ferry, the first one we had seen since leaving Green river, east of Great Salt Lake City. We put up for the night at a hotel in Bidwell's bar. Here we saw our first orange tree. On this bar John Bidwell, who had about twenty Indians working for him, took out one hundred thousand dollars in gold dust during the years 1848 and 1849. Samuel Neal, who came into California with Lieutenant Fremont in 1844, also had about twenty Indians working for him. He took out of Feather river, during those two years, one hundred and ten thousand dollars in clear gold dust. I heard him tell that each Indian's task was to bring him one hundred dollars a day and that several of them often brought it by ten o'clock in the morning, and that they did not have to work any more that day, but laid in the sun and had all the fresh beef they could eat, and that was no small quantity. He and Bidwell had Spanish grants of land, each owning two leagues square, equal to one American township. The Indians belonged absolutely to the owners of the grant, but as far as my observation extended, this was not a great hardship to them, for they were taught to work and were well treated and well fed. As they were a gentle docile race they soon became semi-civilized and able to take care of themselves. When the Americans took possession of the country they became free, but most of them remained in their old homes, and lived practically as before. In the spring of 1850, Sam Neal, who had bought cattle and horses with some of his money had eighty thousand dollars on hand which he divided, and sent forty thousand dollars to his parents in Pennsylvania. The remaining forty thousand dollars he kept for himself.

To resume our journey. From Bidwell's bar we went down Feather river a few miles, and laid over at White Rock camp. We saw the river where a dam was placed across it, and all of that good sized stream turned into a large flume, for about a quarter of a mile, leaving the bed of the river practically dry. Here was a large number of men busily engaged in washing the sand and gravel, and taking out large quantities of gold dust so called, but very little of it was dust. It was in pieces from the size of a pinhead, some the size of grains of wheat, and corn and pumpkin seed, and much of it much larger than that called nuggets. While we were here the foreman of one gang of the miners came up from the river with a sheet iron gold pan in which he had about a gallon of gold of all sizes, which looked mighty good to us. The next morning we went on down the river a few miles, and then crossed it on a ferry, and went up Morrison's ravine, which split Table mountain in two, and in a few miles emerged into the famous Sacramento valley. We went on across Dry creek, reaching Sam Neal's ranch, where we stopped at a large two-story hotel, on September 26, 1852. Thus ended our trip of about two thousand miles across the great plains and mountains.

Experiences in California

We spent a week at Sam Neal's ranch in the Sacramento valley, but as every meal we ate cost each of us one dollar James and I determined to leave and go up into the mountains to the gold mines. We went sixteen miles up in the foothills to a little village on the ridge between the west branch of Feather river and Little Butte creek. This little village was known as Butte Mills, because there was a sawmill near by run by water power from Little Butte creek, but it soon got its proper and well deserved name of Dog Town, for although there were only ten houses, there were sixteen fully developed dogs. From the edge of town one looked down into the West branch, where its waters flowed in a cañon a thousand feet deep, which in the course of about a million years it had worn down through talcose slate. This stream had been rich in placer gold, and was still being worked by many miners. James and I looked it over, but it was all claimed, and as we knew absolutely nothing about mining, we thought we had best hunt for some place that was easier to work than a small river that was full of large boulders, over which the water dashed and foamed.

We became acquainted with two young men, Wyatt M. Smith, eighteen years of age and Fountain J. Sweeney, age nineteen years, and being about our ages we were soon fast friends. They told us about six miles up Little Butte creek, there were some gulches (ravines) known as "Tom Neal's dry diggins," that they thought were rich, and they proposed to us to go up there and go in with them in mining. They had been in California for about a year, and already knew a little about how to mine. We thought it a good chance to learn from them and accepted their kind offer. They already had some tools, and a part of a kitchen outfit to cook with. James and I bought some additional things and rolling up our blankets, with an extra shirt apiece, took them on our backs and started for the "diggins." Thus we entered upon a new, strange, and untried life. Although our loads were not very heavy, we found it necessary to sit down and rest several times in going that six miles.

The country through which we passed was an open forest with beautiful large trees of many kinds. We selected a spot for our log cabin, near a clear cold little spring in a wide gulch where the trees were smaller and more suitable for building our cabin. This we made sixteen feet square, and seven feet high at the eaves, roofed it with clapboards that we made out of sugar pine trees, which split so easily and accurately that many of the clapboards were twelve inches wide, and four feet long and only a half inch thick, and almost as smooth as if they had been sawed. Never can I forget the pleasure with which I roamed through the beautiful forests that covered the region where we lived and mined for a year and a half. There were the lofty smooth-trunked sugar pines, six feet in diameter, three hundred feet high; and from sixty to eighty feet from the ground there was not a limb or a blemish. Many large gray squirrels, almost double the size of the squirrels in the eastern states, made their home in the tree tops. There were also yellow pine trees, a little smaller than the sugar pines, and several species of fir trees and black oaks, large cedars, some beautiful madrona or laurel trees, dogwood trees, thirty feet high with large glossy leaves and snow white blossoms as large as a dollar, manzanita, and many other flowering bushes, that perfumed the air, and in the little open park-like spots, lovely flowers grew among the grass. In the forests about here I saw for the first time birds putting away food for winter. They were small, black and white woodpeckers, not very numerous, and always traveled in pairs, a male and female. For a storehouse they selected a large dry limb on a pine or oak tree and carefully removed every particle of bark, then with their bills pecked small holes into which they deposited an acorn. The acorns exactly fitted the holes and it was impossible to remove one without cutting it out with a knife. The birds would fill large limbs just as full of acorns as they could possibly be filled. It was a delight to me to watch these clever little woodsmen store their winter food and to listen to their cheerful cry of "Yacob, Yacob," repeated very rapidly.[16]

In the vicinity of our cabin were some patches of brush in which there lived a covey of California quails. Never was I guilty of killing one. In going to and from work we often saw them scurrying along in the grass and undergrowth.

The large gray squirrels were interesting and beautiful also, but our appetites and love for hunting got the better of our tender-heartedness and we killed and ate any number of them. My dog Watch, the one that

---

[16] The size and general description would suggest the Nuttall woodpecker (*dryobates nuttallii*) but the habits and call suggest either the ant-eating woodpecker (*melanerpes formicivorus*) or the Californian woodpecker (*M. f bairdi*). Possibly Stuart saw all these different varieties and confused them. – ED.

I coaxed from his master's grave on the Platte river, was still my constant companion and he delighted to hunt squirrels and was an exceedingly clever squirrel dog.

Wyatt M. Smith and I each had a good muzzle loading rifle and we in turn hunted squirrels for dinner. The squirrels lived in the tops of the lofty sugar pines and fed on pine nuts and it was no easy matter to discover them high up in the tree. Watch had a very keen scent and he would track one to a tree and then bark until one of us came and shot it. We tanned the skins and made money bags out of them. When well tanned and carefully sewed they would last years and made a most excellent bag in which to carry gold.

I felt as though I had been transplanted to another planet. There was nothing here that I had ever seen or heard of before. The great forests, the deep cañons with rivers of clear water dashing over the boulders, the azure sky with never a cloud were all new to me, and the country swarmed with game, such as elk, deer and antelope, with occasionally a grizzly bear, and in the valleys were many water fowls. Tall bearded men were digging up the ground and washing it in long toms and rockers, and on the banks by their sides was a sheet iron pan in which were various amounts of yellow gold.

The gold coins used then were also different from any that I had seen. They were coined at the mint in San Francisco and were ten, twenty, and fifty dollar pieces. The great octagon fifty dollar pieces were especially strange to me.[17]

---

[17] John H. Landis formerly superintendent of the Philadelphia mint writes in the *Encyclopedia Americana* under COINAGE: "The largest gold pieces ever coined by the United States government are the six hundred $50 pieces coined as mementoes of the Panama-Pacific International Exposition." – ED.

These men had neither tents nor houses. They camped under lofty pine or spreading oak trees as the case might be, for it never rained there in the summer time. They were strong and healthy and lived a life as free as the air they breathed. No finer specimens of mankind existed anywhere than were these California miners of the days of forty-nine. Men without ambition never started for California. The faint-hearted turned back before they reached the Missouri river. The puny sickly ones either recovered or perished on the road. Only the courageous determined man crossed the plains and reached the land of gold.

Where all the gold came from was a much mooted question, and they pondered deeply over it and finally settled down to the belief that it must have been thrown out by volcanoes, as the country bore evidence of ancient volcanic convulsions. In 1851 a report was started (but no one knew who started it) that high up in the Sierra Nevada was a lake, evidently the crater of a large volcano, and that the shores of this lake were covered with gold so plentiful that there was little sand or gravel there. As soon as the miners heard this rumor they at once said, "That's just where we thought all this gold came from, and what is the use of us digging here in the mud and water for a few hundred dollars a day when we can go up there and just shovel it up by the ton?" And incredible as it now seems, several hundred of them abandoned rich claims and went up into the mountains and spent all summer looking for the "Gold lake." This of course did not exist, and when they came back in the fall, ragged and footsore, all their rich claims were taken by others. Later I personally knew two men who, in 1851, were working in Rich gulch on the West branch of Feather river, taking out three hundred dollars a day apiece. As soon as they heard of Gold lake they at once quit their rich claims and spent months and all the money they had searching for this imaginary lake, and on their return found their claims being worked by others and irrecoverably lost to them.

I once asked some of those who, I knew had families in the states, "Why don't you quit drinking and gambling and save your money and go back home to your families?" To which they all answered, "So I would, but don't you see that at the rate the gold is being taken out, by the time I got home with a lot of it it wouldn't be worth any more than so much copper, therefore, I am going to stay right here and have a hell of a good time while it is worth something." And so they stayed, and had that kind of a time. No such enormous amounts of gold had been found anywhere before, and as they all believed that the supply was inexhaustible, there was some justification for their thinking it would soon lose most of its value.

Even as at Great Salt Lake City I found myself in company with the twelve Apostles, so in the foothills of Sacramento valley I thought, in my eighteen-year-old innocence, that I must unconsciously have strolled into the Garden of Eden, for the good looking Indians who lived there wore no clothes, there were no fig trees there either; but they managed to get along, when the weather was cold, by wearing a small, I believe I am justified in saying, a very small apron, made of wisps of grass. These women felt no embarrassment because they were naked for they never knew what clothes were. They were as modest as their white sisters. In a short time we became accustomed to seeing them clad in their limited wardrobe and thought nothing of it.

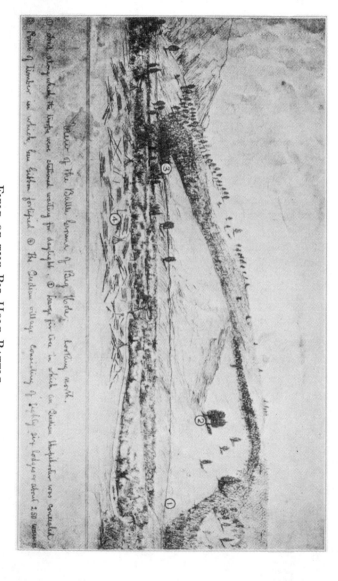

FIELD OF THE BIG HOLE BATTLE

From an original pencil sketch made by Granville Stuart, May 11, 1878

These Indians lived in moderate sized huts dug partly in the ground. They would dig about three feet deep, then around that in a circular form would set up poles which would meet, tying them together with bark strings. On this they would put thatch and cover with mud mortar. The mud mortar was used to prevent their leaking. They had no fires in their huts. Their cooking was done out of doors. They had a small oval door about two feet in diameter at one side, by which they entered. These thatched huts were always warm. Their food in winter consisted largely of fish and acorn bread. There were quantities of acorns on the oak trees and in the fall the Indians gathered and stored them for winter use. They had baskets that held from one to two bushels of acorns. These were carried on their backs suspended from a broad band that passed across their forehead. These heavy loads caused them to stoop over and hold their heads low, consequently most of the older Indians were very stooped. They stored the acorns in little store-houses built upon poles about four feet from the ground. These little houses would hold from six to ten bushels of acorns. I was pleased to see that the men did as much work as the women and always carried the heavier load. They crushed the acorns with stone pestles into a sort of paste, and having no shortening they dug angleworms and crushed them up with the acorns. This made a sort of dough, which they made into little flat cakes and baked in hot ashes. This was their bread and largely their winter food. These little cakes of acorn bread were bitter to taste but highly nutritious.

The women also gathered many grasshoppers. On frosty mornings the hoppers would be stiff with cold and easily caught. After collecting a small basket half full they would put them in the edge of the fire and cover them with hot ashes. When they were roasted a nice brown they were scraped up carefully and restored to the basket. Then shaking them up and down and blowing them they got rid of the legs, wings, and ashes, leaving the body brown and crisp. They tasted like a bit of marrow.

These Indians were always anxious to work. They especially liked to go hunting with us. When we wanted to get a deer or elk we would have an Indian accompany us. They, being accustomed to those woods, would invariably see the game first. They would stop still and point to the brush and we could almost always get a shot before the game discovered us. After killing a deer we would give the Indian our hunting knife and he would butcher it. He always cleaned the paunch and filled it with the blood of the animal. This he carried home and made into a blood pudding, a great delicacy among them. He would then take the deer, tie its feet together and carry it to camp for us. His pay would be, head, neck and hide, though we usually gave him a quarter of the deer.

Often when passing under spreading trees he would discover wild pigeons and very often get one or more with his bow and arrow. These Indians were not allowed to have firearms at all. We often sent one of them to the village to get supplies. He would walk six miles to the store and return with fifty pounds of flour and as much bacon and other things, carrying it all on his back. His pay for this would be one hickory cotton shirt which cost seventy-five cents. They were strictly honest and never carried off anything that they were to bring us. After a few years the men wore clothes, but up to the time I left there the women had felt no need of additional clothing.[18]

In the years from 1852 to 1857 placer mining in California may be said to have been at its best. On all the streams in all the gulches and high up in the Sierras to the north, clear to the Oregon line every little camp was crowded with miners and gold was being taken out in such profusion as almost to lead one to believe that there would be an over-production and everybody seemed to be trying to find some way to spend all he had.

In the smaller towns the gambling halls were the chief attraction. They were magnificently fitted up with plate glass mirrors, brilliant lights shown from chandeliers, and upon a balcony at one end of the hall would be a string band, usually consisting of two violins, and banjo. About the room were numerous tables, large enough to accommodate eight people at each. All known gambling games were furnished, but monte and faro were the two favorite games. It was no unusual sight to see a man place a fifty dollar slug on a monte card or to place a thousand dollar bet on a faro card. Some won, some lost, but of course in the long run the dealers were sure winners. The supply of gambling suckers was endless. All of the halls would be crowded until two or three o'clock in the morning. Enormous sums of money changed hands in these places. Women gambled as well as men.

In an alcove at one side of the room would be a

---

[18] It is more difficult to classify the Indian of central California than it is the woodpeckers. There were many tribes in this region with customs similar to those described by Stuart. H. H. Bancroft, *Native Races of North America*, in *Works* (San Francisco, 1882-90) vol. i, p. 362 ff., describes these Indians in much the same way as Stuart does. – ED.

saloon bar stocked up with all kinds of choice liquors and cigars. The liquors were sold at twenty-five cents a drink and the cigars at twenty-five cents each. The cigars were generally very good. Considering the circumstances better order was preserved in these places than could have been reasonably expected. Of course there was a great deal of drunkenness of all stages, from gentle elation up to maudlin foolishness. Quarreling, shooting, and stabbing were comparatively rare. It was to the interest of the owners to keep as good order as possible. Many of the gamblers did not drink at all. They would keep sober and watch the game carefully, and sometimes make large winnings.

One night I strolled into one of these gambling halls to listen to the music and watch the players and it was here I lost my faith in the preachers of the Gospel. At our home in Iowa we had always attended preaching regularly and our house had been a favorite stopping place for the circuit rider, as mother was an excellent cook and there was always plenty of nice chickens on hand.

Of these preachers one, Brother Briar, gave a most lurid description of hell-fire and painted a most vivid picture of what would become of us if we did not repent. We hardly knew what we were expected to repent of, but he scared us up plenty. James and I felt that we must do something quick in the way of getting good or something terrible would happen. We would go home from meeting, climb up into the loft where we slept, with our hair standing on end, and dream all night of lakes of fire and brimstone and devils, big and little with pitch forks. We thought Brother Briar a lucky man to be so good as to be safe from such a pitfall.

Well time went on and in the many changes and
events of our journey across the plains and the strange
new life in California I had almost forgotten Brother
Briar and his hell-fire sermons and certainly when I
strolled into the great glittering room full of light and
music and excited men and women crowded about the
tables, betting their gold on the lucky or unlucky card,
nothing could have been further from my thoughts
than Brother Briar.   When, lo! at one of the tables sat
the self-same man coolly and calmly dealing faro.   I
said to myself then, he don't believe in hell-fire and
never did, and neither do I.

Every Sunday there were horse racing, cock fights,
and dog fights.   In the larger towns of Marysville and
Sacramento were the magnificent gambling houses,
saloons, dance halls, music halls, theatres, horse races,
and an occasional bull fight.   Bull fighting never appealed to the miners and never became popular.

October 26, 1852, the rainy season set in with a down-
pour such as I have never seen since, not even in the
tropics.   It rained six days and nights without cessa-
tion.   The west branch of Feather river rose fifty feet;
sweeping away nearly all the miners' cabins on its banks
and all of their tools, such as long toms, rockers, picks,
shovels, and gold pans.   The water poured down the
hillside back of our cabin about four inches deep all
over the ground.   At no time during the six days could
we get an armful of wood without being soaked to the
skin (rubber coats and shoes were unknown at that
time) but it was what we, of the dry diggings, had been
waiting for.

We had finished our cabin, did some prospecting in
the gulches in the vicinity, and found some ground that
we thought would pay.   We had a few boards hauled

by wagon from the mill at Dog Town to within a mile
of our cabin; but, there being no road further, we carried the boards the rest of the distance on our shoulders,
which were sore for a week after. We used the boards
for a door to the cabin and to make a long tom. We
made our long tom in this manner – the bottom was a
twelve-foot board twenty-four inches wide; nailed on
each side of the bottom, and about three feet longer
than the bottom were the sides which were about ten
inches high. The projections beyond the bottom on
each side were sloped up a gentle curve, from the end
of the bottom up to the top of the two side boards and
on the curve was nailed heavy sheet iron, the lower
edge of which was closely nailed fast to the ends of the
bottom. It was punched full of half-inch holes to the
number of thirty-five or forty. The tom was placed
in the gulch with the sheet iron end from twelve to
twenty inches lower than the upper or open end, in
which a considerable stream of water was turned from
a water ditch. Under the iron end of the tom was
placed a wooden box about four inches deep, and about
the size of the perforated iron above it. This box was
placed on the ground with the same slope as the tom
above, and had several bars of wood about two inches
high placed at intervals across the inside of its bottom.

In using the long tom after it was properly set in
place, two of us took our places, one on each side of the
tom, where, with pick and shovel, we dug up and
shoveled into the tom the sand and gravel of the gulch,
which the stream of water washed down to the perforated iron plate at the lower end where the third
person was stationed with a shovel with which he
stirred the sand and gravel back and forth on the half-
inch holes down into the flat box underneath where the

water carried all the sand and gravel off over the lower end of the box, leaving the gold, and some black sand, lodged against the two inch bars placed across the bottom of the box. The man at the plate threw out all the pebbles and rocks, which were too large to go through the holes, as soon as they were washed clean; but he had to carefully examine what he threw out, lest, as sometimes happened, there might be some nuggets of gold too large to go through the holes, in the iron. However, they were usually seen and picked up off the iron, which event, when it did occur, caused great joy and excitement, for a nugget too large to drop through the holes would be worth at least forty dollars, and might be large enough to be worth one hundred dollars or more. We had enough water in our gulches to work our long tom until about the first of March, but they did not prove as rich in gold as we anticipated. We could only make from three to five dollars a day, each one of us, but occasionally we would find some little nuggets worth from eight to sixteen dollars, which helped. One day just before our water supply failed I was digging on the right side of our long tom, with Wyatt M. Smith on the left side, and Fountain J. Sweeney at the iron plate, throwing out the rocks. On my side lay a flat rock about ten inches long and seven inches wide. I had dug past it, but as it slid about six inches of it stuck out of the bank right where I wanted to put my foot as I worked so I stuck my shovel under the side of it and gradually pried it up, when Lo!, there beneath it lay a bright nugget of pure gold that weighed sixteen ounces, which at sixteen dollars an ounce (the value of gold then) was worth two hundred and forty dollars. We also took out nine dollars in small gold that day, so that we made eighty-three dollars apiece, and there were three jovial boys in camp that night. This was the largest piece of gold I found while in California, although some localities yielded larger ones.

About the time the water failed in the spring in our gulch diggings, Sam Neal of Neal's ranch began to build a sawmill on Little Butte creek, about half a mile below Dog Town, and I hired to him to herd six yoke of oxen which were used for hauling pine logs to the mill.

In July the sawmill shut down and the oxen were taken down to Neal's ranch and I had to hunt other fields and pastures. During this time brother James had been prospecting for "diggins," and in company with other men had found a place on the West branch that looked good, so we bought a "rocker" and moved down into the deep cañon and went to work. There was a deep crevice in the soft talcose slate filled with sand and gravel amongst which there was considerable quantity of beautiful bright gold, resembling in size and shape muskmelon seeds, and up to the size of pumpkin seeds. It paid big, but in a week we dug it all out and although it was a good neighborhood in which to look for more, we accepted the opinion of our partners and abandoned it. This was unfortunate, for we learned later that much gold was taken out all around there that summer. We then fell in with two men who had mined over in Big Butte creek cañon. They said they knew of a spot in that creek that had not been mined out and that they knew it must be rich. They proposed to James and me that we go in with them, and turn the water out of the creek, which was then at a low stage, and work in the bed of the stream, taking out big returns in gold. We went with them carrying our blankets, tools, and grub on our backs about five miles. We did not need even a tent for shelter. We spent six weeks digging a small canal through the soft black slate on one side of the stream into which we turned the creek by building a dam across it as the head of our little canal. This dam we made by building two walls of stone about three feet apart and carrying the red soil of the hillside in sacks, and filling it in between the walls all of which was very hard work, and when done the greater part of the stream ran through our canal all right, but we then found, to our disgust, that quite a quantity of water seeped through the sand and gravel under our dam and this we could not stop, or at least we thought we couldn't. We found that there were many boulders of considerable size in the bed of the stream where we expected to work, which we had no means of moving. The seepage water running over and between these boulders was only a few inches deep and we could shovel up sand and gravel out of that water and get as high as twenty-five cents to a pan full. But that was very slow and unsatisfactory work, and our partners said we could not make it pay and that we had best abandon it, which we did. After we had, a year later, left that part of the state and saw mining elsewhere, I knew that if we had stayed there and used a little judgment we could have made enough to have paid us good wages for all our labor. James and I thought it highly probable that our two partners did that very thing, that they returned to the claim and worked it till the high water from the fall rains drove them out, thus getting the benefit of our labor for nothing.

We returned to Dog Town from our river claims and after a few days rest we, in company with a friend, Abe

Folk, went up to our gulch diggings and on our way passed by a gulch from which several thousand dollars of gold had been mined in 1850 (three years before) but the pay-streak gave out and no more could be found and it was abandoned. We began scratching in the bank at the side of the old workings and in a few minutes scratched out of the dirt, on the bed rock, four dollars in coarse gold. We then knew that we had found the pay-streak of the old workings where it left the gulch as it made a bend around the point of a hill and evidently went under the hill. We had neither paper nor pencil with which to claim the ground by putting up a notice stating the size and direction of our claim, so went on to our cabin about two miles beyond, intending to return and put up our claim notice the next morning, which was Sunday, but the next morning brother James and our friend took a notion to wash some clothes instead of going to our new found mine and putting up our claim notice. I had a feeling that we ought to do it without delay and told them so and urged them to go with me to the place and claim it. They laughed at me, saying that all that region was dry as bone and that there was no danger of anyone finding the pay or even coming into the district until just before the rains set in, which would be over two months yet, so I finally gave in and also washed clothes. It was by far the most costly washing that ever any three men indulged in, for when we went to the mine on Monday morning, Lo and behold! there was Tom Neal with several friends, with their notices up claiming the mine for a long distance, leaving us entirely out. Tom told us that he with a couple of friends happened along there on Sunday afternoon on their way to some gulches further up the ridge, and as he was of those who had mined there in 1850, he was showing them where he had mined and seeing where we had scratched out the place in the bank, and that convenient old case knife lying right there, he, as we had done, picked it up and began scratching in the place where we had dug. He soon found some pieces of gold and then he also knew that he had found the rich, lost pay-streak, and some of them having paper they at once claimed the rest of the gulch.

Now, if we had taken a little trouble to cover up the place where we had dug, with dry dirt and thrown that tell-tale old knife away Tom and party would doubtless have passed on, as he had often done before, and done no scratching. We were so confident that there was no chance of anybody coming along there that we did not even think of concealing the sign we had made. When the winter rains set in and furnished water in the gulch to wash the pay dirt, that party took out over twenty-five thousand dollars in beautiful coarse gold, some nuggets weighing from one hundred to three hundred dollars. To tide over the interval, before the winter rains set in, we busied ourselves making clapboards or shakes out of sugar pines. These were in good demand down in the valley and we made good wages.

In 1853 a man from Dog Town brought to our cabin a young man, just the age of brother James, who was very pale and weak. He was shaking with the ague every alternate day. He told us that his name was Rezin Anderson, that he had just crossed the plains from Iowa and come in by the Carson river route. Reaching Sacramento valley he was at once taken sick with the ague and no medicine would break it. The doctor there told him to go on up to the mines, the higher in the mountains the better. He got a little acquainted and met a man from Dog Town, who told him of men going up there with the ague and getting well in a short time. He managed to get there a few days later, and was told that there were two young men from Iowa in the dry diggings six miles further up in the mountains, so he hired a man to bring him to our camp and he told us that if we would take him into our cabin and mess, that he would work for us to pay what he would owe as soon as he got strong enough, for he was broke. Of course we did not refuse him and he became one of our mess, but his ague would not stop, and he looked so feeble that I feared he would not live more than a month or two.

Before we left Iowa James read and became interested in the Presnitz Water Cure System, just then coming into notice and into use in Germany. He told Anderson, if he would let him try, he believed he could cure him and Reece, as we ever afterwards called him, was glad to take the treatment. James stripped him and then rolled him up in a blanket wet with cold water and gave him hot tea to drink, at the same time covering him up with dry blankets. The cabin being quite warm, of course he soon broke into a profuse perspiration in which he was kept for an hour. He was then unrolled, rubbed dry, and put to bed for the night. After the second night the ague left him and after four nights of this treatment he was cured; his appetite, which had been poor, soon became good and he rapidly gained in strength. In two weeks he was able to do light work. His rapid convalescence I think was largely due to the large fat squirrels that my dog Watch and I got out of the lofty sugar pines in the neighborhood, which when nicely fried in bacon grease left nothing to be desired, except more squirrels.

One Sunday I happened to be at Dog Town and there being no amusement, except watching the several poker games that always ran on Sunday and as I never took any part or cared to look on at them, I took my rifle and went slowly down along the side of the cañon of West branch: occasionally sitting down on some projections of rock to enjoy the sunshine and soft air and watch the water dashing over the boulders far below. I heard something walking in the chapparal a little below me, so I picked up a stone and threw it where the slight noise seemed to come from, and out jumped a large deer with handsome horns. I at once shot, butchered, and quartered him, and went to Dog Town (only a little over a quarter of a mile away) and got three friends to help me bring up the meat, each of us carrying a quarter. When I got into the little town (in the West there are no villages, no matter how small they are they are always called towns) and the people saw the fine fat venison they wanted it, and in a few minutes I sold three quarters of it for twenty-one dollars and seventy-five cents. I have often thought that this little incident should have shown Brother and I a sure way of making a steady income, by buying two or three burros to pack, and then devote ourselves to hunting and delivering the meat to the various little towns scattered everywhere through the mines. It would have been a sure thing, as the demand was always good. But like everybody else in those days, we were bitten by the gold bug, and mine we must, and mine we did, which is not to be wondered at, when one considers the vast quantities of gold which were then being taken out in California, much of it with very little exertion.

At Dog Town we knew a man who in daytime followed the occupation of a crevice miner, and at night that of a professional gambler. In the morning he would put a little lunch in his pocket and taking a small pick and a gold pan, and crevice spoon, he would go down into the deep cañon of the West branch and carefully scan its shores along near the water; searching for the fissures or cracks in the bedrock which often contained sand and gravel forced into them in past ages, and in among which was usually considerable gold. When he found one of these crevices he would dig its contents up loose with his little pick and then scrape it all out carefully with his crevice spoon, and put it into the shallow circular iron pan, always called, "a little gold pan," which he would then take to the edge of the water, and squatting down begin to wash the sand and fine gravel by a circular motion that would gradually carry it out over the edge of the pan, leaving the gold in the bottom. He told us he had been crevicing for over two years and that he had learned where to look for favorable places to hunt for rich crevices, but was not always successful. We asked him what were his usual gains in a day. He said that the first year he would frequently find two or three ounces of gold a day and some lucky day considerably more, but for the past year he could only average one ounce a day for the mines were now more carefully worked. One day he returned to town about noon and joyfully showed me a beautiful bright nugget of pure gold that he had just found. It weighed six and one-fourth ounces and was worth one hundred dollars. He said it was the largest nugget that he had ever found, but that he had found several of from one to five ounces.

In the summer of 1853 our father returned home to

Iowa by way of the Nicaragua route, which was by steamer from San Francisco to San Juan Del Sur, on the west coast of Nicaragua then across Lake Nicaragua thence down the San Juan river on Garrison's line of steamers and thence to New Orleans, thence up the Mississippi river to Dubuque and home.

In July, 1853, some Concow Indians, whose village was over on the North fork of Feather river, came over to the West branch and killed two Chinamen who were mining there and wounded two others. These Indians, in common with all those living on the western slope of the Sierra Nevada, were not allowed by the miners to have firearms and the Chinamen were killed with bows and arrows. Considerable numbers of Chinamen were by this time in California, mostly all engaged in mining on claims worked out and abandoned by white men. The Indians disliked them because they thought them other kinds of Indians, but I never heard of them killing any others, although they often robbed them. The West branch Chinamen brought their dead up to Dog Town for burial and their wounded excited much feeling against the Indians. The result was that the white miners offered to go and drive the murderers out of that part of the mines, if the Chinamen would go with them and carry their food and blankets, which they gladly agreed to do. My recollection is that sixteen well armed men went, accompanied by twelve Chinamen carrying food and blankets. The Indians discovered their approach and fled like deer, the miners firing on them as they ran. I think only two were killed and several wounded. A few of the Chinamen carried shot guns and when the miniature battle began the men said the Chinamen were widely excited and would shut both eyes and fire both barrels of their shot guns at once, the recoil nearly knocking them down, while the buckshot from their guns went tearing through the tops of the oak trees. The men said they were in greater danger from the Chinamen than from the Indians, because they did not know how to handle firearms. The little army was absent three days. I thought at the time that most of them were ashamed of the raid after it was over. The Indians moved and I never heard of them making any trouble afterwards. Brother James happened to be in Dog Town when the foray started and went with it. I was up at our diggings and knew nothing of it until he got back. The grateful Chinamen sent to San Francisco and presented each of their white allies with a large embroidered red silk handkerchief and a quart of brandy.

In the winter of 1852 after the rains began, the roads became so bad and the Sacramento valley was mostly flooded so that no food supplies could be brought up to Dog Town for over a month. Fortunately there was food enough of all kinds except flour. We had none of that for over two weeks, but we had beans and bacon and squirrels. When the pack train got in with the flour the packers swore that they would not make another trip that winter and demanded fifty dollars per one hundred pounds. We thought it well to buy a sack (fifty pound sacks were unknown until three years later) rather than to do without for the remainder of the winter and did so. By the time we had eaten half of it two pack trains loaded with flour arrived and the price fell to twelve cents a pound. Nearly all the flour used in California that winter came from Chile, South America. It had a yellow color and was first class. Large quantities of beans were also brought from there.

In fact if these two articles had not been brought from Chile everybody would have been reduced to meat straight.

In the spring of 1853 we grew tired of our diggings because we were entirely dependent on the rains for water and determined to seek a better place to mine. So James, Rezin Anderson, and I took our respective rolls of bedding on our backs and our rifles on our shoulders and started for Rabbit creek in Sierra county. We went by way of Morrison's ravine, then across Feather river at the ferry, then up the slope between Feather and Yuba rivers, stopping one night at Forbestown, first known as "Boles Dry Diggins," then up the ridge to "Mountain cottage," where we entered the snow of the Sierra Nevadas. We found the snow constantly becoming deeper, but here was a well beaten pack trail.

We arrived at Rabbit creek when the snow was sixteen feet deep. All the miners' cabins had steps cut in the snow down to the doors. There being no stoves, all cabins had open fire places, the chimneys of which were made to extend six or seven feet above the roof, so as to get to the surface of the snow. These chimneys gave plenty of air and the snow kept it so warm that the doors were open all day. The mines were all deep gravel channels from twenty-five to one hundred and twenty-five feet deep on the mountain spurs and ridges, and were worked by hydraulic pipes in which the water was piped down into the cuts and thrown against the banks which were composed of white quartz gravel and sand. These immense gravel beds were once ancient river beds before the mountains and ridges were upheaved, and all contained enough fine gold to pay richly for washing them away by hydrau-

lic process. Through lines of sluice boxes the sand
and gravel was dumped into the surrounding cañons
which drained into the North fork of the Yuba
river. Here the claims were two hundred feet
square. No man could have more than one claim.
All the claims along the water front were being worked
so we located ours further back, but had to wait for
those in front to wash their claims before we could
work ours. Every mining district in California in those
days had their own laws made by the miners and by
them enforced. As we could not work our mines at
once we went to work in a nearby mine where the
gravel was forty feet deep. Part of us worked on day
shift and the others on night shift.

We would work all week, but on Saturday night the
miners would get up a stag dance, there being very few
women in the camp. There were two fiddlers, one
played first violin and the other played second. The
first player was left handed but he was a good one and
such fun as we would have. Among the young men
was one named Clyde Hammon who, ten or twelve
years later became one of the famous lawyers of California.

The Rogue River War

On Sunday, June 4, 1854, our cousin, Clinton Bozarth, who had been mining and running a pack train decided to return to his home in Iowa. He went by way of steamer from San Francisco to Nicaragua. This made us, who were left behind, rather homesick, but we were not yet ready to go home. While Bozarth was with us he told us that at Yreka, a town up near the boundary between Oregon and California, there were some flats that contained gold enough to pay well, if mined by hydraulic process. This news coupled with our inexperience and the desires of youth to seek better things though far away, determined us to go to Yreka. So on June 29, 1854, we quit work and bought two mules. On one we packed our blankets, clothes, and a little grub. One by one we took turns riding the other mule and started for Yreka, on pack trails that zigzagged along the western slope of the Sierras. We took this route to avoid the fierce heat of the route through the Sacramento valley, and to enjoy traveling among cool shady mountains. Our party consisted of James and Granville Stuart, Rezin Anderson, and John L. Good. Some parts of our journey were through unsettled regions, that were not occupied because no mines had been found there. James and I kept a brief diary of our trip, which I here insert.

JUNE 29, 1854. Left Warren hill and traveled seven miles and camped in the little village of Grass Valley.

JUNE 30. Nooned on top of Middle fork of Feather

river hill above the mouth of Nelson creek. Then
went down a long hill (said to be seven miles long and
our legs said it was ten miles, but our eyes said it was
only four and a half miles) then crossed the middle
fork and climbed up the big hill on the north side of
this awful steep cañon, and camped in the head of
American valley near where we entered it in September, 1852. Traveled twenty miles today.

JULY 1. Nooned on the divide between American
and Indian valleys and camped for the night down in
Indian valley. It was sure enough down, for it looks
just as if it had sunk right down for about one thousand
feet. Our knees before we got down the long steep
hill felt it was two thousand feet. Traveled eighteen
miles to-day.

JULY 2. Stopped for noon near the west end of Indian valley, and as our feet and legs felt sore, we stayed
there until the next morning. Only traveled eight
miles to-day. This valley is a long narrow one, with
steep timbered mountains rising up on each side and is
very beautiful, but has considerable tule swamp land
in it, but even the tules, six feet high and very dense,
waving in the wind like a green field are beautiful.

JULY 3. Nooned on the divide between Indian valley and the Big meadows, on the North fork of Feather
river, and there camped for the night in the lower end
of the Big meadows. Traveled eighteen miles to-day.
These meadows are in a beautiful little valley through
which runs the North fork of Feather river, a clear ice
cold stream about twenty-five yards wide and two and
a half feet deep. James rode over, leading the pack
mule and then came back and took us three across, one
at a time behind him. The mule nearly threw us in the
creek.

JULY 4. Camped on the head of Deer creek, a cold clear gravelly stream about sixteen feet wide and deep, which we thought we could wade at the crossing. We took off our boots and stockings, rolled up our pants and did wade it, but Oh! we never felt such cold water before and when we got across our feet and legs were almost paralyzed and ached frightfully. The cobble stones were so slippery and hurt our feet so that we had to wade slowly, and one and all said no more wading of creeks went with us while we had these mules for ferry boats. Traveled twenty-five miles today.

JULY 5. Started at sunrise as we feared we would find no water until we got down into the Sacramento valley, which lay like a map in plain sight below us, while we were parched with thirst under a burning sun. About noon the branch of the Old Larson emigrant road which we are now following, went down into the right hand cañon, but to our great discomfort, it was dry. We found a little water among some big boulders, but it was stagnant, and so hot that we could not drink it until we dipped it up with tin cups and waited a quarter of an hour until it partly cooled, and then we were afraid to drink it for fear it might be poisonous. We washed our mouths with it and wet our hair and went on. The road climbed out of the cañon up onto the other ridge. The day was very hot and there was no shade. We suffered greatly from the heat, and thirst. We reached the valley after dark and hearing frogs nearby we went to them and found a slough of warm stagnant water into which our mules and ourselves waded. We cooked our suppers which we enjoyed very much, having eaten nothing since daylight this morning. Traveled thirty miles.

JULY 7. Traveled twenty miles up the river and

camped at the "Blue Tent," which was a saloon, but as none of us drank any liquor, we were not desirable visitors.

JULY 9. Camped at the "Milk ranch," and had good fresh milk and bread and butter for supper. Traveled up the river for twenty miles.

JULY 10. Stopped in the town of Shasta at the St. Charles hotel. Traveled fifteen miles, weather red-hot.

JULY 11. Went up to the mountains, six miles. Camped a little below a rather lively little village called "Whiskey Town," and from the maudlin songs, yells, and cuss words, that enlivened the night we decided that the place was rightly named.

JULY 12. Went to "Mad Ox canyon," to look for placer diggins.

JULY 13. Prospected.

JULY 14. Moved three miles to Oak bottom on Clear creek. Now a very muddy creek, but the surroundings are beautiful.

JULY 15. Bought one-third of a water ditch and went to work on Oak hill with a small hydraulic. Lovely place to work, the hill being sparsely covered with oak trees. During July and August the thermometer often rose to one hundred and twelve degrees in the shade. As we were always soaking wet and mostly in the shade while working, we did not suffer much and we would all go and lie down in the creek with only our heads out of the water from twelve-thirty to one-thirty nearly every day. Frank Vandeventer and sister kept the Oak Bottom House across the creek and she made delicious pies, of which we bought many to eke out our miner fare. We worked here until September 28th and only made good our expenses from the time we left Warren hill until we sold out and quit work here. Bought a blue mare for seventy dollars and two mules for one hundred and thirty-one dollars and made another start for Yreka, being all mounted with one pack mule. Camped at Mountain House for the night. Traveled sixteen miles.

SEPTEMBER 28. Traveled twenty-two miles and camped at Seley's ranch on Trinity river, a beautiful clear swift stream, with some grassy meadows along it, but country mostly timbered. No mines on the river above here, but said to be many good placers a few miles below this point.

SEPTEMBER 30. Traveled sixteen miles and camped on Trinity five miles from the divide, between Trinity river and Scott's valley.

OCTOBER 1. Traveled eighteen miles and camped in Scott's valley which is perfectly beautiful, with a clear stream flowing through. The valley is different from most we have seen. There is beautiful yellow pine timber on the hills, and low mountains, while all the valley proper is covered with yellow bunch grass, knee high, and waving in the wind like fields of grain, being the first of its kind that we have seen in California.

OCTOBER 2. Traveled four miles and camped in same valley. In the night we were awakened by our mules snorting and trying to break loose from the picket pine. Getting up (we were sleeping in the open air without tents) we saw a huge grizzly bear shambling off and disappearing in the brush along the stream. We finally got our animals calmed down and went back to our beds, thankful that the bear had not come any nearer, and hoping that the next call would be on some-one else. During the night we heard continual splash-ing in the water near where we were sleeping, and couldn't imagine what kind of an animal was in the stream all night, as we had seen no sign of beavers in California. We would have gotten up and investigated, but as we didn't know just where that grizzly might be, we thought it safer to wait until morning. In the morning we went to the place whence came the noise and found that all that splashing in the river was caused by salmon fish, from three to four feet long, flopping and jumping in, forcing their way up the stream over the riffles where the water was not deep enough for them to swim. These were the first salmon any of us had ever seen. We walked in and killed one of them with a club, and while pounding her she splashed water all over us and soaked us plenty. We finally got her out and had fish to eat for two days, and being fish-hungry we enjoyed it hugely. Upon inquiry we were told that every fall these large fish came up from the Pacific ocean to the upper branches of all the streams as far as they can possibly go and there lay their eggs, then start back to the ocean, but most of them are so bruised and exhausted that they die on the way.

The bears follow along these salmon streams and in shallow places throw the fish out on the bank with their fore paws and then eat them at leisure. During this season bears become very fat. The grizzly that had so alarmed our horses and ourselves was only out on a little fishing trip and not looking for us at all.

OCTOBER 3. Camped six and a half miles from Yreka, fearing we would not find grass for our animals if we went any farther.

OCTOBER 4. Went to town and sent our animals out on a ranch to winter. Rented a cabin just west of town near the mines, examined the mining ground that we had come so far to secure and great was our disappointment. It lay so level and so low that it could not be worked by hydraulic process, and around it were only shallow gulches that would not afford any place for sluices to dump tailings, and would not drain much of the flat. The ground would not pay to work with pick and shovel, and to cap the climax the water was scarce in those mines and was already in use. None could be obtained except at high prices and winter was near at hand. Little work could be done as it was occasionally some degrees below zero, with a foot of snow. We began to wish ourselves back in Dog Town with its balmy climate.

We bought a claim for fifty dollars and worked it until cold weather set in and the ground froze. We purchased water from a ditch company for our sluices, all the water in this vicinity being taken from creeks to the mines on Yreka flats which caused much bitter feeling and no end of trouble. After the mines on the flat were discovered and much of the water turned from the creeks into ditches to supply these mines, other mines were discovered in the creek bottoms and many miners scattered along the creek bed were able to make good wages. During the summer months the water became scarce and there was not enough to supply all. The ditch company having first right to the water turned it all into the ditches for the Yreka flat diggins. This enraged the creek bottom miners and they cut the ditches and turned the water back into the creek. The ditch owners had a number of the miners arrested and placed in jail. This enraged their comrades and they swore that they would storm the jail and release the imprisoned men. Accordingly on the night of February 28, 1855, they made the attack. Had they been secretive they might have succeeded, but so much talk and so many threats had been made that the officers of the law prepared for an attack and had the jail filled with armed men. When the rescue party of miners attacked the jail they were met with a volley of shots with the result that four of their number were killed and fifteen or twenty wounded. The wounded were carried off by their comrades and concealed in cabins scattered along the gulches near the creek. Doctors sworn to secrecy, attended them at night for sometime. If any more died it was not known. The officers of the law let the matter drop and did not try to find the raiders. They thought they were punished severely enough as it was. None of the jail defenders were hurt.

MARCH 18, 1855. We bought another placer claim for three hundred dollars, out of which we took considerable gold. Rezin Anderson, being a blacksmith, hired to a shop in town at five dollars a day and did not mine with us anymore.

On the tenth of April, James joined a party of prospectors that was going around Mount Shasta (called Shasta Butte in those days) to the south side. This proved to be an unprofitable as well as a most disagreeable trip. They were gone a month and it stormed on them almost every day. They had no tents and it rained and snowed so hard that they were unable to build fires half the time. At night they rolled up in water-soaked blankets and shivered until morning. They found no mines that would pay. During this time I mined on Shasta river a few miles from Yreka and made some money.

About the twentieth of June, 1855, seven of us started on a prospecting trip about fifty miles up Klamath river, the party consisted of Hugh Bratton, John Cotton, Tom Burns, Tom Duffy, Ed. Tolts, and James and Granville Stuart. Duffy had a Shasta squaw for a wife and she told him that on a certain stream called Butte creek that came into Klamath river on the south side, that Indians knew where there was much gold. So we went in search of these supposed rich diggings. There being no trail up the Klamath we took the emigrant wagon road out to Klamath lake, then along the Oregon road to the crossing of Klamath river. Here we left the road and about ten o'clock in the morning started up along a well beaten trail which showed many barefoot Indian tracks. We had gone about a half mile when without warning a number of shots came from the steep timbered mountain side high above us. None struck us however. All the balls apparently passed over our heads as they always go high when fired down a steep mountain. We at once turned back and before the Indians could reload their guns (muzzle loaders) we got out of their sight behind a thick grove of cottonwoods. We went up the Klamath about a quarter of a mile and chose a strong position on a flat among some big oak trees, and awaited developments. In a short time several Indians appeared among the rocks on both sides of the river below us, but avoided exposing themselves to a shot. We called to them in Chinook jargon, which is understood by all Indians from here up to Russian America (now Alaska) and told them who we were, and asked them what was the matter and why they shot at us, but they only answered that they knew us, and would not tell us why they fired at us. Burns and Duffy by this time recognized several of them, one being the brother of Duffy's wife. Duffy tried to get him to come to us assuring him that

he would not be hurt, but he would not come. He as
well as others had often been to Yreka and had been
at Duffy's house.   His tribe were friendly Indians and
there were no wars at this time with any of the tribes
all of which made more unaccountable their conduct.
Their actions were so suspicious that we became convinced that there was trouble brewing.   We saw several other Indians join the first ones.   We did not know
how many more might be camped near where they fired
at us.

This put a stop to our prospecting in Butte creek and
we decided to return to Yreka.   We packed up at three
in the morning and climbed up out of the cañon to the
timbered table-land which lay between us and Klamath
lake.   We traveled ten or twelve miles through the
forest without any trail, when, coming to a meadow on
the little creek, camped for the night.   At sunrise we
saddled up and struck the emigrant wagon road a few
miles from Klamath lake and from there to Yreka, we
saw no Indians, and met with no further incidents.

We were not long in getting the key to the hostile
conduct of these erstwhile friendly Shasta and Klamath
Indians.   A few days after we had started on our trip
the Indians on the Klamath river below where we
were, had killed fifteen miners, who were scattered
along the river for ten or fifteen miles. Most of the
poor fellows were murdered just after they had risen
in the morning, without any suspicion of danger from
the Indians who had been camped among them for
months.   Those who fired on us knew about the massacre below, and some of them may have been implicated in it.   After we escaped their first fire and took
up a strong position they knew us, and knew that we
were all well armed with rifles and revolvers and if

they followed up their attack many of them would be killed.

This kind of warfare is not liked by Indians. The miners whom they murdered were only one, two, or three, in a place and being taken unawares were killed without any risk to the Indians and their cabins robbed of everything. In some of them was considerable gold. The murderers soon fled across the Siskiyou mountains to Rogue river in Oregon, where, joining the disaffected Rogue river and Modoc Indians, they brought on the second Rogue river Indian war. The first one was in 1852-3, and Tom Duffy was in it and was shot twice through his thigh just above the knee at the Battle of the Cave. The bone was not broken and he did not limp.

Soon after our return to Yreka, Duffy and Burns saw two of the Indians that had fired at us and promptly had them arrested. They refused to talk and it seemed probable that, they, being acquainted in town, came in to see what the whites were intending to do about the murders. They were tried and sentenced to be hung. There was no moving for a new trial in those days (1855) for the purpose of defeating the ends of justice, as has now become the custom.

I will here give a brief account of the depredations committed by the Modoc and Rogue river Indians in 1852-53 and which finally led up to the second Rogue river war in which we enlisted.

The emigration by way of Snake river plains in 1852 consisted of large well equipped trains, and perhaps for this reason, was suffered to pass with less bloodshed than might have been anticipated, though there was much annoyance from pilferings and horse stealings. The emigration by the northern route was less favored.

This route crossed the Sierra Nevada by the old Lawson route and passed by Goose lake, Clear lake, Tule lake, and Klamath lake in northern California. At the latter lake the road forked, the left hand road going to Yreka in Shasta valley, California, on the north side of Mount Shasta. The right hand road turned north along the shore of Klamath lake, a sagebrush and lava bed country, then leaving the lake passed through a pine forest a few miles to Klamath river, which is crossed by a bad rocky ford and then ascended the pine clad Siskiyou mountains. The summit is the dividing line between California and Oregon. The emigrants from the States would separate at Klamath lake, part going to Oregon and part to California. The road to California ran through the lake country. Here in 1843 Fremont's camp was attacked, and here Capt. W. H. Warner, in 1849 was murdered while surveying for a Pacific railroad. Parties traveling through this region were compelled to exercise extreme care, particularly at a pass now known as "Bloody Pass," where the road ran between an overhanging cliff and the waters of the lake. In 1852, between sixty and one hundred men, women, and children died at the hands of the Modoc Indians, and a large amount of property was stolen or destroyed.

The first large train arriving at Yreka reported that they had not been molested, but that there were many companies on the road, some of them with families, and that the Indians were burning signal fires on the mountains which boded no good to travelers.

On this report Charles McDermit of Yreka raised a company of between thirty and forty volunteers to meet and escort these companies over the most dangerous portion of the road through the Modoc country.

At Tule lake the volunteers met a company of male emigrants going to Yreka. They sent two of their men, Smith and Toland, back with the emigrants to act as guides and guards. This party came through to Yreka without being attacked.

The next party to reach Tule lake consisted of about twenty poorly armed men five of them with families, and ten wagons. They found McDermit's company on the west shore of Goose lake and were warned of the danger ahead, and Toland with two of the volunteers accompanied them as guides. On coming to the high hill one mile east of the south end of the Tule lake on the nineteenth of August, no Indians in sight, the guides having in mind James Bridger's caution, "When there are no Indians in sight, then look out," decided to avoid a probable ambush by taking a northerly course across a sagebrush flat.

The women and children were placed in the wagons, and the covers fastened down to hide them from view, while the firearms were made ready for use. In this manner the company had nearly reached the open valley when the yells of Indians in pursuit disclosed to them that they were being pursued. By making all possible speed, open ground was reached just as a shower of arrows whizzed through the air. The emigrants replied with a volley from their rifles and the Modocs withdrew to the shelter of the rocks, but reappeared again on a high ridge, gesticulating and uttering demonical cries expressive of their rage and disappointment.

Seeing that they were working themselves up to a fighting pitch, and would probably attack at some other point, it was thought best to return to hold a talk. Acting on this plan, the wagons were corraled and

Toland with a half dozen others, making a great show of arms went back within speaking distance and challenged the Indians, through one of the guides, who could speak the jargon, to come and fight. Like all the people who practice treachery, they feared it, and not knowing what might be inside the wagon covers, declined, but the head chief proposed to meet the interpreter unarmed and talk with him.

While the talk was progressing, at a safe distance from the wagons, it was observed, by Toland, that every now and then a Modoc had tied his bow to his toe, secreted his arrows, and pretending to be disarmed, joined the chief in the sagebrush. The interpreter, on being warned ordered the Indians sent back, and the chief seeing no opportunity for obtaining an advantage, agreed to return whence he came, and leave the party to pursue its way unmolested. They had not proceeded far, however, before they discovered a reserve of Indians mounted, who had been placed where they could intercept any persons escaping from the narrow pass along Tule lake. Finding themselves outwitted, they also returned, hoping for better luck next time. Camp was made that night fifteen miles from Tule lake. A severe rain storm doubtless prevented a night attack, the Indians being unable to use their bows in wet weather. The train made a very early start next morning and thus averted further trouble.

On the twenty-third of August, at nine o'clock in the evening, Toland's camp was visited by a man on a poor and jaded horse, whose condition excited the utmost pity. He had to be lifted from his horse and fed and nursed back to life before he could give any account of himself. It then appeared that he belonged to a party of eight men who had been surprised by the

Modocs, and all killed except himself. His horse being shot he sprang upon another, which ran with him, carrying him several miles up the valley of Lost river, until he fell exhausted. From here the man whose mind was evidently unsettled by the shock he had received, wandered to Klamath lake, but seeing an Indian, turned back and the next day discovered his horse feeding. He remounted and rode, for three days without dismounting until he came to Toland's camp. He had eaten nothing, but had tied up a handful of rosebuds in his handkerchief as he said that he expected to be out all winter and should need them. This demented creature was taken by the company to Yreka, where his story in connection with the report of Toland and the guides of trouble in the Modoc country, led to the organization of a second company of volunteers.

A meeting was called on the evening of the twenty-fourth of August, at which means to put the men in the field was subscribed by the citizens and miners, and Ben Wright was chosen captain. He was at the time mining on Cottonwood creek, twenty miles distant, but by daylight he was in Yreka surrounded by men eager to assist the emigration through the dangerous country and to punish the Modocs for depredations already committed. A peculiar enthusiasm was imparted to volunteering by the fact that Toland's train was the first to arrive with women and children. The homeless miners were having their minds harrowed by the suggestion of what might have been the fate of these but for the warning and guidance given by McDermit's party, and what might even after all befall others on some part of the route. Three days were consumed in getting together the equipment of men and horses with provision wagons and everything necessary. On the

sixth day after the meeting at Yreka, Wright reached
Tule lake just in time to rescue a train that was surrounded and fighting the Modocs. The sight of
Wright's company advancing sent the savages into
places of concealment among the tules, and on the
island in the lake, and equally alarmed the emigrants
who mistook them for mounted Indians and prepared
for a yet more desperate encounter. Their fears were
changed to joy when Wright, discovering their alarm,
rode forward alone. This train was escorted beyond
danger, and the company returned to the Modoc country.

Wright found the mutilated bodies of the eight men
before mentioned and those of three of his acquaintances, members of McDermit's party, who had been
sent to guide trains and who had been killed. Filled
with rage and grief, Wright and his men made haste to
attack the Indians in their stronghold. To do this they
had to wade in water among the tules up to their arm-
pits, and fight the Modocs concealed in ambuscades
constructed of tules, having portholes. Such was the
vigor of their charge, however, that the ambuscades
were quickly depopulated, and thirty or more Modocs
killed while escaping to the rock island in the lake.

After the battle, Wright proceeded east to Clear
lake where he met a large party of emigrants and
planned a stratagem to draw the Indians out of their
stronghold on the island. He unloaded several ox
wagons, filled them with armed men, a few of whom
he clothed in women's apparel, and placed them in
wagons in plain sight, and loitering along in true emigrant fashion along the dangerous pass. But the Indians either had spies out who reported the trick, or

were too severely punished to feel like attacking white men again and they remained in their fastnesses.

Wright then went to Yreka and had boats built with which to reach the island, spending the time of waiting in patrolling the road through the Modoc country. In the meantime accounts of the massacres had reached Jacksonville, Oregon, and another company, commanded by John E. Ross of that place, proceeded to the Modoc country where it remained on the road until the season to travel was past. On the arrival of Ross, Wright returned to Yreka for supplies, and to bring out his boats. He was unable to find the Indians, who retreated to the lava beds, inaccessible then as now to white men.

That which Wright did find among the plunder left behind on the islands was women's and children's wearing apparel and many evidences that men, women, and children had been taken captive and cruelly tortured and murdered. One of the Indians captured by Wright had a cradle-quilt wrapped about his shoulders. He also learned that there were two white women held captive by the Modocs and however much he desired to exterminate these savages, he knew that the rescue of the women and the safety of all who passed through this section of country, depended upon a treaty with the Modocs.

Wright had an Indian boy for a servant who was part Modoc, and spoke their language. Using this boy as an ambassador, he finally persuaded four of their head men to visit his camp, for the purpose of discussing the terms of a treaty. His proposition was that if they would bring in the two captives, and the stock taken from the emigrants, he would leave their country and trouble them no more, or if they wished, he would trade with them for their furs and feathers. To this the chiefs gave their assent, and while one was sent to fetch the women and the property, the other three were detained as hostages. When the chief returned to camp instead of bringing with him the captive women and the stolen stock, he brought only a few broken down horses and a shotgun; but he was accompanied by forty-five armed warriors. When remonstrated with for his violation of his pledge, he replied that Wright had required three hostages, and now his men greatly out-numbering Wright's he should hold him and his company hostages for the good conduct of the white people. The place where Wright was encamped was on the north side of Lost river, near the stone ford, the Modocs encamping on the same side. The situation was critical, it being plain to Wright that a net was spread for him, which would surely close about him unless, he met the danger with a desperate measure.

The orders for the night were for the men to quietly slip out at midnight and conceal themselves in the sage-brush. They were arranged in groups of three and placed so that they could shoot into the Indian camp. They were to lay so concealed until they heard the crack of Wright's rifle when all were to fire simultaneously. The order was scrupulously carried out. The men rushing upon the surprised Indians at the crack of the signal gun finished the fight with their pistols. The fight was over in five minutes and forty Indians were slain. Wright had four men wounded. These were carried, on litters made by lashing guns together, fifteen miles to the nearest settlement. From there a messenger was sent to Yreka for aid. On the company arriving at that place – thin, sunburned, and nearly naked – they were met by cheers, and bonfires were built and banquets given.

The only regret felt was that the two captive women were left to the fiendish cruelty, which no one doubted, would end their lives before they could be rescued. As a matter of fact, they were never seen alive, but years after their bleaching bones were pointed out by the Indians to curious investigators of Indian history.[19]

Captain Ben Wright appointed agent for the Indians about the mouth of Rogue river, and Captain John Toland, of a volunteer company, were lured to an ostensibly friendly camp of Mackanotin Indians [20] and both cruelly murdered on February 22, 1856. Wright's heart was cut out, cooked and eaten by the Indians. They thought by so doing that they would become as brave as he was.[21]   Again the news came that the Rogue river Indians were in active hostility, aided and abetted by the Klamath Indians who had gone over to Rogue river.

The Oregon authorities called California to aid them in quelling these Indians as most of the hostiles were from across the line and the renegade Klamath Indians had incited the Rogue river Indians to take the war path.   California responded by raising a regiment of volunteers, known as the First California Mounted Riflemen.   They furnished their own horses, arms, and ammunition and received the promise of three dollars a day.

[19] These incidents of the Rogue river war are not found in the published histories.   Stuart's description is from a remote part of the war.   The condemnation he gives to the Indians is more severe than that given by other historians. – ED.

[20] Mackanotin.   Bancroft, *Oregon*, vol. ii (*Works*, xxx) p. 405, spells it Mackanootenais.   These were a group of the Rogue river Indians. – ED.

[21] This account of the renewal of hostilities is more specific than that in Bancroft.   *Ibid.*, p. 369. – ED.

My brother James, Reece Anderson, and myself promptly enlisted. We were armed with muzzle loading rifles, Colt's navy cap and ball revolvers (brass cartridges had not been invented then) and were well mounted. We formed a part of Captain White's company of scouts and were sent to the Klamath lake lava beds to ascertain if possible whether the Modocs had joined the Rogue river Indians. Our company consisted of twenty-five men. Our supplies, food, blankets, and ammunition were carried on pack mules. We scouted all through the lake country until satisfied that the Modocs had nothing to do with the outbreak of the Rogue river Indians. We then returned home, having been gone a month.

On our return to Yreka we found that the Oregon troops assisted by the Californians had subdued the hostiles and the war was over. We were accordingly mustered out and disbanded. James, Reece Anderson, and I resumed mining near Yreka until the spring of 1856.

In July emigrant trains begun to arrive and the Modoc Indians again went on the war path and as these Indians had been so troublesome, constantly breaking treaties, it was decided to go after them good and strong and teach them a lesson that they would not forget.

The state again called for troops and James Stuart and Reece Anderson again enlisted. I remained at Yreka and continued mining, working our placer claims. This time one thousand men enlisted. They took boats out to the lakes and followed the Indians on to the islands and killed great numbers of them. It had been the custom of these Indians to carry stores to the islands in little rafts made of tules and leaving the women, children and supplies, go out and attack any emigrant train they could find unprepared and unsuspecting, then with their loot take to the islands again. Without boats the whites were unable to follow them. In 1856 the volunteers with their boats hunted the last one down and either killed them or caused them to surrender. This put a stop to their depredations for that season. The volunteers returned, disbanded and James and Reece joined me at the mine and we continued mining until June 1857.

From California to Montana

In the spring of 1857 we decided to visit our parents and our old home in Iowa. We arranged to cross the plains horseback, taking pack horses to carry our bedding and supplies. Others hearing of our contemplated trip wished to join us and soon there were eleven of us ready for the trip. Our party consisted of Frank L. Stone, P. H. Redick, S. S. Dickerman, Samuel B. Byall, James Chapin, Rezin Anderson, James Stuart, Granville Stuart, John Dickey, Enos Dickey, and Henry Buckingham.

All our preparations being made on the fourteenth day of June, 1857, we started from Yreka, California, on our journey east. Each man had a horse or mule to ride and a pack horse or pack mule for every two. Two of the party had double barreled shot guns. All the others had muzzle loading rifles and all had Colt revolvers. Each man had blankets and a change of under clothing, and food for about fifty or sixty days.

The first day we traveled twenty miles diagonally across Shasta valley, with Mount Shasta looming up grandly to the southeast. We followed the old emigrant road as far as Sheep rock, which is a rough granite upheaval covering about two acres and from one hundred to one hundred and fifty feet high (so called because many mountain sheep used it as a place of refuge from the Indians and their dogs, before the white men came). The Indians had no guns, but when the white men came they soon exterminated the unfortunate sheep with their rifles.

JUNE 15, 1857. We left the emigrant road which
went east to the Klamath, Tule, Clear, and Goose lakes
and turned to the southeast on a new road that had
recently been opened through the woods to Pit river,[22]
where it connected with the old Lawson 1849-road
across the Sierra Nevadas.

JUNE 16. We traveled twenty miles and camped on
a creek three miles from Pit river. No grass for our
tired horses, the country being heavily timbered.

JUNE 17. Traveled ten miles and then camped in
Pit river valley, where we found good grass for hungry
horses. Traveled eighteen miles and camped at the
ferry on Pit river. Here was a good hewed log house,
stable, corral, and a small field fenced, but not a human
being. The family that lived here had all been murdered by the Indians a short time before. We all
bathed in Pit river, and enjoyed it greatly.

JUNE 19. We here took the old Lawson emigrant
trail, went sixteen miles through open pine forest and
camped for the night at a spring. We are now one
hundred and eight miles from Yreka.

JUNE 20. Traveled eight miles and camped at a
water hole. We found it safer to camp wherever we

---

[22] Pit river was so named because the emigrants, who crossed the plains
to California in 1849 (of whom my father was one) found many pits about
three or four feet wide and six feet long and from six to seven feet deep, in
the game trails in the valley along this river. The dirt taken out of these
pits and all taken away from the vicinity of the pits, they were then covered
over with dry, almost rotten willow sticks, then lightly covered over with
dry grass and leaves and a little sprinkle of earth put on so that it was
similar to the ground around it. The Indians who made the pits would
watch the deer, antelope, and elk that came into valley, and then surround and
frighten them, when they would run in their old trails and some would jump
on the covered pits and would at once give way and they would fall to the
bottom. Unable to get out they fell a prey to the Indians. These Indians
had no tools to dig with and these many pits were dug with prongs of deer
and elk horns and the dirt carried away in little tule and willow baskets, a

found water, for in a strange country we did not know how far it might be to the next water.

JUNE 21. Traveled fifteen miles and camped at a spring. Road is rising all the time, with some stone stretches here and there. Since leaving Pit river we have been in open country, pine woods of rather poor scrubby trees, but no brush. Saw a few deer, but they always saw us first and fled.

JUNE 22. Traveled thirty-five miles over timbered ridges, stony, bad road. From the top of this ridge the plains of the Great Basin were in sight far, far, below us, and a good sized lake near the foot of the mountain. We made this long day's journey because we found no water. We passed no creeks since leaving Pit river, and not much grass. The descent down the mountain, which is the summit of the Sierra Nevada, was very long and very steep and was hard on our horses, although we walked and led them most of the way. We finally reached the lake which is called Honey lake and found good grass, but the water in the lake was hardly fit to drink. Men and horses all very tired. There are a few people living around the lake, but I would not care to live in such a disagreeable region. Not a tree or even a bush, since leaving the foot of the mountains, and the gnats and mosquitoes are bad. They almost devoured us and worried the horses greatly.

JUNE 23. Traveled fifteen miles over a stony road and camped on Little Willow creek (I do not know why it should be called Willow creek, as but few willows grow along its course). No trees anywhere, which

___

long hard labor which of course had to be done by the patient women. These Indians were not friendly to the whites and were dangerous. Along the road to Pit river were occasional little grassy parks in one of which called Elk park, we camped for the night.

makes me homesick for the noble trees of California. We are now one hundred and eighty miles from Yreka.

JUNE 24. Traveled eighteen miles over a stony road, camped at Mud springs, pretty fair grass, but no timber.

JUNE 25. Traveled eighteen miles and camped on Smoke creek. On the way we passed a pool of water under a shelving ledge of rock, and as we came to it about thirty or forty magpies flew up from it. Never saw so many together before. We camped on Smoke creek, a little crooked stream with not a bush on it, but in the narrow crooked bottom along the stream is the finest clover growing that I ever saw. It is as thick as the hair on a dog and fully three feet high. How our horses enjoyed it. They ate until they could hold no more and then laid down and rolled in it.

JUNE 26. Traveled twenty-five miles before we came to a spring. Much of the road rocky and bad. This spring is a wonderful one. It is about fifteen feet across, very clear, and apparently about eighteen feet deep. The water runs down a little slope about one hundred yards and then flows over a meadow of good grass about two hundred yards long by one hundred and fifty yards wide. The country around the spring is of a barren, sandy nature, with some small sage, but not a tree or bush in sight anywhere. The water is very cold and delicious, which is the more remarkable in a region where the water is usually bad and scarce, and where any is found, it is usually boiling hot. There are two other lovely springs in the group, all sending their water into the little meadow below them. There are no mountains or hills near these springs, and their

FRENCH GULCH, DEER LODGE COUNTY, M.T.

Here Mortimer Lott began mining gold shortly after the Stuarts began
operations on Gold creek
From an original drawing made by Granville Stuart, in 1869

GOLD CREEK MOUNTAINS, FROM DEER LODGE CITY (LOOKING WEST)

Scene of the first gold mining in Montana
From an original drawing made by Granville Stuart, August 22, 1865

water, after irrigating the little meadow, sinks in the thirsty desert plains.[23]

JUNE 27. Only traveled twelve miles when we came to a forked mountain of considerable size in the midst of sagebrush four and five feet high. At its foot we suddenly came to a lovely stream six or seven feet wide, and one foot deep of clear cold water. This stream comes out of a cañon that extends back into the forked mountain, on which we see a few scattering trees, apparently fir trees. The mountain is of granite and the creek is called Granite creek. These are the first trees we have seen since we left the Sierra Nevadas and they looked good to us. This lovely creek runs about one-half mile down through the big sage which it nourishes and then sinks in the bare white bed of a dry alkali lake. We camped here for the rest of the day and night, for we knew that there was no water ahead of us for sixty miles and the weather burning hot. There is much loose granite sand on the hillside where the creek emerges from its cañon into the plain and in this sand we find many tracks of mountain sheep. We possibly might kill one by climbing up the mountain, but we are too tired and besides the weather is very hot, so although we want fresh meat very much, we decided not to risk climbing mountains in this fierce heat.

JUNE 28. We started from Granite creek at daybreak. Our road lay over the smooth level dry bed of Mud lake. The greater part of the way this is white and so hard that our horses' feet scarcely made a mark. About half-way across we unexpectedly came to a big boiling spring that sent up lots of steam, but this water

_____

[23] No doubt someone has a fine ranch there now with fruit and ornamental trees in plenty. — 1916.

did us no good, for we had nothing in which to cool it and besides it smelt badly. We feared it might be poisonous and there was not a blade of grass for our hungry horses. They have traveled thirty miles since daybreak in a boiling sun, but we did not stop. We were glad when the sun went down. About dark the road left the level bed of the dried lake and passed over low ridges with sagebrush and some greasewood brush. We arrived at Rabbit spring wells sometime after midnight. These springs do not flow any water, and are only a marshy piece of ground a few acres in extent. By digging holes from two to four feet deep we got some very poor alkali water in limited quantities, bad, but it was wet. There is no fuel here, but a few sprigs of greasewood and we are all too tired to hunt for it in the dark, so after picketing our horses on rather scanty grass and putting two men on guard, we made down our beds and slept sweetly until daybreak.

JUNE 29. Traveled fifteen miles to the Little meadows [24] on the Humboldt river. It is a pleasure to see our horses drink their full of its good clear water and eat all they could hold of the splendid grass and then lie down and roll in it with great grunts of satisfaction. We arrived here about two in the afternoon and for the benefit of our horses we remained all the rest of the day and all night.

JUNE 30. Traveled up the river twenty miles. Had good grass and good water. There was fine grass in the river bottom, with dense clumps of willows along the river banks. Back from the river the valley and low hills were covered with sagebrush. No timber along this curious river.

---

[24] Lassen's meadows. *Montana As It Is*, p. 138. – ED.

JULY 1. Traveled up the river twenty miles. We are traveling slowly to keep our horses in good condition. Good grass and good water, but no wood, use sagebrush for cooking. Road is often a mile or more from the river. Mosquitoes are very annoying. We are now in a section of country where the Indians are hostile and we do not camp near the willows along the river. We make a stop, cook our supper, then when it is quite dark, saddle up, travel five or six miles and make camp without fire or any noise. In this way we keep out of reach of any prowling bands of Indians.

JULY 3. Traveled only ten miles, as a big storm of some kind seems brewing. We made each of ourselves a kind of tent by cutting long slender willows about eight or nine feet long and sharpened both ends and bent them over and stuck them in the ground, thus making arches about three and one-half feet high and about three and one-half feet wide on the ground which we roofed over with a pair of blankets. Then we made down our bed on the ground, and under this shelter we were dry and comfortable. We had completed our shelters and were getting ready for bed when it began to rain. Two stood guard over the horses. Before morning it turned cold and snowed and then it was mighty uncomfortable for the guards. We do not leave our horses alone a minute on this part of the road, for although we have not seen any Indians we know that they are lurking near.

JULY 4. We did not move camp as it is impossible to travel in this storm. It rained and snowed in turn all day. We had no fire on account of the rain and stayed in bed when not on duty herding. In the evening it cleared up and we made a big fire of sagebrush, cooked our suppers, and partially dried out our clothes and bedding. Everything including our provisions was soaked. Both we and our horses have suffered severely during the past two days. None of us can say that we enjoyed the way we were compelled to celebrate the Glorious Fourth of this year 1856.

JULY 5. Traveled twenty miles to-day, passed Stony point, a very dangerous place on the road. Here some emigrants have been killed every year since 1848. Much of the trouble comes from carelessness on the part of the whites. Most of them know little about the habits of Indians and camp in dangerous places. They see no Indians and thinking there are none about become careless and allow their stock to stray too far from camp and the next thing they know the Indians have either stampeded and run off their stock or the train has been attacked. These Indians are mostly armed with bows and arrows and will not attack a train unless they can effect a surprise. We have seen no Indians, but being constantly on the lookout we have seen signs and every night we have seen their signal fires, but we keep our arms ready for instant use and never leave the horses unguarded nor do we camp in places where the Indians could slip up and surprise us. They are not apt to tackle eleven well armed men.

JULY 6. Traveled twenty miles and camped at Gravelly ford on the Humboldt river. Several Indians came into camp this morning and also in the evening. They are apparently very friendly, but as most of us kept our guns in our hands they had no chance to be otherwise. We are all well aware that "eternal vigilance is the price of safety" anywhere on the plains. We are now four hundred and forty-four miles from Yreka. Mosquitoes and gnats nearly set our horses crazy and also tapped us for a considerable quantity of blood.

JULY 7. Traveled twenty-five miles across the mountains to where we came to the Humboldt river again. Plenty of Indian signs, saw signal fires on the mountains to westward. Clouds of mosquitoes and gnats.

JULY 8. Traveled thirty miles up the river. Met two Mormons with a little one horse wagon and a loaded pack horse. They are the first white men we have seen since we left Honey lake valley, and the Sierra Nevada mountains of blessed memory. To-day saw a great many hawks for the first time on trip. The mosquitoes and gnats have tormented our horses and ourselves all day and everything and everybody are about played out.

JULY 9. Traveled thirty miles. Crossed the North fork of the Humboldt. Gnats and mosquitoes are untiring and still busy. Will they never let up? John Dickey rode ahead from our noon halt to try to kill a sage hen or rabbit. We heard him shoot twice and soon after saw him sitting on a big rock pounding the fragments of his double barreled rifle with another rock. He had beaten the stock of his gun into small pieces and bent the barrels into a curve and was busily engaged in beating the fine locks to pieces with another rock. When we asked him what was the matter, he said that he had fired twice at a sage cock and missed him both times and he'd be d—d if he was going to carry any such a d—d gun any further. The rifle was of German make and well finished and we felt sure that the fault lay with John and not with the gun. John was a man of passionate and ungovernable temper. He frequently beat his fine mule unmercifully without good cause. We are now five hundred and twenty-nine miles from Yreka. To-day we met one lone Indian riding a little colt. I am sure there are many Indians not far off or he would not be so bold.

JULY 10. Traveled twenty miles, crossed the river on an apology for a bridge and bade a long farewell to the Humboldt river. We have traveled up the Humboldt three hundred and two miles and it is quite a stream still. We camped at a spring on the mountain. Here plenty of Indians came into camp; they seemed very friendly and tried to talk with us, but as they did not understand English, or at least pretended they didn't (which is a common trick among Indians everywhere) and we did not understand the Snake language, we did not make much progress.

JULY 11. Traveled thirty miles. Pass through Thousand spring valley, a noted place and well remembered by all who crossed the plains in 1849. The valley is swampy owing to the many springs. We camped for the night at a spring to the left of the road. Today we passed a Mormon wagon in which were two men and a woman.

JULY 12. Traveled fifteen miles and then laid up on the head of Goose creek where we found good grass and good water. Here we met the first trains of emigrants bound for California. They looked very natural to us who went through the same experience five years ago. I could not help thinking of all the wonderful things I had seen and felt in that five years and now I had turned my back on them and was going home. Quite a number of wagons, mostly ox teams and about five hundred cattle passed us early this morning while we were cooking our breakfast.

JULY 13. Traveled twenty miles down Goose creek nearly north to where the road leaves it. Met lots of emigrants. Some of our party bought a few food supplies from them, mostly sugar, coffee, and bacon, which they sold us at a very reasonable price when one considers the twelve hundred to fifteen hundred miles they had hauled these things, across vast plains and mountains. Their teams were mostly in fair condition and would get through all right.

JULY 14. Traveled twenty miles. Bid a long farewell to Goose creek. Met scores of emigrants to-day and passed the forks of the roads. The right-hand one goes east to Great Salt Lake City and the left-hand one goes north-east and is known as the Hudspeth "Cut Off" [25] from Soda springs on Bear river to this place. It was considerably shorter than the old emigrant road, that went from Soda springs to Old Fort Hall on Snake river. Camped on West branch of Raft river at junction of Fort Hall road with the Hudspeth "Cut Off." Today we passed through the "City of Rocks," which is a great natural curiosity; huge rocks, some square, some round, some resembling houses, and all kinds of strange and fantastic shapes stand scattered over a space of about three miles long, and one mile wide. I never saw anything like this anywhere else in all my wanderings.

JULY 15. Traveled twenty miles and camped on the east branch of Raft river. Good camp, plenty of wood, water, and grass. The road crossed the river here. Here we found a couple of Mormons camped selling provisions to the emigrants.

JULY 16. Traveled twenty miles over hilly country and camped at a good spring where the grass is good

25 *Ibid.*, p. 143. – ED.

and plentiful. Met many emigrant wagons mostly
families with some small droves of cattle.

JULY 17. Traveled thirty-one miles to Malad creek
sometimes called Gravel Bottom creek. Nice clear
water, some wood and plenty of good grass. We passed
over two high ridges and through two cañons. Leading up to and down through these there were some
quaking aspen timber and some brush. But for twenty-two miles before reaching Malad creek we found
no water and weather quite warm. The crossing of
Malad creek is two hundred and forty miles north of
Great Salt Lake City. Passed or rather met many
emigrant teams. All were anxious to get to water as
the teams were suffering greatly for it.

On the head of Malad creek, in the same region
where I fell ill on my way to California in 1852, I was
again taken sick. On July 17, 1857, I was so ill that
my companions felt, that if I recovered at all it would
be a long time before I would be able to travel. Accordingly it was decided that Reece Anderson and
James Stuart remain with me and the other eight resume their long journey east. Here on the great Overland emigrant road about sixty miles north of where
the town of Corinne was afterwards built, I lay for
seven weeks too ill to travel. My brother succeeded
in breaking the fever, but not until it had brought me
nigh to death's door. My recovery was very slow.

Early one morning we heard a great hubbub followed
by a number of shots fired into the camp of a train of
emigrants camped nearby. They had let some of their
horses graze away from their camp about two hundred
yards. Suddenly four mounted Indians, who were
concealed in a dense patch of willows, dashed out
among them and with loud yells and shaking of their

blankets stamped all the loose horses.   By the time
the astonished emigrants got their rifles in action the
Indians and frightened horses were three hundred
yards away and going at full speed.   A number of shots
were fired, but no one was hit.   The Indians stopped
and fired back, wounding one man in the heel and then
resumed their flight and were soon out of sight among
the hills.   They got away with eight horses.   This
sort of thing happened very often on the overland road
because of the carelessness of the emigrants.

Camped near us was a man named Jake Meek, who
some years before, had been in the employ of the Hudson's Bay Fur Company, carrying their mail and express between Fort Hall and Fort Boise on Snake
river, near where is now the thriving town of Caldwell,
Idaho.   At the time of which I am writing both forts
were in Oregon.   Meek was engaged in trading ponies,
dressed skins, and buckskin clothing to the emigrants,
for money and tired out cattle and horses.

The emigrants at once accused him of being in
league with the Indians in stealing their horses and
made dire threats as to what they would do to him.
He protested his innocence, but they were in an ugly
mood and I think they would have killed him had not
James Stuart and Reece Anderson taken his part. James
told them that we had been camped near Meek for
some time and knew him to be innocent; that only two
days before the Indians had got away with two of his
horses and came near getting ours and would have done
so but for our always standing guard over them day and
night.   Eternal, sleepless, vigilance was the only way
to save one's horses from being stolen when traveling
through an Indian country.

During the time we were delayed here many important events had taken place. Brigham Young, President of the Mormon church, had, as we now learned, declared the state of Deseret now Utah, free and independent of the United States. In fact he had seceded from the Union.

I remember hearing Brigham Young in 1852 preaching and abusing the United States, calling them, "a Union with hell and the devil" and assuring the "Saints," "that the Mormon Church would overcome all its enemies, that the Lord would yet guide them back to Jackson, Missouri, that He would deliver the United States over to them and they would establish the Kingdom of God over the world." I thought at the time that Brigham was tackling too big a job, but I found that now five years later he had started in to make good. The government at Washington tried to reason him out of seceding, but Brigham refused to listen saying that, "The Lord was on the side of the Saints and that they could and would lick the United States, and all the legions of hell that were helping the United States." The government finally started five thousand troops commanded by General Albert Sidney Johnson to Utah to squelch him. While I lay sick Brigham declared Utah under martial law, organized and drilled the Saints and made it high crime to sell or give away any food or ammunition to a gentile, and got ready for war.

By this time the United States troops with long slow moving ox trains of supplies, were coming up North Platte and Sweetwater rivers and the Mormon troops patrolled and guarded all the roads, and when at last I was able to mount my horse, we found all the roads guarded, and we could neither go forward to the States nor back to California. To attempt it would cause us to be arrested as government spies and that meant sure death. A few persons found traveling were arrested and were never heard of afterwards. No doubt Brigham's corps of "Destroying Angels," under Porter Rockwell, and Bill Hickman, could have pointed out their graves. Five years later I became acquainted with Hickman at Gold Creek, Montana, and found him a genial sort of man. I think Byron's description of "The Corsair," "He was the mildest mannered man that ever scuttled ship or cut a human throat," would have fitted him quite well. We now found ourselves in a very dangerous situation. We could not long remain where we were, and if we tried to go anywhere else we ran the risk of losing our lives.

We discussed our forlorn situation with Meek, finding him familiar with the country generally. He told us that the past winter (that of 1856) he had wintered in Beaverhead valley some three hundred miles north, and that the Indians in that region were friendly, that the winters were not severe, and game was plentiful there, and that he intended to go there and winter as soon as the cattle and horses he had traded for had rested up enough to stand the trip. He said the best thing we could do would be to go with him and winter there and come back in the spring, as the Mormon war would probably be over then. We had never heard of Beaverhead valley, and knew nothing of the country, but as we could not safely go anywhere else we determined to go with him. Then came the problem of getting supplies in a hostile country in time of war. Meek told us that forty miles down the stream on which we were camped, was an outlying Mormon fort and a small settlement. He thought the bishop who ruled the settlement, as was always the case among the Mor-

mons, might possibly be induced by a good price to sell
us some food and ammunition secretly, in spite of
Brigham Young's prohibition against letting gentiles
have anything. Brother James and Meek, who also
wanted supplies, went down to Bishop Barnard's fort
at Malad City, as these few adobe huts were called, and
found the bishop kind enough to sell them secretly a
limited quantity of flour, bacon, coffee, and sugar, provided Meek, who had bought a wagon and two yoke
of oxen from the emigrants, would bring his wagon to
the fort at midnight, and get his food and drive the
rest of the night, so as to be far away before day
dawned. Of course these conditions were gladly accepted. He also sold James a small quantity of powder, lead, and percussion caps, for our muzzle loading
rifles. We were also armed with the old style powder
and ball Colt's navy revolvers and they were mighty
good weapons, too, as I often proved by killing deer,
antelope, and mountain sheep, with mine at one hundred yards distance.

While we were still at our camp on Malad creek preparing to go North, the massacre at Mountain meadows
in southern Utah took place. On September 11, 1857,
there was murdered, in cold blood, by the Mormon
militia an entire train of emigrants, consisting of one
hundred and twenty men, women, and children. Only
seventeen little children from three to seven years old
were spared alive.

This train of emigrants was camped at the meadows
resting their horses and cattle before starting across the
desert between there and California. They were first
attacked by Indians and Mormon militia disguised as
Indians. The train hastily entrenched themselves inside their corral of wagons and fought for four days.

Seven were killed and several were wounded and several Mormons were killed.

John D. Lee, who led the Mormons found the train too well equipped to be easily taken and decided to try another plan. His Mormons threw off their disguise and then appeared on the scene as a rescuing party. John D. Lee induced the train to surrender promising them protection and assistance to go to California. After giving up their arms all except the seventeen children before mentioned, were shot down in cold blood.[26]

The reason afterwards alleged for this dreadful massacre, by the Mormons, was, that this train was from Arkansas, where one of the twelve apostles of the Mormon church, Parley P. Pratt, was killed on May 13, 1857, by a man named Hector McLean, whose wife it was alleged Pratt had seduced. This was probably true, for Mrs. McLean left her husband and children and went with the Mormons to Salt Lake City. It was also alleged by the Mormons that the men of this emigrant train, while passing through the Mormon settlements, boasted that they were glad that Pratt was killed and that they would like to kill a lot more Mormons, and were abusive generally. The seventeen little children were sent back to their friends in Arkansas in 1859, by means of an appropriation made by congress for that purpose. Only one man was ever punished for this horrible crime. John Doyle Lee was duly

[26] R. L. Baskin, *Reminiscences of Early Utah* (1914) pp. 83-88, 108-149, gives a documentary account of the massacre and the evidence bearing on the guilt of the heads of the Mormon Church. His opinions are very hostile to the Mormons. Orson F. Whitney, *History of Utah* (3 vols., Salt Lake City, 1892) vol. i, pp. 692-709, blames the emigrants for hostile talk against the Mormons, and implicates only two white men in the massacre, Lee and Klingensmith. Even from his statement however there seems to be no doubt but that many other Mormons were implicated. – ED.

convicted of being the principal leader of those who murdered these emigrants and was taken to the spot of the massacre twenty years later and shot, March 23, 1877. The laws of Utah allowed murderers to choose whether they would be hanged or shot. Lee chose to be shot. Lee was convicted on the evidence given by a man named Philip Klingensmith, who turned state's evidence. He was second in command under Lee and ought to have been shot also, as he led the final massacre.

Had we known on the eleventh day of September, 1857, as we were packing up, of the dreadful deed being done at Mountain meadows, instead of traveling leisurely along, we would doubtless have traveled, without camping day or night, as long as our stock could go, in our desire to get as far away as we could in the shortest space of time. We did not hear of the massacre until June 26, 1858, when James, Anderson, Ross, and I went to Fort Bridger, Utah, for supplies.

We crossed the Rocky Mountain divide on the tenth day of October, 1857, where the station called Monida now is on the Oregon Short Line railroad. As soon as we had crossed the divide a wonderful change appeared in the country. Instead of the gray sagebrush covered plains of Snake river, we saw smooth rounded hills and sloping bench land covered with yellow bunch grass that waved in the wind like a field of grain. A beautiful little clear stream ran northwest on its way to join the Missouri river. This is now known as Red Rock creek. The forepart of October gave days of brilliant sunshine, warm and pleasant with no snow anywhere except on the tops of higher mountains and very little even there.

We had seen no game except an occasional lone antelope on the plains of Snake river. Soon as we came to the divide of the Rocky mountains bands of antelope of from four to five, to fifteen and twenty together, were in sight all the time, but the Indians had evidently been hunting them, for they were exceedingly shy, making it very difficult to get within gunshot of them on the smooth treeless benches of Red Rock creek. Our muzzle-loading rifles were not sighted for long range shooting, but we soon managed to circumvent them sufficiently to have meat. We also discovered as we moved on our way down the valley to Beaverhead that there was plenty of game, consisting of black tailed deer, big horn or mountain sheep, and also many bands of elk.

On the twenty-fourth of October we left Sage creek and crossed the rather high ridge of Blacktail Deer creek. That night a furious snow storm set in which lasted all the next day. Twelve inches of snow fell and it turned quite cold so that ice formed on pools of still water. Fortunately we were camped where wood was reasonably plentiful and we did not suffer. Having arrived at our destination, the Beaverhead valley, we chose as a camping place a spot in the valley at the mouth of Blacktail Deer creek. Here we remained until Christmas. At our camp were Reece Anderson, James Stuart, Jake Meek, Robert Dempsey with his wife, Antoine Le Clair and wife, and his two grown sons, and myself. We all lived in elk skin Indian lodges and were very comfortable. The winter was mild with very little snow. It was our custom to go hunting without a coat. There was plenty of game and the camp was kept well supplied with meat.

Fifteen miles further down the Beaverhead at the mouth of the Stinking Water was another camp of mountain men. Captain Richard Grant, an old Scotch gentleman formerly with the Hudson's Bay Company, with his family, John F. Grant and family, James C. Grant, Thomas Pambrun and family, L. R. Maillet, John Jacobs and family, Robert Hereford and family, John W. Powell, John Saunders, Ross, Antoine Pourrier, and several men in the employ of Hereford and the Grants.[27]   Captain Grant built a good three room log house for his family to live in, but the others occupied Indian lodges made of dressed elk skins.

A mile further down the river was Antoine Courtei and family, and two Delaware Indians, named Jim and Ben Simonds, both very large men, weighing over

[27] The families were Indian women and half-breed children with the exception of Captain Grant's family. His wife was a quarter-Indian from the Red river of the North and had been educated in a convent as were his three charming daughters. G. S. One of these daughters married C. P. Higgins of Hell Gate and Missoula. Angus MacDonald, a son of the old trader at Fort Connah believes that Mrs. C. P. Higgins made the contraction of an Indian sentence meaning, "Where the waters flow from opposite directions" to form the word Missoula. On the other hand his half-brother Duncan MacDonald asserts that Missoula came from an Indian expression *In May soo let que* meaning Quaking river. Father Palladino gives still another meaning. He believes that the expression *lm-i-sul-e* meaning "by the cold, chilling waters," is the origin of the word. *Indian and White in the Northwest* (Lancaster, Pennsylvania, 1922) p. 358.

Robert Hereford was a trader along the Emigrant road. It was probably he who informed the Stuarts of the signs of gold in Deer Lodge valley. Michael A. Leeson, *A History of Montana* (Chicago, 1885) p. 209. He was later in the Bitter Root associated with Major John Owen (*Fort Owen Journals* edited by Seymour Dunbar and Paul C. Phillips, 1925). He was engrossing clerk of the first territorial legislature of Montana, and later was assessor of Lewis and Clark county. MONTANA, *House Journal of First Legislative Assembly.* F. H. Woody, Sketch of the Early History of Western Montana in *Montana Historical Society Contributions*, vol. ii (Helena, Montana, 1896) p. 95. Maillet was a partner of Neil McArthur an old Hudson's Bay Company employe. He came into the Bitter Root in 1855, and had gone into the Beaverhead country to trade when Stuart met him. A semi-autobiographical sketch of his life is in *Montana Historical Society Contributions*, vol. iv (Helena, 1903) pp. 197-228. Thomas Pambrun is frequently mentioned in the *Fort Owen Journals.* Delaware Jim was for several years after this in the employ of Major Owen and accompanied him on many of his trading trips. Jake Meeks was also often associated with Major Owen. – ED.

two hundred pounds.   These Indians had considerable quantity of goods to sell and trade to the Indians as did Hereford, and the Grants.

The time during the winter was passed trading with the Indians and in visiting one another's camps and in hunting.   The price of a common horse was two blankets, one shirt, one pair of cloth leggins, one small mirror, one knife, one paper of vermillion, and usually a few other trifles.   A dressed deer skin cost from fifteen to twenty rifle balls and powder; one elk skin, twenty to twenty-five balls and powder; antelope, five to ten balls and powder; beaver, twenty to twenty-five balls and powder; moccasins per pair, ten balls and powder.   The Grants and the Hudson's Bay men generally, complained bitterly of the American hunters and adventurers for having more than doubled the price of all those articles among the Indians in the last ten years, which was doubtless true.

Simonds and Hereford each had considerable whiskey in their outfits but it was only for the whites, as they did not trade it to the Indians who were scattered about.   These Indians were mostly Snakes and Bannocks, with a few Flatheads.   They did not seem to crave liquor as most Indians do, but were quiet and unobtrusive, and as respectable as Indians ever get to be.   The whites and half breeds drank enough while it lasted (which fortunately was not long) for themselves and all the Indians in the country.   At times it seemed that blood must be shed, but the Providence that seems to watch over the lives of drunken men stood by them and the end of the liquor was reached before anyone was killed.   As we three never drank, we often wished that the devil had them all.

Gambling was a popular pastime.   The Indian is an

inveterate gambler and will gamble even the shirt off his back and walk home naked. The mountain men as a rule were almost as bad, and much of the time during these long winter nights and short winter days, was taken up by playing the Indian gambling game of "Hands." Those inclined for a game would collect at some lodge. Inside there would be a pole usually a lodge pole, about six feet long and on either side a number of Indians and often white men. They would sit and sing or drone a sort of song, all the time beating on the pole with the sticks. One always knew by these sounds that a game was in progress within the tepee. The gamblers would sit opposite each other and they would have a polished stick or bone about an inch long and an inch or inch and a half in diameter. The man who starts the game takes the piece of bone in his hand and he shifts it back and forth holding his hands over his head in front and behind him and when he thinks he has sufficiently bewildered his opponent he stops and the other guesses which hand the bone is in. If he makes a right guess he wins and wrong he loses.

They take turns hiding the bone whether the man who had the bone wins or loses the next man takes his turn. They wager everything they possess on this game; horses, blankets, belts, war bonnets, skins, robes, vermillion paint, saddles, shirts, leggins, moccasins, and tobacco. Usually the gambler has a pile of his belongings beside him and will wager first one article and then another, and the pile grows or diminishes as luck is good or bad. It is no uncommon thing to see one man in camp with about everything in his possession and next day perhaps be almost naked, having lost one day what he has won the day before. The singing and beating on the pole is not solely to furnish music to the players. The musicians are usually unsuccessful gamblers, pounding and singing to make, "medicine," so that the next time they would be lucky.

On Christmas day Captain Grant invited Reece Anderson, Ross, James Stuart, Jacob Meek, and myself to dine with him. The menu consisted of buffalo meat, boiled smoked tongue, bread, dried fruit, a preserve made from the choke-cherries, and coffee. This was an elaborate dinner for those days. Supplies were scarce and hard to get, and most of us were living on meat straight.

Late in the fall some ten lodges of Nez Percé Indians came into the Beaverhead valley, and spent the winter camped there. They were peaceable among the whites and gave no trouble. A number of them had the smallpox during the winter, but it was of a mild type. We often met them riding along the trails all broken out with the disease. The weather was quite cold, with no snow on the ground, yet none of them died. They remained outside of our lodges when they called on us as they knew the disease was contagious. This was thoughtful of them and saved us the trouble of keeping them out of camp. A Bannock woman, the wife of Robert Hereford, took the disease and died. Strange to say her husband and three other white men who occupied the same lodge with her during her illness did not take the disease.

About January 1, 1858, there arrived ten men, under the command of B. F. Ficklin, who had been teamsters in the employ of Johnston's army. They were enlisted as volunteers, and sent out from the winter quarters at Fort Bridger to purchase beef cattle from the mountaineers. They were guided by Ned Williamson, and reported very little snow on the route. They could not

purchase cattle on terms to suit them, and fearing to
return in mid-winter, remained on the Big Hole until
the general exodus in the spring, when they returned to
Fort Bridger.   They were compelled to eat some of
their horses on their way, as indeed did also some of
the mountaineers, game being very scarce.   The spring
was stormy and bad, although the winter had been mild
and pleasant.

Just after Christmas we moved from the Beaverhead
over on the Big Hole river a short distance below where
Brown's bridge now stands and just above the curious
ridge of naked broken rock known as the "Backbone." [28]   We thought this a better hunting ground but
the game was all poor and getting scarce.   We decided
that we would get out and go to Fort Bridger just as
soon as the snow had melted enough to enable us to
cross the divide.   We were entirely out of provisions
and had been for sometime living on wild game without salt. We knew that as soon as we crossed the Rocky
mountain divide onto the sagebrush plains of Snake
river, there would be no game of any kind and also
none from there to Fort Bridger.   We four visited
Captain Richard Grant's camp at the junction of Stinking Water creek and the Beaverhead river.   The Captain was getting ready to move his camp to Bitter Root
valley by way of Deer Lodge valley and on down
through it and Hell Gate cañon to the junction of the
Hell Gate and Bitter Root rivers.

On the twenty-eighth of March, 1858, Reece Ander-
son, Ross, Brother James, and myself tried to cross the
Rocky mountain divide at the head of Dry creek, above
Pleasant valley (then known as "Lodge Pole Camp").
We had twenty horses and forced our way over near

[28] About thirty miles north of Dillon. – ED.

where the Summit stage station stood in 1876.[29] Not far from where Monida now is, we encountered a driving snow storm and as the snow was about six feet deep and soft, the labor of breaking a trail was so severe that our horses became exhausted and night coming on we were compelled to return to our camp on Red Rock creek. Here we discovered that the roots of the wild thistles which we dug out of the frozen ground with an axe, were large and firm and tasted very much like the inside of a cabbage stalk. When boiled with our deer and antelope meat it improved it greatly.

It being found impossible to cross the Dry creek pass, and it was resolved to move over and try the next one south known as the Medicine Lodge pass.[30] At this time everybody was reduced to meat straight and it took energetic hunting to get even that for game of all kind had become unaccountably scarce.

[29] Where the Oregon Short Line now crosses the mountains. – ED.
[30] This pass is southwest of the one above described. – ED.

The Discovery of Gold

While camped in Sheep Horn cañon, endeavoring to kill meat enough to do us over the divide, it became apparent that if we remained here longer, a resort must soon be made to horse flesh, so we resolved to go over to Deer Lodge where game was said to be abundant and kill and dry enough meat to do us to Fort Bridger. We were also actuated by a desire to investigate the reported finding of float gold by a Red river half-breed, named Benetsee, in the lower end of Deer Lodge, 1852.

On the fourth of April we moved to Deer Lodge valley and on the seventh made camp about where the town of Stuart now is. Reece Anderson and I went hunting in the mountains where the station of Durant now is. About the rocks in the cañon we encountered numerous bands of mountain sheep. I succeeded in killing one ewe that had not had kids that year and she was very fat; I also killed two yearlings. This was the first fat meat we had had for several months, and was a great treat to us. We packed the sheep on our horses and took them to camp and after dressing them carefully cut the meat in thin strips and dried it and used it as a seasoning for the poor antelope meat that we killed later.

We then went down the Deer Lodge valley to the mouth of Flint creek where we found John M. Jacobs camped with a small herd of cattle that he had taken from John F. Grant on the shares. Grant had gone to the Bitter Root. Here we luxuriated on milk and wild game. Jacobs had broken several cows to milk.

Later we joined camp with Thomas Adams now of Washington, D.C., and all moved up Flint creek to a point three miles above where the town of Philipsburg now is. Here we built a corral, strong enough to bid defiance to the Blackfoot Indians, into which we put our horses each night. We remained here but a short time as there was little game, and then moved down to the West fork of Flint creek near where the town of Hall now is. Here we were joined by Jacobs and we built another strong corral.

These Blackfoot Indians were not blood thirsty at this time, for they could have ambushed and killed us almost any day or night. But to be an expert and successful horse thief gave the Indian great prestige, and he was emphatically "It" among the damsels of his tribe. Except in actual war it was considered a greater achievement to get the horses without blood-shed and without being seen than it was to murder the owner in order to secure his horses.

Not long after this they succeeded in getting four of our horses. We had not seen any Blackfeet for sometime and had allowed our horses to run loose and feed on the luxuriant grass along the creek bottom. Just below us on the creek were camped eight lodges of Flathead Indians. They had a number of ponies that fed with ours. One morning I arose just at day break and went to bring our horses to camp as was our custom. I had gone only a short distance from the lodge when I saw hanging on a willow an old worn out pair of moccasins. Right then I knew what had happened. Investigation showed that four of our horses and eight of the Flatheads were gone. The Indians started out in pursuit but we knew it would be useless as the thieves had several hours start and as soon as they reached the top of the mountain about forty miles distant would be in the country of the Blackfeet. The Flatheads followed the trail to the divide and then returned. They knew that it meant certain death to them for a small party to go over into the enemies' country.

The Indians of the eastern states have always been described as a saturnian, gloomy, mirthless race, which may have been so, but it is not true of those living in the western states, for they love a practical joke and villages and encampments are often scenes of jollity and laughter. They have a keen sense of ludicrous humorous situations, as when that thief hung up his worn out moccasins where we would be sure to see them he told us very plainly, "I have walked until my moccasins are all worn out, and now I will ride home and you can take my old moccasins and walk in search of more horses."

John M. Jacobs had an English rifle made by Westly Richards, for tiger shooting in India, that he bought from a Hudson's Bay trader. It had a two foot barrel of sixty-five calibre, which chambered a one ounce round lead ball. It had a small back action lock of exquisite finish; also a spring to regulate the trigger pull, an iron ram-rod with a screw on its end for extracting balls, and moulds for making ounce balls, and a fine sole leather case for the gun, which only weighed eight pounds. Jacobs complained that he could not kill any game with it. I examined it carefully and made up my mind that the fault lay in Jacobs and not in the highly finished rifle, and offered to trade him my old reliable Kentucky rifle for it. He accepted my offer and we were both satisfied. I tried the rifle and found it a fine shooter when enough powder was used, and found that Jacobs used only half enough because he feared the recoil, which was tremendous, for it would turn me half around to the right every time I fired it.

Game of all kinds, found in this part of the Rocky mountains, was abundant in Flint creek valley and we were in no danger of starving especially after I traded for that mighty tiger rifle. With it I provided plenty of lean antelope, and deer meat without a speck of fat on it. This with plenty of clear water out of the creek was all we had. Our principal object in coming over into the Deer Lodge country was to kill game and dry meat enough to last us to Fort Bridger and to do a little prospecting.

We had been told that Benetsee, a half-breed from the Red river of the North had found gold on Benetsee creek, about twelve miles from where we were camped.

On May 2, 1858, James Stuart, Reece Anderson, Thomas Adams, and myself packed up the tools we had, which was an old square pointed spade with the hand hold broken out of the top of the handle, that Adams had found in his wagon when he had bought it in Salt Lake, and a tin bread pan that we had brought with us from California and started for Benetsee creek on a prospecting trip.

We followed up the creek about five miles carefully searching for any prospect or evidences of prospecting but found nothing. Near the bank of the creek at the foot of the mountain we sunk a hole about five feet deep and found ten cents in fine gold to the pan of sand and gravel. This convinced us that there were rich gold mines in this vicinity, but as we had no tools or provisions we could not do much prospecting. This prospect hole dug by us was the first prospecting for gold done in what is now Montana and this is the account of the first real discovery of gold within the state.[31]

It was now almost sundown and we built a fire and cooked our supper and sat around the camp fire dis-

---

[31] Stuart wrote in 1864: "About the year 1852, a French half-breed from Red river of the north, named Francois Finlay, but commonly known by the sobriquet of 'Benetsee,' who had been to California, began to 'prospect' on a branch of the Hell Gate now known as Gold creek. He found small quantities of light float gold in the surface along this stream, but not in sufficient abundance to pay. This became noised about among the mountaineers; and when Reece Anderson, my brother James, and I, were delayed by sickness at the head of Malad creek, on the Hudspeths 'Cut-Off,' as we were on our way from California to the states in the summer of 1857, we saw some men who had passed 'Benetsee's creek,' as it was then called, in 1856, and they said they had good prospects there, and as we had an inclination to see a little mountain life, we concluded to go out to that region, and winter, and look around a little. We accordingly wintered on Big Hole, just above the 'Backbone,' in company with Robert Dempsey, Jake Meeks, and others; and in the spring of 1858, we went over to Deer Lodge and prospected a little on 'Benetsee's creek;' but not having any 'grub' or tools to work with, we soon quit in disgust, without having found anything that would pay, or done enough to enable us to form a reliable estimate of the richness of this vicinity." *Montana As It Is*, pp. 7-8.

About 1875 Stuart again wrote of his party and the reasons for going to the Deer Lodge valley: "They were actuated by a desire to investigate the reported finding of float gold by a Red river half-breed, named Benetsee, in the lower end of Deer Lodge, in 1852, and its subsequent discovery, in 1856, by a party on their way to Salt Lake, from the Bitter Root valley." *Montana Historical Society Contributions*, vol. i (Helena, Montana, 1876) p. 37.

In 1876 Stuart again wrote: "In 1852 a Scotch half-breed from the Red river of the north, named Francois Finlay, but who was known among his associates as 'Benetsee' and who had just returned from California to the Rocky mountains, began to prospect on what is now Gold creek, in Deer Lodge county and found light float gold but as his prospecting was necessarily of a superficial character he found no mines that would pay. The fact of gold being discovered there, however became noised about among the mountaineers still in the country, and in the spring of 1856, a party among whom were Robert Hereford, late of Helena, John Saunders called Long John, Bill Madison and one or two others who were passing Benetsee creek on their way to Salt Lake from the Bitter Root valley where they had spent the winter trading with the Indians, and prospecting a little found more gold than had been obtained by Finlay. One piece weighed about ten cents and they gave it to old Captain Grant, who used to show it, up to the time of his death in 1862 as the first piece of gold found in the country. Granville Stuart, A Historical Sketch of Deer Lodge County, Valley, and City, July

cussing the situation until dark. We decided to stick
to our original plan – kill and dry meat enough to last
us to Fort Bridger and then buy supplies and return
and prospect for mines.

4, 1876, *Montana Historical Society Contributions*, vol. ii (Helena, 1896)
p. 121.

Stuart wrote as a note to his Journals as follows: "Francois Finlay,
better known as 'Benetsee' perhaps did find a few colors of gold in Benetsee
creek, but his prospecting was of a very superficial nature and he was never
certain whether he had found gold or not. I first became acquainted with
him in November, 1860. I had located at a point where the Mullan road
crosses Gold creek; a village of Flathead Indians camped near me and
with them was Benetsee, who made himself known to me. Naturally our
conversation was about gold in Gold creek. I asked him if he had ever
dug a hole and he said 'No, I had nothing to dig with, and I never cared to
prospect.' I am certain that this was true, because although we prospected
on Gold creek and in all the gulches and streams leading into the creek, I
never found the slightest trace of holes being dug or of any prospecting
being done and the slightest disturbance of the sod would be noticed by
us at that time.

"So far as I ever knew Benetsee was not an Indian trader and he posi-
tively never located a ranch on Gold creek nor made any particular place
his habitation in that vicinity. In November, 1860, I built a log house at
Mullan road crossing of Gold creek and was the first person to build a
house and live on that stream, not a tree had ever been cut before that time,
and I found the least evidence that even a corral had ever been built anywhere on that stream. He lived with the Indians and, as the Indians, lived
by hunting. He roamed over the Flathead country as did the Flatheads,
going out to the plains to hunt buffalo and returning, after the hunt, with the
Indians. I saw him occasionally so long as I lived on Gold creek, but when
I left there in 1863 I lost track of him."

Benetsee has a most loyal partisan in Duncan MacDonald of Dixon,
Montana, the son of Angus MacDonald who completed Fort Connah in 1847
for the Hudson's Bay Company and remained in charge for many years.
In 1916 he submitted a strong statement for Finlay which was quoted in an
article by Paul C. Phillips and H. A. Trexler, Note on the Discovery of
Gold in the Northwest in *Mississippi Valley Historical Review*, vol. ix, pp.
92, 93.

May 5, 1924, he wrote the editor another letter in which he says in part:
"As I have stated before about Benetsee Finlay which no one disputes in his
finding gold on a creek named after him in the early days long before Mr.
Stuart ever put his foot on the ground . . . Sand Bar Brown yelled like
hell if Finlay did find gold, why did he not work the gravel? A child, a
babe, knows better. That Finlay was a British subject and had an Indian,
a Salish Flathead wife. That under no circumstances that he could locate

The Blackfoot Indians were becoming very trouble-some and horse stealing parties lurked about every-where. We selected a dense patch of willows near the creek and as soon as it became quite dark so that we

a claim and was further advised by the H. B. Co. to never mention gold for fear their fur business would be ruined, which is true. How did Stuart or why did he turn from his winter quarters north in the spring? . . . It was at his camping quarters towards spring that a gentleman from Fort Owen enlightened him that a talk about gold being discovered by Finlay at the creek in question. Instead of proceeding for his home, started for the place mentioned and found the gold, but Finlay found it years before. . . Angus McDonald sent seventeen pounds gold dust to Victoria for the H. B. Co. obtained from the Pend' Oreille mines where the Clark fork runs into the Columbia. . . Now Pend' Oreille mines was very rich and mined for years. This was found by little Joe Morelle a teamster under Angus MacDonald . . . Antoine Plant was one of the men with Finlay in California; when he returned Finlay told him. He has an Indian wife and a member of the tribe could not locate. . . And I ask again why did Stuart start for that particular creek when he was to start direct for his home? No, he did not start for Iowa but turned north made a straight line for as we call Benetsee creek and when he arrived with others and sure enough there was gold in the gravel but he never noticed any holes dug by Benetsee Finlay. That is a rather weak excuse any man who has experience regarding Montana streams knows that holes would be covered by first high water."

In the *Fort Owen Journals* for Feb. 15, 1852, there is this entry: "Gold Hunting found some." Charles S. Warren, The Territory of Montana in *Montana Historical Society Contributions*, vol. ii, p. 63, states: "In the spring of 1852 Samuel M. Caldwell discovered gold on what was then known as Mill creek, nearly opposite Fort Owen, west [east] of the Bitter Root river."

Lieutenant James H. Bradley in a letter to the *Helena Herald* of September 1, 1875, claimed the honor of first discovery for John W. Silverthorne who, he claimed brought about $1500 worth of gold to Fort Benton in 1856. Letter quoted in Leeson, *Montana*, pp. 210, 211. Another pioneer, Matthew Carroll, of good reputation for honesty claimed he knew Silverthorne well and that the gold brought to Fort Benton came from mines in the Kootenai country in Canada.

The claims for the discovery of gold by Father De Smet and by Lieutenant John Mullan rest on no definite evidence and other claims are nothing more than rumors.

The evidence would seem to indicate that Finlay found gold in Gold creek about 1852 and traded it at Fort Connah where he was cautioned not to spread any report of his discovery. While the Stuarts were encamped at Malad creek some one from the Deer Lodge country reported to them the prospects for gold in this region. Led by this hope they turned north could not be seen, we extinguished our fire and quietly led our horses into the center of the willows. Here each one selected the softest spot he could find, rolled up in his blanket and went to sleep leaving one man, gun in hand to keep watch over the horses and ourselves. The guard was relieved every two hours.

(see page 136) and discovered gold as described in the text. Finlay probably found the gold first but it was left to the Stuarts and their companions to spread the news. – ED.

Trading Experiences

Our horses were all in good condition; we had a supply of moose meat dried and on June 16, 1858, Reece Anderson, Ross, James Stuart, and myself packed up and started for Fort Bridger, intending to sell most of our horses (we had about twenty-five in all) purchase supplies and return. Adams remained on Flint creek with a small herd of cattle that he had taken from John Grant on shares. We were all well armed; James, Reece, and I each had rifles and Colt revolvers, and plenty of ammunition, Ross had a revolver.

We traveled up the south side of the Hell Gate river to where the town of Deer Lodge now is; then on the west side of Deer Lodge river past Warm springs; finding the river fordable we crossed and went through the gap known as "The Hump;" then recrossed the stream below Silver Bow and then went south through Deer Lodge pass, over the summit of the Rocky mountains and down Divide creek to Moose creek hill, which we crossed and struck the Big Hole river near where Melrose now is.[32] The river was very high; out of its banks over the low bottom and running ten miles an hour, frightful to look at and yet we must cross it.

A short distance below, where the Oregon Short Line railway bridge now spans the river, we found a few dead cottonwood trees. We cut these down and then cut them into twelve foot lengths. Finding a little

[32] This was the route of the old Northwest Company and Hudson's Bay Company fur traders. Major Owen crossed this pass in 1852. *Journal of John Work, opus citra*, pp. 100-101. – ED.

eddy and putting our logs in we lashed them together and made a raft. We tested it by all standing on it and found it would likely carry us and what little baggage we had.

We hewed out four good strong paddles and cut and piled a lot of brush on the middle of the raft. On this we put our clothes, keeping nothing but our shirts on ourselves. With our clothes we put our dried meat, two rifles and two revolvers and ammunition for them. Then we lashed all fast to the raft so that, if it wrecked, our things could not wash off and be lost. We could swim and push the raft to shore some place below.

We then saddled our horses putting half our blankets on them under the saddles and each man tied what clothes he had left to the saddle. We also tied one rifle and one revolver with ammuntion to the saddles. This was done so in case we lost the raft we would still have some blankets, a few clothes, and guns and ammunition. If dire necessity forced us to it we could kill a horse and dry the meat and we would not starve.

Having hedged in every possible manner against disaster, we each armed ourselves with a long slender willow pole and gathering the horses to a place where the bank sloped gradually into the water, we made a sudden rush upon them and with our poles we beat the poor things into the river. Some of them had swam rivers before and they at once struck out for the other shore and the others followed them. Great was our relief when we saw them ascend the bank after being carried down stream over one hundred yards by the swift current, and this, too, when the river was but a little over one hundred yards wide.

We then seized our paddles and seating ourselves two on the front end and two on the rear end of the raft we pushed out from the shore and paddled with all our might. The raft was a good one and did not overflow, but in spite of our efforts we drifted rapidly down stream and reached the other shore about fifty yards below where our horses landed. As we struck the bank we grasped some willows that stood in the edge of the water with one hand and hung to the raft with the other; the sudden stopping threw us down and the water rushed over us giving us a good soaking but our baggage on the brush remained dry. We hastily unloaded the raft, two holding it against the bank while the others carried our things on shore. Taking the ropes from the logs, that had served us so well, we regretfully saw them one by one float away.

We gathered our horses together, untied our clothes and weapons from the saddles, wrung the water out of them and spread them on the bushes to dry. We prepared a meal of dried moose meat, by cutting it into small bits and boiling it in our only kitchen utensil, a large frying pan, until it softened somewhat, then adding a little tallow, and frying it awhile so that we could chew it. After dark we saddled up and rode six miles to Birch creek. There selecting a place where there was good grass, we camped. Without any noise we picketed our horses and leaving one man at a time on guard, the others slept until dawn, when we arose, picketed our horses on fresh grass, prepared breakfast, like our supper; devoured it, saddled and packed up and lit out at a fast gait, for we expected to travel about fifty miles a day.

We reached the Beaverhead river at the mouth of Blacktail Deer creek where we had spent part of last winter. It too, was very high, but we searched until we found a place where we thought we could ford it.

Fearing it might be deep we held our most precious things in our arms and plunged in. Sure enough as we neared the farther bank the horses had to swim for about thirty feet. As usual we camped just before sundown and let our horses graze and cooked supper, and as soon as it was dark saddled up and went several miles up Blacktail Deer creek and silently made our all night camp.

Next day we passed Sage creek to Red Rock creek, then up Junction creek past the timbered butte and on over the Rocky mountains divide where is now Monida and camped in a pouring rain under some big fir trees just beyond Pleasant valley. The trees gave some shelter, but soon the water ran down the sloping ground and under our beds thoroughly saturating us. This was certainly a disagreeable night and we were glad when dawn came. We crawled out of our watery beds and finding some pieces of pitch wood in an old partially burned tree and lots of dry limbs we soon had a big fire and stood around it drying our dripping clothes and warming our benumbed bodies.

The sun rose in a clear sky and we were soon warm and dry. We saddled up and struck the trail. When we reached Camas creek, which had been a beautiful little clear stream flowing through the sagebrush, when we were there the preceding October, we found it out of its banks and about forty yards wide. We knew the channel must be deep but we had to cross it. Putting our saddles on the best swimmers among our horses we mounted and spurred them into the water, and away we went across that stream.

Our next stop was at Market lake so named because in the fall there were many wild water fowls here and the old trappers were always sure of fresh meat. They called going to the lake, "going to market" hence the name, "Market lake." This lake is fed from some under-ground cracks in the lava beds.

About two miles beyond Market lake is Snake river and at this time of year was at flood water. It was four times as large as the Big Hole river and was clear out of its banks, overflowing all the low ground on both sides and clear out into the sagebrush. At this place there was no timber to make a raft and there was no place where we could ford it, so we rode along down the bank looking for some opportunity to cross. A few miles further down there was a place where this large river turned up on edge and rushed through a crack in the solid lava about forty feet wide with another crack about twenty feet wide on the east side of the large one, forming a small island of hard lava about twenty feet wide and a hundred feet long. The water in these two cracks must have been a hundred feet deep and it went through them with such velocity as to make us poor devils giddy to look at it. Following on down the stream we finally spied some dead cottonwood timber in a little bend. The little bottom was all overflowed but we camped, stripped down to our shirts and waded out into the icy water to those dry trees. It was a close call to get them for while cutting them down we stood in the swift water to our hips, but we just had to have those logs. Even the old dry moose meat was getting low and we had exhausted our supply of tallow. We had not seen so much as a jack rabbit on the trip and there was no possibility of game between Snake river and Fort Bridger. As fast as we cut down a tree it was floated out to shore and when we had enough we towed them into a little eddy and constructed the raft. Then dividing our belongings as we did at the Big Hole river, we proceeded to make the crossing.

Our horses made most strenuous objections to taking the water. It looked quite as bad to them as it did to us and we had to use energetic measures to get them started into the turbid flood. They were swept down the river almost a quarter of a mile and landed on a small island, covered with a thick growth of willows, near the far shore. Now we were up against the necessity of making a landing on that island to drive the horses off.

The raft was all ready and we pushed off. When she struck the strong current, the water rushed over her about six inches deep and our hearts almost rose into our throats for we feared our raft was overloaded, but we paddled with all our strength and in a few seconds it rose and floated high in the water. Paddle as hard as we could we were drifting down stream very rapidly and it looked as though we would miss that island, but we managed to grab a bunch of over-hanging willows as we were being swept past the lower point of land, and although it almost jerked our arms off we succeeded in making the landing. Driving the horses off we returned to the raft: It was only about forty yards to the shore and we had no trouble in getting across.

At this place Ross discovered a raven's nest in a cottonwood tree a short distance from camp. He declared his intention of having fresh meat and, as the moose meat was about as dry and hard as flint and getting very scarce at that, almost anything in the way of food was tempting. Climbing the tree, in spite of the protests of the old ravens, he threw down four half grown birds, just one a piece he said, and in a short time he and Reece had them dressed and roasting before the fire. There was a peculiar flavor and smell about the flesh that soon sent James and me back to our dried meat, but Ross and Anderson picked the bones of all four and rose chuckling saying: "Such nice young fowls would not go to waste around us."

From this place we traveled down the river to near Old Fort Hall where we struck the Emigrant road leading to Oregon and California.

At Soda springs on Bear river we drank our fill of soda water from a spring on the bank, just above the river water. One can make excellent soda biscuits from this water, but at this time we had no flour.

We crossed Tommaws fork, a mean sluggish stream, on a bridge built by the emigrants. It was a pleasure to cross on a bridge, as we had had enough of constructing rafts.

We reached Fort Bridger on the evening of June 28, 1858, having eaten the last of our dried meat eight hours before. We had traveled six hundred miles in twelve days without encountering Indians or seeing any game.

We remained two weeks at Fort Bridger where we found several of those who had wintered in the Beaverhead valley where we had become acquainted with them. They treated us very hospitably and we enjoyed our stay. We then went to Camp Floyd where we remained about two weeks selling our horses to the soldiers and camp followers.

This fort reminded us strongly of the good old days in California. Money, all in twenty, ten, and five dollar gold pieces, was plentiful, and the way everybody drank, gambled, and scattered it around was almost equal to the days of forty-nine. A host of gamblers had congregated there and many of them were at the top of their profession. When the outsiders were "busted" they preyed upon one another and it was amazing to see the way they stacked up their coin on their favorite card. I saw them win and lose five thousand dollars on the turn of a single monte card.

We were unable to get mining supplies at Camp Floyd and we discovered that there was considerable money to be made by trading with the emigrants on the road to and from California and Oregon and thought best to try to increase our capital somewhat before returning to mining.

Reece Anderson and Ross purchased some supplies for the Indian trade, and went north to the Flathead country. We never again saw poor Ross. He was drowned in June, 1860, while attempting to drive a band of horses across Bear river, when the water was very high.

The latter part of July, 1858, James and I went to Green river, east of Fort Bridger and began buying and trading for poor and tired out oxen and horses, with the army supply trains and with the emigrants. On the long journey across the plains many of the horses and oxen became footsore and tired out and unable to travel. In this condition, they were a burden to the train. We would trade for, or purchase such stock for a very small sum and after caring for them and resting them up for a month or two, they were fit as ever and could then be disposed of for a good price.

Here I met Jim Baker, one of the trappers well known from the borders of Mexico to the British line. He was six feet, one inch high, and weighed two hundred pounds, a perfect blonde with large blue eyes. He remined me of pictures of the old Vikings who sailed the north sea. Jim was much too good natured to make a real genuine pirate. It made me sad to see him ruining himself drinking whiskey.

Robert Dempsey and his man, "Friday" Jackson, were there. They both kept saturated and, when in this state, Dempsey was said to be the best trader on the Emigrant road. He certainly had a faculty of sizing up the possibilities in a lame or jaded ox or horse and never paid too much for such an animal.

In October, 1858, we moved from the Emigrant crossing of Green river to Henry's fork, a distance of fifty miles. Here we remained until April, 1859. Near us was a French Canadian, named Marjeau, who had brought a lot of groceries and some trinkets for the Indian trade, in a big wagon with four yoke of oxen all the way from Council Bluffs. Dempsey and Jackson also came over here and camped near by, and later another French Canadian moved in with a stock of goods for the Indian trade. The winter was very mild with no snow, and bright sunny days. There was no game in the country and consequently there were no Indians.

Marjeau later moved down Green river to Brown's Hole, some thirty-five miles and there struck a village of Ute Indians and had a good trade, although the Utes were of a mean insolent character and difficult to trade with.

Hearing these Canadians speak French, put me in the notion of trying to learn the language, but only being with them occasionally I made little progress. It was my custom to make weekly trips, ten miles west, to Fort Bridger to get our mail. There I became acquainted with another French man named Ely Dufour, who finding that I was trying to learn French, presented me with a pocket dictionary of French and English, which I still have, in a somewhat damaged condition from frequent pressures of the lash rope on our pack horses.

In April we moved from Henry's fork to the mouth of Ham's fork, where we remained a month. Here I saw the first of the Pony Express riders. This rider did not stop to make any acquaintances, but came tearing up the road to the station, dismounted, threw his saddle on a fresh horse and was away again before I realized what had taken place.

The Pony Express was established by W. H. Russell of the firm of Russell, Majors, and Waddell, in 1860. The first trip was started April fourth. The route was from St. Joseph, Missouri, to Sacramento, California, a distance of nineteen hundred and fifty miles, through an uninhabited country infested with road agents and hostile Indians. There were relay stations along the route, where two minutes were allowed to change horses and mail. Each rider covered a distance of from sixty-five to one hundred miles, according to the character of the country. The dispatches were written on tissue paper, no rider carrying more than ten pounds. The horses used were California mustangs, noted for their sure footedness, speed, and endurance. The cost of delivering these dispatches was five dollars in gold for every half ounce. Although this seems to us at this day an exorbitant price, yet it did not cover one-tenth of the expense of maintenance to say nothing of the investment.

The time in which to make this trip was ten days and the wages paid the riders was one hundred and twenty-five dollars a month. As a tribute to the courage and fidelity of these riders be it said that never once during the two years that the Pony Express was in existence, did a dispatch reach its destination behind the schedule. The inaugural address of President Lincoln, March 4, 1861, was carried through in seven days and seventeen hours. Through rain and snow, across rivers, deserts, and mountain ranges, in the darkest nights, pursued by Indians, or robbers; often reaching a station wounded and dying; often finding their relief murdered, the station burned and horses driven off, nothing daunted, they kept right on until they delivered the goods and it never occurred to one of them that any obstacle, no matter what it was, was great enough to delay them one minute. I want to say right here that for nerve, courage, and fidelity, there never was a body of men that excelled the Pony Express riders.[33]

While camped here a mule train of sixteen wagons loaded with freight for Salt Lake City camped a short distance above us on the stream. In a few minutes we heard a shot fired and as there seemed to be some excitement we walked up to the wagons, and were shocked to see one of the drivers lying on the ground, shot through the heart. The wagon boss had gotten drunk at Green river, about fifteen miles back, was cussing the driver about some trifle, the driver had talked back and the "boss" who was J. A. Slade,[34] drew his revolver and shot the man dead. Later the teamsters dug a grave by the roadside, wrapped the dead man in his blankets and buried him. The train went on to Salt Lake and nothing was done about the murder.

[33] For a brief account of the pony express see Frederick L. Paxson, *Last American Frontier* (1910) pp. 182-185. – ED.

[34] For account of Slade see Dimsdale, *opus citra* (1913) pp. 143-151 and Langford *opus citra*, vol. ii, pp. 288-321. – ED.

Late in the summer we were joined by Reece Anderson, who brought twenty horses from the Flathead country, as Bitter Root valley was then called.

While here a tragic incident occurred that made me so mad that it was with great difficulty I kept from inflicting summary vengeance on two of the parties. Near by us was camped a man with a wife and five small children and a hanger-on friend of theirs. There came along a disreputable looking man with a five gallon keg of whiskey and camped with them. The three men at once proceeded to get drunk.

A few days prior to this time there came to our lodge a young man apparently about twenty years of age. He was on foot carrying a pair of blankets and a change of underwear. He was making his way to California and asked to stay with us until he could join some passing emigrant trains. We, of course, bade him welcome.

One day he told me that the drunken men, who were then nearing delirium tremens had threatened to kill him. I asked him what the trouble was and he said he did not know. I told him to keep away from them and gave him my Colt's navy revolver, telling him that if they came over to our camp after him to defend himself.

James, Reece and I went out to look after our stock and when returning, and about two hundred yards from our lodge, we heard three shots in rapid succession and saw the young man run out and fall close by. The three drunken men also came out, one of them limping, and went to their camp. When we reached the fallen man he was dead. We were furious, Reece and I were for going over and having it out with them, but James reasoned that we did not know who fired the fatal shot and that if we went over there while they were in their present condition we would likely have to kill them all and that we could not do on account of the women and little children. There was no civil law so James's council prevailed and we wrapped the unfortunate young man in his blankets and buried him beneath the cottonwood tree on which I would have liked to hang his murderers.

In October, 1859, we again moved over to Henry's fork of Green river with our horses and cattle and wintered near our former camp. There was very little snow and scarcely any cold weather; our stock came out fat in the spring, without having any shelter, excepting the willows along the streams, and nothing to eat, but bunch grass.

In April, 1860, we took our stock, and with our baggage loaded in a large wagon drawn by three yoke of oxen, started for Salt river valley, a branch of Snake river, and spent the summer there trading with the emigrants. This is the most beautiful spot that I have ever seen. In 1860 the bunch grass all over the valley waved in the wind like a field of grain. The creek in the center of the valley, bordered by a heavy growth of willows was clear as glass and icy cold, the home of many beautiful mountain trout.

In September, 1860, we raised camp and started for the Beaverhead valley, where we intended to winter and then in the spring to cross over to Benetsee creek and do some more prospecting for gold.

At the lower end of Salt river valley we found a little flat of some three or four acres that was as white as snow although the grass was green and beautiful all around. We camped near by and went to examine this white spot and found it to be a layer of pure white salt about four inches thick which had been deposited by a spring flowing from the side of a low bench about fifteen feet high. The spring furnished a stream of water, about four inches wide and two inches deep, of the strongest brine. This ran down into the little flat and covered it with salt as above described. We scraped up enough to fill a two bushel sack and took it with us. Later when the gold mines brought a rush of people to Montana and Idaho a company from Salt Lake established salt works there and supplied all this section with the finest quality of salt and from 1864 to the present time have paid dividends that far exceed those of any of the gold mines that we were interested in.

We traveled slowly allowing our horses and cattle plenty of time to graze. Snake river was now a clear beautiful stream, and we found a shallow place and forded it. We returned to Beaverhead by the same route that we had traveled before.

After we crossed the divide by way of Lodge Pole pass we found plenty of game and killed fat antelope whenever needed. On the Beaverhead river at the mouth of the "Pak-sam-ma-oi," [35] which in the Indian language means cottonwood grove, we established our winter camp. There game was abundant, the grass good, and the willows along the streams furnished shelter for our cattle and horses. We were soon joined by a middle aged trapper named Louis Simmons and a young Snake Indian boy named Tabbabo. This boy we employed as a horse herder, and he proved to be a good and faithful one.

[35] According to Mr. John E. Rees, an old Indian trader well acquainted with Indian tongues, this word should be Pah-mamar-roi, meaning literally "cottonwood grove by a water." Mr. Rees thinks that Robert Dempsey gave the stream this name. It was originally called Stinkingwater, and now appears on the map as Passamari. – ED.

By trading we had acquired a considerable number of beaver skins and other furs and as we needed powder and lead and percussion caps for our own use and some clothing and blankets and various other articles for trading with the Indians, Reece and I saddled up our horses and putting our furs and some bedding on pack horses, we started for a Hudson's Bay trading post on Crow creek not far from St. Ignatius Mission,[36] a little horseback ride of four hundred sixty miles altogether to do a little shopping.

We made the trip all right, but were greatly surprised to meet, on our return, James, Simmons, and Tabbabo, with all our stock at Camp creek, on the Big Hole river, moving to Deer Lodge valley. They told us that soon after we had left a large camp of Bannock Indians came into the valley and soon began to show an insolent semi-hostile disposition, and game being scarce, they killed one of our cattle. So to avoid serious trouble James packed up and started for Deer Lodge. We held a consultation and decided to go on to Gold creek and locate and work our gold prospect of 1858.

This insolent band of Indians was under a chief named Ar-ro-ka-kee, who was six feet, two inches tall and weighed two hundred and seventy-five pounds. Captain Grant and his retainers called him, "LeGran Coquin," which in French means "The Big Rogue," and our experience with him convinced us that they had rightly named him.

It was thought best that I should at once hasten on to Gold creek and locate a claim. I saddled up for a ride of sixty miles more, and putting a little food and bed-

---

[36] Fort Connah on Post creek or Crow creek. Built by Angus McDonald in 1847. One building of this fort still stands. – ED.

ding and our elk skin lodge on a pack horse, started, accompanied by Simmons and the young Indian.

At Cottonwood creek was camped Thomas Lavatta, Joseph Hill, and some others. Louis Simmons and Tabbabo remained there. I went down to Gold creek and begun cutting poles for a corral. Four days later Anderson and James arrived with the ox team, horses and cattle.

Settlement of Deer Lodge Valley

The winter of 1860 was more severe than either of the three preceding ones that we had spent in the Rocky mountains. Our cattle and horses were in good condition in the spring although they had no food except the native bunch grass which grows from twelve to thirteen inches high everywhere. They had no shelter except the willows along the streams and in some of the ravines. We spent the winter very pleasantly. Antelope, deer, and mountain sheep, were available most of the time, and although usually thin in flesh, the meat was good, for we had plenty of good army bacon to fry it with. We occasionally had visitors, as people passed coming from Fort Owen, in the Bitter Root valley, and from Hell Gate, three miles below where Missoula now is, and going on up to John Grant's at the mouth of Little Blackfoot creek, and sometimes on up to the little settlement on Cottonwood creek, where is now the beautiful town of Deer Lodge.

After a week or two they would come back on their return home and everybody always stopped over night with us and if it stormed they often stayed two or three days, and were hospitably entertained. In those days, nobody ever charged traveling visitors a cent for food and lodging, and this also extended to any scattering Indians that came along, but of course, we did not feed the villages of combined Nez Percés, Yakimas, Coeur d'Alenes, and Flatheads that passed every fall on their way to the plains of the Missouri and Yellowstone to

spend the winter hunting buffalo. Those Indians did
not hang around and beg, but had considerable self respect, and we usually asked the chiefs to dine with us
when passing. We kept a small assortment of Indian
trading goods and when passing they would buy what
they needed. The Nez Percés often had money to pay
for what they purchased, but the others seldom had
any. If they did possess any and were asked where
they got it the answer was, "We won it gambling with
the Nez Percés."

We never refused any of these Indians credit for the
few things they wanted, such as calico, red cloth for the
ladies' leggings, calico shirts, vermillion paint, beads,
knives, handkerchiefs, powder, lead, percussion caps,
combs, and sometimes blankets. To their honor be it
said, they always paid when they passed on their return
from the buffalo range. We never lost a dollar through
crediting them, for even if the purchaser was dead, or
sick, the wife or husband or some relative, as the case
might be, came and paid us in buffalo robes, dried
meat, dried tongues, skins or something they had. If
a white man came to an Indian's camp he was always
welcome to the best he had without money.

In the fall of 1860, Frank L. Worden and Captain
C. P. Higgins came up from Fort Walla Walla with a
pack train of cayuse horses, loaded with a small stock
of merchandise, and located on the north bank of the
Hell Gate river, three miles below where is now the
town of Missoula. Here they built a log store and a
log cabin and named the place Hell Gate. They also
brought up some garden seeds, and we determined to
plant a garden and raise some vegetables as we had not
had any for almost four years except for a short time
while at Camp Floyd, south of Great Salt Lake City.

John Owen had among other things bought a plow at Fort Benton in the summer of 1860.[37] While camped on Greenhorn gulch just east of the summit of the Rocky mountains, the Blackfoot Indians stampeded the pack animals and got away with a number of the horses. This left them so short of pack animals that they left the plow there and we, hearing about it, bought it from Owen. We were mighty anxious to get at that garden, so early in April a young man by the name of John Seeber and I took a pack horse and went for the plow. We packed it with the greatest difficulty and in due time we arrived home.

We selected a place down in the damp river bottom and plowed up a piece of ground. After putting it in condition, we planted our seeds, expecting great things from this garden, but alas! our hopes in this direction were blasted. Frost visited this low land every month in the year, and no sooner did a vegetable poke its nose out of the ground than it was immediately frozen. Had we selected a spot on the bench east of the house, we could have watered it out of Gold creek and had a beautiful garden free from frost. As it was, we had nothing to speak of.

James and I were both great readers and we had been all winter without so much as an almanac to look at. We were famished for something to read when some Indians coming from the Bitter Root told us that a white man had come up from below, with a trunk full of books, and was camped with all that wealth, in Bitter

---

[37] Major John Owen had come to the Bitter Root in 1850 as an Indian trader. He purchased St. Mary's mission of the Jesuits and built a fort there which he named Fort Owen. Major Owen carried on extensive farming operations and built a sawmill and a grist mill. He also acted as Indian agent. Frank H. Woody, Sketch of the Early History of Western Montana written in 1876 in *Montana Historical Society Contributions*, 1896, vol. ii, pp. 91-92. *Fort Owen Journal.* – Ed.

Root valley. On receipt of these glad tidings, we saddled our horses and putting our blankets, and some dried meat for food, on a pack horse, we started for those books, a hundred and fifty miles away, without a house, or anybody on the route, and with three big dangerous rivers to cross, the Big Blackfoot, the Hell Gate, and the Bitter Root. As the spring rise had not yet begun, by careful searching we found fords on these rivers, but they were dangerous, and at times we were almost swept away. Arriving in the Bitter Root valley we learned that the man who brought the books had gone back to the lower country, but he had left the precious trunk in charge of a man named Henry Brooks, whom we finally found living in a tepee, at a point on Sweathouse creek, near where the town of Victor now stands. We gradually and diplomatically approached the subject of books, and "our hearts were on the ground" when Brooks told us that Neil Mc-Arthur,[38] a Hudson's Bay Company trader, who left the books in his care, told him to keep them until he re-

---

[38] Henry Brooks came into the Bitter Root in 1855. He was the first justice of the peace of Missoula county. Woody, *opus citra*, pp. 93, 103. Neil McArthur had started, in 1846, the construction of the post on Crow creek which Angus MacDonald finished and named Fort Connah. After retiring from the Hudson's Bay Company employ, in 1856, McArthur came into the Bitter Root and later built a trading post at Hell Gate. *Ibid.*, p. 97.

McArthur and Louis R. Maillet became partners and they also established a trading post at Fort Colville. The business apparently prospered. In 1858 Maillet went on a trip to the "states and Canada to visit his family." During his absence of some two years he had no news from McArthur. On his return he found McArthur gone and with him their herd of stock. Apparently McArthur had gone to Fraser river. Maillet declared that the property when last valued by the two partners had amounted to $150,000, but Maillet now learned that his partner's bad management, debts, and numerous undertakings had lost everything. The last he ever heard of McArthur was a letter from him, in which he said that he was broke, had a bad horse, and was prospecting "so farewell." W. F. Wheeler, Historical Sketch of Louis R. Maillet in *Montana Historical Society Contributions*, vol. iv (Helena, 1903) p. 217. This sketch was written in part by Maillet and dictated in part to Mr. Wheeler. – ED.

turned.   He gave him no authority to sell any of them. We told him how long we had been without anything to read, and how we had ridden many days, seeking that trunk, and that we would take all the blame and would make good with McArthur when he returned. At last we won him over, and he agreed to let us have five books, for five dollars each, and if McArthur was not satisfied we were to pay him more.

How we feasted our eyes on those books.   We could hardly make up our minds which ones to choose, but we finally settled upon Shakespeare and Byron, both fine illustrated editions, Headley's *Napoleon and his Marshals*, a Bible in French, and Adam Smith's *Wealth of Nations*.   After paying for them we had just twenty-five dollars left, but then we had the blessed books, which we packed carefully in our blankets, and joyfully started on our return ride of a hundred and fifty miles.   Many were the happy hours we spent reading those books, and I have them yet, all except the *Wealth of Nations*, which being loose in the binding, has gradually disappeared, until only a few fragments remain.   McArthur never returned to the Bitter Root valley, and I do not know what became of the rest of the books, but I hope they gave as much pleasure to some others, as did the five to Brother James and myself.

In the summer of 1860, a mining enthusiast by the name of Henry Thomas (but who as his peculiarities became known I designated "Gold Tom," by which name he ever after went) came up from below by way of Pend d'Orielle lake and begun to prospect on Benetsee creek about one mile west of where the mining town of Pioneer now stands.   Some Frenchman told him where the creek was.

He started out to find the prospect hole that we had dug in 1858, when we made the discovery of gold. He had no difficulty in finding the place and began prospecting and got the same prospects that we did, ten cents to the pan of gravel. The place was full of enormous granite boulders and he saw at once that he could not dig there. He went out on the side of the creek some twenty-five or thirty yards from where we had sunk this hole and entirely unaided sunk a shaft twenty feet deep in the glacial detritus along the creek, getting a little gold all the way down.

He made a primitive windlass, and hewed out and pinned together with wooden pins and bound around with a picket rope, a bucket with which he hoisted the dirt while sinking the shaft. He would slide down the rope, fill the bucket with gravel, then climb up a notched pole aided by the windlass rope, and hoist the bucket of gravel. He encountered many boulders too large to go into the bucket. Around these he would put a rope and windlass them out. After we located at the crossing of Gold creek, I visited him several times and was amazed to see the amount of work he had done under exceedingly difficult conditions. He also hewed out boards eight inches wide and about seven feet long and made four little sluice boxes. He had no nails, but put them together with wooden pegs. He placed them near his shaft and then dug a ditch from the creek around to the sluice boxes, where he washed the gravel from his shaft and some of the surface dirt. He worked the summers of 1860 and 1861, but could not make more than one dollar and fifty cents a day and often less than that sum, owing to the great disadvantage under which he labored.

When I visited Gold creek in 1876, his windlass and

MISSOULA IN 1865 (LOOKING NORTH)
The settlement was then only a year old and was made up mostly of
former residents of Hell Gate
From an original pencil drawing made by Granville Stuart, December
25, 1865. [On the drawing is noted "sketched in twelve inches of
snow, thermometer 34° below zero"]

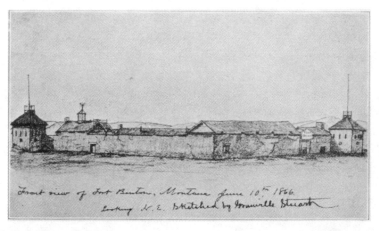

FRONT VIEW OF FORT BENTON, MONTANA (LOOKING NORTHEAST)
Fort Benton was the last great post of the American Fur Company in
Montana. It was at the head of steamboat navigation on the Missouri,
and the eastern terminus of the Mullan Road
From an original sketch made by Granville Stuart, June 10, 1866

four little sluice boxes hewed out with an axe pinned together with wooden pins were still there, but fast falling to decay. Alas! Poor Tom, I lost sight of him in 1864-5 and often wondered if he fell a victim to the *ignius fatus* [ignis fatuus] of Coeur d'Alene, Peace river, Stinkene, Cassiar, White Pine, Pioche, or Yellowstone, and last but not least the Black hills. Wherever he may be, may fortune smile upon him with a broader grin than fell to the lot of the pioneers at Gold creek in 1860-1-2.

He usually preferred to be alone, and would spend days and weeks in the mountains without other companions than his horses and trusty rifle. He was not at all misanthropic, and I never knew him to drink whiskey or to gamble.

As a pen picture of the life we led in Missoula county, Washington Territory,[39] which included all on the west side of the Rocky mountains of the present state of Montana, fifty years ago, I now copy from a daily journal kept by my brother James and myself alternately.

MAY 1, 1861. Finished sowing wheat and oats by two o'clock in the afternoon, will harrow them the last time tomorrow. Killed three large wolves last night with strychnine and probably more if they could be found. We went prospecting in the afternoon. Found tolerable good prospects. There is gold in all the ravines that we have tried. Weather warm and pleasant, strong west wind in the afternoon. Cloudy at dark.

---

[39] Missoula county was first organized by the legislature of Washington Territory, December 14, 1860. Its northern boundary was Canada, its eastern the main ridge of the Rockies, its southern the forty-sixth parallel and its western the one hundred-fifteenth meridian. Woody, *opus citra*, p. 99. – ED.

MAY 2. Finished harrowing the wheat and oats by twelve o'clock. Forenoon, weather calm and warm, but last night froze ice a quarter of an inch thick. In afternoon made hoe and axe handles. Green flies have been about to take possession of the ranch for the last week and some few mosquitoes. Antelope are tolerable plenty. Just now we have more meat than we can use before it spoils. Wish we had a barrel so we could salt some of it down. This had been the warmest day we have had this spring.

MAY 3. Morning calm and cloudy until about eleven o'clock when there was a shower of rain accompanied with a strong west wind. Planted some peas, onions, cabbage, and radishes. Afternoon planted some potatoes. Occasional showers of rain, and wind moderate.

MAY 6. Planted some corn in the forenoon. After dinner Granville went to Dempsey's camp six miles down the river, to try to get some beet seed, and gathered up the cattle as he came back.

MAY 7. Cold strong west wind, with occasional snow squalls, too cold to work. Caught a lovely trout that weighed four pounds, and Oh! but it tasted good, when nicely fried.

MAY 8. Chilly east wind this morning until ten o'clock. Froze ice one-half inch thick last night. In afternoon west wind with showers of rain and hail. Worked some today getting out timber for fence. Had a visitor. A Blackfoot Indian on his way from the Flathead country. Gave him his dinner and sent him on his way. Doubtless he will stay all night at Johnny Grant's at the mouth of Little Blackfoot creek, eight miles up the river and try to eat enough to do him to

Sun river, for there is no one living this side of there. Our settlement is now known as American Fork. Johnnie Grant's at the mouth of Little Blackfoot is Grantsville and the one above on Cottonwood creek is Cottonwood.[40] We are becoming somewhat civilized as we remain long enough in one spot to give it a name.

MAY 12. Worked on fence because we must get it done soon or cattle and horses will destroy our little crop. Froze ice a quarter of an inch thick last night. Light wind from the east in the morning and from the west the greater part of the day. Not so cold as it has been for several days past. F. H. Burr and Doctor Atkinson arrived today from the Missouri side of the mountains. They had bad stormy weather on the trip and say that vegetation is not as forward over there as it is on this side of the mountains.

MAY 15. Gathered up the cattle. Froze a little ice last night. Today east wind in the afternoon, with a little rain. Forenoon warm and pleasant. John F. Grant passed on his way home to mouth of Little Blackfoot creek, from Hell Gate where he visited with his father, Captain Richard Grant. With John, was Joe Piou, and an American with twenty gallons of whiskey on their way to trade with the Blackfoot Indians. They say that the Big Blackfoot and Hell Gate rivers are as low as they were in the winter. They have not commenced to rise because of the cold late spring.

MAY 17. Late yesterday evening John W. Powell and two other sports came here for a game of poker and we played all night. Powell lost $97.50, and one of the others lost $65.00. The other one and I were

---

40 Later Deer Lodge. – ED.

the winners.   Occasional showers last night and in the
forenoon.   Afternoon cloudy, east and north wind all
day.   J. S.

MAY 18.   Granville built a corral.   I went hunting
and killed one black-tailed deer, and three elk, all very
poor.   Only brought the meat of one elk home with
me.   I killed them with a Maynard breech-loading
rifle, that uses a brass cartridge shell that can be re-
loaded many times, and is water-proof.   The cartridge
is fired by a tape cap, which is automatically put on the
nipple, which enables the rifle to be fired very rapidly.
J. S.

MAY 22.   Prospected some, found one and a half
cent dirt to a pan of gravel.   Bercier and party passed
on their way to Bitter Root valley.

MAY 23.   Froze a little last night.   Today warm,
calm, and clear.   Prospected some, raised the color.
I have been sick for about a week.   A stranger arrived
from Fort Benton going to Coeur d'Alene Mission.[41]
He is probably a lay brother.   He stayed all night.

MAY 24.   Prospected, Granville and I.   We found
good gold prospects.   Received a letter from Bitter
Root valley from Thomas Adams.   Brought here by
Nine Pipes,[42] a Flathead Indian, a good reliable man.
He says the weather is very cold and stormy down there.

MAY 25.   Nine Pipes and quite a number of Flatheads passed on their way to hunt buffalo bulls on the
Missouri.   (The Indians only kill the bulls at this time
of the year because the cows already have calves or soon
will have them.)   I went to Dempsey's [43] ranch today,

---

[41] Coeur d'Alene Mission was started by Father Pierre de Smet in 1842.
H. M. Chittenden and A. T. Richardson, *opus citra*, vol. i, p. 372.

[42] His name is perpetuated in the Nine Pipes reservoir in the Flathead
irrigation project. – ED.

[43] This ranch was up Dempsey creek south of the present Deer Lodge. –
ED.

found everyone drunk and three strangers there with fifteen gallons of Minnie Rifle whiskey. Fortunately, Granville and I do not drink any kind of liquor. This kind is usually composed of one part alcohol and ten parts of water, with a considerable quantity of tobacco and cayenne pepper to strengthen it. These two men report that the crops in Bitter Root valley are damaged considerably by the frost. The season here is also very backward. The cottonwoods, alders, quaking-aspens, and willows are only commencing to leaf out.

MAY 26, SUNDAY. This has been a beautiful day. Warm, calm, and nearly clear. Thomas Pambrum and Oliver LeClaire arrived from Bear river, near Box Elder, Utah, Mormon settlement. They do not bring any news of any consequence. They went down there with Van Etten's [44] party to help drive a band of horses that Van traded from the Flatheads last winter. They all got through safely. Van's home is down near Salt Lake City. Gold Tom visited our ranch today. He had found some tolerable good prospects up the creek.

MAY 29. Planted beets, potatoes, muskmelons, pumpkins, and squashes. Froze ice a quarter of an inch thick last night. Also a very heavy frost.

MAY 30. Rained the greater part of last night and today. Bercier and party passed on their way home to Johnny Grant's from Bitter Root valley. They brought no news from any part of the world.

MAY 31. Went up to Little Blackfoot settlement and found the majority of the inhabitants on a drunk. Returned home in the evening. Little Blackfoot creek is high, nearly swimming.

---

[44] Van Etten was a Mormon trader who bought stock along the Emigrant trail and drove it to the Bitter Root to recuperate. In his employ at one time or another was a number of the settlers of the Bitter Root. Woody, *opus citra*, p. 98. – ED.

SUNDAY, JUNE 2, 1861. Frost last night. Forenoon warm, calm, and clear. Afternoon warm, nearly
clear, very light breezes of wind from the east. Went
to Grantsburg, returned in the evening. Gold Tom
visited us today. Showed us several pieces of gold that
weigh from ten to fifteen cents each.

JUNE 3. Hauled wood and made ready to start to
Fort Benton to meet the steamboat that is expected
there, intending to buy a good supply of food and mining tools. Going on horseback one hundred and ninety
miles to get it. Surely this is a country of fine large
distance and a great scarcity of inhabitants.

JUNE 4. James and Fred H. Burr,[45] wife and infant
daughter, started for Fort Benton. Burr has a good
elkskin lodge and the necessary poles with which to set
it up, so they will be well sheltered. Forenoon, quite
warm and calm. Afternoon, strong west wind and
showers of rain. I went to Bercier's, his wife gave me
a hen and a rooster, for which I thanked her most sincerely. Prospected a little, killed my daily ration, a
duck. Tolman, Johnny Carr and Co., are on a drunk
and as I never drink of course they had to come up and
visit me. Oh! for a lodge in some vast wilderness
where drunks could never come and where whiskey
was unknown. Fat Jack went by, going to Bitter Root.

JUNE 7. Beautiful sunset. Washed my duds today.
Gold Tom came down and stayed part of the day. He
has abandoned his gold diggings in disgust. Did not
look for my ration. The streams are falling a little
today. It snowed upon the mountains south of here
last night. Saw Indians after dark this evening, two

---

[45] Burr came into Montana in 1853 with Lieutenant Mullan's party. In
1856 he brought four hundred cattle into the Bitter Root and settled. Charles
S. Warren, The Territory of Montana in *Montana Historical Society Contributions*, vol. i, pp. 62, 63. – ED.

on one horse, apparently somebody will have horses stolen or I will be surprised.

JUNE 8. Rained hard all last night and today. James Minesinger [46] came down from Grantsburg in the afternoon and stayed all night with me. I am glad to have someone come, as it is frightfully lonesome since James and Burr left. The frost night before last cut down the corn and potatoes, but did not hurt the peas, cabbage, onions, or radishes. It slayed my one melon. Ned Williamson's horse is missing. I fear those Indians took him.

JUNE 9. We have now nineteen young calves, four yearlings, thirty-three cows, fifteen oxen, two young steers, and three bulls. Frank Newell and Oliver Le-Claire came up from Bitter Root on their way to Grantsburg. They found the river ford, at the point of the hill, swimming and came back and stayed with me.

JUNE 10. Heavy frost last night. Forenoon, warm and pleasant. Afternoon one heavy shower. Three Flathead Indians passed in hot haste in the forenoon after some of their horses that were stolen from Camas prairie last night. Gave one of them some bullets and some percussion caps. The same Indians that stole their horses must have stolen Ned Williamson's horse. I have searched the country and cannot find him. The folks up at Cottonwood saw three Indians on Friday, one on foot and two on one horse, supposed to be Bannocks. Louis tried to catch them and turn them back but they hid and got away. It was they I saw on Friday night. I killed antelope with Adam's Maynard rifle, two hundred and forty yards, shot it off-hand. The bullet passed through the butt of its heart. Jack-

---

[46] Minesinger came in with Burr in 1856. *Ibid.* – ED.

son, Dempsey's friend, Oliver LeClaire, Tolman, and
Oliver left for a hunt up Flint creek.   They took several milk cows intending to catch young moose calves
and have them suck the cows until they are old enough
to eat grass and willow twigs.   I do not believe they
will catch moose calves enough to start any big herd.
Frank Newell and John Seeber start to the Bitter Root
tomorrow by way of the valley of Big Blackfoot river.
I saw a party on horseback passing along the foot of
the mountains south of here, and thought they were
probably those horse thieves.   Oliver and I gave chase
and overtook them in six miles.   They proved to be a
party of squaws from John Grant's on a root digging
expedition.

JUNE 11.   Forenoon, cloudy and calm.   I remod-
eled an old hat, making it look quite respectable.   Afternoon cloudy, with one shower of rain and hail inter-
mixed.   Those Flathead Indians returned this morning.   They did not recover their horses, felt sorry for
them and gave them a piece of bread and an antelope
ham and sent them on their way rejoicing.   Received
a call from Lady Catherine and Mrs. Powell, Indian
women, who are going from Grantsburg to visit Mrs.
Dempsey, a country woman of theirs.   They told me
that the prowling Indian thieves stole one horse from
old Michael (a Nez Percé half breed) one from the
Frenchman Le Gris, one from Chas. DeLabreche, one
from Joe Piou, who was camped on Blackfoot creek a
few miles above Grant's, on his way to Fort Benton.
The river and creek are both falling considerable.

JUNE 12.   Forenoon, clear with a strong east wind.
Found the horses in two bands this morning.   They
are all in very ill humor.   They fight each other like
devils.   Afternoon, strong south wind with light fleecy

clouds. The women returned from Dempsey's going home. Seeber and Newell came back being afraid of the high water in all the streams here. The potatoes, corn, peas, and beets that were planted last are coming up fine. Began to enlarge my prospecting out in the ravine, looks good. This has been a beautiful day, smoky like Indian summer. Read "Byron" and indulged in many reveries while lying on the bank under the trees by the lovely creek and soothed by its gentle murmur. Woke up by having to return to earth and wash the dishes and roast some coffee. I am becoming very lonesome and long for brother James to return. Was bitten by several mosquitoes and saw the first horse fly of the season.

JUNE 15. Forenoon, calm clear and warm, but alas! A heavy frost last night. Dug some more, enlarging my cut in the ravine, got good prospects in beautiful gold. Joe, Powell's young Indian horse herder, came along and told me lots of news. He says that on the night of the eleventh there were stolen about ten head of Johnny Grant's horses, five of his mother-in-law's, (old squaw Giomman) three from Powell, one from Joe himself. I think they tried to catch some of ours and Burr's that same night as I found them split into two bands in the morning and very cross. Tied our best horses at the cabin door tonight and lay in the door with my rifle and revolver at my side. The three horses are Brooks, Old Fiend, and Cawhaw. Last night's frost does not show any effect in our garden yet. This day three years ago, we left Sheep rock, California, en route for the states and we have not gotten there yet. Today I received a visit from Johnny Carr and Frank Newell. They told me of a fierce single combat they had witnessed up at Dempsey's between Mrs. Dempsey

and Charles Allen.   Mrs. Dempsey was busy at the
wood pile, chopping the day's supply, when Charlie,
"half-shot" came along and begun to issue orders.
Right there the fight began. Mrs. Dempsey landed away
with the axe, but missed.   Thereupon Charlie grabbed
for the lady's hair.   His aim was more certain and he
got one hand full, whereupon the lady lit in with both
hands and in two seconds Charlie's face looked like he
had had an encounter with a wild cat.   This desperate
onslaught caused him to loose hold on her hair.   She
grabbed a stick of wood and used it with such good
effect that she put the enemy to flight, but not until she
had blacked both eyes, knocked out a tooth and
scratched his face until his best friend would fail to
recognize him.   Mrs. Dempsey is known in these parts
to be a lady of uncertain temper, but "more power to
her elbow," say we all, for who could put up with the
gang of drunken loafers that hang around Dempsey's
without losing their temper.

JUNE 17.   Clear and warm light west wind.   I
made a quick trip up to Johnny Grant's settlement and
back to hear what was on up there.   Those thieves who
have lately been stealing horses were Blackfoot Indians.
They came suddenly on a camp of Flatheads over the
other side of the mountains.   The Flathead camp outnumbered them and as they could not get away with all
the stolen horses they took a few of the best and fled,
leaving most of the stolen horses behind.   The Flatheads (honest fellows) brought them over the mountains to Johnny Grant's and delivered them to their
owners. Eight to Johnny, Jim Minesinger one,
Johnny's young Indian one, and another stray returned
with Johnny's.   Twelve in all recovered.   The Blackfoot thieves got away with Old Michael's one, and La

Breche's one, Joe Piou's one, Johnny's mother-in-law's five! Eight whose owners are known, but it is estimated that there are about forty missing from the Indians and whites from this side of the mountains. Lucky Williamson (the Indians did steal his horse as I thought) the good Flatheads recovered him and brought him back. River and creek rising a little. Some of the corn and melons that were planted on May 6, are just coming up. Plenty of mosquitoes at dark. Tied up our three best horses tonight as usual.

JUNE 18. Nearly clear, with a strong west wind cool and pleasant. Hoed corn and cleaned up around the house. Old Michael found four horses a few days ago, supposed to have been lost by the Nez Percés, and last night they were stolen from him, it is thought, by the Flatheads. Truly our horses have fallen among perilous times. The trees and bushes have just finished leafing out, river and creek rising a little. The snow is going fast upon the mountains. Too cool for mosquitoes at dark. Tied up our four [three] best horses tonight as usual.

JUNE 20. Another deadly black frost last night. Froze ice one-eighth of an inch thick. It cut down the wheat and oats and killed many of the wild flowers. All kinds of vegetation show the effect of it today, looking somewhat wilted. Went hunting, saw a cinnamon bear, two little white tailed deer, four antelope and did not get a shot, all very wild. River and creek falling a little. The Flathead war party that passed going south on the sixteenth, came back on the other side of the river this morning. They had ten loose horses and halted on the hill and sang me a war song and waved something on a pole that they wanted me to consider a scalp. I was quite willing to so consider it and glad to have the number of horse thieves that infest this neighborhood reduced by one.   Tied up the three horses again tonight and watched them.

JUNE 21.   Went hunting, killed a bull moose, saw one white tailed deer and five antelope.   Two Flat-heads passed going after two horses that the war party left somewhere tired out.   They say that all eleven recovered their horses except one, and that they killed one Bannock (guess that was a scalp sure enough). One Flathead had a lock of hair cut off the back of his head by a bullet.   Fred's bay filly got her skin cut somehow and is lame.   River and creek falling a little. Can see many bare spots on the south mountains where the snow has lately gone off.   Many mosquitoes and a few horse flies.   Tied up the three horses and slept with one eye and both ears open.   The entire band of horses was stolen last night with the exception of the three I had at the cabin door.   Fred H. Burr lost eight good mares and six colts, and we lost six good mares and three colts.   While I was gone looking for the trail which I found, leading southeast towards Deer Lodge valley, one of our mares and colt, and Fred's little lame bay filly came back.   They were the least valuable and contrary to drive so the Indians left them on the road. Last night just at dark I saw two Indians, one on foot run out of the first ravine south of the house and to the brush south of the creek.   My first impulse was to jump on my horse and dash across the creek and try to find the horses somewhere on the bench west of the creek before the Indians got to them.   Then came the thought that some of the party of Indians were in all probability hidden in the brush along the creek just below the house, watching for a chance to get the three horses tied at the door which were worth as much as all our six on the bench.   Oh! how I wish brother James were here with me for we would have sprung on two of the horses and the third one would have followed us and each of us armed with rifles and revolvers, we could have overtaken any Indians that might be driving off the horses.   These eleven Flatheads overtook the thieves and the horses at Moose creek on Big Hole river, and killed two of them.   There were four Bannocks in the party.   They had the horses belonging to LeGris's party and had four horses packed with meat. They have probably been in the vicinity for a long time. The Flatheads said they could have killed the other two Bannocks, but let them go as a warning to the rest of their tribe.   Only one of them offered to fight.   San Pablo (St. Paul) took his bow away from him and told him to "go" and he went.   O! mercy, ill bestowed, for I am sure that it was those Bannocks who stole our horses.   It was evident that at first these Indians did not want to steal from the whites, for they had passed by the same horses twice before without molesting them, but after their misfortune at the hands of the Flatheads they ceased to be respectors of person.   This is the Indian's ethics anyhow.   In the evening James Minesinger came down from Grant's and stayed all night with me.   How unfortunate he did not come last night, for if he had done so he and I would have saved our horses and very likely have killed the two thieves, for the horses that I tied were faster than others.   A Frenchman named Decoteau, who lived forty miles south from here at Warm Springs saw the two Indians pass at sunrise the morning of the twenty-third driving about twenty horses.   Kept our three horses tied at the door as usual.

JUNE 28.   Rained all day, with the exception of a

little while about noon.   Took some ammunition down
to Dempsey's for Tolman to take to Tom Adams at
Fort Owen in Bitter Root valley.   Tolman and Jackson start for that place in the morning and Frank
Newell and John Seeber start to Walla Walla, four
hundred and twenty-five miles west.   The wind blew
from all points of the compass today, coming from the
west at night.   River and creek falling a little and the
water getting clear.   Tolman, Jackson, and Oliver got
back from their hunt day before yesterday and they did
not catch any moose.   I would have been greatly surprised if they had.   I gave Jackson an order on Mc-
Donald for three bushels of wheat and Tolman an order
for two bushels.   The wild flax and bitter-root are in
full bloom now and very beautiful.   Kept the horses
staked out all day, and tied them up at night at the
cabin door.

JUNE 29.   Rained all the forepart of last night.
Weather today very cloudy, warm, and sprinkling rain
occasionally.   River and creek rising fast, and are up
to their highest mark again.   I found a ripe strawberry and a rose in bloom, the first of the season.   The
potatoes are coming up again.   They are certainly
bound to win out in spite of their hard luck.   Jim
Minesinger came down and stayed all night.   I found
a new species of flower today.   Kept the horses staked
out within gunshot all day and tied them at the door
at night.

JULY 1.   Saw a huge comet last night in the northwest.   Its tail reached half across the heavens.   It has
probably been visible for sometime, but as it has been
cloudy lately I had not observed it before.   The cottonwood trees are in full bloom.   It is the first time I have
ever seen them in blossom.   Nine Pipes, a Flathead,

came to get a nipple put in his yager rifle, but I had none that would fit it.   Sorry, for he is a good Indian.

JULY 2.   Plenty of mosquitoes, horse flies, gnats, and deer flies.   River and creek are falling a very little. Kept the horses staked out in the daytime, and tied them at night.   Saw the comet again.   It is not the one we saw in October, 1858, or at least it does not have the same appearance.   That party of Flatheads passed today, returning home after their buffalo hunt.   They had three buffalo calves, which they had caught over about the Three forks of the Missouri.   I traded three plew [47] of beaver skins and four buffalo tongues for them.   Four hills of melon seeds that we planted are just now coming up, having been in the ground fifty-six days.   Never saw the like before.

JULY 11.   Insect pests very bad.   We have now twenty-one calves, thirteen females, and eight males. Took a short hunt, found no game.   River and creek are now quite low.   Doctor Atkinson passed en route for Bitter Root.   Brother James arrived home to my great relief and joy for I have had a trying time during his long absence and have been very lonesome.   He was absent thirty-eight days.   He now keeps the journal.

---

[47] Plew or pluie is a French-Canadian word meaning pelt, probably derived from the French word *poil*.   It generally referred to beaver. — ED.

Life in Early Montana

I arrived home at ten o'clock today (July 11, 1861) and I have ridden ninety miles since the sun was two hours high yesterday morning. I have had a very disagreeable trip. The American Fur Company's steamboat burned and blew up at the mouth of Milk river. Cargo total loss, no lives lost. Higgins and Worden of Hell Gate lost a big stock of goods, no full particulars have reached Fort Benton as yet, except that the fire was caused by a deckhand who went down into the hold to steal some alcohol, of which there were several barrels. There were also several of whiskey. The d— fool had a lighted candle and when he bored a large gimlet hole in a barrel to fill his jug the fumes of the alcohol took fire and spread instantly and here is a failure of the retributive justice, for the cause of this great misfortune escaped with some slight burns. As it was known that there were twenty-five kegs of gunpowder on board, the steamer was run to the shore as quickly as possible and everybody ran ashore and out into the woods some distance and almost immediately the steamer blew up with a terrific report and sank. The greater part of the time I have been absent I had neither tea, coffee, sugar, nor bread. Only poor buffalo bull meat and water to live on. It reminded me of our experience here in 1858. There were no supplies of food at the fort, all having been eaten up and everybody waiting for the arrival of that steamboat to procure more. Now it is destroyed and those people,

as well as ourselves, will have to get food supplies from
Salt Lake City, five hundred miles away.   While I was
at Fort Benton the Crow Indians killed ten Blackfeet,
and Little Dog, head chief of the Blackfeet, killed two
of his own tribe and wounded one other very badly.
It will probably be the cause of civil war among the
Blackfeet for those killed were all sub-chiefs.   The
night of the fifteenth of June, I camped at the great
falls of the Missouri river.   Sun river was not fordable
then.

JULY 12.   F. H. Burr and Ned Williamson arrived
this evening from Fort Benton.   Gold Tom, who was
with the party left at Prickly Pear creek to hunt on the
Missouri river.   Horse flies and mosquitoes are very
bad here and torture me plenty.   Clear, warm and
strong west wind in the afternoon.   Granville went
hunting, but the flies were so bad in the pines that he
had to come home without meat.

JULY 13.   Clear and warm.   Granville went hunting and killed a black-tailed deer.   It was fat enough
to be very good eating and we just needed it too.   I
cut out and made a raw-hide rope today.   Jim Minesinger came down on a visit.   Fat Jack passed here on
his way to Walla Walla.

JULY 15.   Wash day in camp.   Granville and Burr
went to Dempsey's ranch after two of Burr's cows.
They borrowed a small fragment of a newspaper that
Tolman and Jackson brought from Fort Owen in Bitter
Root valley.   Bad news from the states.   The North
and South are fighting.   Tom Adams, John Grant,
John W. Powell and party arrived from Benton.

JULY 16.   Forenoon clear and warm.   Ned Williamson returned from Grant's ranch accompanied by
Michel Le Claire.   I hoed potatoes.   Afternoon, light

wind, cloudy and cool. Killed time by discussing the outbreak of war in the states.

JULY 22. Frank L. Worden and party passed here at sunrise this morning on their way to Hell Gate. Michel returned about noon. Adams killed an antelope. Worked leveling ditch. John Grant, John W. Powell, Thomas Pambrum, Louis Simmons and others passed en route for the Hudson's Bay trading post near the St. Ignatius Mission. Paid John F. Grant twenty-eight pluie of beaver skins. War parties of Bannocks have the mountains on fire in all directions. Somebody will probably lose some more horses.

JULY 24. Afternoon, Michel and I went hunting. Michel killed an antelope. Adams returned, only went as far as Flint creek divide. Frank Goodwin returned from Hell Gate. Nez Percés gold mines are paying from five to fifty dollars per day per man. Eight thousand miners there. I think that number should be cut down to about two thousand.[48]

JULY 27. F. Goodwin came and got Pambrum's gun. Party passed returning home from Hudson Bay post. I went with them to Grant's and stayed all night. Insects very bad.

JULY 29. Warm, clear. Gentle west wind. Tried to stop a fire at the foot of the mountain from coming down the creek to our ranch. From here to Flint creek, about thirteen miles the land on the south side of the river has been all burned over along the face of the mountains, we do not know whether it was started by whites, Indians, or lightning. The fire is still going south towards Deer Lodge valley. Michel returned home today. Powell came on a visit. Afternoon, very

---

[48] This refers to the district around Florence, Idaho.

warm. Cloudy with strong south-west wind. Laid foundation for calf corral.

JULY 31. Warm, clear, nearly calm. Fire still coming down the creek. Worked on corral for calves. Insect nuisance visibly on the decrease for which we are truly thankful. Doubtless our live stock is equally so, as the poor things have been the greatest sufferers for over six weeks. Last Sunday Granville lent Dempsey's employees a mowing scythe. I sent Michel after it last evening and instead of giving it to him they sent word that "they were using it and could not do without it for a few days yet." Now the weather is hot, but by jings, that is cool enough to bring on a heavy frost.

AUGUST 3, 1861. Very warm, clear and nearly calm. Three miners from the Nez Percé passed here today on their way to the states. They report plenty of people in those mines and some of them are doing very well. Worked on milk house and mowed. Insects bad.

AUGUST 5. Thomas Pambrum passed here going to Walla Walla. I wrote a letter to Clinton Bozarth, a cousin in Iowa, and sent it by Pambrum. Walla Walla is four hundred and twenty-five miles west, being our nearest postoffice. Johnny Grant's Indian wife was with Pambrum. She is going to stop at Hell Gate cañon below Flint creek and gather service berries.

AUGUST 10. Forenoon, calm, clear and warm. Cut and put up hay. Oliver went home. We had Mrs. Catherine and Mrs. Pambrum for dinner with us. Both well behaved Snake Indian women.

AUGUST 11. We had green peas of our own raising for dinner, but how they ever survived the many frosts beats me. Mosquitoes and flies are not so bad as they have been. Gnats are seemingly worse. Cuss a gnat anyhow, or anytime. We have had plenty of wild

goose-berries for about ten days and now the raspberries are ripe. High living these days.

AUGUST 14. Clear, warm, and nearly calm, very
smoky. Heavy frost last night. It came very near
ruining our farm and garden and probably has done so,
but we can't tell for certain for two or three days yet.
Fires still burning on the mountains. Went prospecting, washed seven pans of dirt and got six cents, not
quite a cent per pan. Gnats very bad, a few horse-flies
and mosquitoes. Margaret, Thos. Pambrum's Indian
wife, passed here from Grantsburg on her way to
Dempsey's ranch. Adams and Michel escorted her
down there. She had a fight with her relatives at
Johnny Grant's and left them in disgust, which strikes
us "out of the frying pan into the fire."

AUGUST 16. Prospected, washed six pans of dirt
and got ten cents which is better than usual. Adams
and Michel went to Pete Martin's today.

AUGUST 17. Prospected, washed seven pans of dirt
and got six cents. Adams returned from above. He
saw two men from the Nez Percé mines en route for
the states. They are planning on going down the
Missouri in a boat from Fort Benton. We feel certain
they will perish if they start, for two men are too few
to protect themselves from the Indians.

AUGUST 22. Capt. Richard Grant and Thomas
Pambrum arrived from Hell Gate, and stayed all
night with us. It is the first time we have seen the
Captain since the winter of 1859. His rheumatism is
much better than it has been. He is going on a visit
to his son John. He brought us four letters from the
states that were brought from Walla Walla by Bachelder's Express to Hell Gate, to Worden and Higgin's
store. One letter was from our mother, one from Uncle

Valentine Bozarth, one from Cousin Sallie Bozarth, and one from brother Samuel. Great was our rejoicing at their arrival.

AUGUST 29. I returned home this evening. A Mr. Paris from Sun river government farm, arrived here this evening, en route to Bitter Root valley. Stayed all night.

SEPTEMBER 5, 1861. Warm and smoky. Frank Goodwin came down to see us. He contracted to build a log house for F. H. Burr for two horses and fifty pounds of flour.

SEPTEMBER 6. Rained hard last night and until ten o'clock today. I hope it will put a stop to all the fires in the mountains. Went fishing, caught twenty lovely trout, one very large one, over four pounds. Did not see the sun today.

SEPTEMBER 7. Rained a little. Very cold for this season of the year. The mountains are covered with snow almost down to the edges of the valleys. Robert Pelky and party of three wagons arrived from the states en route to Bitter Root valley and passed here in the afternoon. I went up to John Grant's.

SEPTEMBER 9. Frank Goodwin moved down from above with his camp, consisting of his Nez Percé wife, an elk skin lodge, and several horses. Last night Jack Collins and Ned Williamson arrived from Hell Gate en route for Fort Benton with whiskey for Indian trade.

SEPTEMBER 21. The Flathead Indians are camped in the bottom below here on their trip to the buffalo range for their usual winter hunt, and there are plenty of drunken Indians passing from Grantsville to their camp. I wish those whiskey traders would go on to the Blackfoot country or to Hades. Michel went to Grantsville.

SEPTEMBER 23. The Flathead camp passed on their way to hunt buffalo all winter. Am glad they are gone because of the d—d whiskey.

SUNDAY, SEPTEMBER 29. Warm cloudy. Jacobs [50] and Gwin had a shooting match for one and two dollars a shot. It was a standoff, for both quit even. Frank Goodwin went up to John Grant's and got into a drunken row and shot Michel LeClaire twice, with a navy Colt's revolver, wounding him (it is supposed) mortally. Poor little Michel he was under middle size but active and strong and only twenty years old. Goodwin was much larger, weighing about one hundred and sixty-five pounds and could have handled poor Michel without shooting him. It is a shame. This is the effect of bringing whiskey into a peaceful quiet community. I have expected that some of the Indians would kill each other while drunk, but so far have not heard of any fatalities among them. James returned from Grantsville this evening having been absent six days. He won four hundred and twenty-five dollars from a man named McCulloch playing poker.

OCTOBER 1, 1861. Four men from New York state passed en route for Walla Walla. A Frenchman named Le Gris who lives with his Assiniboine wife at Grantsville, and McCullough passed going to Bitter Root and Ned Williamson with them. Ned Collins has sold all of his whiskey and is going below for more.

OCTOBER 2. James, Powell, and Louis Maillet went to Hell Gate and Bitter Root valley. I bought a sore backed horse from Goodwin for ten dollars, and bought a small lot of gunsmith's tools from him for twenty-five dollars in ammunition. Bought two picks and shovels

[50] John M. Jacobs and John M. Bozeman constructed the Bozeman road. – ED.

and a pair of gold scales from him for cutting out his gun. Goodwin and Gwin have left this vicinity.

OCTOBER 5. Smith camped just above here with John Owen's pack train. They are packing hard bread from Fort Benton for the Flathead Indian agency on the Jocko river.

OCTOBER 9. Cold and stormy with west wind. I banked earth up against the house, preparing for cold weather. Dempsey's and Joe Blodget's wagons passed, loaded with flour and other goods, which were bought in Salt Lake City, five hundred miles away, but there is no food any nearer except at Fort Walla Walla, four hundred and twenty-five miles west, over a nearly impassable road for wagons. Two emigrant teams were with Dempsey and Blodget. Brother James and F. H. Burr arrived home.

OCTOBER 10. Nearly clear, and quite pleasant. I helped Jacobs haul house logs and fire wood. Powell, L. R. Maillet, and Jimmy Grant passed. James bought a steel rifle, light and handy about thirty-five calibre, made by Fisk of New York, for which he paid twenty dollars. It is entirely new and a bargain, but I would not exchange my trusty Maynard breech-loading brass cartridge rifle, which I bought from Thomas Adams for forty dollars for three like the Fisk rifles. Peter McDonald gave Brother James his double barreled Mortimer shot gun. James sold our wheat crop to Henry Brooks of Bitter Root valley for four dollars a bushel.

SUNDAY, OCTOBER 13. I went down to Dempseys. Jack Collins and A. K. Gurd, arrived from the Bitter Root valley with a wagon load of vegetables. One hundred and forty miles is a long haul to get to market, but they will make a good profit selling to the folks at Grantsville and Cottonwood, who are all hungry for vegetables.

OCTOBER 14. I churned five pounds of fine quality butter. Put handles in the picks and sharpened the shovels, and got ready to dig on our mining ditch. These tools were brought up for us from Walla Walla by Worden and Higgin's pack train. James Minesinger abandoned Grantsville and moved down to our pleasant little village.

OCTOBER 25. Clear, calm, and warm. Finished building dam. John Grant and his wife, a Bannock woman, passed en route for Bitter Root valley. Doctor Atkinson and Major William Graham arrived from Fort Owen in Bitter Root valley.

NOVEMBER 11, 1861. Snowed nearly all day. Meeks and party arrived from above. John Grant and Burr arrived from Hell Gate. They brought us a letter from Rezin Anderson. He wrote that he was going to enlist in the Federal Army. We hope he won't. Anderson is now visiting in Iowa.

NOVEMBER 12. All the Frenchmen from Cottonwood and Warm Springs passed here today, going to Hell Gate.

NOVEMBER 22. Calm, cloudy, and cold. Thawed a little about noon. "Old Sport Allen" went home. Allen is a peculiar character. He is continually after some of us to teach him to play poker. As he looses every time he gets into a game we have rather discouraged him in his ambition to become a real sport. Gold Tom and Jacobs hauled puncheons for Burr's floor.

DECEMBER 2, 1861. Cloudy and warm. A strong southwest wind, known as a Chinook, began about sundown, and in twenty minutes the water was running off the roofs and the warm wind caused the snow to settle down very fast and this morning it was all gone. The ground was covered with water. It looks good to see the bare ground again, after having been covered with snow so long, and so early in the fall. A camp of Pend d'Oreilles of eight lodges passed here. They are going over the mountains to hunt on the Missouri side during the winter. They will, no doubt, be joined by a much larger camp of Nez Percés, Yakimas, Spokanes, Flatheads, and Kootenais.

When Thomas Adams returned from Fort Benton he brought Granville a new breech-loading fifty caliber Maynard carbine rifle taking reloading brass cartridges intended to contain forty grains of black powder. This was the first gun of its kind seen out here and Granville being an excellent shot had an idea that he could beat anything or anybody shooting with that particular gun. The first lot of cartridges that he loaded he had used his powder flask and measured the powder exact, and he had been doing some remarkable shooting on his recent hunting trips and we had all been bragging a good deal on the gun and his markmanship.

John Grant had a brother-in-law, an old Indian named Pushigan. He had a long, heavy muzzle loading rifle of about forty calibre on which he had a sight made of hoop iron. With this old gun and the hoop iron sights, this Indian had been doing some fine shooting himself. John Grant had been bragging about what his brother-in-law could do so one Sunday morning Sterne Blake, Powell, Bud McAdow, Jim Minesinger, Tom Adams, Granville and I went up to Grantsville for a shooting match.

John Grant, James Grant, Chas. Jackson, Bob Dempsey, and Tendoy (the old Snake Indian chief, a brother-in-law of John Grant) were there ready to back Pushigan.

We took the end gate out of John Grant's wagon for a target and in the center marked a bulls-eye. Pushigan fired the first shot and made the bulls-eye. Granville stepped up to the mark, took deliberate aim, and missed the target entirely, and each one on our side was out one dollar. The match went on and the distance had been increased from one hundred yards to five hundred yards Pushigan having decidedly the best of it. Up to this point only light bets had been made. Granville was considerably crestfallen. He couldn't account for the inaccuracy of his little Maynard. At six hundred yards Pushigan made a bad score and Granville made a bulls-eye. Confidence was at once restored and Powell bet two horses to one. Our joy was short lived. Old Pushigan began carefully manipulating his hoop iron sights and made a bulls-eye at every crack of the rifle, while Granville made but one good score. By this time our side was flat broke and afoot. I offered to bet my trusty long range rifle with old Tendoy for a good little roan horse, but the old fellow refused so I suppose I lost my chance of handing my gun over to the wily old chief.

We all hoofed it back to camp arriving late in the evening, tired, cold, and hungry. Granville had little to say about that gun and only remarked that, "He never did believe in gambling," to which remark Powell made answer, "Too bad you didn't bet that gun and lose it."

Next day Granville was busily engaged loading brass cartridges. He carefully measured the powder putting in exactly forty grains to the cartridge and then taking his Maynard out back of the house he set up a target and found that he could make a bulls-eye almost every crack of the gun at two, three, five and six hundred yards. The trouble the day before was that he had loaded his shells by guess and there was too much powder in some, and in others not enough, which accounted for the bad shooting on Sunday.

DECEMBER 25, 1861. We went up to Cottonwood to Pete's grand ball. Had a fine supper and then danced all night till sunrise. There were a few students of toxicology occasionally, but they were well behaved and gave the rest of us no trouble. Snowed a little last night. Tom Campbell arrived from Sun river yesterday.

DECEMBER 26. I returned home. Had a visit from Pierre Ish Tab-ba-bo and his wife, a good young couple. He had married a Snake girl. Bud (P. W. McAdow) started to Salt Lake. I fear he will have a very hard, cold trip. Let Powell have the Arkansas steer to butcher for beef.

DECEMBER 27. Very cold and disagreeable. Stayed in the house all day. Roland and another man passed with Jack Williams, prisoner for stealing horses (first [49] arrest for this offense here). They passed last night. Kiplinger and Eaton went above today.

DECEMBER 30. Very cold. Caught my cream colored horse, that I bought from Frank Goodwin, and doctored his sore back. Dempsey and Major Graham got back from their Indian trading expedition. They traded for eighteen horses and about six hundred skins from the Sheep Eaters, and Digger Snakes. It snowed considerably today.

---

[49] I cannot recall what became of this horse thief; he was not hung and he had no trial. There were not at this time any courts nearer than Walla Walla.

JANUARY 1, 1862. Snowed in the forenoon. Very cold in afternoon. Raw east wind. Everybody went to grand ball given by John Grant at Grantsville and a severe blizzard blew up and raged all night. We danced all night, no outside storm could dampen the festivities.

JANUARY 2. Still blowing a gale this morning. Forty below zero and the air filled with driving, drifting snow. No one ventured to even try to go home (we lived eight miles below and many couples lived ten to fifteen miles up in Deer Lodge valley). Johnny Grant, good hospitable soul, invited everyone to stay until the storm should cease. We accepted his invitation without a dissenting voice. After breakfast we laid down on the floor of the several rooms, on buffalo robes that Johnny furnished, all dressed as we were and slept until about two o'clock in the afternoon, when we arose, ate a fine dinner that Johnny's wife, assisted by the other women, had prepared, then resumed dancing which we kept up with unabated pleasure until about nine in the evening, when we paused long enough to eat an excellent supper. We then began where we left off and danced until sunrise.

JANUARY 3. The blizzard ceased about daylight, but it was very cold with about fourteen inches of snow badly drifted in places and the ground bare in spots. We estimated the cold at about thirty-five below, but fortunately there was but little wind. After breakfast all the visitors left for home, men, women, and children, all on horseback. Everyone got home without frost bites.

The music for these dances was two violins; and the dance most popular, was the old-fashioned quadrille. The floors were all of puncheon hence not smooth or waxed. Some men called the figures. The women were Indian or half-breed and there were never enough to go around. A man with a handkerchief tied around his arm supplied the place of a woman in some of the sets. There was as much rivalry among the women of those days, as to their finery, as there is now among their white sisters. At these balls they wore their brightest calicoes with new scarlet leggings and handsomely beaded moccasins with gay plaid blankets and ornaments of feathers, shells, silver money, beads, and a generous supply of vermillion paint. The children were also gotten up in the most elaborate beaded costumes that their mothers could supply. It was no uncommon thing for an Indian woman to spend all of her spare time for six months, preparing a suit beaded and embroidered with colored porcupine quills, for her young son to wear to these festivities. Nor were the men without vanity. We always wore our best flannel shirt, a highly ornamented buckskin suit, and best moccasins and trimmed our hair and beards. I kept my handsomely beaded buckskin suit with its decorations of fringe until 1880 when it was stolen from my cabin on the cattle range.

JANUARY 17. All the women in this part of the country have been at John Grant's, having I suppose an Indian Dorcas Society something after the manner of their white sisters, and like them it has broken up in a row. All the women have left for home. That is, they have joined their own people, leaving a goodly number of widowers. Next thing the aforesaid widowers will have to hunt up their absconding wives and the chances are most of them will have to yield up a number of good blankets or horse or two to father-in-law to persuade the lady to return.

JANUARY 18. It is a little warmer today. Cloudy, and nearly calm. Snowed a little. It has been bitter cold every day since the first of the month and the snow constantly becoming deeper. It is now about twenty inches deep with a pretty strong crust on top and another one about eight inches below the surface. The river is frozen over solid for miles, not a single air-hole anywhere and many of the cattle are walking up and down on the ice seeking water. At first we thought that they would have to have water or die, but fortunately Granville and I remembered that when we were wintering on Henry's fork of Green river in 1858-59, Majeau, the French mountaineer trader, told us that when a severe winter came the Ute Indians, who often wintered on Green river, below Brown's Hole (a warm sheltered little valley) would put their horses out among the cedar hills where there was good bunch grass, and good wind shelter among the cedar groves, and would not let them have any water while the cold and deep snow lasted, saying that if the horses were allowed to drink the ice cold water they would become chilled and rapidly lose flesh and many freeze to death. Out in the hills they could not bite the grass without getting enough snow to moisten it sufficiently, and they stayed fat all winter. So we gathered our cattle and drove them up into a deep little cañon on the north side of the river just opposite our houses. There was no water in it, but plenty of big willows also a great deal of tall rye grass and the cañon extended north and south and as the wind almost always blew from the west it blew across it and did not get down into it at all. We took our horses and broke paths through the snow up the east side of the cañon to the bench land above. We then drove all the cattle up these paths to the top of the bench and left them there with our horses. The horses pawed the snow off the grass so they could get it and the cattle at once learned to stay with the horses and help eat the abundant bunch grass that they exposed.

JANUARY 19. Cloudy, and a little milder and calm. Today we put the remainder of the cattle across the river with the first lot and we noticed that just before dark they all came down the paths into the cañon where there was no wind at all and slept among the willows and tall rye grass.

FEBRUARY 1, 1862. Clear, cold, and nearly calm. Hauled two loads of fire wood. Danced last night. Oh! joy. It is not often that we have a fiddler and when we do have one, we try to keep him in practice by having a dance every evening.

FEBRUARY 2. Danced again last night.

FEBRUARY 4. Calm, clear, not quite so cold. Powell and I went to Grantsville. A party of Flatheads passed here with some Bannock horses that they had stolen from the camp at Beaverhead valley. Danced last night. J. S.

FEBRUARY 5. Clear and cold. Light west wind. Last night about nine o'clock a party of Bannocks passed here. They were following those Flatheads. This morning they returned with two Flathead scalps and a band of horses. Danced last night.

FEBRUARY 13. Little Aeneas, the Flathead, or rather the Iroquois, adopted into the Flathead tribe, camped here with his lodge and family on his return home from hunting buffalo. Killed many and dried the meat. Another family joined him this evening. It is Narcisses and family. Tom Gold Digger came down from Grantsville and stayed all night. He says that Dave Contois, Louis Descheneau, and Jake Meek have left their ranches up in the valley and moved down to Cottonwood creek village. Too many Indians prowling about.

FEBRUARY 25. Snowed ten inches last night. Oh! oh! Aeneas, and Narcisses, the Flathead, went up to Cottonwood last night and found a Snake Indian named Peed-ge-gee camped near there. They killed him and took his lodge and camp fixtures and one of his wives. He had eight horses. This has been a horrible day, snowing and blowing furiously. About three inches of snow fell.

FEBRUARY 26. Snowed one inch in the night and is still at it this morning. Narcisses came down from Cottonwood with the captured woman. Powell and I [J. S.] ransomed the captive woman, thinking it just as well not to allow Narcisses to take her down to the Flathead country.   It is usual when they take a captive to turn her over to the women of their tribe and they promptly make a slave of her; imposing all of the drudgery of the camp on her, and making her life anything but a bed of roses. This woman is fair with red cheeks and brown hair and eyes and is evidently half white. The two other women of Peed-ge-gee made their escape the night of the murder and made their way to the white settlement on Cottonwood where they were cared for by some Bannock women until they had a chance to join their own tribe the following summer. Powell killed the black Wiley ox for beef. He was fat, which speaks well for the nutritive quality of the bunch grass, for this has been a very severe winter. Snowed slowly all day but melted nearly as fast as it fell.

FEBRUARY 27. Put two more weak cows up in the calf corral to feed, making four now being fed. We think our small haystack will last them from now until snow goes off. We could not begin feeding sooner as we only have a limited supply of hay, and cattle after being taken up and fed will not return to the range and "rustle" feed but will stand around until they starve hoping to be fed. No news from the states. I suppose Bachelder's Express from Walla Walla to Hell Gate and Cantonment Wright is snowed under. Thos. Adams took unto himself a wife last night. The bride is Louise, Lone-penny's step-daughter, a Flathead damsel.

MARCH 1, 1862. Cold, nearly clear. Snow is drifting very bad. I brought with me the Indian woman ransomed from Narcisses, the Flathead. Powell's wife objected to having her and as we have no cook it seems to fall to my lot to take her and take care of her at least until we can turn her over to some of her own people, should she wish to go. I might do worse. She is neat and rather good looking and seems to be of a good disposition. So, I find myself a married man. Granville says "Marrying is rapidly becoming an epidemic in our little village." J. S.

MARCH 3. Adams's wife left him today. They dissolved partnership by mutual agreement.

MARCH 20. Cloudy and calm. Thawed a little. Worden gives Burr ten dollars a day to take him and Baptiste to Sun river. We played poker last night. I won forty dollars. Worden was the loser. Powell and I came home today.

Sterne Blake comes with a good story of doings down at Hell Gate. Hell Gate is putting on "States Airs," and has a justice of the peace, and has held court and tried one of the distinguished citizens of that section for killing a neighbor's horse.

The trial was held in Bolt's saloon, a log building near Worden and Higgins' store. Suit was brought by "Tin Cup Joe" against Baron O'Keefe for killing a horse. Henry Brooks was judge; Bob Pelkey, constable; Frank Woody, prosecuting attorney; Sterne Blake was one of the twelve jurors and Bud McAdow was an onlooker. Baron O'Keefe conducted his own defense. (Anyone knowing the Baron would feel confident that he was well able to look out for himself.)

"Tin Cup Joe" accused the Baron of injuring one of his horses so seriously as to cause its death. The Baron denied the charge of malicious mischief and said that the horses had been in the habit of breaking down fences around hay stacks, that he put up for his own stock and that he had warned "Tin Cup Joe" to keep them away, a thing he had failed to do.

Frank Woody began for the prosecution and he had not proceeded far before some of his remarks about "Good Citizenship," were taken to be personal by O'Keefe. The Baron straightened up with eyes flashing and snorting like a war horse yelled, "Who are you, what kind of a court is this anyhow?" Then addressing himself to the Bench began, "Say Old Brooks, who in hell made you judge? You are an old fraud. You are no judge; you are a squaw man, you have two squaws now. Your business is to populate the country with half breeds. You —— —— ——." The Baron made a lunge at the person nearest him and in an instant the fight became general. Everybody took a hand, and as both sides had about an equal number of sympathizers, when the dust of battle cleared away it was considered to be a draw. But judge, jurors, constable, and prosecuting attorney, had disappeared and the fiery Baron held the center of the room declaring that "no Frenchman's horses can nibble hay from one of my stacks without suffering the consequences."

Quiet was finally restored, the judge and jury returned and the trial proceeded without further interruption. The jury brought in a verdict for "Tin Cup Joe" and awarded him forty dollars damages, but I do not know that anyone ever tried to collect the money from Baron O'Keefe. I do know that I would not have cared for the job. Such was the very first trial by court in what is now the state of Montana.[51]

The winter of 1861-2 was one of unprecedented severity. Severe cold set in about December 1. The snow was two feet deep and the thermometer registered above zero only four times in three months. The game was scarce and toward spring deadly poor. The Indians that were over in the buffalo country suffered terribly. They lost most of their horses and were unable to kill many buffalo, consequently, they were without meat and were in a starving condition.

Captain Grant lost many cattle and horses. We escaped loss by not allowing our stock to get cold and by keeping them in a sheltered coulees and by keeping horses and cattle together. The horses would paw snow and uncover the grass for the cattle. For sixty days our stock was without water to drink and only had the snow that they ate with the bunch grass. In the spring they were all in good condition, the young ones being fat.

The latter part of March a Chinook struck the country and in less than twenty-four hours the ice was breaking up in the streams, all the creeks and river were out of their banks. There were snow slides on all the steep

---

[51] F. H. Woody denied that he ran away from the fight. Mr. Woody states also that O'Keefe paid the judgment. *Opus citra*, p. 101. – ED.

mountains. It was impossible to travel any distance. The smallest creek became a raging torrent. There were so few settlers in the country that there was not much loss from the floods. There was a big ice gorge in the river above Bold creek and the water and ice covered all of the river bottom below there. Large cakes of ice scattered over the bottoms and laid there until June before they melted.[52]

MARCH 29, 1862. Cold and stormy with west wind. John Jacobs, Brown, and Smith came down from above, on their way to the Bitter Root. The river is just barely fordable. Jacobs told us lots of news. Frank Goodwin arrived at Cottonwood, from Fort Benton (he had gone there accompanied by Gwin when they left here so suddenly after he shot poor little Michel LeClaire). The Gros Ventre Indians came on him near Fort Benton and killed his Nez Percé wife and robbed him of all he had in the world. It is a pity that they did not kill him and let the unfortunate woman escape. Tom Campbell and Jack Collins also arrived from Fort Benton. They did not make anything trading with the Indians, very probably because they were their own best customers. William Kiplinger, Eaton, and John Seeber also arrived from Fort Benton. They, likewise, made nothing trading with the Indians. Great excitement at Benton about reported gold mines at Chief mountains near the British line (a humbug). There is a war on between the Gros Ventres, and Piegan Blackfeet. Seven Nez Percés

---

[52] Judge F. H. Woody wrote, "Prior to this time stock raisers had never made any preparation to feed their stock, consequently no feed had been put up. . . In February, 1862, a thaw came, and while the snow was soft it turned cold and the snow was frozen perfectly solid rendering it impossible for stock to move or get feed and the result was that hundreds of cattle died as did many horses." *Ibid.*, p. 100. – ED.

went to Beaverhead valley to steal horses from Bannock
Indians wintering there. They found four lodges of
Bannocks and tried to take their horses, but the Bannocks overtook them and killed two of them. The
other five got away, with one horse belonging to Tendoy, Grant's brother-in-law. Johnny saw the horse
as they passed by Cottonwood and succeeded in getting
it away from them.

MARCH 31. Snowed four inches last night, rather
raw and cold today, but it thawed a little in the afternoon. Thomas Adams, John M. Jacobs, and party left
for Hell Gate. The Nez Percés are moving camp
down the river past here today. To-losh-to-nau, a
Flathead, camped opposite here on the other side of
the river. He told us that he went to drink in a creek
over the mountains when he saw several pieces of yellow metal (the old story) lying on the bottom of the
stream and that he picked one piece up, about the size
of this thumb (what a whopper, and why didn't he pick
up all those pieces of yellow metal) and that he had it
yet, over at his lodge. We told him to bring it over
and let us see it and we would tell him whether it was
gold or not. He went, but did not come back today.
Good lie that.

APRIL 1, 1862. Cloudy and cold. Sprinkling snow.
That "Siwash" came over today and said that some of
his friends told him that that piece of yellow metal was
not gold and he gave it to his child to play with. Now
if we should go over to his lodge to see it he would
doubtless say that his child had lost it. Nez Percés
still moving camp by here. Pierre Ish, Little Wolf,
and company gave us a call. Rather drunk. Traded
two buffalo tongues and a little dried meat from two
squaws. River falling.

APRIL 5. Cloudy and cold. Nearly calm and snows a little nearly every night. Many Flatheads, Spokanes, and Pend d'Oreilles are passing on their return from buffalo hunting. Powell has been catching a few fish for about a week.

APRIL 6. Granville went to Cottonwood. Nine Pipes came to Victor's camp to hear the news. The Nez Percés have been lying about Johnny Grant, and Victor,[53] the Flathead chief, wanted to hear what we had to say about it. Fred Burr, who speaks the Flathead language fluently, made matters all right with him. I sold a mare (the Jacobs mare) to a Spokane Indian for eighty dollars in gold. Old Allen (Old Sport) came down here yesterday and returned home today. Tried to trade some furs from him but he asked too much.

APRIL 7. Victor's camp passed here today. We had a long talk with him about our Indian affairs. He thinks it is very probable that we will have trouble with the Pend d'Oreilles after awhile on account of our Snake and Bannock women. Maillet came from Cottonwood today to see Victor. Victor is much dissatisfied with John Grant's conduct this winter and is on his way to see Grant and try to have some settlement with him. He says Grant has Snake and Bannock wives and plenty of Indians (Snakes and Bannocks) coming to visit him and when they leave they steal horses from the Flatheads. He says Grant will have to keep the Snake and Bannocks away from his place,

---

[53] Victor was the "great chief" of the Flatheads. He was a Christian and a friend of the whites. It was with him, in 1855, that Governor Stevens negotiated the treaty at Council Grove near the mouth of the Bitter Root river that purported to surrender the Bitter Root valley to the whites. Father De Smet and Lieutenant John Mullan regarded him affectionately. Chittenden and Richardson, *opus citra*, vol. iv, pp. 1337-1341.

etc. As Deer Lodge valley and the valleys of the Big Hole, Beaverhead, and Jefferson have been, from times immemorial, a neutral ground for the Snakes, Bannocks, Nez Percés, Pend d'Oreilles, Flatheads, Spokanes, Coeur d'Alenes, and Kootenais, it looks like the old chief is too arbitrary in insisting that the Snakes and Bannocks should be forbidden to spend the winter and hunt there the same as all others, because of little squabbles common to all tribes. Maillet returned home today very much disgusted with Indians in general, and Victor in particular. Maillet also speaks Salish or Flathead. Tom Campbell and party started for Fort Benton yesterday.

APRIL 10. Many Indians still passing. Granville returned from Cottonwood. Jake Meek and several others are going to start to the Emigrant road in about eight days to spend the summer trading there. Some of the Fort Benton men camped on the other side of the river. They have a pack train loaded with supplies and clothing for Lieutenant Mullan's cantonment at the mouth of Big Blackfoot river.[54]

---

[54] This was Cantonment Wright built by Mullan in the fall of 1861 for winter quarters. It was named for General Wright. Captain John Mullan, *Report on the Construction of a Military Road from Fort Walla-Walla to Fort Benton.* (Washington, 1863) pp. 32, 33.

Gold Mining in Deer Lodge Valley

Our little settlement at American Fork has begun to take on the lively bustling appearance of a new placer camp.[55] Several parties were out prospecting with fair results. We have succeeded in getting one thousand feet of lumber, at ten cents per foot, whipsawed for sluice boxes. P. W. McAdow and A. Sterne Blake have been washing dirt in a short gulch on Gold creek and have taken out three dollars in nice clean gold dust from one hundred pans of dirt.

APRIL 30. Burr went down to Lieutenant Mullan's camp to deliver his two American horses (Old John and his bay stallion) that he sold to Mullan for three hundred dollars, when he was down there. McAdow came down and got his horses, he is going to move camp up the creek as the water has failed in his gulch. Johnny Grant sent Pierre Ish down to tell us that "Tom Gold Digger" and Tom Campbell had arrived from Fort Benton and say that there is a war party of Blackfeet on the road over to steal horses from this side of the mountains. Baptiste Quesnelle and Paul Michel came down and stayed all night. Napoleon went back. Tied up our best horses tonight. Powell killed an antelope and saw a band of elk.

---

[55] "In the fall of 1861 A. S. Blake came here [to Hell Gate] with the intention of prospecting and in the spring of 1862 in company with "Bud" McAdow, W. B. S. Higgins, Doctor Atkinson, C. P. Higgins, and E. D. Dukes went to Gold creek and commenced operations." F. H. Woody, *opus citra* 101. See also letter of McAdow of August 4, 1908, in Montana Historical Library. – ED.

MAY 2, 1862. Granville was married today to Aubony, a Snake Indian girl, a sister of Fred Burr's wife. She had been living with Burr's family, is a fairly good cook, of an amiable disposition, and with few relatives.[56] Clear and warm. Minesinger and I went up to the mountains after lumber with the wagon and three yoke of oxen. We brought down about seven hundred and fifty feet. Martineau and Sam Hugo moved down. Old man Hugo started to Hell Gate to see about building a bridge for Lieutenant Mullan. Doctor Atkinson, Higgins, Blake, and company all moved to Gold Tom's old place on the creek to try it for diggings. Tom Campbell came down and stayed all night. He says that "Tom Gold Digger" and Brown are prospecting up on Cottonwood creek. The Bannocks left Cottonwood today on foot. They said they were going to the Flathead country to steal horses, but I think they will steal any horses they can, whether they belong to white men or Indians. F. H. Burr returned from Hell Gate. He brought a lot of late papers.

Doctor Atkinson is a most original character. He is always traveling about the country with a pack horse and one or more companions, prospecting. He carries a large pair of field glasses, rides up the cañons keeping along on the ridges when possible, from points of vantage he will take out his field glasses, take a look at the surrounding country and declare that, "There, the country does not look good." Then putting away his field glasses he will ride on. I never knew of his dig-

---

[56] Aubony or Ellen became the mother of nine children of whom three, Charlie, Sam, and Mary (Mrs. E. C. Abbott, wife of "Teddy Blue" of Gilt Edge, Montana) still live. She also adopted two sons of James Stuart. One of these, Robert, is still living. Aubony died in 1887 at Maiden, Montana. This information is from the son, Sam. – ED.

ging a hole or of panning a pan of dirt.   He does buy into claims occasionally and then resells them.   On the whole he was about as lucky as some of us who dig many holes and wash innumerable pans of gravel and succeed in "just missing the pay streak."

MAY 5, 1862.   Cloudy and cold with some rain.   Jim and I hauled a log and put it across the creek for the dam to rest against at the head of the ditch.   Cossette and Joe dug six rods of ditch.   James and Tony made some of the sluice boxes, these being the first ever made in the Rocky mountains north of Pikes peak.   They also made some of the horses to set the sluice boxes on. Those Bannocks tried to cut down the corral gate last night and we repaired it this afternoon.   Oh! yes, certainly, they only wanted Flathead horses, d— them!

MAY 6.   Cloudy with rain, Joe, Cossette, and I dug fifteen and three quarters rods of ditch.   Finished the sluices and horses, and hauled them up to the ravine. Adams, Blake, and Creighton arrived from the Bitter Root.   McAdow, Blake, and Higgins are finding good prospects in a small creek up at the foot of the mountains, five miles above here. Adams commenced boarding with us today.

MAY 7.   Clear and warm and strong west wind. Finished the dam today and turned the water into the ditch.   It broke away at the steep hill side by the three pines.   Hauled up lumber and repaired the break by putting three joints of flume.   Then we set our flume boxes ready to begin washing.   Tony, Joe, and I dug several rods of ditch.   Tebow came down and got two yoke of oxen and the wagon to haul Higgins's sluice lumber to his camp.   Powell killed an antelope.   L. L. Blake and Creighton went above.

MAY 8.   Clear and warm.   Adams, Brother James,

Jim Minesinger and I began to wash gravel with the
sluices, but the ditch soon broke on the hillside, which
was composed of soft clay shale. Repaired it and
worked until nearly night when it broke again. Tony
Cossette and Joe dug ten rods of ditch. Jimmy Grant
and David Pattee arrived from Hell Gate. Nothing
new down there. Tom Campbell and Joe Hill came
down from above and report that those Bannocks stole
about twenty-five horses from Johnny Grant. Gold
Tom, Brown, Ish, Chas. DeLabreche and several others
are in pursuit of them and I surely hope they may overtake them and return home loaded with Bannock
scalps. They also report that Jack Collins and Frank
Goodwin started to Fort Benton.[57]

MAY 11. Blake, Creighton, La Breche, and Napoleon, came down from above. Creighton bought five
head of cattle. He and Napoleon went on down to
Dempsey's. Napoleon is on his way to Walla Walla.
McAdow came down from his diggings and showed a
prospect of twenty cents to the pan of dirt. Martineau
and Ball hauled down another load of logs for Pete
Martin. Gold Tom came down from above. He says
they overtook those Bannock horse thieves, but did not
get their horses, because the Indians "bluffed" them
off. I suppose there were six or seven whites and but
ten Indians. They should have gotten those horses.

MAY 13. Tony, Joe, and Cossette dug on ditch.

---

[57] While in Benton Frank Goodwin became involved in a quarrel with a
Greek over a gambling game and beat him over the head with his revolver
inflicting severe injuries. Goodwin then left the fort and remained away
until he thought the incident had been forgotten and then returned. The
Greek was appraised of Goodwin's return and taking his rifle posted himself
in a room upstairs, on watch for Goodwin who was in a store across the
street. When Goodwin came out into the street he stepped to the window
and shot him dead. There was no civil law and those at the fort thought
the Greek was justified in killing Goodwin, nothing was done in the case.
Thus was poor little Michel Le Claire's unprovoked murder avenged.

James, Jim, and I washed with the sluices in the forenoon. In the afternoon they dug a hole to look for the pay streak. I killed a two year old beef, assisted by Pete Martin. Powell, Burr, and Adams also dug a hole looking for the pay streak, which I regret to state none of them found. LaBreche returned with Little Jake, who came to hire to Adams. Gold Tom and Brown moved their camp up to the upper diggings today. River and creek on a stand, but still high.

MAY 14. James, Jim, and Adams set the sluices in another place and washed all day. Powell went hunting and killed nothing. Burr and I went up to the diggings now called "Dixie," to take a look at them. Rather liked their appearance and took up three claims just below Blake's and McAdow's on Pioneer gulch. I took up a hundred and fifteen pounds of beef to them and salted down half a barrel of beef, with salt that we brought from Salt river in 1860. Leon Quesnelle and DeMars came down from Cottonwood to look at the diggings and stayed all night.

MAY 20. Working at ditch and sluices. Burr, Powell, and I went to Dixie, found everyone hard at work. Blake and McAdow made ten dollars yesterday and nine dollars today. Higgins worked about three hours on bed rock and made three dollars and a half. Doctor Atkinson and Gold Tom are digging tail races to their claims. We sponged on Blake and McAdow for our grub. We had rice, etc., for dinner; beans, etc., for supper. Blake was the cook, enjoyed our visit very much. They are a jovial set of miners and we had much fun at one another's expense in the way of jokes. I like the appearance of the diggings better than I thought I would. There is plenty of hard work, but I think there is good pay doing it. Maillet came down this evening on a collecting tour. Also Jim Grant and Pattee. They are on their way to Hell Gate. Peter Martin went to Cottonwood.

MAY 21. Dempsey and Jackson came to see us at work mining. Cleaned up the sluices and only had twelve dollars, most of it being in one nugget. This is the first nugget found here and there may be quartz ledges in this vicinity.[58]

MAY 27. F. H. Burr started for Fort Benton with Mullan's party. Cleaned up the sluices and had four dollars and twenty-five cents for two days' work. We have concluded to quit here for the present and all go up to the Dixie diggings.

MAY 28. A party of Flatheads and Pend d'Oreilles passed on the creek above us with twelve horses that they had stolen from the Bannocks. I am glad that those Bannocks are having to take some of their own medicine.

JUNE 4, 1862. Tony came down from Dixie today. They have gone down eleven feet in our tail race and no sign of bed rock. They sunk a hole about sixty yards up-stream above the end of the race, and found bed rock at nine feet with one inch of gravel that prospects one cent per pan of dirt. "BAD EGG."

JUNE 17. David Pattee arrived here en route for Salmon river mines, with a band of cattle for John Grant. Bill Hamilton moved down here today. I wish he had gone somewhere else. Granville and crew made seventeen dollars and sixty cents today. J. S.

JUNE 24. I went to Dixie. Granville's crew made seven dollars and twenty cents. Prospected Higgins's claim (the one he bought from Doctor Atkinson).

[58] This was the first gold nugget found in what is now Montana and I still have it in my possession, September 8, 1916.

Doctor Mullan and the Lieutenant's messenger passed en route to meet Lieutenant Mullan at Fort Benton. Arrived here today a party of sixteen from Colorado. Acquaintances of our brother Thomas Stuart. Thomas expected to come with this party, but was detained and will come later with another party.[59] They have gone up on Pioneer creek to prospect. Word came that Captain Richard Grant is seriously ill at Walla Walla, and his sons, John and Jimmie have gone to see him. The doctors say he cannot live long. This has cast a gloom over the entire settlement. Captain Grant was a jovial kind hearted gentleman and very popular with the mountaineers.[60]

JUNE 25. Barcier and others arrived from Fort Benton. They say three steamboats have arrived there loaded with emigrants, provisions, and mining tools and supplies. Now everybody talks of going to Fort Benton.

JUNE 29. Mr. Louthan, S. T. Hauser, John Ault, Doctor McKellops, and Jake Mauttie arrived here from St. Louis, having come up the river on one of the steamboats. They are en route for Salmon river gold mines, never having heard of this place.[61]

JULY 4, 1862. Five emigrants arrived last night and twelve or fifteen today. All from Benton. Came up the river on those four [three] steamboats. I [J. S.] made arrangements about going into partnership with Frank H. Woody.

---

[59] Among these was James M. Bozeman, who discovered the Bozeman pass. He was murdered by the Indians on the Yellowstone in 1877. G. S. See also Grace M. Hebard and E. A. Brininstool. *The Bozeman Trail* (2 vols., Cleveland, 1922). Vol. i, p. 214. Doctor Mullan was a brother of the builder of the Mullan road. — ED.

[60] Captain Grant did not recover from this illness. His descendants are now scattered over the Northwest. – ED.

[61] Speaking of the early days in the rich and almost inaccessible mining

JULY 5. There are about forty-five emigrants in the mines at this time. C. P. Higgins arrived from Walla Walla this evening. He brought some letters for us from folks at home.

JULY 6. Capt. C. P. Higgins went to meet his teams coming from Fort Benton. We received one letter from Brother Samuel and one from Cousin Sallie Bozarth, both living in Iowa. The Colorado party are finding some good prospects in a gulch about two miles north of Pioneer.[62] We call the place "Pikes Peak." [63]

JULY 10. Returned from Cottonwood. That whiskey enabled Powell to buy nine cows and a yearling

---

camp of Florence. A bill of goods bought there in the spring of 1862, by one of my friends, who later came to Bannack. Here it is verbatim:

100 lbs. beans	@ 1.25	$125.00
300 lbs. flour	1.00	300.00
11 lbs. coffee	1.25	13.75
300 lbs. beef	.25	75.00
9 lbs. beans	1.00	9.00
3 sacks salt, 5 lbs. each		
1 lb. bar soap		3.00
6 lbs. nails	1.00	6.00
10 lbs. sugar	1.50	15.00
25 lbs. bacon	1.25	31.25
1 paper salaratus		6.00

$596.50

[62] Pioneer: a small fork of Gold creek where the Stuarts mined in 1862, named by Lieut. John Mullan. – ED.

[63] Stuart in *Montana As It Is*, pp. 8, 9, describes the naming of Pike's Peak. After telling of the settlement at Gold creek in 1861 he continued, "We succeeded during the following summer in finding prospects that we considered very good, upon which we began to make preparations to take it out 'big,' and wrote to our brother Thomas, who was at 'Pike's Peak,' as Colorado was then called, to come out and join us, as we thought this a better country than the 'peak.' How events have fulfilled this prediction will be seen hereafter. Thomas showed our letters to quite a number of his friends, and they became quite excited over them, and in the spring of 1862 many of them started out to find us, but became lost, and went to Old Fort Limhi, on Salmon river, and from there they scattered all over the country, a few of them reaching us about the first of July. We were then mining on

for beef.   Adams, Burr, and Major Graham arrived from Benton today.   I bought two hundred pounds of flour at twenty dollars a hundred and thirty-six pounds of salt at twenty-five cents per pound from Dave Contois.   How I wish we had that spring on Salt river.

JULY 11.   I visited Dixie.[64]   Worden arrived from the states via Missouri river.   Many emigrants arriving every day now.   J. S.

JULY 12.   With the emigrants today is a Mr. B. B. Burchett with his family, consisting of his wife, two very handsome daughters, one a blonde and the other a brunette, and two little tow-headed boys.   It looks like home to see little blonde children playing about and to see white women.   Miss Sallie Burchett is sixteen years old and a very beautiful girl.   Every man in camp has shaved and changed his shirt since this family arrived. We are all trying to appear like civilized men.

JULY 13.   Many emigrants arriving some going back to the states and some adventurous spirits are going to Salmon river, others to Walla Walla.

JULY 14.   Clear, calm, and warm.   This place here before known as American fork, has been re-christened

Pioneer creek, a small fork of Gold creek, without making more than a living, although some adjacent claims paid good wages.

"About this time quite a number of people arrived who had come up the Missouri river, intending to go to the mines at Florence and Oro Fino; but not liking the news from that region, when they arrived in Deer Lodge, a part of them went no farther, but scattered out and began to prospect, and most of them are still in Montana with a 'pocket full of rocks,' and stout and robust as grizzly bears, although some of them are suffering from a severe attack of an epidemic known as 'quartz on the brain,' which is now raging furiously all over Montana.   It seldom proves fatal, however; the victim generally recovering after being bled freely in the pocket.   The 'Pike's-peakers,' soon after their arrival, struck some good pay on a small branch of Gold creek, now known as 'Pike's Peak gulch.'   The diggings of this region did not, as a general thing, pay very well that summer, and they have not been much worked or prospected since from the following cause." – ED.

[64] Dixie, a mining camp nearby. – ED.

Gold creek and so it is now called. We held an election today. Great excitement, but nobody was hurt except with an overdose of whiskey.[65]

JULY 17. Cool, with west wind. Woody and Worden arrived from Hell Gate. Fred Burr and Jack Mendenhall started for the old Mormon fort on Salmon river to get the things hid there by Jack and his party.

JULY 18. James Stuart played poker with Worden, Hamilton, and Woody and lost forty dollars. Powell has been above since yesterday morning.

JULY 20. Worden and Higgins's wagon arrived from Fort Benton loaded with merchandise for their store at Hell Gate. Our mining claims at Dixie are not paying expenses. The emigrants are still leaving for Salmon river mines and some are returning to the states.

JULY 22. John Grant's team arrived from Benton. Louthan and Hauser returned from their trip in Salmon river mountains. They started out for the Elk City mines, but as Salmon river flows for many miles

---

[65] This was the second election in what is now Montana, it being Missoula county, Washington territory. Polls were opened at Gold creek, Fort Owen, and Hell Gate. The following persons were elected: Representative to the Washington territorial legislature, L. L. Blake, with thirty votes; for county commissioners, Granville Stuart, and Thomas Harris, both with thirty votes. F. L. Worden, treasurer with thirty votes; for justice of the peace, Charles Allen, with thirty votes; for coroner, John W. Powell with twenty-nine votes. There were no party lines drawn in this election and only one ticket except that C. P. Higgins and L. L. Blake both ran for representative. Blake won, he receiving twenty-four votes and Higgins six. Names of those voting are as follows: John Franks, John J. Hall, J. W. Powell, James Conlin, Ed. Hibbard, Henry Thomas (Gold Tom) David Brown, John Carr, Louis Mat, Peter Martin, James Spence, Edwin Dikes, James Stuart, Thomas Adams, W. B. Higgins, James Minesinger, Thomas W. Hamilton, Granville Stuart, F. H. Burr, P. W. McAdow, and Major William Graham.

through an impassable box cañon, and there was no well defined trail over the mountains, and they had no guide, they became lost in the mountains.   After wandering about, suffering untold hardships and almost starving to death, they finally gave up and returned to Gold creek.

JULY 23.   Arrived at our town to-day a fine violin player accompanied by his handsome, seventeen year old wife.   His name is J. B. Caven.[66]   We purchased a good violin sometime ago, so we have the Cavens over often and enjoy the society of an intellectual white woman and good music.   Certainly we are approaching civilization or rather civilization is coming to us. All the men are shaving nowadays and most of them indulge in an occasional hair cut.   The blue flannel shirt with a black necktie has taken the place of the elaborately beaded buckskin one.   The white men wear shoes instead of moccasins and most of us have selected some other day than Sunday for wash day.

JULY 24.   There is plenty of whiskey in camp now and rows are of frequent occurrence.   To-day a drunken Salmon river chap became insulting to Worden who walked into him with a pick handle.   Captain Higgins took a hand at the finish or Worden would have been worsted in the fight.

JULY 25.   Very warm.   Whiskey business very dull. Tony Cosgrove and I started to Cottonwood for a horse thief.   J. S.

JULY 26.   Clear warm.   Stayed all night at Dave Contois'.   Started on the road to Benton after our man and overtook him at sundown.   Camped all night with him on a branch of little Prickly Pear creek.   J. S.

---

[66] J. B. Caven was sheriff of the Fairweather mining district for a few weeks in 1863, but resigned to be succeeded by Henry Plummer. – ED.

JULY 27. Very warm. Arrested our man at daylight and arrived home with him at sundown. J. S.

JULY 28. Cloudy and warm. We called a miners' meeting, tried him and found him guilty. In consideration of his age and contrition, his sentence was only to refund all of the stolen property that he had and to leave the country within twelve hours. As he was utterly destitute, the court, which embraced nearly all in the camp, gave him fifteen dollars and some provisions. He then departed from Hell Gate river toward Walla Walla and was seen no more.[67] J. S.

JULY 29. Worden and Higgins concluded to start a branch store in our village and leave a portion of their goods here and to-day I began helping them put up a log store. G. S.

JULY 31. Cool, and nearly calm. John M. Jacobs arrived from Soda springs with a train of forty wagons en route for Walla Walla. He reports many more behind. Some emigrants and Dempsey are on a spree to-day.

AUGUST 1, 1862. The grocery is doing a flourishing business. Several gambling houses started.

AUGUST 2. Monte tables going every day. The bank is ahead. We gave a company of emigrants permission to work our upper claims.

AUGUST 4. Many emigrants arriving from Pikes Peak. I bought two wagons and the harness with them for eighty dollars. The grocery is doing a fine business.

AUGUST 5. Dr. H. J. McKellops, dentist, pulled a tooth for me.

AUGUST 7. Worden and Higgins started for Benton after their goods. Captain Higgins went to Hell Gate.

---

[67] Hubert H. Bancroft, History of Montana (*Works*, vol. xxxi, San Francisco, 1890) p. 619, tells this story.

Powell arrived from prospecting and reports finding good prospects, east of the Rocky mountains on Boulder creek.

AUGUST 9.   Louis Maillett started for Fort Benton. He left his blacksmith tools and other things with me. Powell has been on a big spree since he arrived here.

AUGUST 10.   The little village is all astir today. There is a general stampede over the mountains to Powell's new discovery.   Some are buying horses, some trading, everybody packing grub and mining tools, each one in a hurry to get out ahead of the rest.

AUGUST 15.   Rezin Anderson arrived from the states (he having gone down the Missouri river from Fort Benton with Worden on the Fur Company's Mackinaw boat on March 25, 1861).   We talked nearly all night and then could not relate all that had happened since we parted.   He brought letters and news from home. It makes Granville and me homesick, although we enjoy getting all the news and meeting Reece again. We thought he had joined the army.

AUGUST 16.   More emigrants arriving en route for Walla Walla.   Rezin Anderson's train arrived here.

AUGUST 17.   Powell sold his house to Terry's man and started to Deer Lodge valley with his family. Dempsey sold his ranch a few days ago and is now moving up to Deer Lodge valley.

AUGUST 19.   Woody arrived from Hell Gate with a load of vegetables and thirteen chickens.   He reports that there has been a good placer gold prospect found in Big Hole valley as much as two dollars and a half to pan of gravel.[68]

[68] These were the mines discovered by Mortimer H. Lott. G. S. For account of Lott and his discoveries see Thomas J. Dimsdale, *opus citra* (third edition) pp. 216-221. – ED.

AUGUST 20. Considerable excitement about the news that Woody brought about new placer discoveries.

AUGUST 21. Cloudy with a little rain. A number of persons are preparing to go to Big Hole valley to examine the reported new placer mines there. On the fourteenth inst., three men arrived at Gold creek from the lower country. They had six good horses, but very little in the shape of a traveling outfit. One of them, B. F. Jermagin, had no saddle on the horse he rode, but only some folded blankets strapped on the horse's back in lieu of a saddle. The other two men showed that they were on the gamble and one of them William Arnett, kept his belt and revolver on and rather posed as being a "bad man." The third, C. W. Spillman, was a rather quiet reserved pleasant young man, of about twenty-five years, he being the youngest of the three.

AUGUST 22. Woody, Burr, and several others started for Big Hole on a prospecting tour.

AUGUST 23. I have lost three hundred dollars staking a man to deal monte for me in the past three days. Think I will take Granville's advice and quit gambling. J. S.

AUGUST 24. Our monte sharps are about to take the town. Getting decidedly obstreperous in their conduct. J. S.

AUGUST 25. Our stranger monte sharps opened a two hundred dollar monte bank and I broke it in about twenty minutes. About four o'clock in the afternoon two men arrived here from Elk City in the Clearwater mountains.[69] They were in pursuit of our monte sharps for stealing the horses they rode from that place. One of the arrivals was armed with a double barreled shot

---

[69] The gold fields of Idaho.

gun heavily loaded with buckshot and a Colt's navy revolver. Their names were Fox and Bull. Bull had the gun. They slipped quietly into town in the dusk of the evening and meeting me inquired if the three men above described were there. Upon being informed that they were, they stated that they were in pursuit of them for stealing the horses on which they had come from the vicinity of Elk City. They requested the coöperation of the citizens in arresting them. I assured them that they should have all the assistance necessary and went with them to look for their men. They found Spillman in Worden and Company's store and bringing their shot gun to bear on him, ordered him to surrender, which he did without a word. They left him under guard and went after the other two, who had just opened a monte game in a saloon. Arnett was dealing and Jermagin was "lookout" for him. They stepped inside of the door and ordered them to "throw up their hands." Arnett, who kept his Colt's navy revolver lying in his lap ready for business, instantly grabbed it, but before he could raise it, Bull shot him through the breast with a heavy charge of buckshot, killing him instantly. Jermagin ran into a corner of the room, exclaiming, "Don't shoot, don't shoot, I give up." He and Spillman were then tied and placed under guard till morning. J. S.

AUGUST 26. Proceedings commenced by burying Arnett who had died with the monte cards clenched so tightly in his left hand and his revolver in the right that they could not be wrenched from his grasp, so were buried with him. Jermagin plead that the other two overtook him on the trail and gave him a horse to ride and that he had no knowledge of the horses being stolen, and what saved him, was Spillman saying that

he and Arnett had found him on the trail packing his
blankets and a little food on his back and that they gave
him a horse to ride on which he strapped his blankets.
On this testimony Jermagin was acquitted and given
six hours to leave the country and it is needless to say
he left a little ahead of time. Spillman who was a
large, fine looking man was found guilty and sentenced
to be hung in a half hour. He made no defense and
seemed to take little interest in the proceedings. When
I asked him if he had any request to make he said he
"would like to write a letter." He was furnished with
writing material and wrote a letter to his father stating
that he was to be hung in half an hour; that keeping
bad company had brought him to it, begged his father's
forgiveness for bringing disgrace upon his family and
concluded by hoping that his fate would be a warning
to all to avoid evil associates.

He wrote and addressed the letter with a hand that
never trembled and when asked if there was anything
else he wished to do said "No." Although the time was
not up he said he was ready and walked to his death
with a step as firm and countenance as unchanged as if
he had been the nearest spectator instead of the principal actor in the tragedy. It was evident that he was
not a hardened criminal and there was no reckless
bravado in his calmness. It was the firmness of a brave
man, who saw that death was inevitable, and nerved
himself to meet it. He was hung at twenty-two minutes
past two o'clock August 26, 1862. He was buried by
the side of Arnett in the river bottom just below town.[70]
J. S.

AUGUST 27. My birthday. I am twenty-eight years

---

[70] This was the first execution in what is now Montana and it caused

old.   Weather very warm.   Everything very quiet in town.   Fox and Bull started back to Elk City with the six horses.   No news from the states.   The grocery is doing a very poor business.   Michel Ogden, Major Graham,[71] and a stranger arrived from Hell Gate.   G. S.

AUGUST 29.   I won fifteen dollars bucking at monte, last night and forty dollars to-day playing poker with Louthan, Parker, and Pete Martin.   J. S.

AUGUST 30.   Very warm. Dull times in town. Burr and party returned from Big Hole, did not find anything that would pay to work.   J. S.

AUGUST 31.   Granville quit mining and moved down here.   Rezin Anderson hauled some coal and is now ready to go to work blacksmithing.   J. S.

SEPTEMBER 5, 1862.   Jim Brown had an extra gun and some clothing that he wished to dispose of for a good price and decided to raffle them.   As almost ev-

---

the little town of Gold creek to be put down as "Hangtown," on some of the western maps for some years after.   It was never known by that name in this vicinity.

Justice was swift and sure in those days.   There was no moving for a new trial or any of the thousand other clogs upon the wheels of justice, which but too often render the execution of the law a mockery.   It may be claimed that the punishment was severe beyond all proportion to the crime, but it must be remembered that there was no recognized court in the country and the nearest jail was at Walla Walla, four hundred and twenty-five miles distant, over rugged mountains.   The communities were too small and too poor to indulge in costly criminal prosecutions and hence it was advisable to inflict such punishment as would strike terror to the minds of the evil doers, and exercise a restraining influence over them.   I have always regretted that Spillman did not plead for his life, because if he had, I think he could have made such a good showing that the death penalty would have been commuted to banishment.   I now think that he was so stunned by the fearful calamity that had overtaken him, that despair seized him and he thought it useless to try to escape death.   As to the letter he wrote I have an indistinct impression that Brother James destroyed it for, of course, we would not send such a letter to anyone's father.

[71] Michael Ogden was in charge of Fort Connah.   Major Graham was a guest of Major John Owen. – ED.

erybody is on the gamble it did not take long to gather a crowd. The raffle was held in the saloon and the contestants threw dice at one dollar a throw. Clark won the gun, Burr the clothing, and Worden the gum boots, which were the first ever seen here. J. S.

SEPTEMBER 9. Cool and windy. Played poker and won a little. J. S.

SEPTEMBER 10. Granville and Woody started to Hell Gate to try and organize our county government, Granville having been elected county commissioner at our election last July, and Frank Woody having been elected auditor. I gave bonds and took the oath of office, having been elected sheriff of Missoula county, Washington Territory. J. S.

SEPTEMBER 12. Powell came down on a visit. We had a social game of poker. Fred Burr won some little. J. S.

SEPTEMBER 13. Cold and cloudy. Powell and I went up to some new placer mines on the head of Pioneer creek. Saw some men take out one piece that would weigh one dollar or more. They are working with rockers. Sunday went with a party of comrades to Blackfoot. As there are no churches around here to attend and not even a Sunday school, we passed the time playing poker. Funny how often our little testament gets lost, but we can always dig up a deck of cards any place or anywhere. I lost twenty-three dollars. J. S.

SEPTEMBER 14. Balanced accounts with Worden and Co. Are four hundred and fifty dollars in debt. J. S.

SEPTEMBER 18. Woody and Granville arrived from Hell Gate accompanied by two lower country-men.

We played poker last night. Worden was winner. I lost twenty-two dollars. J. S.[72]

SEPTEMBER 20. Played poker, lost eighteen dollars. Granville and Reece Anderson mended Plummer's double barreled shot gun, which he had broken off at the grip, coming through the timber from Elk City. Reece forged four strips of iron about five-eighths in. wide and three and one-half in. long and Granville set them into the gunstock on top and bottom of the grip, and screwed them down solid so that the gun stock was stronger than before it was broken. J. S.

SEPTEMBER 21. Woody and York started to the gold placer mines near Beaverhead. Plummer and Reeves went with them. I played poker and won one hundred fifty-two dollars. Ed. and Freeman House were the victims. Granville found the out crop of coal in Pikes Peak gulch. J. S.

SEPTEMBER 22. Mrs. Burchett and family dined with us and will remain here with us while Mr. Burchett, Ed. and Freeman House go over to look at the Beaverhead mines.

SEPTEMBER 25. James went to Dempsey's. Bob Nelson and I begun hauling hay. Bought Charlie Allen's colt. Mailette, John Grant, Thos. Pamburm stayed all night en route from Hell Gate. Minesinger

---

[72] On our way to Hell Gate at Beaver Dam hill we met two fine looking young men. One of them said his name was Henry Plummer, the other was Charles Reeves. Woody and I told them who we were. They were from Elk City on Clearwater, and enquired about the mines at Gold creek and at Beaverhead. They rode two good horses and had another packed with their blankets and provisions. We liked their looks and told them that we were only going down to Hell Gate and would return to Gold creek in a few days and asked them to return to Hell Gate with us and then we could all go up the cañon together. They accepted our invitation and in a few days we all went up to Gold creek together. These men proved to be notorious road agents and were hanged later.

and Jimmy busy hauling logs for Woody and Stuart's grocery. Burr went hunting. The boys up at the head of Pioneer creek making good wages working with rockers. Reece and I have made fifty-eight dollars in the shop in the past few days. G. S.

SEPTEMBER 26. Rained slowly most of the day. Mountains white with snow. Captain James Fisk,[73] who lately arrived with a large emigrant train that he brought across the plains from St. Paul, Minnesota, and a small party passed and camped just below here. He is inspecting Captain John Mullan's military wagon road from Fort Benton to Walla Walla. He has a brass mountain howitzer with him. Fred Burr killed four black-tail deer this evening. Reece and I did eleven dollars worth of work in the blacksmith shop.

SEPTEMBER 27. Raw and cold. James returned from above. Bob Nelson hauled a load of charcoal. Reece and I did twenty-two dollars worth of work in the shop.

SEPTEMBER 28. Sunday. Decidedly cold, I dined with Captain Fisk and had a splendid dinner. He was considerably "high" in the evening. The boys had lots of fun with him. Sullivan and P. C. Wood tried to get up a party to take the Captain's howitzer, but they failed. Jack Mendenhall started for Salt Lake.

SEPTEMBER 29. Captain Fisk started below. Several parties quite drunk. Reece and Granville busy in the shop. P. C. Woods and "Buzz" Caven moved here from Little Blackfoot. We are glad to have Caven for we will enjoy some good music and like to

---

73 This was the first of Fisk's expeditions to Montana. Fisk's *Journals* are in the library of the Minnesota Historical Society. Bancroft, *Montana*, pp. 622, 634-637, describes briefly the expeditions. – ED.

have his white wife about. We have had no white
women in camp since Mrs. Burchett and family went
to Beaverhead mines.   J. S.

SEPTEMBER 30. Woody returned from Beaverhead
mines. He reports that nearly everybody is making
money over there. Everybody excited.

OCTOBER 5, 1862. York and Irvine came from
Beaverhead mines yesterday. They report two hundred Pah-Ute Indians over there when they left, under
the old chief Winnemucca and as these Indians are an
insolent treacherous band it is feared that they will
make trouble so a party of us are going to start over
there to help if it becomes necessary.

OCTOBER 22. We went to the Beaverhead mines, so
called although they are not on that stream at all, but
on a small creek that comes into the Beaverhead from
the west a little below the junction of it and Red Rock
creek.[74] We had fine weather during the ten days that

---

[74] These were the Bannack mines on Grasshopper or Willard creek discovered by John White in July, 1862. He was one of the Pike's peakers
whom Stuart described in 1864 as follows: "Many of the 'Pike's peakers'
became rather lost and bewildered in their attempts to reach Deer Lodge
and were scattered all about through the mountains; this, though a source
of infinite vexation to them at the time, proved of great ultimate benefit to
the country, for one small party of them discovered some gulch mines at the
head of Big Hole prairie that paid tolerable well during the summer of
1862, but they seem to have been exhausted, as they have not been worked
since that time. I have been told by men who worked there, that they
worked across a vein of good coal thirty feet wide in the bed of the gulch,
and that they put some of it on the fire and it burned brilliantly. If this is
the case, this locality will become valuable in a short time.

Another party happening to camp on Willard's creek, began to prospect
and found very rich diggings, where a great many men made fortunes during that summer and winter. This attracted almost every man in the country to the spot, and the mines at Gold creek were deserted for the richer
ones at "Bannack City," as a small town that had sprung up at the head of
the cañon of Willard's creek was called, and have virtually remained so
ever since, for about the time that the Bannack mines began to decline a little
and people began to think of branching out again, a party of six who had

we were gone. We found everybody making money and well satisfied. There are about four hundred men there. We have decided to move over. Woody remained to look after things, until I can get back with a load of goods. We hired Butler to build us a log building twenty feet square for which we are to pay $140.00. There was no Indian trouble. The Pah-Utes have gone over to the Yellowstone to hunt buffalo and there were only a few Digger Indians there when we arrived. They are always very peaceable. Hired William Babcock to haul about a ton of freight over for us.

OCTOBER 23. Hugh Bratton, an old friend of ours from California, arrived yesterday.

OCTOBER 25. Below zero. A severe change in the weather. James, Hugh Bratton, Bob Nelson, and James Collins started for the Beaverhead mines with the "Old Steamboat" wagon full of goods. Lots of Flathead Indians in town to-day. Snow twelve inches deep – awful!

OCTOBER 27. Gathered up all of our cattle, and Reece and I did some work in the shop for Indians.

---

started to the Yellowstone country, on a prospecting tour, and had been driven back by the Crow Indians, who robbed them of nearly everything they had, camped, as they were returning, on a small branch of Stinking-water river, afterwards called Alder creek, because of the heavy growth of that wood along it, not a single tree of which is now to be seen, the wants of the miners having used them up long ago, and the banks and bed of the stream are dug up and piled about in a most extraordinary manner, considering the short time that has elapsed since its discovery. But to return to the discoveries. They camped on the creek about half a mile above where the city of Virginia now stands, and on washing a few pans of dirt they "struck it big," getting as high as four dollars to the pan. They staked off their claims and went to Bannack City to get a supply of provisions, and to tell their friends to return with them and take claims, which they did. The creek proved almost fabulously rich. Thousands of men having made fortunes in it, and still it is not half worked out. *Montana As It is*, pp. 9, 10.

They did not move to-day.   The town women folks are doing a big business trading for dried service berries, camas, bitter root, etc.   I bought a hair rope for one dollar.

OCTOBER 28.   Indian village moved to-day.   Everybody trading for Indian horses.   Reece busy in blacksmith shop.   Thomas Adams captured his little boy from the Indians.   The boy's mother left Adams; going back to her tribe and Adams had not seen the child before, but when he found him with the village he took him.   The little fellow cannot speak English and is weeping bitterly for his Indian relatives.

OCTOBER 29.   Daubed part of the walls of our house with mud mortar.   Kiplinger and Knuckols arrived from Beaverhead mines and said everybody is taking out big wages in placer gold.

OCTOBER 30.   Adams's little boy wept all night and we persuaded him to let the child join his Indian mother.   He has finally consented and handed the boy over to a couple of Flatheads, who will join the village tomorrow.   The child is once more happy.   Sold Kiplinger eight head of cows for beef at $60.00 a head.   He paid me $164.50 and is to pay the balance, $315.50 when he returns from the mines.   I paid Worden and Co. $280.00 in clean gold dust at $16.00 per oz.

NOVEMBER 1, 1862.   Reece and I went up to Pioneer creek and hauled down the rest of the charcoal and sixteen sluice boxes as we need the lumber.

NOVEMBER 3.   Worden and Peter Martin started to Beaverhead mines.

NOVEMBER 4.   Sold Worden and Co. 54 lb. of tea @ $2.00, $108.   Got the sorrel stallion "Brooks" back.

NOVEMBER 5.   I made one bunk to sleep in.   Our puncheon floor was rather solid, while a bunk built against the wall and filled with hay is so restful that we hate to get up of mornings. Reece, while hunting our horses, saw an Indian driving off one of Jack Gunn's oxen late this evening.

NOVEMBER 6. Reece, Burr, Purple, Bill Fairweather,[75] and I went after the Indians that took Gunn's ox and overtook them in Hell Gate cañon, twenty miles below here. We found the ox in their possession and they said they had traded for him with a white man at Charlie Allen's place. We brought him back with us to have him point out to us the man that traded with him. It was dark before we reached home. I think he is lying about any white man having traded that ox.

NOVEMBER 7. Burr had the Indian locked up in his one room log house last night, but he concluded that he did not want to help us hunt up the white man that he traded with for the ox, so in the night he let himself out and fled leaving his pishamore, a buffalo skin rug used under his saddle, horse leggins, and knife behind him. A southern gentleman, named Captain Simms, who had sojourned in our little town since he lodged here sometime last summer, and who was usually engaged in reducing the visible supply of whiskey around town, which he always paid for, however, took possession of the Indian's horse and contemplated keeping him.

NOVEMBER 8. A brilliant day. I felt the *dolce far niente* common name "laziness," pretty strong, but I struggled valiantly against it and succeeded in building another bunk and then went after our cattle to Flint creek, but did not find them. Reece worked in the shop. A crowd of women and men left here for Cottonwood to attend a ball given by Thomas Lavatta's

[75] Bill Fairweather later discovered Alder gulch. – ED.

folks. Everybody in town nearly sick. Cause, tight houses.

Two Coeur d'Alene Indians passed intending to overtake the Flathead village beyond the mountains somewhere. I gave them something to eat and sent them on their way rejoicing.

SUNDAY 9. All the Indian women went up to Johnny Grant's today. Maillett and Tom Lavatta came down and stayed awhile.

NOVEMBER 10. Sent three men from Pikes Peak gulch down into the cañon below the mouth of Flint creek to prospect for gold. It looks like the famous Beaverhead diggings down there. I think rich placers will be found in that vicinity.[76]

NOVEMBER 11. Worden and Pete Martin got back from Beaverhead mines. Brother James and the ox team will stay at Cottonwood tonight. Blake and Higgins had their horses stolen at the spring six miles this side of Beaverhead. Supposed that Snake Indians took them. I sent two yoke of oxen to meet Jim Minesinger in the cañon. He is coming with a wagon load of goods and but one yoke of oxen. They have entirely played out.

NOVEMBER 14. Had a big dance in Minesinger's house tonight.

NOVEMBER 15. Major John Owens, Major William Graham, and C. C. O'Keefe arrived from Fort Benton.

[76] The Pike's Peak men did not find the placers, nor was I one of the discoverers, but four years later, in 1866, my predictions were verified by the discovery of the very rich mines of Bear gulch.

Bannack and Pike's Peak

NOVEMBER 18, 1862.   I have concluded to go to the Beaverhead mines with James and open a butcher shop during the winter.   Woody will run the grocery outfit.

NOVEMBER 19.   Started for the mines with the ox teams loaded with goods and supplies of all kinds. James and I rode horseback and Bratton drove the wagon.   Reece Anderson will remain in charge of the property left at the little town of American Fork.

NOVEMBER 22.   We arrived at the mines and at once moved into our log cabin.   The village is now called Bannack.   We have fixed up our cabin quite cozy and home like.   There is a fire place in one corner, two bunks against the wall, a couple of shelves and a calico curtain does service for a cupboard, another shelf holds our five books and James's tobacco pouch and pipe. The table and some stools complete the outfit.

NOVEMBER 23.   The building which we contracted for the butcher shop is also finished and we will begin business at once.   Most of Fisk's train is located here and quite a number of others among them, Henry Plummer, Charlie Reeves, Louis Cossette, the Burchett family, and "Buz" Caven, and his charming wife.

A number of the men of the Fisk train who had wagons and mules or oxen turned their attention to freighting, going to Salt Lake and returning with sup-plies.   There was so little snow on the divides that these freighters crossed all winter without difficulty. This was most fortunate for there were so many people in the country and no supplies whatever that had the winter been severe with deep snow many must have perished from starvation. It would have been utterly impossible to have furnished game for so many people.

The Bannack mines were very easily worked; being mostly bars of gold bearing gravel on the banks of the creek, lying at from ten to twelve feet above the water in the stream. At the edge of these bars there was but a thin layer of rich gravel on the underlying limestone bed rock and I, several times saw the miners pull up the small sagebrush that grew on the edge of the bars and shaking off the sand and fine gravel, that adhered to the roots, into a pan which they carried to the creek and obtained from twenty-five cents to one dollar to the pan, in small pieces of beautiful gold. This caused the saying at Bannack that "we could pan gold out of the sagebrush."

Bannack City, during this winter gradually drew to itself the greater part of the people then scattered over the region round about, and by spring, mining was assuming large proportions. Many gamblers and desperate characters drifted in, lured by the prospect of acquiring gold dust without digging for it. It became the custom to go armed all the time.

The miners of Bannack met and established a miners' court. B. B. Burchett was elected judge and Henry Crawford, sheriff. A mining claim was one hundred feet up or down the creek and as far out on each side as the pay dirt extended, they were numbered 1, 2, etc., above or below discovery as the case might be. Title to a claim was established by staking it and posting a notice and then taking it to the recorder and having it recorded. The claimant was then obliged to work his claim every day when water was available. An absence of three days constituted a forfeiture and the claim could then be jumped. In case of sickness the claim was protected until such time as the owner was able to resume work. The laws laid down by a miners' court were very simple and absolutely just. There was no appeal from the court's decision. These early day miners were men of unquestionable honesty and integrity and there was little disposition to infringe upon the rights of others, consequently the law was followed to the letter. Neither James nor I did any mining at Bannack.

There were two good fiddlers in camp, "Buz" Caven and Lou P. Smith, and something over thirty white women. Seven were unmarried, but did not remain so very long. We had a number of fine balls attended by all the respectable people and enjoyed by young and old alike. Best suits packed in the bottom of our "war bags" and long forgotten, were dragged out, aired and pressed, as best we could, and made ready for these festive occasions. A very few of the men who had their wives with them, sported white shirts with stiffly starched bosoms, but the majority wore flannel shirts with soft collars and neckties. These dances were very orderly; no man that was drinking was allowed in the hall. The young people danced the waltz, schottish, varsoviane, and polka, but the older ones stuck to the Virginia-reel and quadrille. There were usually about ten men to every woman at these balls so the women danced every dance. These gatherings were very informal and very enjoyable. Tickets were $5.00 gold and there was no supper served.

"Buz" Caven possessed considerable dramatic talent

and he and his wife gave several entertainments consisting of songs, dancing, and recitations. So passed the
winter of 1862 at Bannack City, Dakota territory.

About the fifteenth of March, 1863, I made a trip to
Gold creek to get a load of goods from Worden and
Company's store. In this load were two dozen long-
handled shovels, which I sold quickly at Bannack for
ten dollars each. I also had fifteen pounds of chewing
tobacco for which I received fifteen dollars a pound.
I was certainly glad that I did not use tobacco.

On April 10, 1863, James Stuart, with a party of
fifteen started for the Yellowstone valley to prospect
for gold.[77]

After selling my goods I closed up the business at
Bannack; selling everything but two town lots and two
houses. I had collected all together about three
thousand dollars and on April 24, started for Gold
creek with that gold dust in my cantinas at my saddle
bow.

I had a distinct recollection of the fate of Charlie
Guy and George Edwards,[78] and that their murderers

[77] James Stuart was in command of this expedition. His Journal of the
Yellowstone Expedition of 1863, is published in the *Montana Historical
Society Contributions*. (Helena, Mont., 1876) vol. i, pp. 132-205. – Ed.

[78] The rich "diggings" of Grasshopper creek attracted many undesirable
characters and I believe there were more desperadoes and lawless characters in Bannack the winter of 1862-3 than ever infested any other mining
camp of its size. Murders, robberies, and shooting scrapes were of frequent
occurrence.

In November, 1862, Charles Guy, who had some money and a good team
of horses and a wagon, started to Salt Lake for supplies and was found
murdered and robbed, and his horses gone, on Red Rock creek. No trace
was ever found of his murderers, but it was supposed afterwards that some
of those later known as "road agents," had followed and murdered him.
He had no relatives at the mines.

The second murder this winter was perpetrated in January, 1863. A
young man named George Edwards went to look for some horses that were
on the range and failed to return. After a few days his friends became

were still in town, so I was very careful not to let any
one know that I had the money or that I intended leaving town.   I had my horse brought into town the evening before so that I could get an early start next morning.   I arose very early, ate a hurried breakfast, and
left town just at sunrise.   I saw nobody stirring and
passing along a back street took the road to Deer Lodge
valley.   I was armed with my short breech-loading
rifle, with plenty of cartridges and I knew that there
was not another breech-loader in town, and in my belt
I carried a tried and true Colt's navy revolver and
handled both as quickly as any of the robbers.

I had just begun to congratulate myself on getting
away without being seen, when I heard horses coming
behind me and knew that I was being pursued.   In a
few minutes three men on horseback came in sight
around a bend in the road.   They were Charlie Reeves,
William Graves [79] and a man whom I did not know,

anxious and went to look for him.   Some snow had fallen and they were
unable to find his tracks on the range, but quite by accident found his blood-
stained clothing stuffed into a badger hole, but the body was never found.

Edwards had several hundred dollars on his person when he left town
and this must have become known to some of the bad characters that infested
Bannack that winter.   The murderers stripped the body for two reasons,
first to make sure that they had all the money and second to hide the clothes
to prevent identification of the body if found.   Edwards had no relatives
in the country and I do not think any effort was made to find the body after
the snow melted in the spring.

His murderers were never apprehended.   I have always suspected that
Charlie Reeves and William Graves (Whiskey Bill) committed this murder.
At this time there was no law or courts, save the miner's court and no steps
were taken to do more than to regulate affairs relating strictly to mining
matters.   Every man was expected to take care of himself. G. S. Stuart's
manuscript contains a chapter on "Undesirable Citizens" that closely
parallels the account in Langford, *opus citra* and is omitted. – ED.

[79] Reeves was banished in 1863 but later returned.   He later fled when
the vigilantes became active.   Graves, alias, Whiskey Bill was hanged by
the vigilantes at Fort Owen January 26, 1864.   Dimsdale, *opus citra*, p. 22. –
ED.

but I did know that Reeves and Graves were tough characters.

The road followed up a ravine to the top of the mountain about a mile. I did not think they would attack me so near town, but determined to give them no chance and when they drew near I dismounted and pretended to be cinching my saddle, being careful to keep my horse between me and them. I did not take my eyes off them; intending if they made a move toward their revolvers to shoot with my rifle, which was hung on a shoulder strap and ready for action. They saw that I was watching them and that my rifle was conveniently near. As they rode up Reeves called to me asking where I was going and volunteered the information that they were going to Deer Lodge and rode on. Just at this minute to my dismay I saw another horseman coming up the ravine. I thought I might possibly stand off three, but it would be about impossible to escape from four. I remained by the side of my horse and when the horseman drew near, you may imagine my relief when I discovered him to be my friend, Edwin R. Purple, and that he too was armed with a navy revolver.

As soon as he came up to me I explained the situation to him and we decided to travel together to Deer Lodge. We knew that our safety depended upon our not allowing them to get behind us. It was not long before we overtook them and several times during the day they halted ostensibly to tighten their saddle cinches. We both immediately did the same, always stopping behind them. They were very anxious to do the agreeable, but we kept close together and always a short distance in the rear.

It was sundown when we reached Divide creek,

where it issues from the mountains near the summit of
Deer Lodge pass.   Here Purple and I decided to camp
for the night hoping the others would go on, but they
too decided to camp.   We allowed them to select their
camp first and then we chose ours a spot about fifty
yards below them on the little stream.   We ate our
lunch and then sat down by our camp fire in a position
where we could watch their camp.   Purple smoked his
pipe and then spreading down our saddle blankets for
a bed and our saddles for pillows we lay down.   We
agreed to keep watch all night.   I took the first watch
for two hours.   Our neighbors also retired, but I had
no desire to sleep with those three men only fifty yards
away; I was only anxious that they remain just where
they were.

The night seemed very long, but we all arose at sunrise and eating our breakfast resumed our journey.
All morning our unwelcome companions tried to get
behind us, but this we prevented by stopping every time
they did. When we passed Warm springs they spurred
their horses into a gallop and left us, reaching Deer
Lodge an hour ahead of us.   We spent the night at
Deer Lodge and went on down to Gold creek next day,
but our three companions remained in Deer Lodge.

These were dark days in Bannack; there was no safety
for life or property only so far as each individual
could, with his trusty rifle, protect his own.   The respectable citizens far outnumbered the desperadoes,
but having come from all corners of the earth, they
were unacquainted and did not know whom to trust.
On the other hand the "Roughs" were organized and
under the able leadership of that accomplished villain,
Henry Plummer.   At times it would seem that they
had the upper hand and would run affairs to suit them-

selves. The law abiding citizens were beginning to get better acquainted and although the few attempts made to administer justice had failed they believed that the time would come and that at no distant day, when the community would rid themselves of this undesirable element.

During my brother James's absence I decided to remain at Gold creek, as I was anxious to do some prospecting down the river, at a place some fifteen miles below the mouth of Flint creek. Reece Anderson had remained at Gold creek to look after the cattle and blacksmith shop while we were in Bannack.

APRIL 17, 1863. Killed a young steer for beef and hauled a load of wood. Four Flatheads came along on foot followed by three on horseback. They said they had had nothing to eat for several days and from the way they made beef disappear, I am inclined to believe them. They say the Flathead village will be here in four days.

APRIL 18. Hauled all the lumber we had down out of the mountain; gathered up our cattle. I brought in two milch cows, determined to have some milk and butter. Decided to enlarge our house and am putting in spare time on that.

APRIL 19. Traded four gallon of pure spirits to J. M. Morgan for a good new horse. This would seem to be a rather high price for spirits, but Morgan will add a few pounds of plug tobacco, a quantity of cayenne pepper, some mountain sage tea, and rain water enough to fill a barrel. This will enable him to start in the whiskey trade in first class shape.

APRIL 20. Hugh Bratton and I went "gold hunting" down the river to about fifteen miles below the mouth of Flint creek, where there is a belt of rotten

limestone resembling that around Bannack. We prospected all around there, but could hardly find a "color"
of gold so returned.[80]

MAY 5, 1863. Two pack trains arrived from Walla
Walla. Bought from them the following:

52	lbs.	Tobacco	@ $4.00	$208.00
168	lbs.	Bacon	@ .40	67.20
241	lbs.	Sugar	@ .60	144.60
17½	lbs.	Soap	@ .50	8.75

$428.55

The pack trains brought us our mail, some letters
from the states and some San Francisco papers sent to
us from Hell Gate by Worden.

The letters from Iowa came by way of the Isthmus
of Panama to San Francisco, then to Portland and the
Dalles, and then overland to Walla Walla, and on by
Frush and Sherwood's Express to Hell Gate, then up
here by any reliable person coming this way. We pay
$1.00 express on each letter received and 75c on each
sent out, but letters from home are welcome at that
price.

MAY 9. Worden and Company's teams stopped
over night with us. They are on the way to Fort
Benton after goods which are being brought up the
Missouri river by steamboat. There is a good deal of
travel past here now and Anderson and I are kept busy
in the blacksmith shop shoeing horses, mending wagons,
and repairing fire arms. Took in $62.30 today.

MAY 15. Maillette, Pattee, Eaton, and Peou, left

[80] We were on the right track even if we were not lucky enough to make
a discovery. Three years later the rich Bear gulch diggings was discovered
near where we prospected.

for Cottonwood en route to Fort Benton. Reece Anderson and I hauled wood for a coal pit and while he set up the pit, I tried to fix the meat-house so it would be fly proof. We have been much annoyed by these pests and suffered no small loss by their blowing meat for us. Higgins left a fine black dog skin overcoat hanging in our cabin and when he came for it some weeks later it was white all over with fly blows and they could not be brushed off, but had to remain until the sun came out warm enough to hatch the darned things. This was quite awhile and at a time when Higgins needed his coat. These flies have the ingenuity of the Devil and up to the present time we have been unable to keep them out of the meat-house. We have carefully tacked mosquito netting over our windows and closed every crack, yet they keep getting in. Sunday I took a day off to watch for them and to try to discover how they got in and to my surprise I saw them poke their front feet into the mesh of the mosquito netting and pull it apart enough to get their heads through and then by wiggling and squirming they got the rest of their body in and the hole would close behind them. They seem to have eternal life, for as cold weather sets in they crawl behind loose bark on dead trees or any crack or crevice that will afford a hiding place and then freeze solid. As soon as a Chinook wind comes and it begins to thaw a little, out they come, lively as ever and begin their work. They will repeat this performance as often as thaws come, and freeze again every time it freezes.

MAY 20. James Grant arrived from Hell Gate and reports many men on their way here from "below." We bought four fine Hudson's Bay shirts from him @

$3.00 each.[81] These shirts are far ahead of our American things called "hickory."

MAY 21. Rainy and cold. We opened our coal pit and had about twenty bushels of charcoal. Eight men arrived from Clearwater this morning. They are going to stop and prospect up the creek for awhile. These new arrivals got up a shooting match. We have heard nothing but what fine shots they were and how one of them was "barred out" at a shooting match "below" because he won so many chickens. We think we are "some shots" here so it didn't require much hunting to get up a team. We set up a board five feet long and eight inches wide at one hundred yards distance. We did not do any remarkable shooting, but managed to rake in most of their loose coin. Only one in their party hit the board at all. I suppose the change of climate affected their marksmanship.

MAY 22. A man, by the name of Townsend, has been busy making a lot of saddles, which he intends to take to Benton to sell to emigrants coming up on the steamboats. We made a lot of rings for him.

Fourteen Pend d'Oreille Indians came along well mounted. They said they were going to steal horses from the Crows. They unsaddled and showed a disposition to stay all day and night too, but we were not very cordial, and they left in the afternoon. I burned three warts off my left hand with nitric acid.

MAY 23. Worked in the blacksmith shop and caught cold in my hand where I burned the warts off. My hand and arm are much swollen and very painful. I could not sleep last night for the pain. Worden and Company's store has a bottle labeled, "Merchants

---

[81] Grant was a trader for the Hudson's Bay Company. – ED.

Gargling Oil, a liniment good for man and beast," and this morning I went for it and wrapping my hand in several folds of cotton cloth kept them soaked in it. It felt better and toward evening the pain is less severe. My whole arm is badly swollen and inflamed.

One of the priests passed going to St. Ignatius Mission.[82]

MAY 25. Word came that two Pend d'Oreille Indians had killed a white man in Hell Gate cañon, somewhere near the Beaver Dam hill, and had taken his horses and pack and joined the Flatheads. A party of men left here to go after the Indian and punish him. Reece Anderson joined the party, but my hand was in such bad shape that I could not go.

MAY 26. The priests' wagon from St. Peters Mission [83] passed here today taking a sick man to St. Ignatius. A very remarkable looking man was driving two yoke of oxen to this wagon. His mouth was all on one side and looked as though it had been broken into three pieces and badly put together. His eyes did not match and looked in all directions; one could not tell whether he was looking at you or away from you. I cannot think where he came from, but the Fathers do pick up some queer specimens of humanity. I sent some letters by him to Hell Gate to be mailed; also all the tin pans in Worden and Company's store to Captain Higgins, who wanted them.

[82] St. Ignatius Mission was first established on Lake Pend' Oreille in 1844 by Father De Smet. In 1854 a new location was selected by Father Adrian Hoeken south of Flathead lake and west of the Mission mountains where the mission remains today. Chittenden and Richardson, *opus citra*, vol. ii, p. 474, vol. iv, p. 1234. – ED.

[83] St. Peters Mission was founded in February, 1863, by Fathers Giorda and Imoda for work among the Blackfeet Indians. It was located on the Missouri not far from the mouth of the Sun river. Lawrence B. Palladino s. J., *Indian and White in the Northwest* (Lancaster, Pennsylvania, 1922) p. 194.

ST. IGNATIUS MISSION, 1866

St. Ignatius was, and still remains, the center of Jesuit missionary work with the Indians of western Montana
From an original drawing by Peter Tofft. Tofft was an artist of real ability and made a number of
excellent drawings of early Montana

A man from Prickly Pear stopped with us over night. He reports about fifteen men getting ready to mine there; bringing in a ditch about a mile and a half long. They get small prospects for eighteen feet down and then come to a strata of gravel (thickness as yet unknown) that prospects forty-five cents to the pan of dirt.[84] I churned about three pounds of good butter this evening. My hand is improving, thanks to the Gargling Oil. The priest thought I had blood poison and had it not been for the oil I suppose I would be dead now.

MAY 27. Van Court, the man from Prickly Pear mines, left for home. Charles Frush and G. J. Sherwood arrived and took dinner, then went on to Fort Benton. They brought states [papers] dates to April 18th. From the war news it would seem the South is getting rather the best of it.

Our mail to Hell Gate has fizzled out; as it would not pay to carry it for so great a distance. Louis Mullan, a brother of the Lieutenant, had the contract and lost money on it.

MAY 28. Baptiste Quesnell came down from Cottonwood (La Barge City now). La Barge, a trader from St. Louis, promised to build a store and put in a stock of goods; hence the change of name. Charlie Allen came from Bannack and reported that old Johnson had been killed up near Bird Tail rock by four men and robbed of eight hundred dollars.

MAY 30. The men returned from Hell Gate. They went to the Flatheads and demanded the surrender of the Indian, who had murdered the white. At first the chief refused to give him up saying, that the culprit

---

[84] In this neighborhood was discovered Last Chance Gulch the next year. — ED.

was not of his tribe, but as he was with them the whites insisted that he be given up and after some parley he was brought forward and turned over to them. As there was no question as to his guilt he was sentenced to death and hung at Hell Gate.

MAY 31. The Flathead village arrived here today. The chief rode out into a spot that suited him and dismounting stuck his spear into the ground and sat down beside it. The squaws came up, unsaddled his horse and led it away, while others undid their packs and set up the lodge over his head. Some style about that fellow! These Indians are on the way to hunt buffalo bulls. At this time of year the cows are calving and the bulls go in herds by themselves and are very fat and fine eating. They do not hunt the cows or disturb them, if they can help it, but leave them and the calves until fall when they are fat and the robes fine.

Captain Felix Burton and another man arrived from Three Forks of the Missouri, where is a small settlement called Gallatin City, and took dinner with us. Six Pend d'Oreille Indians came along going on a war party after the Snakes. One of them had a paper from the priest, stating who he was and where he was going and requesting that no one molest him. We told him "all right, but do not get too near any of our horses." I start to Bannack with my wife tomorrow to try and finish collecting some outstanding debts. We go on horseback, a nice little ride of one hundred and ten miles.

JULY 3, 1863. Left our ranch on Gold creek on May 31 and returned today. When we reached the top of the mountain about a mile from Bannack we met a big stampede from town. I inquired what it was all about and learned that six men had come into town a couple of days before to get some provisions, and under promise of strict secrecy had told a few of their friends that they had found a rich gulch and would take them to it. Of course enough leaked out to create a great excitement, and everybody got ready to follow. So here they were, about seventy men. I asked who made the discoveries and they replied, "We only know one of them and his name is Bill Fairweather, and he and the other discoverers are all in front of the crowd." They were strung out for a quarter of a mile, some were on foot carrying a blanket and a few pounds of food on their backs, others were leading pack horses, others horseback leading pack animals. The packs had been hurriedly placed and some had come loose and the frightened animals running about with blankets flying and pots and pans rattling, had frightened others and the hillside was strewn with camp outfits and grub. My wife and I assisted some to round up their animals and collect and re-adjust the packs; soon they were all on their way again hurrying and scurrying lest they get left behind.[85]

This party (Bill Fairweather's) had intended to join James Stuart's Yellowstone expedition but were detained by not having horses. They went to La Barge City to intercept a Flathead village and purchase horses. After securing the horses they started for the mouth of the Stinkingwater, where they expected to join the Stuart party, but found they were too late and

[85] This stampede was on its way to the famous Alder gulch. The discovery was made by Bill Fairweather, Henry Edgar, Bill Sweeny, Tom Cover, Henry Rogers, and Bainey Hughes. G. S. Another account by one of the party of this expedition is the Journal of Henry Edgar, 1863, in *Montana Historical Society Contributions*, vol. iii (Helena, Montana, 1900) pp. 124-142. In the same volume pp. 143-153 is another account of the discovery of Alder gulch by Peter Ronan, who came into Alder gulch with the first rush. – ED.

that the main party had passed. Taking the trail, they followed on expecting to overtake them. Before they did so they were captured by a large band of Crow Indians and led prisoners to the Crow village.[86]

I remained in Bannack all of June and collected about three hundred dollars and rented the store building to a baker, for forty dollars a month, rent in advance. Bannack was almost deserted on account of the new diggings on Stinkingwater. James, my wife and I, returned to our home at Gold creek; found our old California friend, Hugh Bratton, living with Anderson and laid up with a sprained back and hip. Everybody, but two Frenchmen, have abandoned Pioneer gulch and moved over to Pikes Peak gulch, where they have found good placer diggings.

JULY 4. Rested after our journey and talked matters over. James and Clabber, our Indian horse herder, caught twenty-five large trout and we celebrated the national day by having a fine dinner with trout as the principal dish.

JULY 5. Reece and I went up to the upper sink of the stream in Pikes Peak gulch cañon to see if we can bring the stream on down past the sink in a ditch. At the upper sink a stream two thirds the size of Gold creek runs into a hole in the marble limestone bed rock and forever disappears. This water is much needed for the new placer discoveries in Pikes Peak gulch. We think it practicable to bring the water from just above the sink around in a ditch, but the cost will be great. Killed a beef today.

JULY 6. Everybody came down from the mines today, to get their weekly supply of provisions. They

---

[86] Here Granville Stuart inserts the Edgar Journal noted above which the editor omits.

are all anxious to get the water and agree to pay for it, if we will convey the water to their mines. I caught thirty-five trout, using grasshoppers for bait.

JULY 7. James and I went up and made a survey of a ditch to bring the water into the Pikes peak gulch placers. It can be done, but at a high cost, and just now we haven't that much money.

JULY 8. James went to La Barge City with a four horse wagon, after flour and other things. Bratton, Cook, and Bob Nelson bought out Parker Ball and Company, in the old Discovery claim in Pikes Peak gulch for one horse and $120.00 cash. We advanced the cash.

JULY 9. James and I made another survey of that ditch, but there will have to be so much fluming and at the high cost of lumber we think it impracticable. Clabber quit herding for us. We paid him $25.00. This boy has been one of Captain Grant's retainers and this $25.00 is the first wages he ever had. He is a good faithful Indian.

Several men from Walla Walla passed on their way to Bannack. Peter Martin and family returned from Fort Benton yesterday greatly disgusted. No steamboat arrived this season and everybody over there in a semi-starving condition. One steamboat came as far as Dauphins rapids; ninety miles below Fort Benton and had to stop, the river being very low. There are three other boats behind somewhere. Powell and Worden are on them and we are all much concerned about them, and are afraid something may have happened to them. These boats pass through the Sioux country, and when the water is low, as it is this season, they are often stuck on sand bars for days; exposed to hostile attacks from the Indians.

JULY 11.   Strong east wind, cool and pleasant; very smoky for several days past, caused presumably by forest fires west of us. James and I went hunting; he taking the north side, I the south. He only saw one black-tailed deer; shot it with his Sharps rifle, the trusty gun that he carried on his Yellowstone expedition. I had worse luck; saw one white-tailed doe and shot and killed her off hand at seventy-five yards with my Maynard breech-loading rifle. I could only see her head and neck; broke the latter and when I came up to her found she had young ones. I would have given anything to have restored the poor thing to life and to have allowed her to go free with her children.

JULY 12.   Frush and Sherwood's express arrived from Walla Walla. They brought us states papers dates to June 16th. This being Sunday, all the miners are down for supplies; sold all the deer meat to them.

JULY 13.   I went up to Rock creek to see if it was possible to make a ditch from it to Pikes Peak gulch; I found it possible, but at an enormous cost. I followed up the creek to a beautiful little lake about a mile and quarter long and half mile wide. It is surrounded by high mountains in the midst of a lovely forest. There were many trout in it and one lone duck floated on its placid waters. No doubt I was the first human being it had ever seen, for it had no fear of me, and probably thought I was just a new kind of a deer, and my horse only an elk.

I decided to join the duck in a swim in the water, which was as clear as a crystal; found it slightly warm on the surface to a depth of two feet, but below that so icy cold that I could not remain more than a few minutes and came out shivering in the hot July sun.   It lies very high; the creek flowing out of it falls over one thousand feet in the first three-quarter mile. The lake has been formed by several land slides from the mountains which filled up the cañon about one thousand feet deep at the lower end of the lake, which must be that deep. This lake belongs to me, as I am probably the first white man who ever stood on its shores, and tried to bathe in its icy waters. Saw several deer, but not near enough to get a shot, and the horse flies tried to eat up "Old Fiend" my horse.

JULY 14. Reece and I began making a pair of spurs and found it no easy job. James and Peter Martin started to Bannack after a load of flour, and bacon.

JULY 16. Red and Mat Craft returned from Bannack last night; they bring news that Lee's army is within three miles of Washington, D. C., with terrible fighting going on. Charlie Allen started to Bannack to try to settle up the estate of George Carhart, his partner, who was accidentally killed in a saloon row.[87] Reece and I finished my steel spurs, they are noble, noisy ringers. Mat Craft and his wife (the only white woman in camp) moved up to James Minesinger's house. Johnny Grant passed on his way to Hell Gate.

JULY 17. Reece piled up the charcoal. Made shelves and put up the drugs and medicines. Bratton is still laid up with his lame hip and back, and his horse is sick and likely to die. A small band of Pend d'Oreilles passed; returning from a war party and don't look or act as though they had been very successful. They asked for whiskey, but did not get any and passed on.

JULY 19. Am glad I do not have to attend church

---

[87] Langford, *opus citra*, vol. i, p. 314, describes this shooting in detail.

and sit on a bench two hours listening to some fellow telling us how much hotter it would be somewhere else, and that we were headed for that particular spot. We may miss some of the good things of life by being out here, but we escape some mighty disagreeable experiences. All the miners (five now here) came down from Pikes peak gulch and had their tools fixed up. Red and George Craft started on a prospecting trip to the head of Flint creek, by the way of the head of Gold creek. We had a high old game of cribbage.

JULY 20. Sixteen Flatheads and Pend d'Orielles passed, returning from a horse stealing expedition against the Crows. We came near having a row with them, but by a friendly talk it blew over; and we traded with them for a mare and colt that they had stolen from the Crows. They had two horses belonging to Fred Burr, that the Crows had stolen from him at the crossing of the Big Hole river; Te-losh-ten-aw, a good Flathead, had these horses and returned them to Burr, he paying the Indian all that they were worth for his trouble.

JULY 21. I smoothed the interior of our shot gun. Thirteen men are here en route to Fort Benton. They are from the Florence mines: say that the soldiers had a fight with the Indians on Snake river, in which they killed eight hundred Indians and captured two thousand ponies; which is so big a story that we do not believe it.

They have twenty-five thousand dollars worth of gold dust with them in buckskin sacks; and intend building a boat at Benton, and going down the Missouri river to the states in it. We advised them not to do it; and also admonished them against exhibiting so much treasure, as there were some people in the country who were not particular as to how they came into possession of gold dust, just so they got it. They did not seem to pay much attention to our warning and went on their way.[88]

JULY 23. Rained all last night and until ten A. M. to-day, John Grant and Captain Higgins arrived from Hell Gate to-day, and Frush and Sherwood arrived from Bannack. Captain Higgins brought us one dozen fine Hudson's Bay shirts; price three dollars each. They are much better and, thank goodness, have much longer tails than the miserable "high water," hickory, American shirts that we are sometimes obliged to wear.

[88] Their fate was not known until several years later; when William Keyes spent the winter of 1871 on the Missouri river, below Rocky point, and there married an Indian woman. Seeing her husband with gold dust, she told him of a squaw who had some and related to him the story of how she came by it, which is as follows:–

A village of about one hundred lodges of Sioux Indians were camped on the bank of the river, and they saw a boat with white men coming down. The warriors at once began firing at them. The men in the boat had a small cannon, which they loaded and fired at the Indians; but so heavy was the recoil that it loosened a plank in the bottom of the boat and it began to sink. The men beached it on a sand bar, but on it there was no shelter and they were still within reach of the Indians' rifles. The white men had only the cannon and revolvers. They did not use the cannon after the first shot, and the Indians killed them all; then crossing over to the sand bar, they stripped them naked, scalped them, and cut them up in a most horrible way; and then proceeded to plunder the boat. Finding the buckskin bags filled with the gold dust, and not knowing what it was, they emptied it out on the sand and took the sacks, which they could use for many things. One squaw, out of curiosity, kept one bag of gold and put it in her parflash. Keyes's wife persuaded this squaw to show him the bag of dust; later she accompanied him to the scene of the massacre.

Keyes tried to find where they had emptied the gold. In the spring he and his wife came to Fort Benton and told their story to John Lepley, a wealthy cattle owner on the range between Shonkin and Arrow creek, whom they persuaded to go down the river with them to make further investigation. The sands of the bar had washed and were so changed that they found but little of the gold; but were convinced that the party murdered was the men from the Florence mines.

Eighty-five in the shade on the south side of the house, up under the eaves.   If I put the thermometer on the north side, where I can not watch it the Indians will steal it.   It would be of no use to them, but not understanding what it is, they think it is some sort of "medicine" and are very curious about it.

Virginia City

JULY 26, 1863. The new discovery at Stinking-water is now attracting attention from everywhere. The mines are turning out big. People passing here every day on their way over. All the miners here are abandoning their diggings and going over and we have about decided to move also. James and Reece Anderson are going over tomorrow to see what best to do.

JULY 27. Brother James and Anderson started for Stinkingwater mines today. Solitary young man arrived from "below" on his way to the states via Fort Benton. He had a large boil on his cheek, was almost barefooted, poorly mounted, nearly naked, and not much money; but carried a double-barreled shot gun. He invested in $5.25 worth of "grub," shot, and fish lines. I told him that it would be utterly futile for him to try to make his way down the river alone in a boat. He would be murdered as soon as he struck the Sioux country. I advised him to go over to the mines, where he could get work and later return across the plains with some freight outfit. I think he will take my advice.

This evening, while Bratton and I were enjoying a quiet game of cribbage, we were suddenly interrupted by all the women in the village rushing in, headed by Mrs. Craft; all trying to talk at the same time: English, Flathead, Blackfoot, Snake, and Bannock; some were weeping, some, ready for a fight; a regular Tower of Babel performance. We finally learned that all the commotion was caused by Mrs. Craft's having accused Pierrot's squaw of stealing her "shimmy."

They appealed to me to settle the row; but what could one lone man do in a case of this kind? I was no Solomon. I asked Mrs. Craft what the thing looked like. She called me a "fool," and left with her nose in the air. Madam Pierrot denied vehemently ever having touched the thing. I called my wife in and after talking things over, discovered that a young Indian girl visiting with Madam Pierrot saw Mrs. Craft with a new fangled garment brought from the states; and not wishing to be behind with the styles, she had purchased some cloth and seeing the coveted garment on Mrs. Craft's clothes line had "borrowed" it for a model after which to construct her own; but before she had time to return it, Mrs. Craft had missed it, and so great was her wrath that the Indian girl became frightened and hid it instead of returning it.

JULY 30. Captain Higgins arrived today bringing states papers. It is said Vicksburg has been taken and that a mighty battle is in progress on the Potomac.

AUGUST 7, 1863. U. S. Marshal of Idaho Territory, D. S. Payne, arrived en route to Bannack City, Stinkingwater mines, and Boise. His business is to estimate population, resources, etc.; and to establish election precincts through this part of the country, which is now Idaho Territory.[89]

Mrs. Craft, good woman, is introducing many new innovations into society here. She has decided we should wear starched shirts. I have been called upon to make a "bosom board;" which I did, and she has starched front, neck, and wristbands of our shirts; and is busy every day explaining the process of ironing shirts to the "native Americans."

---

[89] Idaho Territory was established by act of Congress in March, 1863, out of parts of Dakota Territory and of Washington Territory. – ED.

AUGUST 13. James and Reece Anderson returned from Stinkingwater mines and reported everything "booming" over there. The mines are turning out very rich and are quite extensive. James hired a man to build a log blacksmith shop for $150.00; we will soon move over bag and baggage.

AUGUST 17. James took a load of lumber to Cottonwood. (It is Cottonwood once more. Captain La Barge failed to start his store there and the inhabitants went back to the old name.) Worden, Powell, Mailette, Louis Demars, and Al. Clark arrived today from Fort Benton. Worden is accompanied by his sister. They all came up the Missouri river on the delayed steamboat. We have made Miss Worden as comfortable as possible. This must seem a strange country to a young lady from the states, but she seems to be very well contented.

AUGUST 21. We have brought all of our cattle over to Robert Dempsey, who is camped at the crossing of the wagon trail from Bannack city to Stinkingwater; and will leave them with him to be wintered.

AUGUST 26. Arrived at the new diggings and camped in Daylight gulch. The new town is called Virginia City, the district Alder Gulch. Our blacksmith shop is almost finished. James bought two thousand pounds of flour at ten dollars per cwt.; and one hundred and fifty pounds of bacon at thirty cents a pound, and stored it in Bannack when he was over before. We have hauled that over here; also all of our things from Gold creek including lumber. James and W. B. Dance formed a partnership and will open a general store as soon as a building can be erected.

AUGUST 30. Reece and I went to work in the blacksmith shop; lots of work. In two weeks we cleared three hundred dollars; and then took in Frank McConnell as a partner and ran two fires, I acting as sledge hammer man for both fires; which was a heavy job as the weather was very warm.

SEPTEMBER 18, 1863.   We have a large lot of boots, shoes, harness, saddlery, and leather coming up the Missouri river.   One lot of 1290 lbs. arrived and I paid $348.30 freight on it, being 27c per pound.

OCTOBER 15, 1863.   Today we moved into our log house down town. James bought a Charter Oak cooking stove No. 8; it and utensils for it cost $150.00; also a heating stove for the store cost $35.00.   Frank McConnell, Reece, and I are very busy in the blacksmith shop.

OCTOBER 27.   Unusual excitement in town today news has just arrived that the coach that left here for Bannack on the twenty-fifth was held up by highwaymen and the passengers robbed.   That morning the driver was ill and as a furious storm was raging no one could be found willing to make the trip.   Finally Billy Rumsey who is a good driver consented to take the coach over to Bannack.   There were three passengers and as they were several hours late Rumsey made the best time possible to Stinkingwater station. Here another delay.   There was no stock ready.   Men were sent out in a hurry to bring in the horses but after being gone for some time the stock herder returned with only a portion of the stock.   Rumsey ordered them to hitch up what they had and he started out on a run.

At Dempsey's they were again delayed because of the stock not being ready.   Daniel McFadden, better known by the sobriquet of "Bummer Dan," and the discoverer of Bummer Dan's bar; one of the richest bars in Alder gulch who had been spending a few days here, took passage on the coach.

At Coplands everything was ready and the horses were quickly changed and all possible speed made to the Rattlesnake ranch but in spite of the best efforts it was almost dark before they arrived, and only to find that the stock had all been turned loose; the excuse given was that it was so late they had ceased to expect them.

Rumsey ordered the herder out to bring in the horses; he went but came back without them. It was impossible to proceed further without fresh stock so there was nothing to do but remain all night where they were. William Bunton who was in charge of the ranch showed himself to be the soul of hospitality being especially liberal with his whiskey. The "crowd" was repeatedly called to the bar and treated. Rumsey would not drink with them, but most of the hangers-on spent the night drinking and gambling. At daybreak Rumsey went himself with the herder to look for the missing horses, but they could not be found and he was obliged to hitch up the jaded team that he had driven in the night before and proceed on his journey. When all was ready he shouted "All aboard for Bannack." Matteson, Percival, and McFadden took seats in the coach, Wilkinson announced that he was going to accompany Bob Zachary and ride one of his horses. Bill Bunton came out with a bottle and glass, and offered everybody a drink; and announcing his intentions of going also, mounted the seat beside the driver.

It was cold and stormy and the passengers inside let down the curtains to the coach. The horses were traveling along at a fairly good gate; Bunton doing the whipping and Rumsey the driving, but as the team was played out before they started they soon settled down to a slow trot.   Bunton complained of being cold and left the seat beside the driver for one inside the coach beside Bummer Dan; Percival and Matteson were on the front seat with their backs to the driver.   They had not gone more than a mile when Rumsey saw two men wrapped in blankets with hoods over their heads and a gun apiece and knew in a flash that they were road agents.   He shouted to the passengers to get their guns; but all were too much surprised to move.   The robbers were coming on a run for the coach and were down on them in an instant.   "Throw up your hands" was the preemptory order.   Rumsey drew up his team and complied.   Bunton began to beg and plead for his life; repeating over and over, "For God's sake, don't shoot. Take what I have, but don't kill me!   For God's sake, spare my life!"   This was all for effect and to distract the others for Bunton was a member of the road agent band.   The driver was ordered down and the passengers out.   Rumsey objected saying he was afraid that the team would get away.   Bunton offered to hold the horses which he did.

Rumsey was next ordered to take the arms from the passengers and throw them in a pile on the ground, and after that to take their valuables and deposit them in the same place.   McFadden handed out two small purses and Rumsey took them and threw them on the ground as directed; whereupon the spokesman shouted to him with the most terrible oath to unload his dust and to be quick about it or he would perforate him with lead.   Dan lost no time in getting off a belt and handing over two more purses of dust.

These preliminaries over, all were ordered back in the coach and Rumsey was told to drive like hell and never to open his mouth or they would kill him sure. The order was obeyed in so far as getting out of that neighborhood in the shortest possible time and the coach proceeded on its way to Bannack where they reported the robbery. Bummer Dan lost $2500.00 and the others about $500.00 between them. So far as I can learn no steps have been taken to discover who the robbers are or to punish them.

NOVEMBER 10, 1863. Have been ill with typhoid. Miss Matilda Dalton, whom I named "Desdemona" in Bannack last winter, because she was beautiful and so good, is also very ill of typhoid.

James and W. B. Dance have opened the store. Virginia City is a very lively place and reminds us of the placer days in California.

NOVEMBER 13. Sam T. Hauser and N. P. Langford [90] started for St. Louis today overland via Salt Lake City. The departure of these dear friends has cast a gloom over us. Before them lies a long perilous journey of eighteen hundred miles; through cold and storm and be-set on all sides by hostile Indians and road agents. It will take six weeks to make the trip. "God be with them."

NOVEMBER 29. Gillette's wagon train arrived from Fort Benton bringing six hundred pairs of heavy leather boots for Dance and Stuart. The freight from St. Louis here has cost thirty-five cents a pound. The boots are not what are liked here by the miners and I see that we will not make any money on these goods. Two men killed and one severely wounded here the past month in drunken rows.

[90] Hauser was territorial governor of Montana from 1885 to 1887 and for many years thereafter was a leading Democratic politician in the state. Langford became noted as a writer and for many years was connected with the Minnesota Historical Library. — ED.

NOVEMBER 30. A man murdered twenty miles below here. I did not learn the particulars, but I surmise robbery was the motive. There has been several robberies on the road between here and Bannack seventy miles away and few are people living between the two camps. There is certainly an organized band of highway men about here and something will have to be done soon to protect life and property.

Louis Maillett and DeMars arrived from Salt Lake with loads of flour. Flour is now selling for $28.00 cwt. It has been as high as $40.00, but a quantity arriving from Salt Lake made it fall to $28.00. Fresh beef sells at 15, 20 and 25 cents a pound according to cuts; beef tallow 30c a pound; sausage, made from beef scraps, 30c lb.; bacon, 40c; sugar, 60c; coffee, 90c; table salt, 50c; keg butter, $1.50 lb.; eggs, $1.50 per doz. (very scarce); turnips, 25c lb.; potatoes, 40c lb.; candy, $1.50 lb.; raisins, $1.00 lb.; board from $16.00 to $18.00 per week.

News of the discovery of gold in Alder gulch spread with incredible rapidity and as soon as claims were staked attention was turned to building a town. The first stampede reached the gulch on June 6, 1863. The stream was marked on either side by a dense growth of beautiful dark green alders and willows and it was because of the presence of the growth that Henry Edgar named the district "Alder Gulch."

Campers, at the upper end of the gulch, accidentally set fire to the dry grass and, as a high wind was blowing, the fire was soon beyond control; sweeping down the creek with such rapidity that many who were camped along the creek and in the brush, had no time to remove their belongings and lost everything they had. This was indeed a serious calamity as there were no supplies to be had in the camp. Those who escaped the fire divided with those who lost everything and, by so doing, managed to get along without serious discomfort until supplies arrived.

On the sixteenth of June the Varina Townsite Company recorded a claim to three hundred and twenty acres of land. A town was laid out, and named Varina, in honor of Mrs. Jefferson Davis. The name was soon changed to Virginia by Judge Bissel, who bluntly refused to use the name of Jeff Davis's wife on any document that he prepared and accordingly as he named it so it remained. The change of name caused us no little inconvenience for several years; when a U. S. mail route was established. There was already a Virginia City, Nevada, and letters and papers intended for us were sent there and their mail found its way to Virginia City, Montana.

People flocked to the new camp from every direction; all the other settlements in the country were deserted. There were no houses to live in and not much in the way of material to construct houses. Every sort of shelter was resorted to, some constructed brush wakiups; some made dug-outs, some utilized a convenient sheltering rock, and by placing brush and blankets around it constructed a living place; others spread their blankets under a pine tree and had no shelter other than that furnished by the green boughs overhead. The nearest sawmill was seventy-five miles away on the creek above Bannack, but the nearby mountains furnished an abundance of house logs and the ring of the axe was a familiar sound and soon log houses made their appearance on all sides. The first building was erected by T. L. Luce, on Cover street and was occupied by a baker, but Henry Morier was soon in the field and had his building up and a saloon started. I think this is about the first time in the history of founding a mining camp where the bakery got ahead of the saloon. Frederick Root and Nathaniel J. Davis were the first to complete their store building, but R. S. Hamilton brought in the first stock of merchandise. John Lyons built and occupied the first residence, but before cold weather set in there were houses all up and down the gulch and most of the families were housed in comfortable log cabins; although windows were not as numerous as they might have been. Sash and glass had to be brought from Salt Lake and there were no panes of glass larger than eight by ten; most being six by eight, and the cost $1.00 per pane. The first lumber brought over from Bannack sold readily for $250.00 gold per thousand feet. P. W. McAdow and Thos. Cover succeeded in getting a sawmill in operation on Granite creek in February, 1864, but the price of lumber did not decrease for some months as the demand exceeded the output about ten to one.

A. J. Oliver and Company started a stage line from Virginia City to Bannack and Salt Lake City in August, 1863. We were rejoiced to pay $1.00 each for any paper or letter received and 75c for all letters despatched. There was no government mail route until November, 1864. George B. Parker was the first postmaster. The first newspaper published in Montana was the *Montana Post*, printed by John Buchanan and issued on my birthday, August 27, 1864.

The winter of 1863-64 was a mild one, building and mining operations were carried on with but little interruption all winter and before spring every branch of business was represented. Gold was coming out in large quantities. The district extended from the foot of Old Baldy to twelve miles down the creek. The bed of the creek and the bars on both sides were uniformly rich; the bed rock being literally paved with gold. The Alder gulch diggings were the richest gold placer diggings ever discovered in the world.

Freight teams from Salt Lake arrived until late in the fall, bringing in supplies; and while we were not provided with luxuries there was no suffering from food shortage. Molasses was considered by us, a great delicacy and it was both scarce and dear. Sam Hauser hit upon a plan all his own whereby he kept the only one gallon of molasses in our mess all to himself. Returning home one evening tired and hungry, we found Sam sitting at the table holding a mouse suspended by the tail: the little animal had every appearance of having been drowned in the molasses. Sam didn't say that he had taken the mouse from the molasses, we just reached that conclusion by inference and immediately lost our fondness for molasses – not so with Hauser – he continued to spread molasses on his bread every meal until it was all gone. One day, in an inquiring mood, he asked us why we all quit on molasses. James replied that he liked molasses but not well enough to eat it after a mouse had drowned in it: whereupon Hauser informed us that he had killed the mouse and smeared it with molasses later just to see how we would take it.

There was a great number of saloons and each dispenser of liquid refreshments had the formula for making "tanglefoot:" – a quantity of boiled mountain sage, two plugs tobacco steeped in water, box cayenne pepper, one gallon water; so if any one got low in whiskey he promptly manufactured more. Saloons, gambling houses, public dance halls (hurdy gurdies) ran wide open and here, as in California, gold dust flowed in a yellow stream from the buckskin bags of the miners into the coffers of the saloons, dance halls, and gambling dens. Gold dust was the sole medium of exchange and it was reckoned at $18.00 an ounce. Every business house had gold scales for weighing the dust. If a man was under the influence of liquor, the bar keepers were not averse to helping themselves liberally to the man's dust, when paying himself for drinks and he more often took $1.00 for a drink than the going price of twenty-five cents. A dance at one of the hurdy gurdies cost one dollar and as each dance wound up with an invitation to visit the bar where drinks for self and partner were expected, the cost of a waltz, schottische, or quadrille was usually $1.50. Dances kept up all night long but were usually orderly. If a man was found to be getting too much under the influence of liquor, some obliging friend would expel him from the hall. Every sort of gambling game was indulged in and it was no uncommon thing to see one thousand dollars staked on the turn of a monte card. The miner who indulged in gambling usually worked six days, then cleaned up his dust; and placing it in a buckskin sack hied himself to the nearest gambling house where he remained until he had transferred the contents of the sack to the professional gambler. If he played in luck he could usually stay in the game twenty-four hours. He would then return to his "diggins" without money and often with little grub; a sadder but no wiser man, for he would repeat the same thing over and over as long as his claim lasted and would then start out, blankets on his back, in search of new "diggins."

There was a hotel and several restaurants in Virginia City, but most of the miners built themselves cabins and did their own cooking. Some of these cabins were the pink of neatness, while others were not so well kept but cleanliness was the rule.

Open-hearted generosity was met with on all sides. There was quite a number of families in Virginia City at this time. All the ladies did their own house work and in case of sickness helped nurse and care for their neighbors. There was quite an epidemic of typhoid fever during the fall and early winter and some people were very ill, but there were no deaths. The women were particularly kind and helpful, leaving their own work to nurse and care for those who were ill. No appeal for assistance ever went unanswered. A subscription paper setting forth its purpose would be circulated up and down the gulch; two or more responsible citizens taking it, was all that was required to get sufficient money to relieve any case of distress. Everybody would contribute a sum of gold dust.

During the winter Prof. Thomas J. Dimsdale[91] opened a private school; all of the children of school age attended. The fee charged was $2.00 per week for each pupil – a very modest sum for those days. The school was a good one.

There were many dances and social gatherings where all the families in town attended, bringing the children with them. There was usually a bed or two provided in some adjoining room and all the little ones were put

[91] Thomas J. Dimsdale was an Englishman, at one time a student at Oxford University and a man of fine culture and character. He taught a private school for a time and was appointed the first territorial superintendent of instruction. He was also the first newspaper editor in Montana and as such wrote the articles in the *Vigilantes of Montana* published first in the *Montana Post* and published in book form in 1865. It has gone through several editions. There is a brief life of Dimsdale imprinted from the *Rocky Mountain Gazette* of March, 1901, in the third edition of the *Vigilantes of Montana* (Helena, Montana, 1915). – ED.

to bed and the folks took turns looking after them. It was no uncommon thing for a man and wife to appear at a ball carrying a clothes basket between them in which was snugly deposited the baby. These parties were very informal and most enjoyable. Dancing would be kept up until an early hour in the morning. A fine supper was usually served at midnight and the tickets cost $5.00 each. J. B. Caven and wife gave several theatrical entertainments and the tickets were $3.00.

Rev. A. M. Torbett [92] arrived early in 1864 and was the first protestant minister in Montana. He started a little church on Idaho street and I think all the protestants of every denomination attended and supported the minister and the church.

Although there was no court except the miners' court there was a number of lawyers in camp: Samuel McLean, G. W. Stapleton, and J. P. A. Smith being the first to arrive. Dr. J. S. Glick, a skilled physician and surgeon, arrived in 1863 and begun the practice of medicine.

In order to make clear how debts were collected in days before courts of law were established, I will here give a notice of a miner's meeting called to settle a question of a debt between two citizens. Copied from the *Montana Post* of November 5, 1865.

"At a meeting of miners of Brown's District, Bevins Gulch, Madison County, Territory of Montana; held at J. H. Hughes' saloon in Bagdad City, October 30, 1864, for the purpose of settling a dispute between W. P. Allen and Company and Caleb Perry.

"Willa Huffaker was called to the chair and N. T.

---

[92] Mr. Torbett did not remain long in Virginia City. He had left before July 18, 1867. Daniel Tuttle, *Reminiscences of a Missionary Bishop*, p. 125.

Headley appointed secretary. On motion, the Chair appointed Clitus Barbour, O. C. Stanley, W. S. Ferris, W. L. Britton, S. McKee, and G. G. Ford, a committee to try the case and render a decision according to the evidence and testimony advanced before them. The committee brought in the following verdict: – 'That we find Allen and Company entitled to receive from Perry the sum of one hundred dollars.' Mr. Perry then declared he would pay nothing. The following resolutions were then offered and adopted.

"Whereas it is a notorious fact that Caleb Perry will pay no debts unless forced to do so; and whereas after having agreed to abide by the decision of a jury of six men, appointed to make such decision, and then disputing the right of such jury to try the case, and refusing to make any settlement.

"Resolved: That the miners of the district put Mr. Allen in possession of the claims of Caleb Perry and assist and protect him in working the same until he shall take out one hundred dollars clear of expenses. On motion, C. Farnham and S. Jeff Perkins were appointed a committee to wait upon Mr. Perry and to notify him that unless he complied within twenty minutes with the decision as rendered by the jury selected to try the dispute between Allen and Perry that Mr. Allen should be put in possession of his (Perry's) claims on the following day.

"The Committee appointed to wait upon Mr. Perry reported that he (Perry) refused to comply with the decision of the meeting.

"On motion the Chair appointed the following committee to put Mr. Allen in possession of Perry's claims:

Bishop Tuttle quotes from some newspaper notices of Torbett in Montana *Historical Society Contributions* (1904) vol. v, p. 292.

James Hunter, C. Farnum, S. Jeff Perkins, Michael Hughes, and Joseph Woodward."

The Perry claims were accordingly turned over to Allen and Company, who worked them until they had taken out one hundred dollars over and above cost of working and then the claims were turned back to Caleb Perry.

About the middle of January, 1864, a regular stampede craze struck Virginia City. The weather had been quite cold and work in the mines was temporarily suspended. A large number of idle men were about town and it required no more than one man with an imaginative mind to start half the population off on a wild goose chase. Somebody would say that somebody said, that somebody had found a good thing and without further inquiry a hundred or more men would start out for the reported diggings.

One report of a discovery on Gallatin river started a large party out in that direction. Every horse that could be found fit to ride was made ready. We had some horses on a ranch near town and brought them in and in less than an hour we had sold them all for about twice what they would have sold for at any other time. Four hundred men left town in mid-winter, with the ground covered with snow, for some place on the Gallatin river; no one seemed to know exactly where they were going, but most of them brought up at Gallatin City. Many, who could not get horses, started on foot. The first night out brought them to a realization of the futility of such a trip and they turned back.

Late in the evening on January 22, a rumor started that a big discovery had been made on Wisconsin creek, a distance of thirty miles from Virginia City. The report said that as much as one hundred dollars to the pan had been found; and away the people flew all anxious to be first on the ground, where they could "just shovel up gold." Virginia City was almost deserted: men did not stop for horses, blankets, or provisions, the sole aim was to get there first and begin to shovel it out at the rate of one hundred to the pan. Fortunately the distance was not great and the weather was mild. Robert Dempsey had a ranch nearby and the stampeders got a supply of beef from him to last them back to town. It is needless to say that they found no diggings and all returned to Virginia in a few days.

The next great excitement was caused by a rumor of new rich discoveries on Boulder creek, a branch of the Jefferson. We sold every horse that we would spare at about three times its real value. Reece Anderson was among those taken with the fever and he joined the expedition. He had a good saddle and pack horses and plenty of food and blankets. There were so many in this stampede who started with little or nothing that those who had good outfits were obliged to share food with those who had none to keep them from starving and in the long run those with good outfits did not fare much better than those who started with none. Our friend, Reece Anderson, returned in about two weeks without having found any big thing in the way of gold mines, but he had accumulated quite a valuable stock of experience and got his nose, ears, and fingers badly frost-bitten.

The next big excitement started right in town. Somebody reported a "find" at the edge of town and in the morning claims were being staked off the main streets and on the rear of all of our lots. One enthusiastic man began to sink a hole in the street, just above the store and it began to look like we would be dug up and washed out without ceremony.   Of course there was no gold found and mining operations in the streets and back yards was soon suspended.

A grand stampede to the Prickley Pear valley in which more than six hundred people took part was the last of the season.   Away they went, crossing the hills into Boulder valley.   They found the snow very deep, but fortunately not cold.   Some good mines had been discovered on one bar about six hundred feet long, but all good ground had been taken when the stampeders arrived.   The little army of disappointed men turned around and returned home once more.

BRIAN TURNER'S
favourite British recipes

Also by Brian Turner

A Yorkshire Lad: My Life with Recipes

BRIAN TURNER'S
favourite British recipes

CLASSIC DISHES from YORKSHIRE PUDDING to SPOTTED DICK

Photographs by William Shaw

headline

DEDICATION

To my mum and dad, sadly no longer with us,
and to Louis Virot, my first mentor

Photographs © **William Shaw 2003**, except for title page © **Trevor Leighton**

First published in **2003** by **HEADLINE BOOK PUBLISHING**

10 9 8 7 6 5 4 3

Cataloguing in Publication Data is available from the British Library

ISBN 0 7553 1092 6

Edited by **Susan Fleming**
Designed by **designsection**
Art direction by **Lisa Pettibone**
Home economy by **Annabel Ford**
Styling by **Roisin Nield**
Reprographics by **Spectrum Colour**, Ipswich
Printed and bound in France by **Imprimerie Pollina**, L93620

HEADLINE BOOK PUBLISHING
A division of Hodder Headline
338 Euston Road
London NW1 3BH
www.headline.co.uk
www.hodderheadline.com

Contents

Introduction

Although my basic training was in French cooking, and most years of my long career as well, I'm an Englishman born and proud of it. I grew up on classic British — Yorkshire — food. My mother cooked for us at home, mostly long-cooked stews and baked vegetables, and my father ran a transport café nearby. I used to help at the café, along with my brothers and sister, and could say that I was a head chef at the tender age of twelve! I'm still a dab hand at breakfasts, my speciality then. And my first professional job, at the age of eighteen, couldn't have been more British, as it was at that bastion of Englishness, Simpson's in the Strand. There I learned the vagaries of the catering trade, and eventually was allowed to carve the roasts in front of the customers, the ultimate accolade for a mere whippersnapper from the kitchen.

So I am not unfamiliar with British food, and in fact when at home, I tend to cook things which are much more British in feel than French. But of course the history of cooking in this country has been as hybrid as the language: the Vikings influenced us, as did the French after 1066, and then later, when what seemed like all the French chefs decamped to London in the nineteenth century. It would appear that there have always been two strands of British cooking and eating: one for the rich in the cities who could absorb foreign influences (because they could afford it), and one for the poor in the north and west, who made do with what they could grow, pick, kill or poach (and the latter is not in the culinary sense). The differential between these strands is now far smaller than it was, because of modern communications and our burgeoning interest in food — although, sadly, some people will always eat less well than others. However different these traditions are, though, both are characteristically British, and both are reflected in this book, which will demonstrate, I hope, that you don't need to have money to eat well.

It's been a revelation researching the background of English, Scottish, Welsh and Irish cooking. I don't think I had quite appreciated how rich our agricultural heritage was, or how lucky we have always been to have such a wealth of indigenous produce. This ranges from the fish and seafood caught along our long coastlines, to the magnificent animals reared on the rich pastures, and the vegetables and fruit — some native, lots introduced — grown in our fields. Home cooking, in any country in the world, is always produce- and season-led. Although we may have lost sight of this slightly these days, because of the advent of the supermarket culture, there is still an inherent knowledge and awareness of what is best when. Nothing could be more delicious than the first English asparagus or broad bean, or the first Scottish raspberry.

I have tried to celebrate the magnificence of what was and is British food in the recipes following. No-one has ever agreed as to the 'original' recipe for something in particular, and of course basics differ from country to country and from county to county, for British cooking is very regional indeed. (As are French and Italian cooking, but somehow we're much simpler here.) All of the recipes are easy (well, most), and all are based on what could be an original way of doing things, but often with a slightly modern or peculiarly Turner twist. I'm quite proud of them, and have thoroughly enjoyed the months of reading, inventing, testing and tasting.

Lastly, this is not a chef's book, although written by a chef, and may not always be appreciated by my fellow professionals. My work with Beefeater and Tesco has made me turn to ideas that are less 'cheffy' in nature and more domestic. And *Ready Steady Cook* has honed me in the fine art of cooking food that people want to cook as well as eat – something many chefs have lost sight of. (Incidentally, why that programme is criticised so much by the profession, I cannot understand. Its premise is the same as the chefs' most revered annual competition, 'Chef of the Year'.) And most chefs wouldn't dare to admit, as I happily do, that their favourite foods to eat at home are basically very simple. I'm a great fan of Welsh rarebit…

Chunky Tomato Soup (see page 22)

Brian Turner's Favourite British Recipes

The words 'soups' and 'starters' signify 'first course of the meal' to us now, but the concept of 'courses' as we know them today is actually fairly recent. At one time dishes in a formal meal were served buffet style, all laid out on the table at the same time. (In fact, we've come full circle now, doing it again in Chinese restaurants, in tapas bars and at Greek mezze tables.) The intention was (and is) to visually impress – and at very grand meals, a groaning table would have been a spectacle indeed. However, there were many drawbacks to this '*service à la française*'. Diners would have to concentrate on

Soups

the dishes in front of them only, or assert themselves and ask fellow guests or servants to pass them something they wanted from elsewhere (difficult if they were shy). And often, of course, the food would be cold by the time it was eaten, particularly soups. It was not until the nineteenth century that the Russian pattern of eating, '*service à la russe*', was introduced and adopted. Foods were carved and plated at the sideboard, served to each diner in a set pattern, and our familiar 'course' system was born.

Soup became and still is a classic starter course, and indeed it can often serve as a complete meal in itself, as a lunch with bread, for instance. In the very earliest times in Britain, soup would have been just that, possibly the only meal the less well off would have all day. 'Pottage' was the early soup, a potful of water in which vegetables, pulses or grains and flavourings – and occasionally some meat, if you were lucky – would be boiled all together. Often the liquid and contents would be poured over bread to serve and this 'sop', as it was known, is probably the origin of the word 'soup' (from the French '*souper*', to taste, as is 'pottage', an anglicisation of '*potage*').

The soups here represent a variety of types. The Scotch broth is perhaps the nearest to the original pottage (and the Scottish porridge is a direct descendant of the medieval grain pottage). The others reveal how tastes gradually changed as new ingredients became available (the tomato and Jerusalem artichoke, for instance), and new influences were introduced (those of the immigrant French and, much later, those returning from India). Fish soup-stews are found all over Europe – think of the French bouillabaisse and garbure, for instance, and there are examples in Britain, from the north of Scotland to Wales to the south of Ireland.

Green Pea and Ham Soup

SERVES 8

The traditional English pea soup was made with dried peas, and its greeny-brown colour was so similar to the dense smog that dominated London in the winter (until as late as the 1960s), that the smog became known as a 'pea-souper'. In *Bleak House*, Dickens referred to the fog as the 'London Particular', and the name has been used for both fog and soup ever since.

There are so many versions of pea soup that to say one is the definitive classical recipe is practically impossible. Soup made from tinned peas is my least favourite but, if made from dried, fresh or a mixture, can work well. The following, however, is the one I like best. It will always remind me of the time Bob Holness came on *Ready Steady Cook*, and I made him some pea soup. This allowed the lovable Fern Britton to utter these immortal lines, 'Can I have a "P" please, Bob?'

85g (3 oz) unsalted butter

1 large onion, peeled and finely diced

900g (2 lb) frozen peas

1 small bunch fresh mint, tied together

85g (3 oz) plain flour

300ml (10 fl oz) double cream

salt and freshly ground black pepper

Ham stock

1 ham hock, about 900g (2 lb) in weight

3.4 litres (6 pints) water

2 carrots, trimmed

2 onions, peeled

1 head celery, washed

12 black peppercorns

1 bay leaf

1 To start the stock, soak the hock for 12 hours in enough cold water to cover.

2 Drain off the soaking water, and cover the ham hock with the measured cold water. Bring to the boil and skim off any scum, then add the carrots, onions and celery, all whole. Leave to simmer gently for about 20 minutes, then add the peppercorns and bay leaf. Gently simmer for a further 1½–2 hours until the ham is cooked through. Watch it carefully: you don't want the liquid to reduce too much. Strain off the stock for the soup – you will need 1.7 litres (3 pints). Put the ham to one side and discard the vegetables and flavourings.

3 Melt the butter in a heavy-bottomed pan, add the finely diced onion and half the frozen peas. Add the mint, and put the lid on the pan. Leave to gently stew for 3–5 minutes. At this point add the flour, and stir in carefully, possibly taking the pan off the heat to stop it sticking. Return the pan to the heat, and cook the pea roux for 2 minutes. Do not let it colour.

4 Slowly add the measured hot ham stock to the roux, beating well with a wooden spoon after each addition to get rid of any lumps of flour. When the stock is all added, make sure that the bottom of the pan is clear of everything. Leave to simmer for 20 minutes.

5 Meanwhile, blanch the remaining peas in boiling water for just 2 minutes. Plunge into a bowl of iced water, which will retain the bright green colour.

6 At the same time it is a good idea to take the skin from the ham hock, to take the meat from the bone and to carefully cut the latter into fine dice. Mix this ham with half of the blanched peas and keep to one side.

7 The soup is now cooked so take out the bunch of mint and put the remaining blanched peas (not those with the ham) into the soup. Liquidise the soup, and then I like to push it through a fine sieve or chinois (conical strainer).

8 When all is through, re-boil the soup gently, adding the double cream, and season as necessary. Put the reserved peas and ham into the soup, and serve immediately.

■ It's not always easy to buy ham hocks these days, except from good butchers. You could use gammon instead (or bacon rinds tied up in muslin, for flavour). Use some boiled ham with peas in the soup at the end.

■ A pea soup is not traditionally served with ham in it, but this addition makes for a much more 'gutsy' dish.

■ This soup is often served with toasted bread triangles, but I prefer it with croûtons, i.e. fried bread dice.

■ Pea soup is great chilled with perhaps extra cream and chopped mint. The French serve stewed lettuce and baby onions with their pea soup.

Cock-a-Leekie

SERVES 4–6 Cock-a-leekie is as much associated in people's minds with Scotland as haggis is, and why the Scots should use prunes always puzzled me. But in fact the soup made from chicken, leeks and prunes is a variant on a dish that occurs elsewhere in Britain, in Wales and Lancashire particularly. The dish from Lancashire is known as Hindle Wakes, probably deriving from 'Hen de la Wake', referring to the holiday Wakes Week in the cotton areas of the country; this is a boiled chicken stuffed with prunes and coated with a bright yellow lemon sauce. It was thought to have been introduced by weavers coming in from Belgium in the fourteenth century, and the dried fruit is a familiar addition to many medieval dishes throughout Europe.

Whatever its history, it is a good family soup-meal, similar to a pot-au-feu. You can use a tough old boiling fowl if you like, probably traditional, and once a capon would have been ideal. Beef stock was usually used to cook the chicken in; I've added the beef to give just a further Scottish taste dimension.

450g (1 lb) topside of beef

1.2 litres (2 pints) chicken stock

900g (2 lb) leeks

1 sprig each fresh parsley and thyme

1 small chicken, approx. 900g (2 lb) in weight

12 large prunes, soaked if necessary

salt and freshly ground black pepper

1 Put the beef into a large pot and add the chicken stock. Bring to the boil and allow to simmer for 20 minutes. Skim off any scum that comes to the top.

2 Meanwhile, trim and wash the leeks, discarding the coarsest of the dark green leaves. Slice the leeks finely.

3 Add the parsley and thyme to the pot along with half of the sliced leeks, and leave to simmer for an hour.

4 Take the meat out and put into a clean pot. Strain the stock over the meat to remove the leeks and herbs. Put the chicken into the pot and make sure it is covered with stock; if not, top up with water. Simmer until the chicken is nearly cooked, about 40 minutes. Test by piercing one of its thighs with a roasting fork: the juices should run slightly pink.

5 Add the prunes and the rest of the leeks, and simmer for a further 20 minutes. Check for seasoning.

6 Take the beef and chicken out of the liquid. Take the chicken meat from the bone, and remove and discard the skin. Chop the meat into large chunks. Slice the beef thinly.

7 Divide the beef, chicken, leeks, prunes and hot stock between warmed bowls, and serve immediately.

■ Once, making something like this would have been the way of life, putting a slow-cooking stew or soup on in the morning, and getting on with everything else – feeding the chickens, hoeing the vegetables, washing the clothes – in the meanwhile. You could still do that today, if you just have the right attitude – think about it in advance, and with a few glances at the pot every now and again, you can get on with the ironing, or read a book or watch television. In fact it's really therapeutic…

■ Prunes can come pre-soaked, in which case all you need to do is add them to the soup (they will be identified as such on the packet). But traditionally dried prunes will need soaking, in plenty of water to cover at least for a couple of hours, and preferably overnight.

Cullen Skink

SERVES 4

'Cullen skink' means a soup-stew which comes from Cullen, a village on the coast of the Moray Firth in Scotland. It is typical coastal fare – dishes like this are traditional throughout Europe – but the difference lies in the smoked fish used. Scotland was the centre of fish smoking, and the fish once used would have been an Arbroath smokie or a Finnan haddock (from the Aberdeenshire village of Findon).

Nick Nairn, Paul Rankin and myself were being taught to drive off-road in the latest brand-new Range Rover, in a programme for the BBC. Our pay-back was that in front of the cameras we would cook a Scottish-type menu, devised by the aforesaid Mr Nairn. He took us through the method for Cullen Skink, and this is a slightly sophisticated variant of his, and the original, using hard-boiled egg and potato to thicken and to add flavour, colour and goodness.

675g (1½ lb) natural, rather than dyed, smoked haddock
25g (1 oz) unsalted butter
300ml (10 fl oz) fish stock or water
salt and freshly ground white pepper

2 hard-boiled eggs, shelled
115g (4 oz) cooked mashed potato
850ml (1½ pints) milk
300ml (10 fl oz) single cream
1 tbsp chopped fresh chives or parsley

1 Preheat the oven to 180°C/350°F/Gas 4.

2 Make sure all the pin bones are taken out of the fish. Use pliers or tweezers.

3 Butter a suitable ovenproof dish, and lay the cut smoked haddock in it, along with the stock or water. Season, put into the preheated oven, and bake for 10 minutes.

4 Take out of the oven and drain, keeping the liquid. Take the flesh off the skin. Discard the skin.

5 Put half the fish in a bowl with the shelled hard-boiled eggs and the mashed potato. Purée this together using a wooden spoon or a pestle. Mix the milk into this, then the cream and strained fish-cooking stock, stirring all well together.

6 Pour into a pan and bring to the boil. If necessary, strain.

7 Add the rest of the flaked fish and the chives or parsley to the soup, check the seasoning and serve hot.

Oxtail Soup

People categorise oxtail as offal, but it is actually an appendage rather than an internal organ, and has a concentrated meaty flavour and texture no organ meat has. We think of oxtail soup and stew as being quintessentially English, but some claim that the inspiration was French: Huguenots fleeing persecution in the seventeenth century settled in East London and had to make their daubes and stews from the cheapest meat available (the tails of the cattle used by the East End tanners). The fame of the soup spread thereafter throughout the country.

675g (1½ lb) meaty oxtail

salt and freshly ground black pepper

25g (1 oz) plain flour

55g (2 oz) beef dripping (or lard)

2 medium onions, peeled and finely chopped

1 large carrot, peeled and finely chopped

4 celery stalks, finely chopped

1 tbsp tomato paste

1.7 litres (3 pints) water or stock

25g (1 oz) unsalted butter

1 tbsp chopped fresh parsley

1 Get the butcher to cut the oxtail between the bones and through the cartilage. Dry off the meat, then season and coat lightly in flour.

2 Heat the dripping until quite hot in a large saucepan, then colour all sides of the oxtail in the fat. Add half the onion and all of the carrot and celery to the oxtail, and colour lightly. Stir in the tomato paste and fry gently for a few minutes. Add the water or stock and bring up to the boil. Cover and simmer for up to 3 hours when the meat is ready to drop off the bones.

3 Take the oxtail out and pick off the meat. Trim off the fat, then throw the bones and fat away, keeping the meat separate. Strain off the liquor and put into the fridge overnight. The next day remove the fat that has set on top and throw this away as well. (This may all seem time-consuming and over-laborious, but I assure you it's well worth it.)

4 Melt the butter in a clean saucepan, add the remaining chopped onion, and sweat until softened. Add the diced oxtail meat and then the strained, de-fatted stock. Bring to the boil, and reduce to taste. Check the seasoning, and serve sprinkled with the chopped parsley.

Jerusalem Artichoke Soup

SERVES 4

What I love about this soup is its silky smooth texture and subtle flavour. It is also known as Palestine soup, presumably because of the vegetable used, Jerusalem artichokes. These were introduced to Europe by French explorers of Canada in the sixteenth century, and were known first as the 'potatoes of Canada'. The name 'Jerusalem' actually comes from a corruption of the Italian word '*girasole*', sunflower, as the vegetable plant is a member of the same family (*Helianthus*). The 'artichoke' bit is just as odd: the Jerusalem artichoke is a tuber, but it does have leaf and stalk growth of up to 3 metres high, as does the globe artichoke. Some say, too, that the flavour of the two artichokes is similar, but I cannot see it.

Try and buy large Jerusalem artichokes, as they will be easier to peel (they are very knobbly). If you don't want to be too sophisticated, just wash the tubers and cook them unpeeled, then sieve; the colour will be different, but the flavour will be just as good.

450g (1 lb) Jerusalem artichokes
salt and freshly ground black pepper
juice of 1 lemon
1 small onion, peeled and finely chopped
1 garlic clove, peeled and crushed
55g (2 oz) celery, chopped

55g (2 oz) unsalted butter
115g (4 oz) smoked bacon rinds, or 2 thick
   rashers smoked bacon
1.2 litres (2 pints) chicken or vegetable stock
300ml (10 fl oz) double cream
2 egg yolks

1 Choose artichokes that are not too knobbly wherever possible. Peel them: I like to use a small knife or potato peeler. Slice finely and, if not using straightaway, keep in cold water with some salt and the lemon juice to stop them from discolouring. Mix the drained sliced artichokes with the onion, garlic and celery.

2 Melt the butter in a saucepan, and add the vegetables and bacon rinds (perhaps tied together with string for ease of removal) or bacon. Sweat carefully over a low heat with a lid on the pan, not allowing anything to colour.

3 Add the stock, bring up to the boil, and simmer until the vegetables are cooked, about 15–20 minutes.

4 Take out the bacon rinds or bacon. Put the mixture through a liquidiser and then pass through a fine chinois or sieve, which makes for a creamy, velvety soup. Put back into a clean pan and add half the double cream. Bring to the boil, and season with salt and pepper.

5 Mix the egg yolks and the remaining double cream in a bowl. Pour some of the hot soup on to this mixture, stirring all the time. Put back into the pan and heat gently, but do not boil. Check the seasoning, and serve immediately.

- Croûtons and parsley are good garnishes. Another thing I like to do is roast or grill some almonds and then add two-thirds of them along with the vegetables (at stage 2). This adds flavour, then you sprinkle the remainder over the top of the soup when serving to add texture.

- If you've ever wondered what to do with the rinds you cut off bacon, well, use them for flavour as here. Freeze them each time you cut them off your breakfast rasher, and you will soon have enough to use.

- In stage 5 I tell you to pour some of the hot soup into the cold cream. Always do it this way round, hot into cold. If cold went into hot, the cold would curdle (i.e. the proteins would set), whereas the hot going into the cold just makes the cold a little warmer…

- To bring this soup bang up to date, you could froth it up at the last minute with one of those new-fangled hand blenders to make a cappuccino-style first course. We did this in 1975 at the Capital Hotel, so eat your heart out, Gordon Ramsay!

Mulligatawny Soup

SERVES 4

I first encountered this soup when I worked at Simpson's in the Strand (my first job, at the tender age of eighteen). It was popular, along with the infamous Brown Windsor soup, with gentlemen of a certain age who had presumably served in India at some time, and learned to love the heat and pepperiness of the cuisine. For the soup and its name are both relics of the Raj, the word 'mulligatawny' coming from two Tamil words meaning 'pepper' and 'water', the nearest thing to soup in India. It was originally a vegetarian sauce apparently, but the British adapted it to include all manner of flavourings and garnishes: the basic pepper water could be served with side bowls of cooked rice, lime wedges, grated coconut, crispy bacon pieces, sliced chillies and hard-boiled eggs.

This version here is a little posher, but lacks the extras!

55g (2 oz) unsalted butter

2 chicken thighs

1 apple, peeled, cored and finely diced

2 small onions, peeled and finely chopped

4 tomatoes, seeded and diced

1 tbsp Madras curry powder

1.2 litres (2 pints) lamb stock

1 tbsp mango chutney, chopped

4 tbsp cooked basmati rice

salt and freshly ground black pepper

1 Melt the butter in a saucepan, add the chicken thighs, allow them to colour lightly, then turn down the heat.

2 Add the diced apple and chopped onion to the pan, then the tomato dice. Do not allow the vegetables to colour. Sprinkle the curry powder over and fry carefully to release its flavour. Do not let it burn.

3 Now add the stock and bring up to the boil, lower the heat and simmer for about 40 minutes.

4 Take the chicken out of the soup, and remove and discard the bones and skin. Cut the meat into dice and put back into the soup along with the chopped mango chutney. Add the rice, warm through briefly, and check for seasoning. Serve hot.

- The soup in Simpson's was passed through a sieve, even the mango chutney, so that all you got in the pepper water was chicken and rice.
- You could make the soup with coconut milk instead of stock – or half and half – and grind your own spices such as cumin and coriander for curry powder, but you must have some heat – preferably chilli powder or a fresh chilli or two.
- Some versions of the recipe use scrag end of lamb instead of the chicken.
- It's often easier to put the rice straight into the cups or bowls, then pour the soup on top.

Scotch Broth

SERVES 4

Also known as barley broth, this soup is simple, but very satisfying, its only necessities being some lamb, barley and vegetables. Barley has become very fashionable nowadays, and many rated restaurants serve barley risottos or pilaffs, but it was a staple in Scotland from very early times, as indeed it was throughout much of the northern hemisphere. It has a good flavour and texture, and here it thickens the broth.

Apparently the famous and acerbic English writer, Dr Johnson, was not too fond of Scotland despite the Gaelic origins of his companion, James Boswell, but did actually approve of Scotch broth!

675g (1½ lb) scrag end or shoulder of lamb, cut into large pieces

55g (2 oz) good pearl barley

1.7 litres (3 pints) cold water

1 bouquet garni (parsley, thyme, bay leaf, black peppercorns)

1 medium onion, peeled and finely diced

2 leeks, cleaned and finely diced

2 carrots, trimmed and finely diced

4 celery stalks, finely diced

1 small white turnip, scrubbed and finely diced

85g (3 oz) shredded cabbage

salt and freshly ground black pepper

1 tbsp chopped fresh parsley

1 Trim the lamb of excess fat.

2 Put the barley into a large saucepan and add the water, then the lamb. Bring up to the boil and put in the bouquet garni. Cover with a lid, but use a wooden spoon to make sure the lid doesn't close properly, and simmer for about 1½ hours, taking off the scum regularly. (If you don't use a spoon, it'll boil over and make an awful mess on the top of your stove.) Stir occasionally as well to make sure the barley doesn't stick.

3 Add the onion, leek, carrot, celery and turnip to the pan, and simmer for about 10 minutes. Take out the meat and dice it.

4 Put the meat back into the pan with the shredded cabbage. Cook for 5–10 minutes more. Check the seasoning, add the parsley and serve.

Cream of Mushroom Soup

SERVES 4

Mushroom soups appear in most cuisines, and on the Continent they would probably be made with wild mushrooms. Here in Britain, however, we seem to have always been a little timid about most fungi, apart from cultivated ones. We took to cultivating them quite early, though, in the mid-eighteenth century, following the example of the French. Around Paris, mushrooms were cultivated in disused quarries; in England, stone mines near Bath were utilised. (In fact, the slightly larger button mushrooms on sale today are still called Paris mushrooms in the trade.)

Field mushrooms have the most intense flavour for a soup, but because of the dark gills, the colour is not good. Use button mushrooms instead, and serve with croûtons if you like.

55g (2 oz) unsalted butter

1 medium onion, peeled and finely chopped

1 medium leek, cleaned and finely chopped

450g (1 lb) button mushrooms, wiped and finely sliced

1 bouquet garni (thyme, parsley, in a leek leaf)

850ml (1½ pints) chicken or vegetable stock, or both

salt and freshly ground black pepper

300ml (10 fl oz) double cream

Garnish

25g (1 oz) unsalted butter

115g (4 oz) button mushrooms, finely diced

1 tbsp chopped fresh parsley

1 Melt the butter in a large pan, and sweat the onion and leek – do not colour – for 5 minutes. Add the mushrooms to the pan, and sweat for another 5 minutes, but still do not colour.

2 Add the bouquet garni, stock and some seasoning, bring to the boil and simmer for 30 minutes. Remove any scum that appears during the cooking.

3 Meanwhile, for the garnish, melt the butter, add the mushrooms and sauté gently. Do not colour them. Season, add the parsley and put to one side.

4 Remove the bouquet garni and liquidise the soup. Put into a clean pan, bring back to the boil, then add the double cream and seasoning to taste.

5 Add the mushroom and parsley mixture, and serve.

Chunky Tomato Soup

SERVES 4

Soup is one of the most traditional of dishes on the British culinary scene, and local 'pot' vegetables were used in the beginning, perhaps with a little grain or, when they were lucky, some meat. When tomatoes gradually came to be accepted, some two centuries or so after they had been introduced from the New World, they were pounded to make soups or acid sauces or ketchups (see page 201). Apparently it wasn't until the twentieth century that we were brave enough to eat these scarlet imports raw!

55g (2 oz) unsalted butter

115g (4 oz) each of carrots, peeled onion and celery, finely chopped

2 garlic cloves, peeled and finely chopped

675g (1½ lb) tomatoes, roughly chopped

basil stalks (see right)

a handful of parsley stalks

1 tbsp chopped fresh thyme

a pinch of unrefined caster sugar

salt and freshly ground black pepper

1.2 litres (2 pints) chicken stock

150ml (5 fl oz) single cream

Garnish

10 tomatoes, skinned and seeded (use skins and seeds in the soup, so do this first)

a splash of olive oil

a bunch of fresh basil, chopped (use the stalks in the soup)

1 garlic clove, peeled and chopped

1 Melt the butter in a large pan, and sweat the finely chopped carrot, onion and celery together. Do not colour. After 3 minutes, add the garlic, the skins and seeds of the garnish tomatoes, and the chopped tomatoes, along with the basil stalks, parsley stalks, thyme, sugar and some salt and pepper to taste. Stew gently for about 10 minutes.

2 When almost all of the liquid has disappeared, add the chicken stock, and cook gently for a further 20 minutes. Pass the soup and vegetables through a sieve.

3 Put back into a clean pan and bring back to the boil. Add the cream and check the seasoning.

4 Chop the skinned garnish tomatoes into neat dice. Warm them in the splash of oil with the basil and garlic. Pour into the soup and serve, with a swirl of cream if desired, as in the photograph on page 8.

Chicken Noodle Soup

SERVES 8

We are famous in this country for making broths or stocks. They were the basis of early pottages, and still add savour to soups and sauces today. The French went one step further, clarifying broths to make consommé, and our clear British soups are probably a borrowing from across the Channel. Almost anything can be used to make a consommé – meat, fish, mushrooms or tomatoes – but the most common is chicken. The classic British clear soup is chicken noodle soup, and the addition of the noodles is probably yet another borrowing, from the Jewish tradition – the *lokshen* (vermicelli) added to the chicken soup known colloquially as 'Jewish penicillin'.

450g (1 lb) raw chicken leg meat,
  off the bone
115g (4 oz) each of prepared carrot, leek,
  onion and celery, chopped
4 tomatoes, chopped
4 egg whites
salt

10 black peppercorns
2.4 litres (4 pints) good chicken stock
85g (3 oz) thin noodles or vermicelli
1 tbsp chopped fresh parsley
2 cold poached chicken breasts,
  skinned and finely diced

1 Chop the chicken leg meat up roughly, and mix with the chopped vegetables. Put all through a coarse mincer. Add the tomatoes.

2 Put this mixture into a heavy-bottomed pan, then mix in the egg whites, some salt and the peppercorns. Add 300ml (10 fl oz) of the cold stock, and mix together. Add the rest of the stock and mix well with a large wooden spoon.

3 Put on to a gentle heat and slowly bring up to the boil, stirring regularly. The proteins in the egg white and chicken will set like a 'cake' on the bottom of the pan. As this cake cooks, it will start to rise in one piece, lifting all the sediment in the stock with it to the top. It's at this moment that care must be taken. As the liquid starts to boil, move the pan to the side, half on and half off the heat, and lower the heat. Try to ensure that the crust is broken on one side only, with the liquid gently simmering through this break. You want to keep it ticking over.

4 At this stage, leave the stock to cook for about 2 hours, uncovered. Taste will tell you when this is ready. It should be lipsmackingly savoury.

5 Carefully strain the majority of the liquid through a folded piece of muslin. Strain the last bit separately, as it might contain some debris which could spoil the bulk of the stock. Degrease the resultant stock using kitchen paper.

6 When you want to serve the soup, season the clarified stock and bring it back to a gentle boil. At the same time, cook the noodles or vermicelli in separate boiling salted water until just cooked. Strain and rinse under cold gently running water.

7 Add the noodles or vermicelli to the stock, along with the parsley and diced chicken. Warm through briefly, then serve.

■ The first secret of a good consommé is the strength of the original stock. If you've got a good strong food processor or mincer, you could put the chicken legs, bones and all, through it, and use that as the clarifying agent, along with the egg whites, for a much more intense flavour. (This works well with fish too, but not, obviously, with the red meats.)

■ Some people like long noodles, some like short, but it's really down to you. As it's a soup, short pieces are probably better – simply break the noodles or vermicelli in your hands before cooking them. I do so in separate boiling water to get rid of the starch which might spoil the clarity of the consommé.

Glamorgan Sausages (see page 36)

'White meats' – the collective name for milk, milk products such as cheese, and eggs – were the food of the poor in medieval times. Unable to afford much red meat, the products of the precious family cow and chickens would have provided important protein in the diet. The eggs would have been cooked very simply: 'roasted', 'poached' and served with collops of bacon (the early form of today's bacon and eggs), or mixed into a grain porridge. The rich would have used eggs in much more sophisticated ways – in pies, custards, and puddings both savoury and sweet. Later people ate buttered or

Eggs, Cheese and Savouries

scrambled eggs, or boiled them in their shells. It surprised me to learn how long it was before the 'foaming' and 'raising' qualities of egg whites were recognised – not until about the late seventeenth century. Thereafter, eggs were used much more widely, particularly in sweet puddings and cakes (see Chapters Seven and Eight).

When I was young, after the war, we had a few chickens in the back garden (as did many a family then), and I used to hate going to collect the eggs, as the hens would peck me! However, I enjoyed eating what I collected (and the chickens themselves occasionally).

Centuries ago the cheese eaten by the poor would have been hard, and local, for not until transport and communications improved did different varieties of cheese become familiar elsewhere in the country. Today, of course, cheese is available in all forms and from all over the world. There's actually been a revolution in Britain: once we only had nine hard cheeses, but now small producers are bringing out some wonderful varieties – fresh, soft and hard – available locally or from farmers' markets. It seems so bizarre, when one of our greatest leaders, Winston Churchill, criticised the French by saying we could never trust a nation that would produce a cheese for every day of the year...

Mrs Beeton wrote that cheese 'is only fit for sedentary people, as an after-dinner stimulant, and in very small quantity'. Which is why the category 'savouries' is here, as many are made with cheese. The savoury is, like afternoon tea, uniquely British and seems to have appeared at some time in the nineteenth century.

Baked Eggs

I've given you two versions of baked eggs here. The first is the equivalent of '*oeufs sur le plat*', but I'm sure we have been preparing eggs like this for far longer than the French… (It's also known as 'shirred' eggs, which suggests 'scrambling' to me.) The second is slightly posher, more like an egg pudding or unrisen soufflé.

Version One

55g (2 oz) unsalted butter

salt and freshly ground black pepper

8 eggs

1 Preheat the oven to 200°C/400°F/Gas 6.

2 Melt a quarter of the butter in each of four flat, eared heatproof dishes of 6cm (2½ in) in diameter. Do not let it colour. Season the dish.

3 Break two eggs per person, one each into separate cups, then carefully pour into the seasoned dishes.

4 Heat on the top of the stove, turning the dishes round to get an even heat, and then put into the preheated oven to set to the desired degree, about 3–4 minutes.

Version Two

55g (2 oz) unsalted butter

8 fresh eggs

150ml (5 fl oz) single cream

2 tbsp chopped fresh parsley

salt and freshly ground black pepper

1 Preheat the oven to 200°C/400°F/Gas 6.

2 Melt the butter and put into an ovenproof pie dish, swirling well to coat all sides.

3 Beat the eggs, cream and parsley together, and season with salt and pepper.

4 Pour the eggs into the pie dish and put into a bain-marie of warm water. Bake in the preheated oven until set, about 8–10 minutes. Spoon out and serve.

■ Both make good snacks, and of course you could tart them up as a starter, lining the dishes with cooked mushrooms, tomatoes, spinach or smoked haddock. I first encountered the idea when I worked in Switzerland; baked eggs were served for breakfast, but on top of slices of cooked ham. (In the kitchen, we cooked this for ourselves in a huge frying pan: sliced sausage then sliced ham with twelve eggs broken on top. We'd eat from the pan.)

■ Use bacon fat instead of butter in both recipes for extra flavour.

Cheesed Eggs

SERVES 4

This is very reminiscent of school days to me, when the only thing they could do properly was a cheese sauce (and no-one can go too far wrong with hard-boiled eggs). Something as simple as this would once have tasted particularly good because of the quality of the eggs, but you can come near if you use the best fresh, free-range and organic eggs you can find. A good Montgomery Cheddar cheese would be delicious.

8 fresh eggs

150ml (5 fl oz) cheese sauce, made with
   single cream (see page 138)

25g (1 oz) unsalted butter

salt and freshly ground black pepper

115g (4 oz) Cheddar, grated

2 egg yolks

1 Boil the eggs for 10 minutes then rest them for 30 minutes in cold water, shell and then slice (a machine for this is perfect).

2 Meanwhile, preheat the oven to 200°C/400°F/Gas 6, and make the cheese sauce.

3 Butter an ovenproof dish well and then season it. Arrange the eggs carefully in the bottom of the dish and season again. Sprinkle with 25g (1 oz) of the grated cheese.

4 Beat the egg yolks into the warm cheese sauce, and pour over the eggs. Sprinkle with the rest of the cheese. Season with pepper and bake in the preheated oven for 10 minutes. Brown the cheesy top under a preheated grill, then serve with lots of bread.

■ The French have a similar dish to this, called *oeufs à la chimay*. The cooked yolks are pounded with mushroom duxelles, and stuffed into the white, then coated with the cheese (sorry, Mornay) sauce.

■ This very grown-up dish is on the children's menu at the Brian Turner Restaurant at the Crowne Plaza NEC Hotel in Birmingham.

Scotch Eggs

MAKES 6

These sausagemeat-wrapped eggs, served for breakfast or as a snack in Scotland, stood alone, I thought, with no obviously similar dishes existing in other cuisines. Some sources have suggested, however, that there is an association with the Indian Moghul 'kofta', which consists of pounded spiced meat wrapped round savoury fillings, sometimes eggs. How the idea came to Scotland, no-one seems to know, but it could be something to do with men returning from service in India during the days of the Raj.

6 hard-boiled eggs (8–10 minutes)
55g (2 oz) plain flour
salt and freshly ground black pepper
350g (12 oz) sausagemeat

115g (4 oz) boiled ham, very finely chopped
2 eggs, beaten
115g (4 oz) fresh white breadcrumbs
vegetable oil for deep-frying

1 Shell the eggs and dry in a clean cloth. Season the flour with salt and pepper. Dip the eggs in this and shake off the excess.
2 Mix the sausagemeat and ham together, and split this mixture into six even parts. Flatten out in your hands to make a meat coating for each egg. Cover each egg with a portion of this mixture, pressing well at the joins to seal.
3 Dip the coated eggs into the seasoned flour again, and shake off the excess. Dip into the beaten egg and finally into the breadcrumbs to coat completely.
4 Re-shape at this stage, and put into the fridge for 10 minutes.
5 Deep-fry in moderately hot fat for about 10 minutes, turning as they cook. Take out, drain well and serve hot or cold.

- Try making the recipe with hard-boiled quails' eggs. Very fiddly, but great for a canapé.
- Many recipes use only sausagemeat, but the addition of ham as well is occasionally found. Try Parma ham, an interesting substitute for boiled ham. And of course you could spice things up by adding some chopped fresh herbs or spices, such as chilli or cayenne, to the mixture.

Omelette Arnold Bennett

SERVES 1

Arnold Bennett based his 1930 novel, *Imperial Palace*, on the Savoy Hotel, where he often ate, and his fictional chef, Roho, on Jean-Baptiste Virlogeux, the then *chef de cuisine*. In return, Virlogeux invented this classic marriage of smoked haddock, eggs and cheese. We made it during my time at the Capital Hotel, and when Egon Ronay once accused us of not changing the menu often enough, I quoted a sad but true story. A Norwegian customer had had this omelette twice on the trot, he liked it so much, and when he went home, he asked his wife to recreate the dish for him. The result was so unlike our original that he brought her straight back on a plane to London. However, we'd changed the menu that very day, so to satisfy his – and her – needs we had to change it back again and make the dish for him!

3 eggs

salt and freshly ground black pepper

15g (½ oz) unsalted butter

85g (3 oz) cooked smoked haddock

3 tbsp double cream

40g (1½ oz) Gruyère cheese, grated

1 Break the eggs into a bowl and beat, then season.

2 Melt the butter in your omelette pan, then add the eggs. Stir regularly until the eggs set. Keep lifting the sides up to make sure the eggs don't stick.

3 When the eggs are cooked enough, but still a little wet, add the smoked haddock. Put the pan under the preheated grill to set the rest of the eggs.

4 In the meantime make the creamy cheese sauce. Reduce the double cream until it begins to thicken, and take off the heat. Season and stir in 25g (1 oz) of the cheese.

5 Turn the omelette over on to a plate. Using the back of a spoon, spread the sauce over the top. Sprinkle with the remaining cheese and put under the preheated grill to brown. Serve immediately.

All-day Breakfast Bap

SERVES 8

The English breakfast is famous the world over, with its egg, bacon, sausage, fried tomato, fried mushroom and fried bread – cholesterol on a plate! Done well, though, it is delicious, but I have played around with the basic idea here to come up with something completely different. The egg, bacon, sausage, tomato and mushroom are served together in a bun, rather like a burger, with lots of different seasonings to taste. I've even added some cheese. It tastes wonderful, at any time of the day!

8 bread buns

Filling
450g (1 lb) Cumberland or
  Lincolnshire sausages
salt and freshly ground black pepper
6 slices best-quality back bacon
vegetable oil
8 button mushrooms

25g (1 oz) butter
3 hard-boiled eggs, shelled and
  roughly chopped
5 sun-blush tomatoes, cut into fine strips
a handful of fresh parsley, finely chopped
1 tbsp tomato ketchup, bought or
  home-made (see page 201)
1 tbsp brown sauce
55g (2 oz) Cheddar, grated (optional)

1 Remove the outer skin from the sausages, and put the meat in a bowl. Season with salt and pepper, gently mix together, and place to one side.

2 Discard the rinds, and cut the bacon rashers into lardons. Fry in a hot pan in 1 tbsp of the oil until golden brown. Drain and cool.

3 Remove the stalks from the mushrooms and cut them and the caps into quarters. Gently fry in the butter and another tbsp of oil. Season and cook until just done. Cool.

4 Incorporate all the ingredients into the sausagemeat and mix well together.

5 Shape the mixture into eight equal-sized patties and store in the fridge for half an hour or so before cooking.

6 To cook, heat a couple of tbsp of oil in a frying pan, to a moderate–high temperature. Add the patties, in batches if necessary, and seal both sides. Cook through well, for about 4–6 minutes each side.

7 Meanwhile, warm the buns through in a low oven, and butter them if you like (I don't). Serve a hot breakfast patty in each bun.

Cheese Pudding

SERVES 4

Very few people make things like this now, but once they would have been a major part of the diet – the protein of the cheese and eggs bulked out with bread. The first version here is a classic Welsh dish, but similar puddings were once known to be popular in East Anglia. If the first is like a savoury bread and butter pudding (something my father used to love – he would have had onions with it), the second is like a savoury queen of puddings.

Version One

6 slices stale bread

55g (2 oz) unsalted butter

salt and freshly ground black pepper

225g (8 oz) mature Cheddar, grated

1 tsp French mustard

freshly grated nutmeg and cayenne pepper

300ml (10 fl oz) milk

300ml (10 fl oz) single cream

2 eggs

1 Preheat the oven to 180°C/350°F/Gas 4.

2 Toast the bread on one side only. Use a little of the butter to grease an ovenproof pie dish, then season it. Take the crusts off the bread, and butter the untoasted side of the bread. Cut each slice into three rectangular pieces each.

3 Place a layer of buttered toast, toasted side down, into the greased pie dish. Mix the cheese with the mustard and some salt, nutmeg and cayenne, and sprinkle over the bread. Lay on more toast, buttered side up, and sprinkle with more cheese. Continue until everything has been used up, finishing with a layer of cheese.

4 Warm the milk and cream together. Beat the eggs to a froth, then strain into the milk. Mix well and pour over the bread.

5 Bake in the preheated oven for 30–40 minutes. Serve hot.

Version Two

115g (4 oz) unsalted butter

salt and freshly ground black pepper

300ml (10 fl oz) single cream

150ml (5 fl oz) milk

115g (4 oz) fresh breadcrumbs

1 tsp English mustard

225g (8 oz) mature Cheddar, grated

3 eggs

1 Use some of the butter to grease a pie dish of about 850ml (1½ pint) capacity. Season with black pepper.

2 Bring the cream and milk to the boil, then add 55g (2 oz) of the butter. Season the breadcrumbs and mix with the mustard in a bowl, then pour in the hot cream mixture. Cover and leave to stand for 20 minutes.

3 Meanwhile, preheat the oven to 200°C/400°F/Gas 6.

4 Stir the grated cheese into the breadcrumb mixture. Beat the eggs well until frothy and strain into the mixture. Stir together well.

5 Pour the cheese mixture into the pie dish, and bake in the preheated oven for 20 minutes. Serve immediately.

■ Version Two is best with ordinary bread, but you could ring the changes in the first one by using more exciting examples – an olive oil one such as ciabatta or focaccia, or even some of the flavoured breads like sun-dried tomato…

Glamorgan Sausages

SERVES 4

Made from cheese, leeks or onions and breadcrumbs, this is more a savoury, meat-free rissole than a sausage, and it can be cooked in either shape. It is attributed to South Wales, where of course there has always been a strong cheese-cooking tradition (think of *Welsh Rarebit*, see page 38), but similar mixtures exist elsewhere. As a cheese lover, I like these very much, but especially since Franco Taruschio (then of the Walnut Tree in Abergavenny) cooked some superb examples at Turner's one St David's Day. And he's an Italian!

140g (5 oz) Caerphilly cheese

175g (6 oz) fresh white breadcrumbs

55g (2 oz) young leeks or spring onions, finely chopped

1 tbsp chopped fresh chives

½ tsp dried thyme

a pinch of dry English mustard powder

salt and freshly ground black pepper

2 egg yolks

1 egg, beaten

lard for frying

1 Preheat the oven to 200°C/400°F/Gas 6.

2 Grate the cheese and mix in a bowl with 115g (4 oz) of the breadcrumbs. Add the chopped leek or spring onion, chives, thyme, mustard, salt and pepper and egg yolks, and mix well together.

3 Divide the mix into eight, and roll each piece into a sausage shape. Dip the sausages into the beaten egg, and then coat with the remaining breadcrumbs.

4 Fry the sausages in a little lard, until they become golden brown on the outside. Finish them in the preheated oven for 3–4 minutes.

- If I were going to serve these as a main course, I would accompany them with a rustic, spicy tomato sauce.
- You could also make the mixture into tiny patties and cook to serve as canapés or an *amuse-gueule*.
- As it stands, this is a great dish for vegetarians, but you could cater for meat-eaters too by adding a dice of smoked bacon, ham or cooked sausage to the basic mixture.

Eggs, Cheese and Savouries **37**

Welsh Rarebit

SERVES 4

There is a huge tradition of 'roasting', 'toasting', 'melting', 'grilling' and 'baking' cheese in Britain, and it dates from very early times. The one which has become the most famous and popular is the Welsh version of toasted cheese, or Welsh rarebit. At its simplest, it can be a piece of bread toasted on both sides then topped with a slice of good cheese and grilled, but 'melting' the cheese with other flavourings, then using as a spread on toast, is much more exciting (and traditional). The research for this book was the greatest excuse I could have for ordering Welsh rarebit at each and every eatery I visited. This in my opinion comes very near the top of the pile.

50ml (2 fl oz) double cream

1 tbsp beer or ale

1 tsp English mustard

225g (8 oz) mature Cheddar, grated

a shake of Worcestershire sauce

2 egg yolks

4 slices from an uncut wholemeal loaf

1 Boil the double cream in a medium pan until it starts to thicken. Add the beer and bring back to the boil. Remove from the heat and stir in the mustard, cheese and Worcestershire sauce. Beat in the egg yolks, pour into a bowl, cool and refrigerate. Use the next day.

2 Cut the bread to doorstop size. Toast the slices lightly on one side, then spread the other side generously with the Welsh rarebit mixture. Toast under a hot preheated grill until golden and sizzling.

■ Serve as a snack or light lunch with a salad, or cut into small pieces as a traditional savoury. I have to admit my favourite way is late at night, with Marmite or *Piccalilli* (see page 204) spread under the cheese...

■ You could use Pommery or grain mustard instead of the French, which gives a different flavour and texture. And recently on *Ready Steady Cook* I was given a Shropshire ale cheese – one that had been soaked in ale – so I had two ingredients ready all in one!

Creamed Mushrooms on Toast

SERVES 4

Grilled or fried mushrooms on toast was one of the most popular – and one of the simplest – of after-dinner savouries. The mushrooms could also be 'devilled' or 'peppered' (kidneys were prepared similarly, see page 105). The finest mushrooms (apart from wild) are the large field mushrooms with the dark gills, and the best way of cooking them is to slow-roast them with garlic, oil and herbs, so that the juices evaporate and concentrate. Using button mushrooms, as here, is more refined, takes much less time, and gives a far nicer colour.

450g (1 lb) small button mushrooms

25g (1 oz) unsalted butter

1 shallot, peeled and finely chopped

150ml (5 fl oz) dry sherry

150ml (5 fl oz) double cream

salt and freshly ground black pepper

1 tbsp chopped fresh chives

4 slices good brown bread, toasted

1   Trim the stalks off the mushrooms (and keep, see below).

2   Melt the butter in a pan, add the mushrooms and sauté them until golden brown.

3   Take the pan off the heat, and add the shallot and dry sherry. Put back on the heat, and boil to reduce the sherry by two-thirds.

4   Add the double cream and bring to the boil. Turn the heat down, and simmer gently until the cream starts to thicken and bind the mushrooms together.

5   Take the pan from the heat and season the mushrooms with salt and pepper. Stir in the chopped chives, spoon over the toast, and serve straightaway.

■ Use the stalks, if there are any, for another dish. A duxelles, such as in the *Beef Wellington* recipe (see page 82), would be perfect.

■ In the restaurant we might take refinement a step further, and cut circles out of each slice of toast as the base for the mushrooms, as for *Scotch Woodcock* (see page 41).

Scotch Woodcock

SERVES 4

This classic after-dinner savoury, the most popular in Victorian times apparently, is basically fancy scrambled eggs on toast. I believe it still appears on the menus of many gentlemen's clubs. The only thing I can see to ally the game bird with the savoury is that both are served on toast. The name of the recipe may also be a snide reference to the parsimony of the Scots (Yorkshiremen stripped of their generosity, as an old joke has it), who might serve scrambled eggs instead of woodcock, the most expensive of the game birds.

4 eggs

4 egg yolks

300ml (10 fl oz) single cream

salt and freshly ground black pepper

55g (2 oz) unsalted butter

4 slices sliced bread

12 anchovy fillets

1 tbsp capers, rinsed

4 fresh parsley leaves

1 Beat the eggs, egg yolks and cream together, then season with salt and pepper. Use 25g (1 oz) of the butter to scramble this mixture.

2 Toast the bread, then butter the slices. Use a round cutter to cut out a large circle from each slice of bread.

3 Load the toast circles with the scrambled eggs. Criss-cross with the anchovy fillets and sprinkle with the capers. Garnish with parsley, and serve immediately.

- Many recipes advocate mashing the anchovy with the butter and spreading it on the toast before topping with the scrambled egg. Or you could use some minced ham mixed with mustard and butter. It's the spiciness you want.
- Don't waste the remnants of buttered toast – eat them!

Angels on Horseback

SERVES 4

Who would have thought this favourite Victorian savoury could be successful, but the sea tang of the oyster with the saltiness of the bacon makes for a perfect marriage. Although a good and tasty mouthful at the end of a meal, the angels (and indeed devils) could also be served as a canapé, a starter or a light lunch. (Incidentally, a scallop cooked in the same way is called an 'archangel'.)

12 rashers streaky bacon

12 large oysters, shelled and cleaned

½ lemon

freshly ground black pepper

a little lard or olive oil, if necessary

4 slices thick white or brown bread

25g (1 oz) unsalted butter

4 sprigs fresh parsley or dill

1 Take the rashers of bacon and stretch out using the back of a large knife so that they are thinner and more elongated than before. Lay out on a chopping board.

2 Meanwhile, take the cleaned oysters, squeeze over the lemon juice and sprinkle on some black pepper.

3 Wrap each oyster with a rasher of bacon and then secure three per person on a wooden skewer (which has been soaked in water if they are to be grilled). Grill until the bacon crisps and the oysters are just cooked. An alternative is to fry them in lard or oil until just cooked.

4 Toast the bread, butter the slices, and cut into your preferred shape. Lay an oyster skewer on each piece of toast and garnish with a sprig of parsley or dill. Serve immediately.

Thinning the bacon rashers by stretching them with the back of a knife will ensure they crisp up quickly.

Devils on Horseback

SERVES 4

We have 'angels' and 'devils' because of colour, I presume – the white of the oysters and the black of the prunes. But why 'horseback', I cannot fathom. Whatever the reason for the name, devils on horseback are almost as delicious as angels, the sweetness of the prunes a good contrast with the salty bacon.

12 large prunes

55g (2 oz) unsalted butter

12 rashers streaky bacon

a little lard or olive oil, if necessary

4 slices thick white or brown bread

4 sprigs fresh parsley or dill

1 Stone the prunes, then fry in a frying pan in half the butter. Drain.
2 Stretch the bacon rashers as in the previous recipe, then wrap them round the stoned prunes.
3 Skewer, cook and serve in exactly the same way as the angels on horseback.

Angels (foreground) and devils on horseback can be served as a canapé, a starter, a light lunch or as a tasty end to a meal.

Salad of Scallops with Bacon (see page 64)

For an island nation, we seem to have had a chequered relationship with foods from the sea. From the very earliest days, fish and shellfish had been a hugely important part of the diet of the British: piles of shells have been found in prehistoric sites from the Orkneys to the Channel Islands. By medieval times, fish was as important as bread in the diet, but for a very different reason. The Roman Catholic Church had decreed that three days of each week must be meat free; and during Lent eggs and dairy foods were forbidden as well. This meant that for virtually half the year fish was the only permitted

Fish and Shellfish 3

protein (although barnacle geese, puffins and beavers were, curiously, classified as fish). For most people living away from the coasts, this fish had to be preserved in some way – dried, salted, smoked or pickled – and this would undoubtedly have proved a little monotonous after a while. It is probably because of this need to preserve the huge catches of fish that there are so many smoked, pickled and potted fish dishes in the British canon. It may also explain why fish was for so long liked *less* than meat: eating fish was mandatory, while meat was special, for high days and holidays.

As the power of the Church diminished, fish did not need to be eaten so often. Ironically, though, transportation began to improve and fresh fish could at last be enjoyed more widely. With the arrival of faster ships, then the railways, salmon from Scotland, for instance, could be brought down to London fresh rather than smoked. Fish became cheaper as a result and soon became the food of the poor: it was nutritious and didn't require much cooking (many homes did not have any means of cooking food). Stalls selling shellfish – oysters, whelks, cockles – sprang up all over the country. Eels became a favourite dish to buy in London, and salmon was so common that London apprentices were said to have complained at having to eat it several times a week. Fried fish was sold too, often with a potato accompaniment, and this was the forerunner of our very British fish and chips.

Turning full circle, fish and shellfish have recently been looked on as luxury foods, principally due to their scarcity because of pollution and over-fishing. However, things seem to be looking up again, and Rick Stein has almost single-handedly been responsible for reintroducing us to the joys of fish cooking at home. I urge you to buy, cook and enjoy.

Herrings in Mustard and Oatmeal

SERVES 4

Herrings used to be a major part of the economy of the east coast of Britain, particularly East Anglia, but sadly they have been over-fished and stocks are in decline. Great Yarmouth in Norfolk was the centre for 'red herrings', whole fish that were brined and then cold smoked so they turned from pale to dark red. I went to a herring fair there once, and I cooked the following recipe on the sand dunes!

Herrings in Scotland are often served with a mustard sauce (a reflection of the Scandinavian influence) or are fried in oatmeal (*the* Scottish grain). Here I've combined the two ideas, but I've used Dijon mustard, as I think English is too strong (although, interestingly, English mustard is as Norfolk based as the red herrings above). Herrings are best in the spring, summer and autumn.

4 herrings

25g (1 oz) plain flour

salt and freshly ground black pepper

2 eggs, beaten

1 tbsp Dijon mustard

225g (8 oz) fine oatmeal

4 rashers bacon

1 tbsp vegetable oil or 55g (2 oz) lard

25g (1 oz) unsalted butter

1 Make sure the herrings are scaled. Take off the fins and the head of each, then cut down each side of the backbone and pull the backbone out so that the fish is split to look like a kipper. Remove the guts and clean well.

2 Put the flour, seasoned with salt and pepper, the beaten eggs mixed with the mustard, and the oatmeal in three separate flattish plates.

3 Rinse and pat the double fillets dry, then coat them with flour on both sides. Shake off any excess. Dip in the eggs and finally into the fine oatmeal.

4 Fry the bacon in the oil and butter in a frying pan until crisp, and the fat has rendered. Remove from the pan and keep warm.

5 Fry the herrings in the fat remaining in the pan until crisp and golden brown on each side. Cook very gently or the oatmeal will fall off. Drain and serve with a bacon rasher over each double fillet.

Mackerel with Gooseberries and Potatoes

SERVES 4

The French and the English disagree as to who invented the magical marriage of oily mackerel and tart gooseberry. Some say it came in at the time of the Norman Conquest, others that it was a natural combination of May's fat, fresh fish (particularly in Cornwall) and the ripening fruit. No less an expert than M. Escoffier himself, however, suggests that it is English in his recipe for '*Maquereau à l'anglaise*', poached fish served with a purée of green gooseberries. That's enough proof for me…

4 mackerel
1 tbsp vegetable oil
25g (1 oz) unsalted butter
salt and freshly ground black pepper

Gooseberries and potatoes
25g (1 oz) unsalted butter
55g (2 oz) unrefined caster sugar
25g (1 oz) chopped fresh root ginger
450g (1 lb) gooseberries, trimmed
450g (1 lb) new potatoes, cooked and warm
1 tbsp chopped fresh parsley

1 Melt the butter in a pan, add the sugar and then the ginger and gooseberries. Cover with a lid and cook slowly for 5 minutes. Take the lid off and cook gently until all the liquid has evaporated.

2 Meanwhile, fillet the mackerel, then take out the pin bones from each fillet. Cut on each side of where the pin bones are, down to the skin but not through it. Then with your knife and thumb, get hold of the piece of flesh and pull away in one fell swoop taking the bones away (much easier than pulling out individual pin bones using tweezers). Slash the fillets across the skin side at the head end to help even cooking.

3 Heat the oil and butter in a frying pan. Cook the fillets in this until golden brown, about 3–4 minutes, then take out, drain and season.

4 When the gooseberries are cooked, add the new potatoes, heat through briefly, and check the seasoning. Add the chopped parsley, then arrange on hot serving plates. Criss-cross the mackerel fillets over the top and serve.

Jubilee Salmon

SERVES 4 Salmon has always been caught in Britain, primarily in Scottish waters, and there are references to 'kippered salmon' in documents from as early as the mid-fifteenth century. Sadly, there are fewer fish now in the wild, due to pollution and over-fishing. Farmed fish can never be quite the same, although the quality is generally good. If you do come across a wild salmon in the early summer, all you need do is simply poach it; it doesn't need much else doing to it.

I cooked this dish for the actress Liza Goddard when she came on Anglia TV's programme, *Brian Turner's All-Star Cooking*, during the Queen's Jubilee year. Liza was on tour in a play in which she actually played the Queen, and the salmon and asparagus combination was chosen because the Queen had apparently eaten that to celebrate her Silver Jubilee.

4 x 175g (6 oz) salmon steaks,
  trimmed and pin-boned
25g (1 oz) unsalted butter
2 shallots, peeled and finely diced
salt and freshly ground black pepper
12 asparagus spears, trimmed
150ml (5 fl oz) white wine
150ml (5 fl oz) fish stock
4 plum tomatoes, seeded and diced

Herb hollandaise
175g (6 oz) clarified butter (see opposite)
3 egg yolks, lightly beaten
1 tbsp white wine vinegar
2 tbsp lightly chopped fresh tarragon
2 tbsp snipped fresh chives

1 Preheat the oven to 180°C/350°F/Gas 4.

2 Lay the steaks skin side down on the work surface, and make an incision through to the skin from back to belly rather than head to tail. Take care not to cut through the skin. Open up the steak so that the skin is folded in on itself in the middle at the back. You should end up with a rough 'heart shape'.

3 Grease an ovenproof baking dish with butter, and sprinkle in the finely diced shallot. Add the salmon steaks, and season. Arrange the asparagus spears around them. Add the wine and fish stock, cover with foil and put into the preheated oven for 10 minutes only, no more.

4 Remove from the oven and take out the salmon. Keep this warm. Take out the asparagus spears and trim off the tips. Chop the remainder of the spears finely, and keep both these dice and the tips warm.

5 Meanwhile, dribble a little clarified butter (from the hollandaise ingredients) into a small pan, add the tomatoes and warm through. Season. At the same time, reduce the salmon cooking liquor by two-thirds in another small pan.

6 To make the hollandaise, over a gentle heat, whisk the egg yolks and vinegar in a round-sided pan to a frothy consistency. Do not overcook. Remove from the heat regularly so that the eggs do not overheat and scramble.

7 Take off the heat and, still whisking continuously, slowly drizzle in the remainder of the clarified butter. (If at any time this starts to curdle, add a tsp of cold water to bring it back.) Add the reduced cooking liquor, some seasoning, the chopped herbs and diced asparagus.

8 Arrange the salmon steaks in the middle of individual warm plates and then spoon over the herb hollandaise. Put a tsp or so of tomato dice on the top, and garnish each steak with three asparagus tips. Serve immediately.

■ To make clarified butter, put a block of butter in a pan and warm very gently over or beside heat until the milk solids sink to the bottom. Very slowly pour off the clarified golden liquid into another container, leaving the milky residue behind. Clarified butter keeps for ages and you can cook at high temperature with it as it now lacks the solids which burn. (Ghee, the fat used in Indian cooking, is a clarified butter.)

Trout with Almonds

SERVES 4

I think this recipe is probably a French import, but I remember that 90 per cent of the fish courses I served at banquets during my college days and immediately after – in the early 1960s – were '*truite amandine*' or '*truite grenobloise*' (like *meunière*, with capers and lemon segments). The former we took to our hearts, and indeed a good trout needs nothing more than a quick frying in butter, and then the added texture and flavour of some toasted almonds.

4 x 280g (10 oz) trout, scaled, gutted and fins removed

25g (1 oz) plain flour

salt and freshly ground black pepper

115g (4 oz) unsalted butter

115g (4 oz) split almonds

juice of 2 lemons

2 tbsp chopped fresh parsley

1 See that the trout are well cleaned, then wash inside and outside and pat dry.

2 Put the flour on a plate, season it, and then dust each fish on both sides, shaking off the excess.

3 Heat half the butter in a frying pan that is large enough to hold at least two fish at a time. Lay the fish carefully in the pan, and cook to golden brown on one side then turn over, turn the heat down, and cook through for 8–10 minutes.

4 Meanwhile, toast the almonds to a light golden brown in a dry frying pan (watch them), then throw them into the pan with the trout for the last 4 minutes. Take out the trout and place on a hot platter.

5 Add the remaining butter to the cooking pan, and let it colour to a golden brown. Taking the pan off the heat, add the lemon juice and parsley. Bring to the boil, and spoon over the fish to serve.

■ I'm sure you already know this, but the correct etiquette when serving trout is to place it on the plate, belly away from the diner (ladies might be offended). I'm not convinced of this, seeing that the heads, eyes and tails are still there, but this is probably why, although it's harder work, fillets of trout are usually served in top restaurants.

Jellied Eels

Eels, those amazing fish that are born in salt water and travel for some three years back to their fresh home waters in Britain, were once very much more abundant than they are now. They were so prolific, along with mussels and oysters, that they became a popular food with the poor of the East End of London, thus the continuing association of eels with Cockneys! Once street stalls and shops selling pie and mash, eel and mash and jellied eels flourished, but sadly these seem now to be diminishing in number. A shame, because eel is delicious, whether baked, poached, grilled or indeed smoked (the latter one of life's joys).

I went eel fishing once in the Fens when filming the Anglia TV series, *Out to Lunch*. We weren't quite blindfolded, as we were in cars, but our guide took us there and back by the most circuitous route so that we couldn't retrace our steps to where his nets were…

675g (1 ½ lb) fresh eel	salt
2 bay leaves	150ml (5 fl oz) white wine
4 fresh parsley stalks	300ml (10 fl oz) white wine vinegar
1 onion, peeled and chopped	2 tbsp chopped fresh parsley
6 black peppercorns	(lots of parsley is essential)

1 Get the fishmonger to kill, bleed, gut and skin the eel to order, then cut it into 5cm (2 in) lengths.

2 Preheat the oven to 140°C/275°F/Gas 1.

3 Lay the eel pieces in a flat deep pot vertically, then add the bay leaves, parsley stalks, onion, peppercorns and a pinch of salt. Pour in the wine and vinegar, and top up with water to cover well.

4 Put a lid on the pot and put into the preheated oven for 2–3 hours, depending on the thickness of the fish.

5 When the eel is cooked, carefully remove the stock and herbs. Strain the juices, discarding the herbs, then add the chopped parsley. Spoon this back over the eel, and leave to cool overnight, when the juices will set to the characteristic jelly (from the dissolved eel bones).

Grilled Dover Sole

SERVES 4

There are various types of sole, but Dover is the very best.

Sole were once filleted at the table for you in old-fashioned restaurants, and in my capacity as Chairman of the Academy of Culinary Arts, I have been helping to bring back some of those old skills we seem to have lost. In this I am very grateful for the work done by Silvano Giraldin, restaurant manager of the Gavroche, and Sergio Rebecchi of Chez Nico, who have been passing on their vast knowledge to a new generation of chefs and waiters.

4 x 450g (1 lb) whole Dover sole
55g (2 oz) plain flour
salt and freshly ground black pepper
55g (2 oz) unsalted butter, melted
2 lemons, halved

Parsley butter
115g (4 oz) unsalted butter
juice of ½ lemon
1 tbsp chopped fresh parsley

1 Make the parsley butter first. Mix the butter with the lemon juice and parsley, and some salt and pepper. Roll up in dampened greaseproof paper to a sausage shape and put in the freezer until needed. Preheat the grill.

2 To clean the soles, remove the black skin first. Dip the tail into boiling water then, using the back of a knife, scrape from the tail end towards the body to loosen a piece of the skin. Hold the fish down and grip the skin piece in a cloth. Pull firmly and all will come away. Turn the fish over and carefully remove the scales from the white-skinned side. Remove the head by chopping it off (optional), then cut the side fins away using scissors. Wash and dry well.

3 Season the flour with some salt and pepper, and dip the sole, skinned side only, into it. Shake off the excess flour and place on a grilling sheet, floured side up. Brush with melted butter, and grill on one side for about 5–6 minutes. If necessary, turn over, but test for doneness first. Do this by pushing your finger on to the backbone: if the meat gives sufficiently for you to feel bone, the sole is ready.

4 Take the parsley butter from the freezer and, using a warm knife, cut into thin slices. Lay two slices on each sole and allow to melt naturally. Serve with half a lemon and new potatoes.

- You probably don't need to know this, but lemon soles, although fine fish, are not true soles — because they are 'left-handed'. True soles like Dovers are dextral or right-handed, because they have both eyes on the right-hand side of their heads. Now you know.
- In restaurants sole are grilled on salamanders, a bottom heat like a barbecue, rather than a top heat. This marks the fish with grid marks, and if you would like to recreate this at home, heat a metal skewer over a flame. Mark the fish before you cook, to scorch the flour.
- You can concoct different savoury butters to accompany grilled fish. Use anchovies, oysters, garlic or tarragon, for instance.

Whitebait

Whitebait, the fry of herrings and sprats, are said to be so called because they are 'white' and were used as bait to catch larger fish. They once shoaled so prolifically on the coasts and estuaries of Essex and Kent that fisheries grew up around them. They were caught in the Thames as well, and wealthy Londoners used to travel downriver for whitebait dinners at Greenwich. Whitebait used to be a big seller at Simpson's in the Strand, and I think they make a very tasty mid-table nibble for people to share.

The whitebait fishery in Britain is discouraged now because of the effect on mature fish stocks, but frozen fish are brought in from abroad. Let the fish defrost and drain well in a colander before cooking.

450g (1 lb) whitebait

150ml (5 fl oz) milk

85g (3 oz) plain flour

1 tsp cayenne pepper

salt

vegetable oil for deep-frying

1 lemon, quartered

1 Simply put the whitebait into the milk and stir round. Handling carefully, drop them into the flour mixed with the cayenne pepper and salt to taste. Shake off any excess.

2 Heat the oil to 190°C/375°F. Drop the tiny fish into the oil in the fryer, not too many at a time. Fry until golden brown, then strain and drain on kitchen paper.

3 Sprinkle with salt and lemon juice, and serve immediately.

- Don't overcook them: it's very easy to let them frazzle. And don't even *think* of coating them in breadcrumbs: the flour will give you the right texture.
- If you don't like the 'devilled' flavour here, simply leave out the cayenne pepper.

Yorkshire Fishcakes

SERVES 4

There are two different types of fishcake in Yorkshire. One is the traditional one with mashed potato, fish and parsley, which is breadcrumbed or battered then fried. This is known as a 'parsley cake'. What I call a real Yorkshire fishcake is two slices of potato with a piece of fish in the middle. Whenever I travel to Yorkshire by car to work, I call in at Norman's Mermaid fish and chip shop in Morley, my home town, to get a piece of fish, a fishcake or two and a bag of chips.

When I was asked by Tetley to present a high tea at a catering competition, we cooked these fishcakes, followed by custard tarts. All the other chefs there were laughing at our simple menu, but the queue outside our back door for a sample was the largest – and Tetley won as well!

16 x 3mm (⅛ in) potato slices
450g (1 lb) fish fillet (cod or haddock)
plain flour for dusting
vegetable oil for deep-frying
 (lard or dripping in the north)

Salt and vinegar batter
175g (6 oz) plain flour
2 tbsp salt
125ml (4 fl oz) water
150ml (5 fl oz) malt vinegar

1 To make the batter, put the flour and salt in a bowl, and make a well in the centre. Add the water and vinegar and whisk until smooth. Leave to rest.

2 Using a 6cm (2½ in) ring, cut the potato slices into even sizes. Cut the fish into thin 55g (2 oz) pieces of a similar size. Dust lightly with flour.

3 Sandwich the pieces of fish between two pieces of potato. Dip the cakes into flour and shake off the excess, then dip into the batter to cover well.

4 Heat the oil in a flat-bottomed pan to about 190°C/375°F. Carefully drop a fishcake into the hot fat and let it settle to the bottom. Add another couple of fishcakes if there is room. They will rise to the top when hot enough, about 5 minutes. Turn over, then cook for another 5 minutes until brown.

5 Take out and drain well on kitchen paper. They're better left for 5 minutes as they are too hot to eat straightaway, and they do need to drain very well. Serve hot with *Tomato Ketchup* and some *Pease Pudding* if you like (see pages 201 and 136), although I prefer just salt and vinegar.

Fish Pie

SERVES 8

In medieval times, mixtures of fish would have been topped with pastry, both to seal in the flavour, and to serve as a carbohydrate accompaniment. Although pastry can of course still be used, we now commonly use the words 'fish pie' to mean fish topped with mashed potato. Comfort food par excellence, but you'll find a few variations here…

225g (8 oz) each of fillets of haddock, white fish, smoked haddock and salmon, skinned
55g (2 oz) unsalted butter
salt and freshly ground black pepper
24 small button onions, peeled
16 small button mushrooms, halved
juice of 1 lemon
75ml (2½ fl oz) dry sherry

Sauce
40g (1½ oz) unsalted butter
40g (1½ oz) plain flour
300ml (10 fl oz) milk
300ml (10 fl oz) double cream
3 tbsp finely chopped spring onion
1 tbsp chopped fresh parsley
a dash of Tabasco sauce

Topping
675g (1½ lb) potatoes
55g (2 oz) unsalted butter
1 tbsp vegetable oil
55g (2 oz) clarified butter (see page 49)

To skin fish fillets: use a sharp knife to make a nick between flesh and skin at the tail end. Either persuade skin from flesh with the blade, or simply pull once you can get proper purchase!

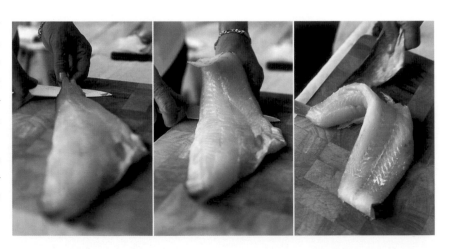

1 Cut the fish into evenly sized 2.5cm (1 in) pieces or cubes.

2 Use the butter to grease a large pie dish, and season it with salt and pepper. Preheat the oven to 200°C/400°F/Gas 6.

3 Put the button onions and mushrooms in a saucepan with 150ml (5 fl oz) water. Add the lemon juice, sherry and some salt and pepper. Cover with greaseproof paper, and leave the vegetables over a gentle heat, covered with the lid, so that they steam and cook, about 15 minutes. Strain off the liquid and cool both liquid and vegetables.

4 To make the sauce, melt the butter in a medium pan, add the flour and stir together to make a blond roux. In another pan, bring the milk, cream and the vegetable cooking liquor to the boil together. Slowly add the hot liquid to the roux, stirring, to make a white sauce. Leave to cook for 5 minutes, then add the spring onion, parsley, Tabasco and some salt and pepper if necessary. Put to one side, and cover with clingfilm to prevent a skin forming.

5 Mix the fish with the onions and mushrooms, then pile into the pie dish and season with salt and pepper.

6 For the topping, peel, wash and dry the potatoes and cut into thin slices. Pan-fry the potatoes in the butter and oil to colour nicely. Drain.

7 Pour the sauce over the fish and tap the pie dish to let the air escape. Carefully place the coloured potatoes over the fish in two layers to make a crust, the top layer being nicely presented. It should look like a hotpot topping.

8 Bake in the preheated oven for 25–30 minutes, brushing with the melted clarified butter every now and again during cooking. Serve hot, straight from the oven.

■ Or follow all the stages of the recipe, but simply cover the fish and its sauce with mashed potato. It needn't be plain mash: horseradish mash, mustard mash or even bubble and squeak mash would look and taste good.

Mussels with Cider

SERVES 8 We think of mussels as being French (*moules marinières*) or Belgian (*moules et frites*), but of course mussels are found all around the coastlines of Britain, and have been eaten here for centuries. Musselburgh in Scotland was actually named for the famous nearby mussel beds, and there are several soup-stews in traditional Scottish cooking. (Mussels are now farmed in Scotland and Ireland, on ropes.) Mussels feature in Welsh and Irish cooking as well – think of Molly Malone plying her live 'cockles and mussels' through the Dublin streets.

Instead of the French wine, I have used our English cider here, along with apples, and the flavours are good.

2.25 litres (4 pints) mussels

2 shallots, peeled and chopped

2 apples, cored and finely diced

300ml (10 fl oz) dry cider

2 tbsp chopped fresh parsley

150ml (5 fl oz) double cream

juice of ½ lemon

25g (1 oz) unsalted butter

salt and freshly ground black pepper

1 Clean the mussels well, removing the beards, and discard any that are cracked, or remain open after you tap them sharply against the edge of the sink. Put into a large heavy-bottomed pan.

2 Add the chopped shallot, the apple dice, cider and half the chopped parsley. Cover with a lid. Cook over a fierce heat until all the mussels have opened, about 6–7 minutes.

3 Lift the mussels out, using a spider sieve, into a colander over a bowl. Strain the cooking liquor into a clean bowl and allow to stand for 5 minutes to allow any sand to sink to the bottom. Discard the vegetables.

4 Carefully strain the liquor into a clean pan, taking care not to disturb any sand at the bottom. Add any liquor from below the mussels as well.

5 Add the cream and lemon juice to the liquor, and boil to reduce by half. Add the butter and remaining parsley, and check the seasoning.

6 Meanwhile, discard any mussels that remain closed. (If in doubt, throw 'em out, they're really quite cheap.) Divide them between eight soup plates, pour the sauce over and serve immediately.

Dressed Crab

SERVES 4

I love crab, and still remember the crab paste we used to have in Yorkshire as kids (once a speciality of Scarborough, I believe). I've been fortunate enough to have worked in three British crab areas. In Cromer, Norfolk, where the crabs are very small but sweet, I met Richard David who catches them at sea and sells them on the High Street. I've also cooked and tasted crab in Whitby, further north, where they are bigger – and indeed they seem to get bigger the further north you go, particularly in Scotland. However, perhaps to gainsay that, I've caught and eaten crab in Guernsey (where they're called 'shankers'), and there they are quite massive.

Most crabs are dressed in their shells, but I think there is complication enough already in getting all the meat out without worrying about keeping the shells whole. I just serve the white and dark meat separately in bowls, and use the shells for quite a different purpose (see opposite).

1 x 1.8kg (4 lb) live male crab
4.5 litres (7½ pints) water
175g (6 oz) salt

To dress the crab

juice of 1 lemon
Tabasco sauce to taste
Worcestershire sauce to taste
55g (2 oz) fresh white breadcrumbs
salt and freshly ground black pepper
4 hard-boiled eggs, shelled
2 tbsp chopped fresh parsley
1 small onion, peeled and finely chopped

1 Bring the salted water up to the boil, plunge in the crab, bring back to the boil and simmer for 25 minutes. Then take off the heat and allow the crab to cool in the liquor. Take out, drain, and put into the fridge. Alternatively, you can buy a fresh cooked crab from a reputable fishmonger.

2 Twist off the legs and claws, and break each joint so that it is easier to remove the meat. Using a small hammer to tap and crack open the pieces, and a skewer, push all the pieces of white meat out into a bowl. The claws

contain the nicest, sweetest and moistest meat, but this needs careful checking for any bones.

3 Next take the body in one hand, then, using a kitchen knife, insert and twist to remove the central case of the body that held the legs and claws. Pull this free then remove the ring of 'dead men's fingers' and throw away. This will reveal the brown crabmeat. Using a spoon remove this from the shell and put into another bowl.

4 Break the brown meat up, adding the lemon juice, Tabasco and Worcestershire sauces to taste, and enough breadcrumbs to form a paste which is not too soft. Season to taste with salt and pepper.

5 Pass the boiled eggs through a sieve, add the parsley and onion, and mix well together.

6 Put the brown meat into a shallow bowl with the egg mixture scattered around the edge to decorate.

7 Serve the white meat in a separate bowl, perhaps with a lemon mayonnaise, brown bread and butter, and even a tomato salad for perfection.

- You may think I have forgotten to season the white meat. But I don't think it needs it. Try it and see.
- Don't waste your time keeping the shells for presentation. Break them up with the claws, using a hammer, and put them in a pot with fish stock, garlic, tomatoes and other vegetable flavourings to make a strong stock. Take the shells out and put some rice in. Pound the shells, and return to the pan until the rice is cooked. Press everything through a fine sieve, squeezing to get as much flavour out as possible. Add double cream and brandy to taste, and you will have a wonderful crab soup.

Lobster with Dill, Tomato and Mustard

SERVES 4

Lobsters have always been highly rated and highly priced, and those of Scotland are said to be the best in Britain, growing sweet in the cold waters of the north. But I have eaten lobsters much further south, in the Channel Islands, and in Alderney, so legend has it, the lobster population flourished and grew fat on the bodies of slave labourers thrown into the sea around the island during the German occupation in the 1940s...

This recipe is similar to a Scottish one, and to many that became popular in Victorian times in gentlemen's clubs. It's my 'almost Thermidor'. A lobster per person is a large main course, but I think if you're pampering yourself, you don't want half measures. However, as a first course, two lobsters between four would be sufficient.

4 x 450g (1 lb) live lobsters
  (approx. weight)
55g (2 oz) unsalted butter
1 shallot, peeled and chopped
150ml (5 fl oz) fish stock
150ml (5 fl oz) white wine
300ml (10 fl oz) double cream

4 tbsp crème fraîche
1 tbsp Dijon mustard
salt and freshly ground black pepper
2 tbsp chopped fresh dill
4 tomatoes, finely diced
2 egg yolks
55g (2 oz) Parmesan, freshly grated

1 Cook the lobsters by plunging in boiling water and boiling for 4 minutes, then take out and leave to cool.

2 Split the carcass in half lengthways. Take out the body meat carefully and put to one side. Break off the claws, and separate into the three different joints, removing the cartilage from the middle of the pincer. Gently tap the joints with the back of a large knife and take out the meat. Keep separate. Discard the intestinal tract from the body then cut the body meat into nice-sized pieces.

3 Preheat the oven to 160°C/325°F/Gas 3. Wash and clean four of the half shells, and put them in the oven to warm through.

4 Meanwhile, melt half the butter in a pan, and sweat off the shallot, not allowing it to colour. Add the fish stock and white wine and reduce by two-thirds. Add the double cream, boil and reduce by half until thickened. Remove from the heat, add the crème fraîche and mustard, mix in and season.

5 Heat the sauce gently then add the lobster meat except for the claws. Heat through gently but well. Dab the claw meat with the remaining butter and heat for a few minutes in the low oven.

6 Add the chopped dill and tomato dice to the sauce, then beat in the egg yolks. Pour this mixture evenly into the four warm half lobster shells.

7 Lay the meat from a claw on top of each mounded half lobster, sprinkle with the Parmesan, colour under the preheated grill and serve.

- If there are eggs in the tail of a female, or a greenish sac in the head (the tomalley), make sure you use these in the sauce.
- Break up the spare half shells, put into a small but tall saucepan, and add some unsalted butter. Leave to stew slowly on the side of the stove. The butter will turn red and taste incredibly of lobster. Strain. You can chill this flavoured butter, or freeze it, to use in sauces.

Salad of Scallops with Bacon

SERVES 4

The combination of scallops and bacon crops up in Scottish, English and Manx cooking, one of those wonderful anomalies of flavour balance, which is similar to oysters and bacon (see page 42) and the Welsh trout cooked with bacon. I've taken it a little into the present time by presenting it in a salad.

Scallops are one of our most delicious shellfish, native to the cold waters of western Scotland and around the Isle of Man (where there has apparently been a scallop fishery for some 3,000 years). Giant or king scallops are the largest, the queens or queenies being much smaller (and, if used instead, you will need six to seven – or even more – instead of three per person).

12 large scallops in the shell

5 tbsp olive oil

salt and freshly ground black pepper

6 rashers smoked back bacon

6 spring onions, chopped

1 tbsp grain mustard

2 tbsp white wine vinegar

2 tbsp groundnut oil

1 tbsp each of chopped fresh parsley, chives and chervil

To serve

mixed salad leaves (more or less, depending on whether for a starter or main course)

1 Trim the scallops, using the white muscle meat only for this dish.

2 Heat 1 tbsp of the olive oil in a solid flat-bottomed frying pan, and sear the

Cut into the side of the shell using a sharp knife. Twist the blade to prise the shell open. Detach the large white muscle from the shell. Take off the skirt (the frill round the muscle), and discard the little black sac.

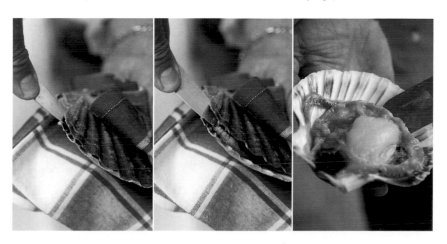

scallops until golden brown, a minute or two only. Turn over just to sear, season and then take out and keep warm.

3   Meanwhile, trim the bacon and cut into thin strips. Sauté and colour these in the frying pan that the scallops were cooked in. Add the chopped spring onion, and sauté until coloured, and then put both bacon and onion into a large bowl.

4   Mix the mustard and vinegar well in a bowl or jar, then add the remaining olive oil, the groundnut oil, herbs and some seasoning. Take some of the dressing and toss with the salad leaves then lay these in the middle of four plates.

5   Add the remaining dressing to the bacon and onion. Balance the three scallops per person on each mound of salad leaves, and then spoon the bacon, onion and dressing over and around.

Potted Shrimps

SERVES 4

Shrimp teas were traditional in the north of England, and potted shrimps became a popular feature of afternoon tea in the late eighteenth century. The shrimp industry in Britain centres on the dangerous shifting sands and shallow waters of Morecambe Bay in Lancashire, where tractors now carry the nets instead of horses. Brown cold-water shrimps, found along many coasts in northern Europe, are very small (which makes them difficult to shell), but taste wonderful. The shelled shrimps widely available now come mostly from Holland, and I urge you to buy those you can shell yourself. The shells will make a fantastic stock. Or, if you can't be bothered with shelling, simply blend the fish, shells and all, to make a great paste for spreading on toast.

Fish or meat has been preserved in butter like this since at least the sixteenth century.

140g (5 oz) clarified butter (see page 49)
350g (12 oz) peeled cooked brown shrimps
a pinch of ground mace
1 tsp anchovy essence
a pinch of cayenne pepper
lemon juice (optional)

1 Preheat the oven to 150°C/300°F/Gas 2.
2 Melt the clarified butter, then take out just less than half and put to one side. Add the brown shrimps to the bulk of the butter in the pan, and season with the mace, anchovy essence and cayenne pepper. You must taste at this stage and if you are unhappy with the balance, add the lemon juice.
3 Now lift the shrimps out using a slotted spoon, and divide between four ramekins or nice oven-to-table dishes.
4 Pour the seasoned butter equally over the shrimps and put the ramekins into a bain-marie (a roasting tray) with warm water. Put this into the preheated oven and cook for 30 minutes. Remove the ramekins from the oven and the tray, and tap the ramekins gently on a carefully folded cloth to get rid of any air bubbles in the mix.
5 Melt the remaining clarified butter and pour gently over the top of the mixture, then leave to cool and set.

Kedgeree

SERVES 4

Although thought of as a quintessentially English dish, kedgeree originated in India during the days of the Raj (as did *Mulligatawny Soup*, see page 18). The original '*khichri*' was a vegetarian combination of rice and lentils. It was thought to be the British Army in India who adapted it to be a rice-only breakfast dish, and who added bits of dried or salted fish. Smoked haddock is the most common fish used now (salmon too), and it's on the menu as such at our Foxtrot Oscar restaurants, very popular with old colonials and old public schoolboys – and, much to my surprise, we sell a lot to young people as well.

550g (1¼ lb) smoked haddock fillet

600ml (1 pint) fish stock

1 bay leaf

juice of 1 lemon

salt and freshly ground black pepper

25g (1 oz) unsalted butter

1 onion, peeled and finely chopped

225g (8 oz) long-grain rice

1 tsp curry powder

a pinch of cayenne pepper

a pinch of freshly grated nutmeg

a pinch of saffron strands (optional)

4 hard-boiled eggs, shelled

1 tbsp chopped fresh coriander

1 Preheat the oven to 180°C/350°F/Gas 4.

2 Make sure the haddock fillet is skinned and boned totally. Put into a large ovenproof dish. Bring the fish stock to the boil, and pour over the fish. Add the bay leaf and lemon juice, and season well. Cook covered in the preheated oven for 5 minutes until just cooked. Strain off the stock.

3 Meanwhile, melt the butter in a saucepan, add the onion and sweat without colouring for a few minutes until soft. Add the rice and stir, then cook until the rice is completely coated with butter. Add the spices.

4 Pour in the strained fish stock topped up with enough water to make twice the volume of the rice. Cover with buttered greaseproof paper and cook in the preheated oven as above for 18 minutes.

5 Take out of the oven, leave to sit for 2 minutes, and then stir with a fork.

6 Cut the eggs into big chunks, add half to the rice and stir in. Check the seasoning of the rice, then pour into a warmed serving bowl. Flake the smoked haddock over the top, sprinkle with the rest of the eggs and coriander, and serve.

Prawn Cocktail

SERVES 4
No-one seems to be quite sure where and when the infamous prawn cocktail originated, but it appeared on restaurant menus in Britain throughout the 1960s, and can still be found today. It may be an American idea. A combination of shredded lettuce, prawns and, usually, a bottled mayo-based sauce, it has been much maligned, but in actual fact when made correctly, can be wonderful. Marco Pierre White even included it on his Mirabelle menu!

350g (12 oz) shelled prawns
1 little gem lettuce
1 tbsp Dijon mustard
1 tbsp white wine vinegar
4 tbsp olive oil
salt and freshly ground black pepper
2 tbsp finely chopped cucumber

Sauce
6 tbsp mayonnaise
2 tbsp *Tomato Ketchup* (see page 201)
1 tbsp double cream
1 tsp each of brandy and
   creamed horseradish
juice of ½ lemon
4 drops Tabasco sauce

To garnish
2 tomatoes, seeded and finely diced
1 shallot, peeled and finely chopped
1 tbsp chopped fresh chives

1 Put the prawns into a bowl. Finely shred the lettuce.
2 Make a vinaigrette with the mustard, vinegar and oil. Season with salt and pepper.
3 Make the sauce by mixing the mayonnaise with the ketchup and cream, then stir in the brandy, horseradish, lemon juice and Tabasco. Check the seasoning.
4 Mix the prawns with 1 tbsp of the sauce and 1 tbsp of the vinaigrette.
5 Mix the shredded lettuce with the cucumber, add the remaining vinaigrette and season.
6 Put the lettuce into four glasses, with the prawns on top. Cover lightly with the rest of the sauce.
7 Mix the tomatoes, shallot and chives, sprinkle over the sauce and serve.

Roast Loin of Pork with Crackling (see page 97)

In the very earliest of times, meat and offal would have been cooked beside or on the fire. Once metal cooking pots were invented, meat could be boiled or stewed in water. Most meat eaten was actually 'game' – even cattle, pigs, sheep and goats were animals of the wild until they were domesticated. Cows, sheep and goats could be milked, so had a dual purpose, while pigs, because they could forage for themselves and be fed on scraps, were perhaps most commonly attached to households large and small.

It was not until the seventeenth century that crops were introduced specifically to

Meat and Offal

feed animals during winter. Before then animals would have been slaughtered during the autumn. The offal would have been cooked then and there, or preserved by salting, drying or smoking. Nowadays we seem only to use the superior 'organ' meats, such as liver, kidneys and sweetbreads, disliking the lesser offal as 'poverty food' perhaps.

The meat of the slaughtered beasts would have been preserved too, by salting principally, but 'corning' was popular in Ireland. Fresh meat was eaten of course, but until the problem of over-wintering was solved it would have been largely seasonal. The tender cuts would have spit-roasted beside the fire (our current 'roasting' in an enclosed space is actually baking), and tougher cuts would have been boiled, often in a pottage, or wrapped in a cloth or a suet casing as a pudding. Once ovens developed, other meat-cooking techniques could evolve, such as braising and baking in or under pastry. Britain was once famous for its meat pies, and we have quite a few still – steak and kidney, veal and ham, the Scottish mutton pie, and Cornish pasties.

Why Britain became so renowned for its roast meats is not easily explained. But, despite increasing French culinary influences throughout the centuries, the love of roast meats, plainly served and sauced, did not diminish. Some say it was because the quality of the meat was so good. In France, animals were worked until old, then slaughtered; the flesh would be tougher and riper, so needed fancy flavourings and longer, more complicated cooking to render it palatable. In Britain, animals were reared specifically for the table, so therefore could be roasted much more successfully.

Why the British still love meat so much is just as unclear, but 'meat and two veg' is almost mandatory, at least for Sunday lunch.

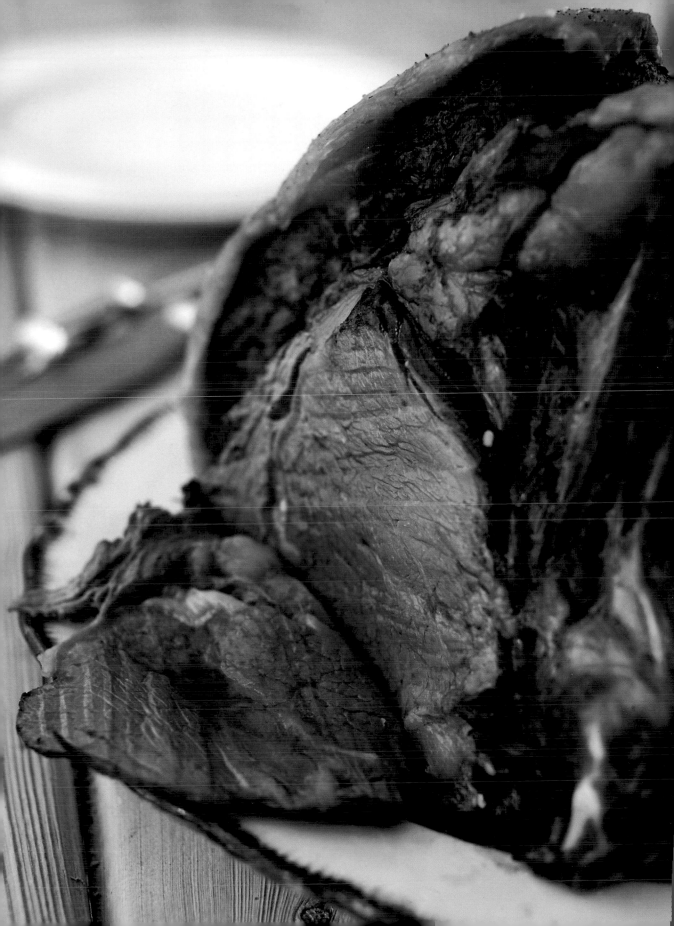

Roast Beef and Yorkshire Pudding

SERVES 8–10 Whatever the reason for the undeniable quality of our beef, Britain wouldn't be so great without its roast beef and Yorkshire pudding. I remember we cooked 25-pound sirloins on the bone at Simpson's in the Strand, and then we took them into the dining room to be carved in front of the guests.

Batter puddings are traditional all over the British Isles, and Yorkshire pudding is the most famous, originally cooked in the tray of dripping under the meat as it turned on the spit. Why it became so associated with Yorkshire, I don't know. Perhaps it was because of the renowned meanness of my fellow countrymen: the pudding was served first, before the meat, in order to fill people up so that they would then eat less meat! To me its main purpose is to soak up the meat juices and the gravy.

1 x 4.5kg (10 lb) rib of beef (5 ribs)
salt and freshly ground black pepper

Yorkshire pudding
1 large cup plain flour
a pinch of salt
1 large cup eggs
1 large cup milk and water mixed
1 tbsp malt vinegar

1 For the Yorkshire pudding batter, sift the flour and salt into a large bowl. Add the eggs and beat well with half the liquid until all the lumps have disappeared. Add the rest of the liquid and the vinegar, and allow to stand.

2 Meanwhile, preheat the oven to 220°C/425°F/Gas 7.

3 Prepare the meat by cutting down the backbone towards the rib bones with the knife angled towards the backbone. Take a chopper and then break the backbones near the bottom of the cut (this is called chining). Lift up the fat from the back and take out the rubbery sinew. Tie the beef with string.

4 Put the joint into a roasting tray and season well. Roast in the preheated oven for 30 minutes and then reduce the heat to 190°C/375°F/Gas 5 for a further 1½ hours. This will give you blood-red beef in the middle. The way to check this is by using a meat thermometer to test to 55°C/130°F or, as I prefer, by plunging a metal skewer through the middle of the beef, holding it

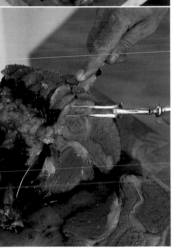

there for 10 seconds and then running it either across the wrist or under the bottom lip. If the skewer is cold the meat is not ready; if warm, it's medium; and if hot, then the meat is well done.

5 When cooked, put the meat in a warm place to rest for 20–30 minutes before carving and serving. Meanwhile, increase the oven temperature again to 200°C/400°F/Gas 6.

6 Heat some of the excess dripping from the roast in a suitably sized ovenproof pan or roasting tray. Whisk up the Yorkshire pudding batter, then pour into the tray and immediately place in the oven. Close the door quickly, and bake for 25 minutes. Turn the pan round and cook on for another 10 minutes.

7 Meanwhile, carve and portion the beef on to hot plates, and make a gravy using the juices left in the roasting tray (see the *Roast Chicken* recipe on page 108). As soon as the Yorkshire pudding is ready, serve with mustard and *Horseradish Sauce* (see page 216), or indeed some horseradish mustard.

- The bigger the joint, the better the meat, and it should always be cooked on the bone. The meat should have a good covering of fat, be dark red in colour (which shows it has been hung properly), and have a good marbling of fat throughout.
- Sprinkling some English mustard powder over the top of the meat halfway through its cooking gives a nice heat.
- This Yorkshire pudding recipe works not by weight, but by volume. Use any size of cup, but measure each ingredient with the same cup. I'm not sure why the vinegar is there, but that's what my gran did. It seems to work, so why change it?
- Yorkshire pudding is very versatile. It can be eaten by itself, with onions and gravy, or can be used in a sweet context as well – not surprising, as the batter is virtually the same as that for popovers and pancakes. In Yorkshire we eat it with sugar and jam, and that's *after* the pudding and the meat!

Toad in the Hole

SERVES 4

Many traditional British batter puddings included some meat, a convenient way of stretching small amounts of protein. Toad in the hole is usually now made with sausages – the Yorkshire beef ones are particularly good – but originally it would have been pieces of leftover meat or, rather posher, pieces of raw rump or fillet steak, or lamb chops.

Yorkshire pudding batter (see page 73)   **12 pork sausages**
55g (2 oz) beef dripping or lard

1 Make the batter as described on page 73, and leave to rest.
2 Preheat the oven to 200°C/400°F/Gas 6.
3 Heat the dripping or lard in a suitably sized ovenproof pan or roasting tray, and colour the sausages on top of the stove. Put the pan into the preheated oven and cook for 10 minutes.
4 Whisk up the batter, and then immediately pour into the tray and return to the oven. Close the door quickly, and bake for 25 minutes. Turn the pan round and cook on for another 10 minutes. Serve immediately.

Boiled Silverside of Beef and Dumplings

SERVES 4–6   Centuries ago, because animals could not be over-wintered, most (apart from breeding stock) were killed in the autumn and the meat was salted to preserve it. Salted meat (except pork) cannot be roasted, grilled or fried, so it had to be boiled, thus the many traditional boiled meat recipes in the British canon. (And indeed in many other European cuisines – think of the French *pot au feu*, the Italian *bollito misto* and the Swiss *Berner Platte*.) Boiled meat has a texture and flavour that is its own, and we shouldn't dismiss it as less interesting than roast. Fresh meat can be used instead of salt.

And the suet dumplings are uniquely British. Apparently they were invented in Norfolk in the sixteenth century, probably evolving from the use of suet crust as the container for boiled meats.

1 x 1.3–1.8kg (3–4 lb) piece of
  salted silverside
2 large onions, peeled
1 leek
2 large carrots
6 black peppercorns
1 bay leaf
2 blades of mace

Vegetables
225g (8 oz) small carrots
225g (8 oz) small onions

450g (1 lb) small leeks (about 4)
225g (8 oz) swede
450g (1 lb) small new potatoes

Dumplings
175g (6 oz) plain flour
1½ tsp baking powder
a pinch of salt
85g (3 oz) chopped beef suet
2 tsp creamed horseradish
water

1 Check with your butcher whether the silverside needs to be soaked: it's often not really necessary these days. Cover the silverside with water, bring to the boil, then refresh in cold water.

2 Put the meat into a clean pan with the onions, leek, carrots, peppercorns,

bay leaf and mace. Bring to the boil, then turn the heat down, and simmer very gently for about 2½–3 hours. Check doneness by strongly ramming a roasting fork into the joint and then carefully lifting up. When done, the meat will slip off the fork easily.

3 Prepare the vegetables and trim into manageable sized pieces. Wrap each type of vegetable in separate cloths and tie with string. About half an hour from the end of cooking, drop all the vegetables into the stock with the meat. They will cook at different rates, usually the potatoes first, then the carrots, swede, onion and then the leeks. Take these out and keep warm.

4 To make the dumplings, mix the flour, baking powder and salt together, then rub in the suet. Mix with the horseradish and enough water to make the mixture come together to a soft, sticky dough.

5 Take some of the liquor out of the silverside pan, strain and bring to the boil in a clean pan. Take 1 tbsp of the dumpling mixture at a time and drop carefully into the liquor. They will swell, so don't put too many in at once. While these are cooking, take the beef out of its liquor and leave to rest, keeping it warm.

6 Serve in large deep bowls. Put the vegetables in first, then slice the beef and lay around the vegetables. Drain the dumplings well, and put on top of the dish. Check the seasoning of the stock, then strain some over each dish, and serve.

- Boiled beef with carrots is the most famed of the boiled beef dishes, but there is no reason why other root vegetables should not be used instead of or as well as.
- You could vary the dumplings. You could add chopped fresh herbs – parsley is very traditional – or even a fried croûton in the middle of the dumpling, which adds a crisp texture.
- Serve with grated fresh horseradish or a horseradish cream.
- There should be plenty of meat left over for sandwiches.

Steak and Kidney Pudding

SERVES 4

The combination of steak and kidney, although it seems as if it might always have existed, was only recorded in a recipe as late as the mid-nineteenth century. Steak puddings, however, had been made for centuries before, bringing together the suet crust used in the early boiled puddings, and the beef for which England in particular was so famous.

A good steak and kidney pudding is a wonderfully traditional British dish, brought to the table steaming in its bowl, often with a clean white napkin wrapped around it. It's a great favourite in gentlemen's clubs, and I remember we made many at Simpson's in the Strand. There, for some reason, they never served the pastry from inside the bowl, which I think is the most flavoursome, imbued with all the juices of the meats. Small individual puddings are now made – I've seen versions in foil, sold in Blackpool's fish and chip shops – and at one time I created a baked version for Beefeater Restaurants (which worked, not becoming too crusty, so long as it wasn't cooked for too long).

25g (1 oz) beef dripping

675g (1½ lb) topside of beef, trimmed
   and cut into 2.5cm (1 in) cubes

350g (12 oz) ox kidney, trimmed and
   cut into 2.5cm (1 in) cubes

1 large onion, peeled and finely chopped

350g (12 oz) field mushrooms, peeled
   and cut into 5mm (¼ in) strips

25g (1 oz) plain flour

300ml (10 fl oz) meat stock

150ml (5 fl oz) red wine

1 tbsp Worcestershire sauce

salt and freshly ground black pepper

unsalted butter for greasing

1 tbsp mixed chopped fresh parsley
   and thyme

Suet pastry

280g (10 oz) self-raising flour

½ tsp baking powder

a pinch of salt

140g (5 oz) chopped beef suet

about 2–3 tbsp iced water

55g (2 oz) unsalted butter

1 Preheat the oven to 180°C/350°F/Gas 4.

2 Heat the dripping in a casserole, add the beef and kidney and colour on all sides. Add the onion and mushroom strips, and cook for 2 minutes. Sprinkle with the plain flour, take off the heat and mix the stock, wine and Worcestershire sauce in well. Season with salt and pepper, then put into the preheated oven, and cook for 1 hour. Remove the casserole from the oven and allow to cool.

3 To make the pastry, put the self-raising flour, baking powder and salt into a bowl and mix. Rub in the suet, then add enough iced water to bind to a fairly soft, pliable dough. Leave to rest for about 20 minutes.

4 Butter a 1.2 litre (2 pint) pudding basin well, and have ready a steamer large enough to hold it, or a large saucepan with a stand in it on which the bowl can sit. Cut a circle of greaseproof paper, larger than the circumference of the top of the bowl. Make a couple of pleats in this, and grease the pleated side.

5 Divide the pastry into three-quarters and one-quarter. Take the larger piece and roll it out to a circle to line the basin, with 1cm (½ in) extra hanging over the edge. Gently line the pudding basin.

6 Mix the herbs into the meat mixture, and pour this mixture into the bowl. Wet the lip of the pastry with water, then roll the remaining pastry out to cover the top. Place on top of the basin, and press down well to seal.

7 Put the greaseproof paper, pleated and greased side down, over the pudding. This pleat allows the pudding to expand. Tie the paper on round the top of the basin, under the lip, with string, and make a handle as well, so that you can lift it in and out easily.

8 Put the pudding in the top of the steamer over boiling water or on the stand in the saucepan, with enough boiling water to come halfway up the pudding. Cover, bring to the boil and cook for 2 hours. Check the water level occasionally.

9 Serve the pudding from the bowl. Slice the top off, lift it off, and spoon out the meat and juices. Serve each person a bit of the top and some of the juicy pastry from the sides.

Beef Olives

SERVES 4

The idea of olives – a flavourful filling encased in a thin slice of meat, and braised – has been around for a long time in Britain. Apparently the veal version was a seventeenth-century variant on the much older beef or mutton olives, which were once called 'allowes' (possibly how the name 'olives' evolved). The idea is not uniquely British, though: think of the French *paupiettes* and the Italian *involtini* or *bocconcini*.

This was one of the first dishes I learned to cook at college, useful because it embodies all of the basic principles of stewing and braising. I've adapted it, though, principally in the sauce: incorporating the braised sieved vegetables into the sauce gives extra flavour, thickness and richness. So serve with separately cooked vegetables, but if you wanted to be more sophisticated, you could do a dice of carrots and add them to the sauce at the last minute to cook and heat through.

4 x 175g (6 oz) slices topside beef

25g (1 oz) unsalted butter

55g (2 oz) fresh breadcrumbs

½ tsp chopped fresh thyme

1 tsp chopped fresh parsley

1 tbsp chopped cooked bacon

1 egg

salt and freshly ground black pepper

55g (2 oz) beef dripping

1 onion, peeled and finely chopped

1 carrot, peeled and finely chopped

1 garlic clove, peeled and crushed

1 tbsp tomato purée

150ml (5 fl oz) red wine

850ml (1½ pints) brown meat stock

1 Tap the slices of topside out evenly between two layers of plastic or clingfilm to make them thinner. Be careful not to tear them.

2 Melt the butter, then add the breadcrumbs, herbs and bacon. Stir in the egg and some salt and pepper, and mix together well. Smear equal parts of this stuffing on to each tapped-out piece of meat, season again and roll up into a cylinder shape. Tie with thin string to hold together, to look like a mini Swiss roll.

3 Meanwhile, preheat the oven to 160°C/325°F/Gas 3.

4 Heat the dripping in a casserole, and seal and colour the olives. Remove from the casserole. Add the chopped vegetables to the hot fat and colour lightly, followed by the garlic and then the tomato purée. Stir in the red wine and boil to reduce by half.

5 Lay the olives in the casserole, and add the brown stock. Stir, then bring to the boil. Cover with greaseproof paper and a lid, then put into the preheated oven and cook for 1–1½ hours.

6 Remove the olives from the sauce and keep warm. Reduce the sauce a little over a high heat, then push through a sieve. Check the seasoning and consistency. Remove the string carefully from the olives, then pour the sauce over them and serve. Delicious with mashed potato.

■ Instead of bacon, you could use Parma ham in the filling or, to be really outrageous, you could use haggis by itself.

Beef Wellington

SERVES 4

I have been unable to discover the origins of this dish, but it was named for the first Duke of Wellington, who defeated Napoleon at Waterloo in 1815. He was no gourmet, it's said, but the pastry-encased fillet, glazed and shiny brown, looks rather like the leather boot that also came to be associated with him. It is most similar in concept, actually, to the Russian dish, *coulibiac*, in that a prime piece of protein is encased in several layers before being baked or roasted.

675g (1½ lb) beef fillet, a piece cut from the centre of the fillet

1 tbsp vegetable oil

salt and freshly ground black pepper

25g (1 oz) unsalted butter

1 shallot, peeled and chopped

55g (2 oz) cooked ham, diced

350g (12 oz) button mushrooms, minced

115g (4 oz) meat pâté or terrine

1 tbsp chopped fresh parsley

6 large, about 25cm (10 in), pancakes (see note opposite)

2 eggs, beaten with a little water

450g (1 lb) puff pastry

1 Tie the fillet with butcher's string to keep a nice round shape.

2 Heat the oil in a frying pan. Seal the beef fillet and colour well on all sides. Leave to cool, then remove the strings and season with salt and pepper.

3 Meanwhile, melt the butter and sweat the shallot without colouring. Add the ham and minced button mushrooms and cook, stirring regularly, until all the liquor has evaporated and the mushrooms are quite dry. Season and leave to cool (this is now what is called a duxelles).

4 Mix the pâté and parsley with the mushrooms. Smear half of this mixture evenly over the top of the beef fillet.

5 Lay the pancakes out to make a 'sheet' of pancakes, side by side and overlapping. Lift the fillet carefully on to the centre of the pancake sheet, upside down so that the 'bare' side is uppermost. Smear the exposed side with the remaining mushroom mixture so that it is now completely covered with the duxelles. Brush the edges of the pancakes with the egg wash and carefully fold these over to completely seal the beef in the pancakes.

6 Roll out the pastry to about 3mm (⅛ in) thick. Trim the pastry into an even oblong just enough to fold over the beef. Brush the edges of the puff pastry

with the egg wash. Lay the pancake-covered beef in the centre, and fold the edges of the pastry in and over to make a neat parcel. Turn over so that the joins are underneath. Reshape if necessary, and cut a cylindrical hole in the top to allow the steam to escape. Egg wash and decorate if wanted, then leave to rest for 30 minutes.

7 Preheat the oven to 200°C/400°F/Gas 6.

8 Egg wash the pastry again, then bake the Wellington in the preheated oven for 25 minutes. Turn the oven down to 160°C/325°F/Gas 3 and cook for another 10–15 minutes until the pastry is brown and the meat inside is nicely rare. Cover with foil if the pastry is getting too brown.

9 Leave to rest for about 15 minutes, just like any other roast meat. One of the best ways to test whether the meat is done is to stick a skewer in the middle, count to ten, and then run the skewer along your bottom lip. You'll feel a variance in temperature, the middle part being the coolest. You should feel hot, hot, cool, cool, hot, hot.

10 When slicing, take off the end bits first, as they will be well done. Serve with a Madeira sauce (see page 219).

- The pancakes and pâté/duxelles layers here are vital to prevent the juices of the fillet running into the pastry.
- You could use brioche pastry instead of puff, but that is considerably more complicated as you have to make it from scratch.
- Other ingredients could be used to encase the fillet inside the pastry, such as sun-dried tomato paste or olive paste, or spinach, but then it would no longer strictly be a Wellington.
- Everyone has a pancake recipe, but if you don't, use the Yorkshire pudding recipe on page 73 to make thin pancakes.

Cornish Pasties

MAKES 12

Variations of this idea – ingredients wrapped in pastry to make individual pies – occur all over Europe, but perhaps the nearest to the most famous one, that of Cornwall, are the Forfar Bridie, from the east of Scotland, and the Lancashire Foot. There are all sorts of legends surrounding the quintessential pasty: it is real only if it is dropped down a Cornish tin mine and the pastry doesn't break; that it is unlucky to take a pasty aboard a ship. In Cornwall, the pasty is occasionally called Tiddy Oggy (a local name for potato).

The basic recipe can also be varied in a number of ways. You could use any meat as a filling, and you could use vegetables alone (common when money for the costly meat was scarce). Whatever and however, the pasty is the ultimate portable food, as handy now for a picnic as it once was for the miner to take into the bowels of the earth or the farmer into the field.

Shortcrust pastry
450g (1 lb) plain flour
a pinch of salt
225g (8 oz) lard
55g (2 oz) butter
approx. 150ml (5 fl oz) water
2 eggs, beaten with a little water
  for egg wash

Filling
450g (1 lb) topside beef
1 medium onion
225g (8 oz) potatoes
55g (2 oz) carrots
55g (2 oz) turnip
salt and freshly ground black pepper
1 tbsp chopped parsley
Worcestershire sauce
Tabasco sauce

1 To make the pastry, sift the flour and salt into a bowl. Chop the lard and butter straight from the fridge into small cubes, then rub into the flour until like breadcrumbs. Add enough water to make the ingredients come together to a dough, then clingfilm and rest for 30 minutes.

2 Preheat the oven to 200°C/400°F/Gas 6.

3 To make the filling, trim the meat of all fat and gristle, cut into small dice then put into a bowl. Peel and finely chop the onion. Peel and cut the

potatoes, carrots and turnip into 1cm (½ in) dice, and add to the bowl along with the onion. Mix well, then season with salt and pepper, and add the parsley and a splash each of the sauces.

4 Cut the pastry into four pieces and roll each of them out thinly. Cut into circles of 15cm (6 in) in diameter. Brush the edges of each pastry circle with egg wash, then pile a quarter of the filling into the middle of each. Spread in a line across the centre of the pastry. Fold the pastry over and up to make a seal on top of the filling. Using your thumb and forefinger, crimp the edges in a wavy fashion. Brush with egg wash and make a hole in the top for the steam to escape.

5 Bake in the preheated oven for 30 minutes, then reduce the oven temperature to 180°C/350°F/Gas 4 and continue to cook for a further 20 minutes. Serve hot or cold.

■ You could use rough puff or hot water crust pastry (see page 92) instead of the shortcrust.

Irish Stew

SERVES 4

The combination of lamb, onions and potatoes is common throughout Europe, but the most famous version is that from Ireland, where potatoes were such a staple, and sheep thrived on the lush grazing. Hogget or mutton was probably used at first, and some say that kid was common as well.

The version here is unusual because of the cabbage, but that's how we used to do it at The Savoy Hotel, plating the lamb chops with a separate braised cabbage 'ball', the whole potatoes and the sauce, flavoured and thickened by the potato and cabbage (and sometimes enriched with cream). The celery leaves were the final touch.

900g (2 lb) large potatoes

3 large onions

½ white cabbage

8 large middle neck lamb chops

salt and freshly ground black pepper

600ml (1 pint) white stock (made from unroasted bones or vegetables)

1 bouquet garni (bay leaf, parsley, thyme etc.)

1 tbsp chopped celery leaves

1 Peel the potatoes and trim into twelve even-sized pieces. Put to one side in water and keep the trimmings.

2 Peel and thinly slice the onions, and lay in the bottom of a large, deep, heatproof stewing pan. Shred the cabbage and place on top of the onion. Put the chops on top. Slice the potato trimmings and scatter over the chops. Season with salt and pepper.

3 Cover the vegetables and meat with the stock and add the bouquet garni. Bring up to the boil, cover with a lid and cook slowly for 1–1½ hours on top of the stove.

4 Put in the trimmed potatoes, and gently simmer for another 20–30 minutes until the potatoes and the chops are cooked. Take out the chops and whole potatoes, put into a serving dish and keep warm.

5 Remove the bouquet garni and purée the liquor in a food processor. Check for seasoning and consistency.

6 Pour the sauce over the meat, sprinkle with the chopped celery leaves and serve.

Pot-roasted Shoulder of Lamb

SERVES 6–8 It is said that until the nineteenth century, sheep were valued more for their wool than their meat. Older sheep would have been slaughtered once past their best fleece days, and probably salted for winter eating. Lambs would have been an occasional treat, whereas now of course it is mutton that is rare.

A piece of sheep – or indeed a whole one – would traditionally have been roasted in front of the fire. Here I'm pot-roasting a boned shoulder, a good way of dealing with and dissolving the fat and cartilage of the cut (once very underrated, now becoming popular again, thank goodness). The meat is rolled round garlic (not very British, I admit) and rosemary, and then served with some traditional accompaniments. They say that these 'tracklements' should be made of foods the animals themselves might have eaten, thus the rosemary here, and sheep might very well have eaten wild mint and redcurrants as well.

I have in my mind that if you tie the lamb correctly, with the remaining bone at the right angle, the lamb looks rather like a duck, which some wag of a parson at some time called Parson's Duck…

1 x 2kg (4½ lb) shoulder of lamb

1 bunch fresh rosemary, leaves separated
   from the stalks (keep the latter)

2 garlic cloves, peeled and crushed

salt and freshly ground black pepper

1 tbsp olive oil

2 onions, peeled and roughly chopped

1 celery stalk, roughly chopped

1 large carrot, roughly chopped

25g (1 oz) unsalted butter

150ml (5 fl oz) white wine

300ml (10 fl oz) meat stock

1 Preheat the oven to 180°C/350°F/Gas 4.

2 There are three bones in shoulder of lamb, and we want to take out two of them. If unhappy, get your butcher to do it, but it's really quite easy and because you can't go too far wrong, it's good boning practice for you! Remove the shoulder blade and the 'upper arm' bone from the flesh side by carefully following the bones round. Open up from the centre to create a two-flap pocket.

3 Chop the rosemary leaves, then mix with the crushed garlic and some salt and pepper, and smear into the inner side of the lamb. Roll the lamb up like a Swiss roll, so that it looks like the body of a duck. Tie the shoulder with string to help keep the shape.

4 Heat the oil in a large frying pan, and sear and colour the outside of the lamb until golden brown.

5 Put the vegetables in the bottom of an ovenproof casserole or roasting tray big enough for the lamb. It should have a tight-fitting lid (if not, foil will have to be used). Put the lamb on top of the vegetables and season it. Put in the butter, the white wine and the stalks from the rosemary.

6 Cover with the lid and cook in the preheated moderate oven for 1½ hours. Turn the heat down to 120°C/250°F/Gas ½, and cook for a further hour. The lamb should be well cooked and ready to melt in the mouth (rather like the Greek *kleftiko*).

7 Take the dish out of the oven and allow the lamb to stand for 10 minutes.

8 Meanwhile, pour off the excess fat from the cooking dish, then add the meat stock. Boil together to reduce by about a third, then skim off the fat, strain and serve hot with the meat.

Lancashire Hotpot

SERVES 4

Slow-cooked dishes such as this only evolved properly once people had ovens. As these were few and far between domestically at first, many hotpots were taken to the local baker or cookshop to be cooked (similar dishes in France bear the adjective '*boulangère*' because of this). At home, a hotpot would be cooked in the baking oven as it cooled after the high heat of baking day.

Speaking as a Yorkshireman, I don't know why Lancashire has the kudos of inventing hotpot. However, it's a fantastic dish, traditionally made with neck end chops. I prefer to use chump chops from the other end, as there's less bone, more meat, and they eat well. So could we call this a Yorkshire hotpot?

4 x 225g (8 oz) lamb chump chops on the bone

55g (2 oz) beef dripping

450g (1 lb) large onions, peeled and finely sliced

900g (2 lb) even-sized potatoes

85g (3 oz) unsalted butter, melted

salt and freshly ground black pepper

4 lambs' kidneys, cored and sliced

600ml (1 pint) lamb or chicken stock

1 tbsp chopped fresh chives

1 Preheat the oven to 200°C/400°F/Gas 6.

2 Trim the chops. Heat the dripping in a large frying pan, and colour the chops well on each side. Put to one side. Add the onion to the pan and colour quickly. Pour out into a dish and leave to cool.

3 Peel the potatoes and, if you can be bothered, cut and trim them to a cylindrical shape. (This is what chefs would do, and it looks very impressive.) Then slice into even slices of about 3mm (⅛ in) thick.

4 Put a third of the melted butter into the bottom of a large casserole dish. Place a layer of potatoes on top of the butter (keep the best shapes for later) and season. Sprinkle with half the onions, then place the chops on top. Season again. Mix the kidneys with the rest of the onions, then sprinkle over the meat. Pat flat.

5 Carefully arrange the rest of the potatoes overlapping each other to cover the top of the meat and onions. Pour the stock over to come just two-thirds of the way up. Season with salt and pepper, then brush the potato layer carefully with most of the remaining melted butter.

6 Cover the pot with a lid and put into the preheated oven for half an hour. Reduce the oven temperature to 180°C/350°F/Gas 4 and cook for a further 1½ hours.

7 Remove the lid, brush the potatoes again with melted butter and cook on until the potatoes are brown. Remove the casserole from the oven and leave to rest for a few minutes. Sprinkle the potato topping with chopped chives and serve.

■ If you like, you could leave out the kidneys and substitute mushrooms as in a steak and kidney pudding or pie.

Mutton Pies

Large and small pies made with mutton or lamb have been popular since the Middle Ages. At first, like so many meat dishes of the time, they would have been quite sweet, mixed with dried fruit, sugar and sweet spices; later they became more savoury. There are lots of such pies in the north of England (perhaps *the* pie centre of the country) and in Scotland. North of the border they use minced, spiced mutton; in places like Northumberland the meat is chunkier, as here. But both are made with a hot water crust pastry, as is the famous British pork pie.

Apparently mutton pies were admired by Dr Johnson (he also liked Scotch broth), and were served at Balmoral and Buckingham Palace receptions by Queen Victoria and King George V. Fine fare indeed.

25g (1 oz) unsalted butter

1 red onion, peeled and finely chopped

1 tsp chopped fresh rosemary

115g (4 oz) mushrooms, finely chopped

a little vegetable oil

450g (1 lb) shoulder of lamb, off the bone,
  trimmed and cut into 5mm (¼ in) pieces

300ml (10 fl oz) lamb stock

salt and freshly ground black pepper

1 tsp freshly grated nutmeg

1 tsp fécule (potato flour) or cornflour,
  slaked in 1 tbsp lamb stock

Hot water crust pastry

350g (12 oz) plain flour

a pinch of salt

150ml (5 fl oz) water

115g (4 oz) white lard

1 egg yolk

1 egg, mixed with a little water, to glaze

1 Make the filling first. Melt the butter and sweat the finely chopped onion and rosemary without colouring for a few minutes. Add the mushrooms and cook for 3 minutes.

2 Put the meat in a frying pan, and pan-fry in the oil to colour on all sides. Add to the onion mixture along with half the lamb stock and season with salt, pepper and nutmeg. Cover and cook for 30 minutes on top of the stove, then allow to cool.

3 Meanwhile, preheat the oven to 190°C/375°F/Gas 5.

4 To start the pastry, sift the flour and salt into a bowl.

5 Bring the water up to boiling in a medium pan, take off the heat, add the lard and allow it to melt. Add the flour and beat well to amalgamate, then knead until smooth. Stir in the egg yolk and keep warm. Try to work quickly.

6 To use, roll out and cut into rounds to fit patty tins or muffin moulds of about 10cm (4 in) in diameter. Keep the leftover pastry covered and warm; you need it for the lids.

7 Spoon the cold filling into the pie cases. Roll out the rest of the pastry and cut out the correct lid shapes. Moisten the edges of the pie cases and put the lids on top, pressing to make a seal. Make a hole in the middle, and brush the tops with mixed egg and water to glaze. Bake in the preheated oven for 45 minutes, until the pastry is crisp and golden.

8 Mix the slaked fécule or cornflour with the remaining lamb stock. Bring to the boil gently, stirring, until thickened (this is what chefs call a 'thickened stock').

9 When the pies come out of the oven, re-cut the hole in the top, and carefully pour some thickened stock into each pie. Serve hot or cold.

■ Pies such as this are very portable, good for picnics. You could make them in smaller moulds if you liked.

■ Note that I haven't asked you to use the pastry in the traditional way, persuading it up around the sides of a jam jar or similar to get the shape. Very hands on and complicated!

Shepherd's Pie

SERVES 4
There are always leftovers from a roast joint, and they can be re-used in a number of ways. Although it's simple, I think shepherd's pie, using lamb, is one of the best – but cottage pie, its beef equivalent, is good too. The recipe is said to have been the creation of shepherds' wives in Cumbria and the Lake District (where the lamb is so good nowadays), who needed to make tough leftover mutton more palatable. Cutting it up small or pounding it would have helped, as would the gravy, but we of course now have the mincer and processor to help us.

Always make plenty of a shepherd's pie, because it's something people always want seconds of. It's more than greed, it's actually psychological!

25g (1 oz) beef dripping or lard

1 large onion, peeled and finely chopped

1 carrot, peeled and diced

450g (1 lb) cooked lamb, minced

1 tsp tomato purée

1–2 garlic cloves, peeled and crushed (optional)

15g (½ oz) plain flour

300ml (10 fl oz) meat stock

a dash of Worcestershire sauce

1 tbsp chopped fresh parsley

salt and freshly ground black pepper

Potato topping

450g (1 lb) potatoes

2 tbsp double cream

115g (4 oz) unsalted butter

a pinch of freshly grated nutmeg

1 Melt the dripping in a pan and add the onion and carrot (you could have chopped them together in a processor). Cook until soft but not coloured.

2 Add the minced lamb and fry for 2 minutes, then add the tomato purée, garlic if using it, and flour, and mix well. Add the stock and bring to the boil, then simmer for 10–15 minutes until the stew thickens but does not stick to the pan. Stir in the Worcestershire sauce, parsley and some salt and pepper, and remove from the heat. Put into a pie dish of about 850ml (1½ pints) and leave to cool.

3 Peel the potatoes then cut them into even pieces and put into cold salted water. Bring to the boil and cook until tender, then drain and return to the pan. Put back on the heat to dry out, carefully stirring all the time.

4 Put the double cream and 85g (3 oz) of the butter into a clean pan and bring to the boil. Pass the potatoes through a potato 'ricer' into the cream mixture. Stir well, season with salt and pepper and add some nutmeg. Allow to cool.

5 Preheat the oven to 180°C/350°F/Gas 4.

6 Put the potato into a piping bag with a 2cm (¾ in) plain nozzle and pipe on to the meat mixture in the pie dish. Put the pie dish into the preheated oven for 10 minutes: this sets the potato topping.

7 Melt the remaining butter and carefully brush over the top of the pie. Put back in the oven for a further 20 minutes or until golden brown. Serve immediately.

- This is essentially a leftover recipe, but you can make it with fresh lamb (or beef). Buy mince, and cook it with the vegetables for longer than above.

- You don't have to use a piping bag for the potato. Spoon it on evenly, and level with a palette knife dipped in olive oil or melted butter, then scroll to make a pattern.

- When we were very good as kids, my mum used to add some grated cheese to the potatoes and then sprinkle some more on top before baking.

- You can leave out the garlic if you like – a modern addition – or you can add something like fried mushrooms or sun-dried tomatoes.

Roast Loin of Pork with Crackling

SERVES 6–8   Wild pigs – or wild boars as they are more commonly known – once ran free in British forests and were hunted by royalty. But pigs, easy to tame, have been domesticated for thousands of years, and in the Middle Ages, most country people, rich and poor, would have kept at least one pig. This would forage in woodlands, accept scraps and household waste, and generally cause little trouble – and then in the autumn it would provide fresh meat for roasting, and sausages, hams, bacon, black puddings and salted joints for the winter. The pig was probably the most useful animal for, as the saying goes, you could eat everything but the squeak.

Unlike other animals, the pig is sold with its skin on, and it is this which crisps up on roasting, to make crackling. The hoary question is whether to leave the crackling on or not during cooking. If you are marinating the meat, you must obviously take the skin off, but it cooks well on the joint. If you take it off, you can roast it separately between two trays to keep it flat. In Mexico, they sell large strips of crackling that look like prawn crackers, but we of course have our own pork scratchings…

1 x 1.8kg (4 lb) loin of pork

fine salt and 1 tbsp coarse sea salt

1 onion, peeled and sliced

150ml (5 fl oz) dry cider

600ml (1 pint) meat stock

1 small bunch fresh sage

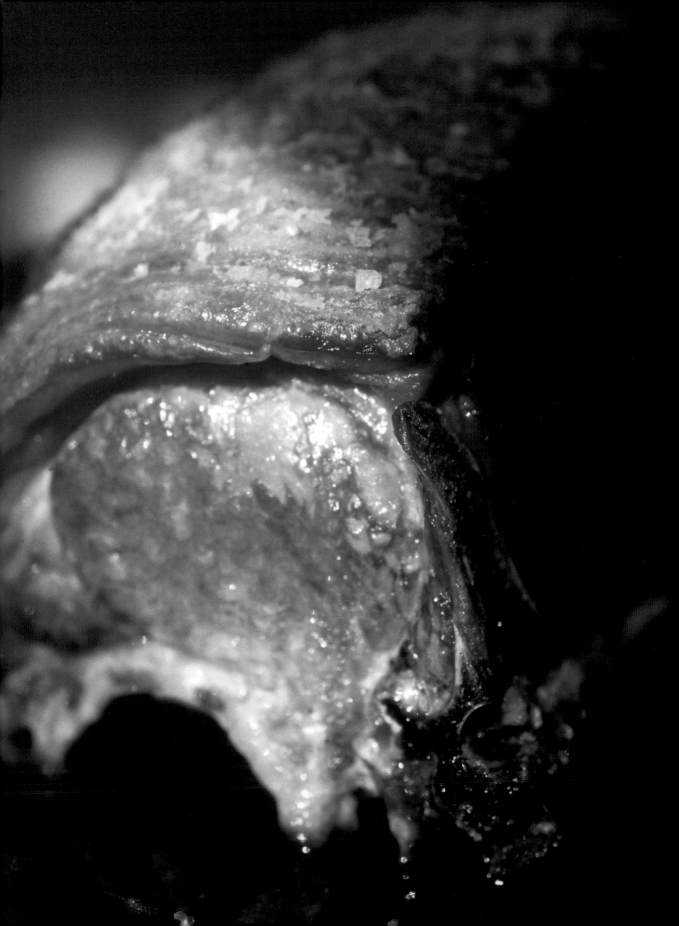

1 Preheat the oven to 220°C/425°F/Gas 7.

2 Wipe the loin with a dry cloth. Using a sharp knife, e.g. a Stanley knife, carefully score the rind of the pork from the back to the belly. Score quite deeply through the rind into the fat, but not into the meat. Score 5mm (¼ in) apart and across the length of the joint. Rub the skin with fine salt.

3 Put the meat on a metal trivet in a roasting tray and then into the hot oven for 25 minutes. Turn the oven down to 190°C/375°F/Gas 5 and cook for another 55 minutes approximately. About 10 minutes before the end of cooking, sprinkle the crackling with the sea salt.

4 When cooked take the pork out of the oven, and leave to rest in a warm dry place. Do not pinch all of the crackling!

5 Add the sliced onion to the fat in the tray and fry to colour slightly. Carefully pour off the excess fat (keep to use as dripping for roast potatoes etc.).

6 Add the cider to the onions, and boil to reduce by half, then pour all of this into a saucepan. Add the stock and sage, bring to the boil and reduce until the desired strength of flavour is achieved. Skim off any scum, and strain.

7 To serve, take off the crackling by cutting from the back down to the belly. Put this to one side. Take the meat off the bone by cutting down the backbone to the ribs and then over the ribs to release the meat. Cut from the side with a longish knife. Serve slices of the meat with strips of crackling, the hot gravy and some *Apple Sauce* (see page 214).

■ Gloucester Old Spot is an old breed with black spots on its skin, said to have been caused by apples falling on them in the orchards where they traditionally foraged. The meat is dense and full of pork flavour.

■ Chop off the backbone using a large knife. Keep the ribs, smear them with a honey/soy glaze and reheat to make great spare ribs.

Roast Ham

SERVES 12–16 Means of preserving hams – the cured legs of pig – vary all over the world. In Italy and Spain, they salt-cure and then 'air-dry' the legs to make Parma and serrano hams respectively. In Britain, though, most hams are for cooking: they are soaked in brines of varying flavours, then hung to mature and dry, sometimes smoked, before being boiled and perhaps roasted or baked thereafter.

I'm telling you how to cook a whole piece of gammon here, which is huge, so before embarking on the recipe, make sure you have a pot and oven big enough to hold it. (You can of course use a smaller piece; cut down the proportions and times accordingly.) It's an ideal dish for a party, for family gatherings, or for that Christmas week when cold turkey begins to pall.

1 x 4.5–5.4kg (10–12 lb) gammon

1 onion, peeled and chopped

2 carrots, chopped

2 leeks, chopped

2 apples, chopped (no need to core)

2 bay leaves

a handful of parsley stalks

12 cloves

12 black peppercorns

600ml (1 pint) cider vinegar

Glaze

1 pineapple

175g (6 oz) unrefined demerara sugar

4 tbsp Dijon mustard

1 Soak the ham overnight in cold water to cover (it might be wise to ask your butcher, when buying, how long he thinks you might need to soak).

2 Put the ham into a large pot, and add the chopped vegetables, apples and the herbs and spices. Pour in the vinegar and cover with cold water. Bring slowly up to the boil and then turn down to a simmer. Skim off the scum. Put on a lid, propping it slightly open with a wooden spoon to prevent boiling over, and allow to simmer gently for approximately 3–4 hours.

3 To test if done, either stick a large roasting fork in (if cooked it will come out easily), or if using a whole gammon (much preferred), a small bone that sticks out at the knuckle end will be easy to release when wiggled.

4 When cooked, leave the ham in the stock for 20 minutes to rest. If serving hot and boiled, drain well and serve.

5 But if roasting, drain, then remove the skin first of all. This will easily pull off from the body end, not the knuckle end. Then trim off the excess fat using a sharp knife, trying all the time to retain the shape of the leg.

6 Preheat the oven to 200°C/400°F/Gas 6.

7 To make the glaze, peel the pineapple and put the chopped flesh through the processor. Drain the flesh well, keeping the juice for the sauce. Mix the pineapple pulp with the sugar.

8 Brush the mustard over the fat of the ham, then carefully press the pineapple mixture over the ham. Score the sugar carefully in parallel lines one way and then at an angle to make diamonds of white lines.

9 Put into the preheated oven for about 20 minutes until the sugar caramelises. Take the ham out, leave to stand for 10 minutes, and then carve.

■ Check the stock. If it's not too salty, keep it for soups (great in the pea soup on page 10), or a parsley sauce which would be perfect with the ham, whether boiled or roasted (see page 110). Otherwise the *Cumberland Sauce* on page 218 would be good with it when served cold, as would the *Piccalilli* (see page 204).

■ You will have plenty of ham left over for sandwiches, cold meats, or for putting into mixtures.

Calf's Liver with Sage, Caper and Sherry Sauce

SERVES 4

We once ate very much more offal than we do now. Liver, as one of the more reasonable *looking* of the various 'off-falls', has always been popular, and has usually been fried with onions or with bacon. It can be stewed too, and one such dish made with ox liver, sage and a sliced potato topping is known as Yorkshireman's Goose…

For this dish I've used calf's liver, but you could substitute lamb's livers if you can find them. I've also used sage, as the Yorkshiremen did above, but have added some capers and sherry for extra flavour. Neither is native to Britain, but both have been appreciated for many centuries, sherry especially. It was Sir Francis Drake who introduced Jerez 'sack' to England when he appropriated several thousand barrels from Cadiz while 'singeing the King of Spain's beard'. The name 'Jerez' was gradually anglicised to 'sherry' (the 'sack' was dropped), and in the succeeding centuries, the popularity of the drink grew. Adventurers from all over Britain went to Jerez to make their fortunes, and many of the names of the great sherry houses – Harvey's, Croft's etc. – reflect this still.

4 x 1cm (½ in) thick slices calf's liver, about 140–175g (5–6 oz) total weight

2 tbsp olive oil

salt and freshly ground black pepper

55g (2 oz) butter

2 shallots, peeled and finely chopped

2 tbsp midget capers (they're tiny and expensive!)

150ml (5 fl oz) dry sherry

1 splash sherry vinegar (or lemon juice)

1 tbsp chopped fresh sage

150ml (5 fl oz) veal stock

1 tsp fécule (potato flour) or cornflour, slaked in 1 tbsp water

1 Trim the liver well, cutting out any large tubes. The butcher should have removed the filmy skin.

2 Heat the olive oil in a frying pan until very hot. Lay the liver slices in carefully, but do not over-fill the pan. Cook in two batches if necessary. When golden brown, turn over, cook quickly and take out. Put to one side, season and keep warm.

3 Throw away excess oil from the pan and melt half of the butter in it. Add the shallots and capers, and sauté to soften, but do not colour. Add the dry sherry and reduce by half. Add the sherry vinegar, sage, stock and the slaked fécule or cornflour. Bring up to the boil, stirring until it thickens, then add the remaining butter. Shake in until melted.

4 Reheat the liver quickly, serve on warm plates and pour the sauce over.

- I think the thickness of liver to be fried is very important, with each slice no thicker than specified overleaf, but it's up to you.
- Good served with buttery mashed potato or *pommes lyonnaise*, sautéed potatoes and onions.

Mustard-devilled Calf's Kidneys

SERVES 4

Lamb's kidneys, still encased in their own suet, were once grilled whole and served, split open, on toast – a favourite breakfast for Edwardian gentlemen. Those same worthies also liked them at the other end of the day, devilled on toast, as a savoury after dinner. I'm using calf's kidney here, but lamb's kidneys can be substituted.

You either love kidneys or hate them, and I'm of the former persuasion. I associate them with José, who opened up at Turner's for fourteen years, and put our stockpots on (he's now retired to Spain). When veal, pork or lamb loins came in, José would take the kidneys off, divest them of their fat, and grill them with garlic. Served on good toast, they were my best start to the day ever.

2 whole calf's kidneys in their fat

a splash of olive oil

25g (1 oz) butter

2 shallots, peeled and finely chopped

150ml (5 fl oz) dry white wine

150ml (5 fl oz) double cream

3 tbsp grain mustard

1 tbsp chopped fresh chervil

salt and freshly ground black pepper

Tabasco sauce

1 Preheat the oven to 220°C/425°F/Gas 7.
2 Trim the excess fat from the kidneys using a knife, but try to retain the original shape. Sear and colour the kidneys on all sides in a little oil in a hot frying pan. Put into the preheated hot oven, and roast for 15 minutes. Take out and leave to rest.
3 Meanwhile, melt the butter and sauté the shallots, but do not let them colour. Add the wine and boil to reduce by two-thirds. Add the cream and bring to the boil. Boil to reduce by a third. Take off the heat and stir in the mustard and chervil. Check for seasoning and consistency.
4 Thinly slice the kidneys and arrange on a hot plate to fill the plate. Collect all the juices from the kidneys and pour into the sauce. Add Tabasco to taste (careful, it's hot), then warm the sauce through again.
5 Spoon the sauce over the kidneys and serve immediately.

Game Pie (see page 121)

At one time, all the meat eaten by the British was 'game' – elk, deer, wild ox, wild pig and birds of every description. As we domesticated cattle, pigs and sheep, so we did the same with birds such as geese, ducks and chickens. The Romans were probably a major influence, for they introduced and intensively reared birds such as peacocks, pheasants and guinea fowl (as well as rabbits, dormice and snails).

For centuries, because of the difficulty of keeping the 'great meat' animals (cattle, sheep and pigs) over the winter, poultry birds and game birds and animals would have

Poultry and Game 5

provided a major source of fresh meat. Nothing was omitted, and many birds we wouldn't dream of eating now were enjoyed: swan, bustard, stork, blackbirds, finches, larks... (I once met a Paris chef who specialised in game of this nature when I was at The Capital. The chef himself was in his eighties, and his kitchen 'boys' must have been in their sixties. They wore aprons that looked as if they hadn't been taken off since the day they started!) Rabbit and hare were eaten by rich and poor alike – when game laws did not bar the latter from hunting – but venison was always for the aristocracy alone.

Almost every household, however poor, would have had a few hens but they were too valuable as egg-layers to eat. Only when old, scrawny and beyond egg-laying might they be consigned to the poor man's cooking pot (and, as we know, the stock from an older chicken is much more flavourful). The rich, however, would have relished poultry much more often: roasting chickens, geese, ducks and pigeons on the spit, cooking them in pottages and pies, and potting them in butter.

Because poultry and game were so readily available on the whole, they were less well thought of in culinary terms than red meat (as was fish). However, curiously, a roasted bird was often considered a food for celebrations – the goose at harvest festival, and originally at Christmas, before the interloper turkey became the norm. I remember chicken – often tasting of the fishmeal in its diet – being a very special treat for Sunday lunch. Nowadays chicken is so common that we are tending to ignore it again. Rabbit too, once the most available of wild meats (and therefore the least appreciated), is making a comeback in popularity.

Seasonality is one of the joys of British food and game is perhaps the prime example.

Roast Chicken with Bread Sauce

SERVES 4

As with all other meats, 'roast' chicken would once have been cooked on a spit in front of a fire, instead of in an oven. A young cockerel would normally have been used, as hens were far too valuable as egg-layers. Nowadays, we can get chickens aplenty, but when cooking them as simply as this, do try and buy the very best you can, preferably corn-fed and free-range.

Bread sauce is perhaps the oldest British sauce, dating from medieval times. The Scots claim it as a northern invention, but it appears all over the islands, and is good with most roast birds, domesticated or wild.

1 x 1.6kg (3½ lb) free-range roasting
  chicken, cleaned weight
salt and freshly ground black pepper
25g (1 oz) lard
55g (2 oz) unsalted butter

Bread sauce
300ml (10 fl oz) milk
150ml (5 fl oz) double cream
1 onion, peeled and stuck with 6 cloves
1 bay leaf
approx. 75g (2¾ oz) fresh white breadcrumbs
25g (1 oz) unsalted butter

1 Preheat the oven to 200°C/400°F/Gas 6.

2 Take out the wishbone, and truss the chicken back to its original shape. Lay it on its side and crush the backbone to allow the chicken to sit on its side and not to spring back to shape. Season the chicken.

3 Heat the lard in a heatproof and ovenproof dish, then add the butter and the chicken lying on one side to start to colour. If the breast touches the fat as well, put a little piece of potato under it to protect it.

4 Roast in the preheated oven for 20 minutes, then turn the chicken on to its other side and cook in the same way, making sure that the legs in both instances are touching the fat, for 20 more minutes.

5 Turn the bird over on to its back and baste with lard and butter. Turn the oven down to 180°C/350°F/Gas 4 and roast until ready. To test after 10 minutes, pierce the thickest part of the thigh: if the juices run clear, the bird is cooked. If not, roast for a little longer.

6 Leave to rest for 10 minutes in a warm place before carving.

7 Meanwhile, make the bread sauce. Bring the milk and cream up to the boil with the onion, cloves and bay leaf. Leave to sit for 10 minutes then add the breadcrumbs. Stir until smooth, then take out the onion. Add the butter and some salt and pepper. Cover with clingfilm or buttered paper.

8 To carve the chicken, first take off the strings. Turn it on to its side and cut the skin between the leg and the breast. Now pull the leg away using a carving knife, pulling away from the neck. This will release the meat. (It will also expose the little hidden nugget of meat, the cook's treat, the oyster. Eat it and don't tell anyone.) Put the leg on a chopping board and chop to separate the thigh from the drumstick. Turn the bird over and repeat.

9 Stand the bird on its back and carve down one side of the breastbone, bringing the knife down between the wing and neck joints. Do the same on the other side. Cut each breast in two.

10 Serve the thigh with the smaller piece of breast, and the drumstick with the other. Offer the bread sauce and gravy if you like (see below) separately. (And some roast potatoes, cooked chipolatas and bacon rolls would make for the full monty!)

- Stages 3–4 may seem complicated, but this is the best way to cook any fleshy bird. As legs are always tougher than breasts, they take longer to cook. By placing the legs directly on the heated dish, in the hot fat – and protecting the breast from that same exposure – both should be cooked at about the same time.

- To make a gravy with the pan juices, thinly slice half an onion and throw into the roasting pan. Fry quickly so that the onion absorbs the juices, then carefully pour away the excess fat (this can be used again). I now like to add a drop of wine, but this isn't classically British. Add some chicken stock, bring to the boil and reduce. Strain into a clean pan, skim off any excess fat, and check for seasoning. Many British gravies have some flour in them to form a sauce-like gravy, but my take on gravy, particularly with chicken, is that it should be thin.

Poached Chicken with Parsley Sauce

SERVES 4

Poaching or boiling would once have been the commonest method of cooking chicken (usually a tough old hen past her best laying days), and there was the added bonus of a delicious stock with which to make a soup. Here I've used the stock to make a wonderful sauce, full of the flavour of the chicken, and thickened with lots of butter and parsley. The sauce is an echo of the traditional green herb sauce of medieval times, in which parsley played a major part.

1 x 1.6kg (3½ lb) free-range chicken,
  cleaned weight

1 lemon, halved

2 onions, peeled and chopped

1 leek, cleaned and chopped

2 celery stalks, chopped

1 bay leaf

6 cloves

salt and freshly ground black pepper

Parsley sauce

600ml (1 pint) reduced chicken stock
  (see method)

300ml (10 fl oz) double cream

115g (4 oz) cold unsalted butter, diced

3 tbsp chopped fresh parsley

1 Remove the wishbone from the chicken. Trim and tie the chicken to its proper shape. Rub the outside of the chicken with the fresh lemon to keep the skin white.

2 Put the chicken into a large pot and add the chopped onion, leek and celery, the bay leaf, cloves and a little salt and pepper. Cover with water and bring up to the boil. Pull to one side, and clean off any scum that arises.

3 Cover with a lid for the first half-hour, simmering slowly, then bring to the boil. Remove the lid, and slowly cook for a further hour, skimming occasionally. To check if the bird is cooked, push a skewer into the thickest part of the thigh: if the juices run clear or a little pinkish, then the bird is cooked. If the juices are at all red, then the bird needs a bit longer.

4 When the chicken is cooked, remove from the stock and keep in a warm place. Use a clean tea towel, dipped in the stock and squeezed out, to cover the bird and keep it from drying out.

5 Strain the stock into a clean pan (or two) and boil to reduce by about half – or until the stock has a good, round, concentrated flavour.

6 Put 600ml (1 pint) of this stock into a separate pan, and the cream into the original stock pan. Reduce the cream until it thickens, and then add the stock. Reduce again until you have a sauce-like consistency.

7 Check for seasoning, then add the butter and swirl the pan to melt the butter dice. Add the chopped parsley.

8 Carve the bird into two drumsticks, two thighs, two wing pieces and then the breast in half. Arrange the pieces in a dish and pour the sauce over and around.

■ At stage 5, using two pans means that the stock reduces more quickly, so the chicken doesn't hang around too long.

■ At stage 7, the professional chef in me would always strain the sauce through a fine sieve to make it absolutely smooth before adding the parsley. However, if you can't be bothered, I can understand...

Roast Goose Stuffed with Apple and Fig

Goose was the celebratory bird in Olde England before the turkey was known, and it still serves that role in much of Europe. Although geese were valued, they had rather a hard time of it. If caught eating someone's corn in Wales, they could be executed (a good excuse to eat goose?). They were force-fattened in much the same way as *foie gras* ducks and geese are in France today. They were plucked regularly throughout the year to supply quills and down (which rendered them rather tough), and then they could be marched off to London (with tarred feet like turkeys) to feed the capital's multitudes.

Geese are traditionally best in September, when they were fattened on stubble and eaten on Michaelmas Day, the 29th.

1 x 7.25kg (16 lb) goose
salt and freshly ground black pepper

Stuffing
10 slices dried bread, broken into pieces
2 Cox's apples, grated
4 ripe figs, pulped with a fork
1 onion, peeled and finely chopped
1 tbsp chopped fresh sage
1 small egg
2 tbsp cider
2 tbsp Calvados
unsalted butter

Glaze
2 tbsp runny honey
1 tbsp Calvados
juice of ½ lemon

1 Preheat the oven to 220°C/425°F/Gas 7.

2 To prepare the goose, take out the wishbone and then remove the excess fat from the cavity end.

3 For the stuffing, mix all the ingredients together except for the butter, and season well with salt and pepper.

4 Use a quarter of this stuffing to stuff the neck end of the goose, and put the rest separately in an ovenproof dish greased with butter.

5 Before roasting the goose, prick all over the breast and neck end to allow the excess fat to be released. Put the bird in a roasting tray on a rack and roast in the preheated oven for 30 minutes. Turn the oven down to 180°C/350°F/Gas 4 and cook for a further 2 hours.

6 Take the bird out and pour the fat from the tray (keep to use for cooking roast potatoes etc.). Put the goose back into the same temperature oven, along with the dish of stuffing, which needs to roast for an hour. Cook the goose for a further 30 minutes on its breast, not on the rack, then turn it on to its back.

7 Mix together the honey, Calvados and lemon juice for the glaze, and brush over the breast of the bird. Cook for a final 30 minutes, basting regularly with the glaze.

8 Remove the goose from the oven, and leave to rest for 20 minutes before carving.

■ A tart sauce or stuffing is normal with goose: apple in the autumn (the fig here is an interesting but not untraditional addition) and, in spring, sorrel would be good.

Braised Duck with Peas

SERVES 4

Ducks from Aylesbury were becoming popular in the London markets of the eighteenth century, and in many cookery books thereafter (although some say it's a Roman or Elizabethan idea) they were boiled with turnips. I remember at The Savoy we used to cook our duck with turnips too, along with olives and cream. However, peas are traditional with ducklings as well – possibly because they are in season at about the same time of year – and that too became a popular braising combination. Lettuce was often added, which is a French touch, and indeed some old cookbooks describe the dish as '*à la française*', in the French fashion.

Some recipes add cream to the peas and then purée them for a sauce, but I don't think this is necessary. The simple step of braising them and the lettuce in with the duck gives amazing flavour.

2 x 1.1kg (2½ lb) ducks, with giblets
600ml (1 pint) duck or chicken stock
85g (3 oz) butter
225g (8 oz) bacon in the piece, cut into stubby strips (lardons) of about 5 x 5mm x 2.5cm (¼ x ¼ x 1 in)
salt and freshly ground black pepper

175g (6 oz) small button onions (12 plus), peeled
1 round lettuce, shredded at the last minute
450g (1 lb) frozen peas
1 tbsp each of chopped fresh sage, mint and parsley

1 Take the giblets out of the ducks. Put the giblets into the stock and leave to gently simmer for 30 minutes.
2 Preheat the oven to 160°C/325°F/Gas 3.
3 Melt 25g (1 oz) of the butter in a casserole dish large enough to hold both ducks. Add the bacon lardons and button onions, and gently colour on all sides. When nicely coloured, take out and keep on one side.
4 Prick the ducks all over with a fork, and rub with a little salt. Colour all over in the same dish as the lardons and onions, then take out of the dish. Drain off all the fat and put the ducks back in the dish.
5 Strain the stock into the dish along with the ducks, bring to the boil and cover with the lid. Put into the preheated oven and cook for 1½ hours.

6 Add the button onions and lardons, and braise for a further 15 minutes.

7 Take the ducks out and allow to rest, keeping them warm.

8 Remove excess fat from the juices in the dish, then add the shredded lettuce, peas and herbs. Simmer to reduce this sauce by a third. Correct the seasoning and consistency, then swirl in the remaining butter.

9 Carve the ducks and put on a flat dish. Pour the sauce over and serve immediately.

Roast Grouse

SERVES 4

The red grouse is said to be the king of game birds, and although the flesh is delicious, its popularity has probably got more to do with its rarity – you almost need the wealth of a king in order to shoot it, buy it or eat it. The Glorious Twelfth, the twelfth of August, is when the season starts, and London restaurateurs still compete to have the first birds flown down from Scotland – the birds' only habitat – to be on their tables that very night. The season is short, only until the tenth of December (although the grouse would probably think it too long). Grouse are not raised for the shoot, as are other game birds like pheasant, but the heather moors where they live are very carefully managed to provide the right conditions, cover, nesting places and food. It is probably their diet that makes their flesh more aromatic – they eat heather shoots, flowers and seeds, as well as any wild blaeberries that come their way.

4 young grouse, with giblets

salt and freshly ground black pepper

4 thin slices pork back fat

85g (3 oz) unsalted butter

1 tbsp vegetable oil

4 slices bread

1 onion, peeled and sliced

300ml (10 fl oz) game stock

4 small bunches watercress

1 Preheat the oven to 200°C/400°F/Gas 6.

2 Season well inside the birds, and keep the livers to one side. Tie the pieces of back fat over the breasts of the birds.

3 Heat 25g (1 oz) of the butter and the oil together in a roasting tray, and colour the birds all over.

4 Put the birds in the preheated oven for 15 minutes, then turn the temperature down to 180°C/350°F/Gas 4 and cook for a further 10 minutes. Take the string and back fat off and colour the birds for a final 10 minutes. Keep medium-rare to medium. There's an art to cooking grouse. It should be pink but not bloody. Take out of the oven and leave to rest.

5 Meanwhile, toast the bread, then cut 5cm (2 in) circles from each slice.

6 Stew the livers in half the remaining butter, then put into a bowl with the rest of the butter, season well and mash together.

7 Put the onion into the fat in the grouse roasting tray and fry quickly to colour. Add the stock and bring to the boil, season and strain.

8 Put the mushed-up livers on the circles of toast and perch a bird on top of each. Put a bunch of watercress into each cavity, and serve immediately. Serve the gravy separately.

- You can tell young grouse by their undeveloped spurs, and downy breast feathers. Hang them in the feather by the neck for two to three days, no longer.

- Try to get sheets of pork fat. They will cover and moisten the breasts better – vital with the lean flesh of game birds – and they will not flavour it like bacon.

- Serve with game chips, a green vegetable, fried breadcrumbs, bread sauce (see page 108) and redcurrant jelly (the *Apple and Rowan Jelly* on page 210 would be good too). Grouse are also delicious when cold.

Braised Pigeons

SERVES 4

It was the Romans in Britain who encouraged wild pigeons to nest in special *columbaria*, tall towers with hundreds of individual nesting boxes. In the many centuries since then, pigeons were one of the few forms of fresh meat available, and the Roman idea was continued, with dovecotes built into the sides of or on top of monasteries and houses. Wild wood pigeons are shot in the countryside – as much a crop pest now as then – but are only available in specialist butchers or poulterers. Squabs, or young pigeons, are now bred for the table, particularly in France.

This recipe is a slightly sophisticated version of more traditional recipes. Once pigeons would have been braised for very much longer because they were older and tougher (for almost as soon as a pigeon takes to flight, its muscles toughen).

6 young pigeons

2 tbsp olive oil

6 shallots, peeled and sliced

1 tsp freshly grated nutmeg

1 small bunch fresh parsley

1 garlic clove, peeled and crushed

1 bay leaf

4 tomatoes

150ml (5 fl oz) Madeira

salt and freshly ground black pepper

150ml (5 fl oz) chicken stock

115g (4 oz) unsalted butter

225g (8 oz) button mushrooms, sliced

1 Preheat the oven to 200°C/400°F/Gas 6.

2 Sprinkle the pigeons with half the oil and roast in the preheated oven for 10 minutes. Remove from the oven, and cut the legs and backbone away from the breasts, leaving what is called the 'crown' of the pigeons.

3 Put the shallots and remaining oil into a casserole and place the pigeon breasts on top. Put the legs into the casserole as well, and add the nutmeg, parsley, garlic, bay leaf, tomatoes (which you have squeezed in your hands first) and Madeira. Season well and add the chicken stock. Bring to the boil, put the lid on and put into the same temperature oven for 15 minutes.

4 Take out of the oven. Remove the breasts and keep them warm while you reduce the sauce by half on the stove top.

5 Melt 25g (1 oz) of the butter in a clean pan and cook the mushrooms until golden brown.

6 Strain the stock, pushing down to extract the last drops of flavour from the vegetables, herbs and pigeon legs. Add the stock to the mushrooms along with the rest of the butter. Shake this into the sauce so that it starts to thicken.

7 Carve the breasts from the bones and put into a serving dish. Add any blood or juices to the sauce. Check the seasoning and pour over the breasts, three per person.

■ Pigeons can be shot all year round, but are best between August and October (when fat from all the summer crop-stealing). Young birds have pink legs: the legs darken as the birds age. Or buy from a reliable butcher or game dealer.

■ Pigeon legs are very difficult to cook and eat as they are so small, so this is a good way of using them, to get flavour into the sauce.

■ This would be an ideal way of cooking pigeon for a game pie. Just put some pastry on the top and put into the oven to get crisp, brown and hot.

Game Pie

SERVES 4

Game was once the most plentiful fresh meat available in Britain, until royal laws were passed and it became an offence for the ordinary man to snare a rabbit or game bird for the family pot. Because the birds obtained (whether legally or by poaching) were often older, they would be encased in suet and steamed for hours as a pudding, or braised first and then covered with a pastry crust as a pie.

Pigeon pie is a speciality of Yorkshire, where young pigeons are cooked with chunks of steak, bacon and hard-boiled eggs under pastry. I've added partridges here as well – in fact you could substitute virtually anything, pheasant or rabbit for instance – and the quails' eggs are a nice modern Turner touch.

225g (8 oz) puff pastry

1 egg yolk, mixed with a little water,
   to glaze

Filling

55g (2 oz) butter

4 smoked bacon rashers, chopped into
   5mm (¼ in) wide strips

2 shallots, peeled and chopped

4 pigeon breasts

4 partridge breasts

salt and freshly ground black pepper

2 tbsp chopped fresh parsley

8 quails' eggs, hard-boiled and shelled

1 tsp Worcestershire sauce

150ml (5 fl oz) chicken stock

1 Melt half the butter in a frying pan and cook the bacon for 2 minutes to colour. Add the finely chopped shallot, cook for a few minutes to soften, then remove both from the pan using a slotted spoon. Put to one side.

2 Melt the remaining butter in the same pan to mix with the bacon fat. Remove the skin from the pigeon and partridge breasts, then seal and colour the flesh in the hot fat. Season and leave to cool.

3 Put a third of the bacon mixture in the bottom of a 1.2 litre (2 pint) pie dish. Lay the pigeon breasts on top and season again. Sprinkle with half of the remaining bacon mixture and half the parsley. Lay the quails' eggs on top along with the partridge breasts, then season. Sprinkle with the remaining bacon mixture and parsley.

4 Mix the Worcestershire sauce with the stock, and pour gently over the ingredients in the pie dish.

5 Preheat the oven to 220°C/425°F/Gas 7.

6 Roll out the puff pastry and cut to make a strip that will fit around the edges of the pie dish, and a large piece to fit the top. Dampen the edges of the dish and lay a thin strip of puff pastry around. Seal to the dish. Dampen the edges of the pastry shape and arrange on top of the strip around the pie dish edges. Crimp the edges to seal. Brush all over the pastry with egg wash, and decorate with a fork. Cut a hole in the centre for the steam to escape.

7 Bake in the preheated oven for 20 minutes, and then reduce the temperature to 180°C/350°F/Gas 4. Cook for a further 40 minutes or so, covering the pastry with foil if getting too brown. Serve hot.

■ Breasts of game birds are now available from supermarkets, but if you buy or acquire the birds whole, cut the breasts off to use in the pie, and use the skins and carcasses to make a wonderful game stock.

Venison Stew

For centuries, the peasants had to stand back when wild deer raided their kitchen gardens, for they were not allowed to kill them. Deer and venison have always been the prerogative of the aristocracy, and the only taste others might have had would be of 'umbles' (offal) pie. Poachers were hung, drawn, quartered, executed and, later, transported. Luckily venison is now farmed, and we can enjoy its gamey flavour without looking over our shoulders…

This is a classic meat stew recipe. You could do exactly the same with beef, lamb or pork, altering the vegetables, and the jelly flavouring.

675g (1½ lb) venison (shoulder or haunch)

2 tbsp olive oil

2 garlic cloves, peeled and crushed

450g (1 lb) tomatoes

2 large carrots, trimmed and finely diced

300ml (10 fl oz) red wine

1 bunch mixed herbs (parsley, sage, thyme), tied together

salt and freshly ground black pepper

a little brown stock (made from roasted bones), to moisten if needed

2 tbsp redcurrant jelly

12 small cooked new potatoes

12 pre-cooked chestnuts

1 Preheat the oven to 160°C/325°F/Gas 3.

2 Cut the venison into large dice of 2.5cm (1 in) square.

3 Heat the oil in a casserole dish and colour the meat on all sides. Add the garlic, tomatoes and carrots, and cook for 5 minutes. Add the wine, herbs and seasoning, cover with a lid and cook in the preheated oven for up to 2 hours, until the meat is tender. Add a little stock if needed.

4 Lift the meat out of the dish and put to one side. Discard the herbs.

5 Add the redcurrant jelly to the juices and vegetables, then liquidise.

6 Put this sauce back on the stove, add the cooked new potatoes and chestnuts, and bring back to the boil. Add the meat and reheat gently.

7 Serve with mashed potato. Some *Apple and Rowan Jelly* (see page 210) would be a good accompaniment.

Rabbit with Mustard

SERVES 6

Like pigeons, rabbits were bred – in special *leporaria* – by the Romans when they came to Britain. Rabbits are actually native to Iberia, and after being introduced to various other parts of the Roman Empire, became a pest as well as a good source of fresh meat. The people of the Balearic Islands had to call for help from the Emperor when they were overrun – and remember what happened more recently in Australia. If we're not careful, according to present-day farmers, and despite myxomatosis, there's a great danger that rabbits will once again become a pest.

Rabbit would once have been the most common game animal, available to rich and poor alike. Although it is not now so popular (probably because of the pet connection, I wasn't allowed to use rabbit on *This Morning* in case children were watching), there are still a good number of recipes in the British tradition. Most of these, as in France and elsewhere in Europe, flavour the generally mild meat with strong spices such as the mustard here, which adds moisture at the same time.

2 small wild rabbits, skinned

600ml (1 pint) chicken stock

150ml (5 fl oz) white wine

3 tbsp Dijon mustard

salt and freshly ground black pepper

1 tbsp olive oil

1 carrot

1 onion

2 celery stalks

½ tsp freshly grated nutmeg

150ml (5 fl oz) double cream

1 tbsp grain mustard

2 tbsp lemon juice

2 tbsp chopped fresh parsley

1 Preheat the oven to 200°C/400°F/Gas 6.

2 Cut the rabbits into pieces: four back legs and four shoulders (the front legs). Trim the saddles, removing the belly, and cut each saddle in half to give four pieces in all.

3 Chop the rest of the carcass and put into a pan with the belly pieces, the chicken stock and white wine. Boil to reduce this stock by half.

4 Meanwhile, mix the Dijon mustard with some salt and pepper and the olive oil. Smear this over the rabbit pieces.

5 Prepare the vegetables and chop into fine dice. Put these in the bottom of a casserole, then lay the rabbit pieces on top. Sprinkle the grated nutmeg over, cover and cook in the preheated oven for 20 minutes.

6 Turn the rabbit pieces over and strain the stock into the casserole. Put back into the oven for a further 20 minutes or until cooked. Take out the pieces of rabbit, place in a clean pan and keep warm.

7 Add the cream to the stock left in the casserole and bring up to the boil. Strain into the clean pan with the rabbit, add the grain mustard and lemon juice, and bring back to the boil.

8 Check the seasoning, add the parsley and serve.

■ I had the most fantastic rabbit dish recently in Menorca. The rabbit pieces – legs and saddle – were marinated in oil and garlic, and then barbecued.

■ Wild rabbits have much more flavour, but less meat, than hutch-bred rabbits. And remember that rabbits have lots of small bones, so do be careful.

Braised Leeks (see page 142)

Vegetables were once a major part of the diet of the poor, who could not afford to eat meat. The native root vegetables such as turnips, parsnips and carrots would be boiled in pottage (probably *over*boiled), with onions and perhaps alongside some grain (or meat if they were lucky). Broad beans and peas would be dried rather than eaten fresh, and it is 'peasant' pulse and protein combinations that have survived, such as beans and bacon and pork and pease pudding. Vegetable cooking was actually rather boring.

Vegetables

After the great transatlantic explorations of the sixteenth century, unknown vegetables were introduced to Europe, among them potatoes, tomatoes, maize (sweetcorn), green beans, peppers and pumpkin. None was accepted very enthusiastically at first, either here or on the Continent, although Ireland, too wet for successful grain cultivation, was quick to adopt the potato, by about 1650. (This disastrous reliance on one crop alone led to the starvation and mass emigration of the populace in the 1840s after potato blight struck.) Gardeners in France, Italy and the Low Countries were also developing new types of vegetable, and as these were introduced to Britain, so vegetables – among them celery, broccoli, Brussels sprouts and artichokes – started to become more popular and more fashionable (at least with the recipe-writing and recipe-reading classes).

It was only at this time that vegetables were defined as a separate category of food, plants grown especially to be eaten. We are fond of vegetables now, and grow them for pleasure, not for necessity. We also cook and treat vegetables properly. Chefs like Paul Gaylor have actually made a speciality of cooking vegetables in an exciting way, and we now have farmers' markets, to which growers bring their produce, often organic, always very fresh.

We are enjoined to eat lots of vegetables for health, and the 'five a day' campaign – eating five portions of fruit and vegetables every day – is a very easy target, especially for children. If we can get children to eat healthy foods as early as possible, and to enjoy them, we will, hopefully, have prevented the tide of obesity that has been worrying us so much lately.

Asparagus

SERVE ABOUT
6 THICK STEMS
PER PORTION The Romans were apparently very fond of asparagus, and perhaps, like so many other foodstuffs, they were responsible for its introduction to Britain. It has always been a vegetable for the rich rather than the poor, as an asparagus bed takes up so much garden space – and only produces a result for less than two months per year.

Asparagus is imported from many countries throughout the world, but I have to say I really do prefer the English spears that arrive in late May, early June – thin (sprue) or fatter, and always green.

1 Using a potato peeler or the back of a strong knife, scrape the lower two-thirds of the stem. Always peel from the tip end to the base and try to get uniformity in look. Much of the flavour and goodness is in the skin, so you only want to remove the outer tough layer. Lay the stems side by side with the tips all levelled up, and cut the lower parts of the stems off so that each stem is the same length. Tie carefully into bundles.

2 One way to cook the asparagus is to stand them upright in an asparagus basket in boiling water up to three-quarters of the height of the asparagus stems with the top section, the tips, steaming. When cooked the stems will just have a little 'give' about 5cm (2 in) down from the top of the tip or, when the tip of a knife is inserted, they feel only just tender. (It is not essential to stand asparagus stems upright to cook, however. You can plunge the untied spears into boiling salted water in a large wide pan.)

3 When they are cooked, plunge into iced water to stop the cooking and then reheat in boiling water before draining and serving.

4 To serve, put the stems on to a plate, with an upturned fork under the stem end side. This means that they are not covered with sauce and can be picked up without dirtying the hands.

5 Serve with a hollandaise sauce (see page 48), or a melted butter sauce (add 225g/8 oz pieces of cold butter to 1 tbsp cold water and the juice of ½ lemon; whisk over heat to make an emulsion).

Potato Salad

SERVES 4

I don't expect this is very traditionally British — is it an American import? — but it has become part of our repertoire and, sadly, is often very badly done. But a good potato salad is a joy, perfect on a buffet or at a barbecue, and deserves much more respect. I give you a couple of ideas below. Both are great with ham, beef or any cold meat.

Version One

450g (1 lb) waxy potatoes, washed

1 onion, peeled and finely chopped

150ml (5 fl oz) mayonnaise

salt and freshly ground black pepper

chopped fresh chives

1 Cook the potatoes in boiling water in their skins. When tender, drain them and leave to cool.

2 Skin the potatoes and cut them into 5mm (¼ in) dice. Mix with the onion, mayonnaise and salt and pepper to taste. Add the chopped chives.

Version Two

450g (1 lb) new potatoes, washed

150ml (5 fl oz) chicken stock

2 tbsp white wine vinegar

2 tbsp olive oil

1 tbsp Dijon mustard

salt and freshly ground black pepper

1 tbsp mayonnaise

1 bunch spring onions, the whites and a bit of the green, finely chopped

1 Cook the new potatoes in boiling water in their skins. When tender, drain them and remove the skins if you like (but I don't).

2 Meanwhile, bring the chicken stock to the boil with the vinegar and oil. Take off the heat and stir in the mustard.

3 Immediately slice the potatoes into the hot liquor. Leave to marinate and cool, during which time the potatoes will absorb most of the liquid.

4 Season with salt and pepper, then stir in the mayonnaise and spring onion. Serve lukewarm.

Champ

Champ is the Irish equivalent of mashed potatoes, but it includes greenery such as young leeks or kale, peas, nettles, salad or spring onions, which have been poached in milk or buttermilk. It is very similar to two other Irish dishes, boxty (see page 137) and colcannon, both of which are traditional at Hallowe'en. Colcannon often contains favours: a wedding ring for marriage, a sixpence for wealth, and a thimble and button for spinsterhood and bachelorhood respectively...

900g (2 lb) floury potatoes
salt and freshly ground black pepper
150ml (5 fl oz) buttermilk
150ml (5 fl oz) double cream

225g (8 oz) spring onions (or young leeks),
 finely chopped
115g (4 oz) unsalted butter

1 Wash, peel and cut the potatoes into large pieces. Cover with water, add salt and bring to the boil. Cook until tender, then strain off and return to the pan over a gentle heat to dry out. Do not colour.

2 Bring the buttermilk and double cream to the boil in a large clean pan. Add the spring onions to the milk-cream mixture, and simmer for 5 minutes. Drain off the spring onions, keeping the cream mixture.

3 Add the spring onions to the potato and mash finely. Add half the butter to the milk mixture, then beat into the potato. Season well.

4 Pour the potatoes into a serving dish and make a well in the middle. Melt the rest of the butter, pour into the well and serve immediately.

■ Today people always seem to want to make things more sophisticated – turning a mixture like this into little moulds, or encasing it in breadcrumbs. Let it be. The good old-fashioned way has always got to be the best.

Baked Beans

A mixture of salted bacon and soaked dried beans was a dish for the poor from very early times. The Pilgrim Fathers took the idea (and the basic ingredients) to America in 1620, where the dish was adopted, adapted and developed into the famous Boston baked beans. And thereafter it was returned to us, in the form of beans canned in a tomato sauce. Such is culinary history!

450g (1 lb) dried white beans
  (haricots blancs)
5 garlic cloves, peeled
2 large onions, peeled and quartered

2 large carrots, trimmed and quartered
1 x 280g (10 oz) tin peeled plum tomatoes
6 medium tomatoes, skinned and seeded
salt and freshly ground black pepper

1 Soak the beans in plenty of cold water to cover for 3 hours (unless it says different on the packet).
2 Drain and put into a saucepan. Cover with water again, bring to the boil and cook for 30 minutes.
3 Put 4 of the garlic cloves, the onions and carrots into the pot, and cook for a further hour.
4 Preheat the oven to 200°C/400°F/Gas 6.
5 Strain off the cooking liquid, and pick out and discard the vegetables and garlic.
6 Chop the tinned tomatoes, fresh tomatoes and remaining garlic clove together. Mix with the drained beans and season well. Put into an ovenproof dish with a lid.
7 Bring up to heat, put the lid on, then cook in the preheated oven for 30 minutes. Give one final check to the seasoning and serve.

- Pick through the beans for grit, stones etc., but it shouldn't be necessary these days. They shouldn't need soaking for too long either.
- Add bacon if you like, cut into strips and sautéed first.

Bubble and Squeak

SERVES 4–6

When I was a child, we always had plenty of cooked potato and cabbage left over after a meal so that we could make bubble and squeak, a classic dish for leftovers. Here, though, I describe how you might do it from scratch. Serve with cold meat, *Piccalilli* (see page 204) and/or brown sauce – and my dad used to serve it with runny fried eggs on top in his café. My own personal favourite accompaniment is black pudding…

The name 'bubble and squeak' is said to come from the noise the dish makes as it cooks, and it was originally a way of utilising leftover meat, made with meat and cabbage only. The potato addition and the gradual loss of the meat made it more like the Irish colcannon.

675g (1½ lb) medium baking potatoes, scrubbed

55g (2 oz) bacon or duck fat

450g (1 lb) Savoy cabbage, cored, finely shredded and cooked until tender

salt and freshly ground black pepper

1 Preheat the oven to 180°C/350°F/Gas 4, and bake the potatoes until tender, about an hour. Take out and leave to cool.

2 Melt the fat in an ovenproof frying pan and add the potato flesh scraped out from the potato skins. Leave until it starts to colour. Crush with a fork, but leave some lumps in.

3 Add the cooked cabbage, season with salt and pepper, and fry well. Keep moving in the pan.

4 When the bottom is coloured, put the pan in the preheated oven for 15 minutes.

■ You can add other ingredients to the basic mix if you like – onions, carrots or peas, say – and you could use mashed instead of baked potato if you had that left over, or sliced cooked Brussels sprouts instead of the cabbage.

■ You could shape the mixture into little cakes before frying, but why bother? It's the taste that counts – and the choice of fat is *vital*.

Punchnep/Clapshot

SERVES 4–6

Outlandish names for a mixture of mashed potato and turnip or swede, the former from Wales, the latter from the Orkney Islands (where they don't tend to use cream). It is the yellow swede that is mostly used, rather than turnip, although the Welsh name reflects the 'nep' or 'turnip' connection (and swedes are actually known as turnips or 'neeps' in Scotland). Turnips, for human and animal consumption, have been around for hundreds of years, but the swede or 'Swedish turnip' was only developed in the seventeenth century (coming from Bohemia, not Sweden).

450g (1 lb) cooked mashed potato
350g (12 oz) cooked mashed swede
115g (4 oz) unsalted butter

salt and freshly ground black pepper
2 tbsp double cream

1 Put the cooked mashed potato and swede into a pan together and dry out over a very gentle heat. Mash together as finely as possible.

2 Beat in the butter and season with salt and pepper.

3 Put into a warm serving dish, and decorate using the flat of a warmed palette knife to make small indentations.

4 Pour the cream over the top and serve.

■ Although you might think it's a bit poncey to decorate the top of the potato (called 'scrolling' in the business), even my dad used to do it. He must have learned this in the Catering Corps, but he used a fish slice rather than a palette knife.

Bashed Neeps

SERVES 6–8 'Bashed neeps' (mashed *swede*, rather than turnip) and 'champit tatties' (mashed potatoes) are the classic accompaniments for the haggis eaten by the Scots at Hogmanay and on Burns Night (25 January). A nip of malt is mandatory!

The lightly spiced vegetable purée is also delicious with roast meats such as roast beef (see below).

675g (1½ lb) swede, peeled and cut into even pieces
salt and freshly ground black pepper
85g (3 oz) unsalted butter

2 tbsp double cream
¼ tsp ground cinnamon
juice of ½ lemon

1 Plunge the swede pieces into boiling salted water, bring back to the boil, and cook until tender. Drain and put back into the pan.

2 Mash with a potato masher until smooth, then add the butter, cream, cinnamon and lemon juice. Season to taste and serve.

Pease Pudding

Dried peas used to be a staple in the diet of poor people in Britain: they were usually cooked to a porridge, perhaps along with a piece of salt bacon (good flavours still). With the invention of the pudding cloth, a more solid pudding could be made, and a round cloth ball of peas, with basic flavourings, would be boiled alongside the bacon or pork. The dish's popularity has waned a little elsewhere, but in the north of England, butchers and market stalls sell slabs of pease pudding for you to take home and reheat.

I have to admit that I'm not keen on ordinary pease pudding – or its cousin, mushy peas – but this rather richer, more sophisticated version is very tasty.

450g (1 lb) dried split peas, soaked

1 large onion, peeled and finely chopped

1 bunch each fresh thyme, parsley
   and mint

1 ham bone, or 4 bacon rashers
   tied together

600ml (1 pint) vegetable stock

salt and freshly ground black pepper

1 tbsp chopped fresh mint

1 tbsp chopped fresh parsley

60g (2¼ oz) unsalted butter

2 eggs and 1 egg yolk, beaten together

1 Strain off and put the peas into a clean pan. Add the onion and bunches of herbs, then the ham or bacon. Add the stock and then pour in enough cold water to cover. Bring to the boil, add pepper to taste, then simmer with the lid on for about an hour, or until tender.

2 Take the lid off and carefully simmer to get rid of the rest of the liquid.

3 Take out the herbs and the ham or bacon, and discard. Put the peas into a food processor and blitz, but do not purée too much. Add the chopped fresh herbs, 55g (2 oz) of the butter and the eggs, and mix well. Check for salt especially.

4 Grease a terrine mould, loaf tin or pudding basin well with the remaining butter. Pour the pea mixture in and steam for an hour in a covered pan, or, as I prefer, bake in a bain-marie in the oven preheated to 180°C/350°F/Gas 4 for an hour.

5 Allow to cool, turn out, slice and serve hot or cold. You can eat straight from the dish!

Boxty Pancakes

SERVES 4 Boxty, like champ and colcannon, is one of the most famous of
Ireland's potato dishes, and again like colcannon, it is traditionally
made for Hallowe'en. It can be baked as a bread (see below), fried as
pancakes as here, boiled as dumplings in the usual way, or boiled then
sliced and fried.

450g (1lb) large floury potatoes

225g (8 oz) plain mashed cooked potato

55g (2 oz) plain flour

½ tsp salt

1 tsp baking powder

2–4 tbsp single cream

25g (1 oz) unsalted butter, melted

To cook

unsalted butter or lard

1 Wash, peel and grate the potatoes. Put into a clean cloth, tie tightly and
   squeeze out all the moisture.
2 Make sure the mashed cooked potato is completely dry, and has had nothing
   added to it (i.e. milk, butter, cream etc.). Mix the raw grated potato and the
   mashed cooked potato together.
3 Sift the flour, salt and baking powder together then add to the mixture and
   stir well. Slowly add the cream and butter to make a sloppier mixture of a
   'drop-pancake' (scone) consistency.
4 Heat a griddle or a heavy frying pan. Use butter for sweet pancakes, i.e.
   if served with treacle etc., or lard when served with something like bacon.
   Use three large 7.5cm (3 in) metal rings to help keep a uniform shape.
5 Drop the mixture into the rings in the frying pan to about 5mm (¼ in)
   thickness. Allow to set and colour golden brown. Take the rings off, and turn
   the pancakes over. Cook them through, a few more minutes until golden,
   and keep warm while you make the remainder.

■ To make into a bread mix, leave out the cream and use a little milk
   instead. Knead well, shape into a round and bake in the oven
   preheated to 180°C/350°F/Gas 4 for 35–40 minutes.

Cauliflower Cheese

SERVES 4

Cauliflowers, which belong to the cabbage family, were developed by the Arabs, and in the eighteenth century in Britain were highly regarded vegetables, suitable for the best treatment, being buttered, coated with a rich white sauce and sprinkled with cheese. It's thought of more now as a supper or high tea dish, on a par with macaroni cheese, but cooked well, it can be great. My grandmother wouldn't recognise the modern additions of Parmesan and breadcrumbs, but they are worthwhile, adding both flavour and texture.

1 large cauliflower

salt and freshly ground black pepper

55g (2 oz) Parmesan, freshly grated

1 tbsp white breadcrumbs

Cheese sauce

40g (1½ oz) unsalted butter

40g (1½ oz) plain flour

300ml (10 fl oz) double cream

150ml (5 fl oz) milk

a dash of Tabasco sauce

1 tsp Dijon mustard

175g (6 oz) Lancashire cheese, grated

1 Preheat the oven to 180°C/350°F/Gas 4.

2 Cut the cauliflower into even-sized florets. Plunge these into boiling salted water and cook until tender, then drain (keep the water).

3 Meanwhile, for the cheese sauce, melt the butter in a medium pan, add the flour and cook for 2 minutes, stirring to avoid lumps. Add the cream and bring back to the boil, still stirring. Add the milk, whisk in and take from the heat. Add the Tabasco and mustard and stir in well, along with the Lancashire cheese. Season to taste. If the sauce is a little thick, add 2 tbsp of the cauliflower water.

4 Arrange the cooked florets of cauliflower in a dish, if possible built to look like a whole cauliflower. Gently pour the sauce over.

5 Sprinkle with the Parmesan and breadcrumbs and bake in the preheated oven for 15 minutes until brown on top. Serve immediately.

- A tendency these days is to undercook cauliflower for this dish. But, although you don't want it to be a mush or purée, it should be soft enough to be able to spoon out easily (soft enough for your grandma to eat without her teeth!).
- Another way of cooking the cauli would be to gouge out the centre stalk, leaving the vegetable whole with a hole in the middle. Cook it for a little longer to ensure the inside parts are cooked.
- Much as I hate to admit it, in my tests the acidity and crumbliness of Lancashire cheese worked better than a Yorkshire Wensleydale. (But if you can't get either, a Cheddar will do fine.)

Brussels Sprouts with Chestnuts

SERVES 4 Brussels sprouts were developed in the Low Countries in the Middle Ages, but did not become popular in Britain until the mid-nineteenth century (and are still not particularly popular in some quarters...). Chestnuts too have been with us for ever, although the French and the Italians have always appreciated them rather more in a culinary sense. The combination of the two is fairly recent, I imagine, created probably because both are in season at the same time.

Although now traditional with our Christmas turkey, the vegetable mixture is so good it deserves to be used more often – delicious with roast pork or poultry, for instance.

225g (8 oz) chestnuts

350g (12 oz) Brussels sprouts

salt and freshly ground black pepper

55g (2 oz) unsalted butter

1 Make a cross with a small sharp knife in the bottom of each chestnut and cook in the preheated oven for 20 minutes or until the shells start to split. Cool a little until you can handle them, then peel.

2 Meanwhile, prepare the Brussels. Trim off the outside leaves and put a cross in the stalk of each. Plunge into boiling salted water and cook until just done. Refresh and drain.

3 Cut the peeled chestnuts and the cooked sprouts in half. Fry in the butter to heat through and brown a little, then season and serve.

■ You could cook the dish in an interesting alternative way. Shred the sprouts before cooking. Stir-fry in butter, add some chopped garlic to taste and the cooked, peeled and crumbled chestnuts. Season and serve.

■ The best chestnuts are those cooked in a special container over an open fire. To test whether a chestnut is ready, shell one, dip it in salt and eat. You'll soon know. (And be sure to buy more chestnuts than you need if, like me, you are obliged to carry on testing to see whether they are ready...)

Laverbread with Bacon

Laver is an edible seaweed which is found on coastlines mainly in the west of Britain, in Wales, Scotland and Ireland (known as 'sloke' in the last two countries). It is gathered, washed and boiled for several hours until it is like a dark-green spinach purée. This is when it is known as 'laverbread' in Wales, where laver is most commonly eaten still. It is served on toast, dressed as a salad, or mixed with oatmeal to make laver cakes, which are fried in bacon fat. I have taken the basic cake idea a little further here. Apparently laver was once mixed with orange juice to make a sauce for roast lamb and mutton.

Laver is known as *nori* in Japan, where it is cultivated. It is mainly available in dried sheets, and in this form has become very much more fashionable than poor old laver, as a wrapping for sushi and similar foods.

225g (8 oz) cooked laver

350g (12 oz) plain mashed cooked potato

25g (1 oz) unsalted butter, melted

salt and freshly ground black pepper

freshly grated nutmeg

4 rashers streaky bacon

225g (8 oz) oatmeal

55g (2 oz) lard

8 rashers smoked back bacon

1 Mix the laver and mashed potato together. Stir in the butter and season with salt, pepper and nutmeg. Leave to stand for a few minutes.

2 Cook the streaky bacon until crisp in a hot pan, and then chop into small dice. Mix into the laver mixture along with half of the oatmeal.

3 Mould into four balls of about 115g (4 oz) each. Roll in the remaining oatmeal and flatten into cakes to look like fishcakes.

4 Fry in the hot lard until golden brown, then turn over and cook through. Meanwhile, cook the smoked bacon.

5 Serve the laver cakes with the rashers of bacon over them.

Braised Leeks

SERVES 4

Leeks have been valued since the time of the ancients. The Emperor Nero apparently ate them in an attempt to improve his singing voice! Everyone grew leeks at one time, as they were a pot (pottage) vegetable, and many towns are actually named after the 'leac-tun', or leek enclosure (such as Leighton). Leeks went into a decline in a fashionable sense, but in the furthest parts of Britain, in Ireland, Scotland and Wales – especially the latter, where it's the national symbol – it survived in many classic recipes. The Welsh make leek pies and braise them, the Scots use in them in *Cock-a-Leekie* (see page 12), and the Irish use them in *Champ* (see page 130).

Most traditional leek recipes have them boiled or braised in butter. I have refined the braising idea a little, which gives good flavour. The leeks are good with any roast meats, particularly lamb and duck.

900g (2 lb) young leeks
salt and freshly ground black pepper
unsalted butter
1 onion, peeled
1 carrot, trimmed

2 celery stalks, trimmed
1 tbsp fresh thyme leaves
300ml (10 fl oz) chicken or vegetable stock
1 tsp fécule (potato flour) or cornflour, slaked in 1 tbsp water

1 Preheat the oven to 180°C/350°F/Gas 4.

2 Trim the leeks of their roots and cut away the dark green tops in a pointed 'v' shape. Wash well, turning them upside down under running water.

3 Plunge the leeks into boiling salted water and cook for 5 minutes, then run under cold water to refresh.

4 Butter a suitably sized ovenproof dish. Chop the vegetables into small dice and put into the dish, along with the thyme.

5 Squeeze excess moisture from each leek. Tap halfway up with a knife and fold in half. Lay on top of the diced vegetables and pour over the stock.

6 Cover with buttered greaseproof paper and cook in the preheated oven for 45 minutes. Take the leeks out of the cooking dish and put into a serving dish. Keep warm.

7 Strain the liquor, discarding the vegetables. Reduce the liquor by one-third and thicken with the slaked fécule or cornflour. Add 25g (1 oz) butter to the sauce, season, then pour over the leeks and serve.

■ You don't have to discard the braising vegetables, although they will have given most of their flavour to the liquor. Simply leave the leeks and veg in the dish (as in the photograph on page 126) and pour the sauce over all.

■ Celery, chicory and other vegetables could be cooked in the same way. You could also sprinkle some grated cheese on the top and brown under the grill at the last moment.

Broad Bean and Bacon Salad

SERVES 4

Before the great explorations of the sixteenth century, we only had the broad bean in Europe, and it would have played a huge part in the diet, being eaten fresh in the summer (pods and all at first, as is becoming popular among fashionable gardeners), then dried for winter use. Dried beans and bacon was a common combination from the very earliest times, and I have brought the idea up to date, using fresh beans instead in a starter salad.

900g (2 lb) broad beans in their pods
salt and freshly ground black pepper
4 rashers back bacon, finely diced
4½ tbsp olive oil
2 tomatoes, skinned and seeded
1 shallot, peeled
½ tsp French mustard

1 tbsp white wine vinegar
1 garlic clove, peeled
1 tbsp chopped mixed fresh parsley, chervil
 and tarragon

To serve
about 55g (2 oz) mixed salad leaves

1 Remove the beans from their pods. Plunge into boiling salted water and simmer for 10 minutes or until tender. Remove, refresh in cold water and drain.

2 If the 'inner' grey skins are tough (more likely in larger and older beans), remove these skins with your thumb and forefinger to reveal the bright green insides, being careful not to crush them.

3 Meanwhile, fry the bacon in ½ tbsp of the olive oil until brown and crisp. Remove from the heat. Cut the tomato flesh into small dice and finely chop the shallot.

4 Mix the shallot with the mustard and then the wine vinegar. Crush the garlic and add to the bacon. Toss and put into a serving bowl with the shallot and mustard mixture.

5 Add the remaining olive oil, and the beans and herbs. Mix and season to taste with salt and pepper. Leave for 30 minutes to marinate and cool.

6 To serve, present on a small bed of mixed leaves, making sure the beans and their dressing coat the leaves. Finish off with a good grinding of black pepper.

Spotted Dick and Custard Sauce (see pages 154 and 220)

Monsieur Misson, a French visitor to England in the 1690s, wrote about the English penchant for puddings. 'Ah, what an excellent thing is an English pudding! To come in pudding-time, is as much as to say, to come in the most lucky moment in the world.' What he was so enthusiastically referring to was mainly the pudding which was made with a mixture of suet or marrow, flour, dried fruits, spices and sugar. This would have been stuffed into an animal gut, and boiled in water, either alone, or with other foods such as meat. These guts were available when the animals were slaughtered, in the

Puddings

autumn, thus his reference to 'pudding-time'. With the invention of the pudding cloth or bag, though, puddings could be made at any time of year. The pudding was the carbohydrate part of a meal, but was not served as a separate course: that came later. Steamed puds, such as spotted dick, Snowdon pudding and jam roly-poly – and indeed Christmas pudding – are current examples of these early puddings.

Gradually the word 'pudding' came to refer to other sweet things, and specifically to sweet things that were served as a separate course at the end of a meal. Many of the other 'sweet things' had as long a heritage as the steamed or boiled pudding. Rice puddings and other grain and milk puddings are an echo of the medieval grain dishes known as 'frumenty', simply using imported ingredients instead of local. Egg custards were popular in the Middle Ages, and they are used in many famous puddings. Bread and butter pudding (now so ubiquitous I didn't think you needed another one here!), apple charlotte and queen of puddings also illustrate another consistent strand in British puddings, the use of bread and breadcrumbs.

But it is perhaps our sweet pies for which we are most famous: our plate pies with one or two layers of pastry, our deep-dish pies, flans, tarts, turnovers and pasties. And there are a host of other fruit puddings with or without pastry, among them apple crumble (well, the crumble topping is *almost* pastry) and the more recent, but famous summer pudding (where bread is used *instead* of pastry). And a final strand represented here is that of the cold creamy puddings such as syllabubs, trifles and fools. They were thought to be less important than other courses in the meal, so all gained rather silly names…

Apple Pie

This must be the most ancient of British apple puddings, a layer of apple between two layers of pastry. This was a medieval idea (taken by the Pilgrim Fathers to America), and it seems to have survived particularly in the north of England. Elsewhere an apple pie usually has a pastry top only (a pastry *bottom* in France), but plate fruit pies are still made in Yorkshire, Lancashire and further north. This is my father's recipe, which he served in his café, often mixing the apple with blackberries, raspberries or (tinned) cherries. My gran used to serve it with Wensleydale cheese: 'Apple pie without cheese is like a kiss without a squeeze.'

Pastry

225g (8 oz) plain flour

3½ tsp salt

25g (1 oz) unrefined caster sugar, plus
  extra for sprinkling

finely grated zest of 1 orange and 1 lemon

85g (3 oz) cold unsalted butter, diced

85g (3 oz) cold lard, diced

about 3 tbsp cold water to mix

1 egg mixed with a little water for egg wash

Filling

450g (1 lb) cooking apples

55g (2 oz) unrefined caster sugar

55g (2 oz) liquid honey

1 To make the pastry, sift the flour and salt together, then add the sugar and lemon and orange zests. With cold fingertips, carefully rub in the butter and lard until like breadcrumbs. Add only enough water to pull it together to a dough. Wrap in clingfilm and put aside to rest for 30 minutes.

2 Peel and core the apples, and cut them into large chunks. Add the sugar and honey and leave to stand for 20 minutes.

3 Meanwhile, preheat the oven to 200°C/400°F/Gas 6.

4 Use a third of the pastry and roll it out into a round shape to fit your chosen non-stick ovenproof pie plate (they used to be enamel). Start with a ball of pastry, it's easier. Lightly grease the oven plate.

5 Lay the pastry gently on the greased plate and pile in the apple mixture. Brush around the edges with egg wash.

6 Roll out the remaining pastry, again from a ball shape to a round which will fit over the mounded tart. Put in place and pat down to seal roughly. Trim around the outside and firmly 'crimp' the edges. Brush with the remaining egg wash, sprinkle with sugar, and cut a hole in the centre for the steam to escape.

7 Bake in the preheated oven for 15 minutes, then turn the temperature down to 180°C/350°F/Gas 4 and bake for a further 20–25 minutes.

8 When out of the oven, dredge with caster sugar and serve hot, with clotted cream, crème Chantilly, ice-cream (as they did at Simpson's in the Strand) or *Custard Sauce* (see page 220) – or a combination of the whole lot!

- You can add spices to the basic apple filling. Cloves are traditional, and I remember one particular occasion when I was at college being taught how to make a deep apple pie. Being a smartie pants, I read the recipe very quickly and, without thinking, chopped up a clove of garlic, and included it in my pie. When mine was ready and the tutor was tasting it, I had to think quickly, having already realised my mistake. 'Sorry, sir, I must have forgotten to wash my knife.'

- Raisins and sultanas can also be added. In fact, there are no end of variations possible.

Bakewell Tart

SERVES 8

Another pudding which includes a layer of jam (see *Queen of Puddings*, page 165), Bakewell tart was originally known as Bakewell pudding and still is in parts of Derbyshire today. There are several stories about how it came into existence, but most are apocryphal as it has long been known in its present form – a pastry case with a jam lining and an almond 'cake' topping. This almond mixture is known as 'frangipane' in the business, and I always wondered what the connection between it and the flower, frangipani, was. It seems a trifle tenuous, but the almond mix was supposedly named after an Italian aristocrat, Frangipani, who invented a perfume, probably using red jasmine, or frangipani, for the gloves of Louis XIII...

Pastry

175g (6 oz) plain flour

a pinch of salt

25g (1 oz) unrefined caster sugar

finely grated zest of 1 orange and 1 lemon

55g (2 oz) cold unsalted butter, diced

25g (1 oz) cold lard, diced

about 2 tbsp ice-cold water to mix

Filling

55g (2 oz) raspberry jam

3 eggs

115g (4 oz) unrefined caster sugar

115g (4 oz) unsalted butter, melted

115g (4 oz) ground almonds

25g (1 oz) icing sugar, mixed with a little
    water to a thin icing

1 Make the pastry as in the recipe on page 152, adding the finely grated citrus zests, and put it aside to rest for about 20 minutes.

2 Meanwhile, preheat the oven to 180°C/350°F/Gas 4.

3 Roll the pastry out to a round to fit a 25cm (10 in) flan ring, and place in the ring. Cut off any excess pastry, and crimp the edges.

4 Warm the jam and then, if you can be bothered (but it's the correct way), press it through a fine sieve to get rid of the seeds. Spread over the base of the tart.

5 Meanwhile, beat the eggs and sugar together, and then slowly fold in the melted butter and the ground almonds. Pour carefully into the pastry-lined flan ring.

6 Bake in the preheated oven until set, about 35 minutes. Take out and cool.

7 Pour the icing into the centre of the tart and, using a palette knife, spread it as thinly as possible. Leave to set.

Treacle Tart

SERVES 4   Treacle tart must be the quintessential British pudding – a pastry
base filled with bread, eggs and sugar. It's made all over Britain, from
Scotland (where a huge amount of sugar came in from the West
Indies) down to Yorkshire. Sometimes the tart is actually a plate pie
(top and bottom pastry); often it is a plate tart, but with interwoven
pastry strips decorating the top. Here I have made little individual
tarts with only one layer of pastry. Whatever you do, it is an
unadulterated sweet delight.

250g (9 oz) *Sweet Pastry* (see page 152)

Filling

25g (1 oz) fine fresh breadcrumbs

275g (9½ oz) golden syrup

1 tbsp dark treacle

juice and finely grated zest of 1 lemon

3 eggs

1 Roll out the sweet pastry and use to line four 10cm (4 in) round, non-stick
tart moulds, 2cm (¾ in) deep. Rest in the fridge for half an hour.

2 Meanwhile, preheat the oven to 180°C/350°F/Gas 4.

3 For the filling, mix together the breadcrumbs, syrup, treacle, lemon juice
and zest.

4 Beat the eggs, then add to the breadcrumb mixture.

5 Pour the filling into the pastry-lined moulds and bake in the preheated oven
for 15–20 minutes. Serve warm with clotted cream.

Lemon Meringue Pie

SERVES 8

Fruit tarts and fruit cheese or curd tarts are long-standing elements of British cooking, but the meringue topping, possibly an American influence – they have 'chiffon' pies – dates from much later. There are several other puds which use a meringue topping – butterscotch tart, Oxford and Cambridge pudding, a Welsh border tart – and, of course, *Queen of Puddings* (see page 165).

Sweet pastry

225g (8 oz) plain flour

a pinch of salt

25g (1 oz) unrefined caster sugar

115g (4 oz) cold unsalted butter

2 egg yolks, beaten

approx. 2 tbsp water

Lemon filling

4 juicy lemons

150ml (5 fl oz) water

55g (2 oz) unsalted butter

85g (3 oz) unrefined caster sugar

25g (1 oz) cornflour, slaked in a little water

3 egg yolks

Meringue topping

3 egg whites

a pinch of salt

115g (4 oz) unrefined caster sugar

icing sugar

1 To make the pastry, sift the flour and salt into a bowl and add the sugar. Chop the cold butter and rub into the flour until the texture resembles breadcrumbs. Add the egg yolks. Mix to a dough, using the water if necessary, and form into a ball. If you have time, chill, wrapped in clingfilm, for about 20 minutes.

2 Roll the pastry dough out to a circle of about 33cm (13 in) to line the base and sides of a 25cm (10 in) flan ring. Place the flan ring on a baking sheet and line with the pastry circle. Neaten the edges, and leave to rest in the fridge for half an hour.

3 Meanwhile, preheat the oven to 180°C/350°F/Gas 4.

4 Fill the pastry casing with a circle of greaseproof paper and fill with beans or rice. Bake in the preheated oven for 15 minutes. Take out of the oven,

remove the beans and paper, and reduce the oven temperature to 140°C/275°F/Gas 1. Bake for 10 more minutes. Remove and turn the oven temperature up to 160°C/325°F/Gas 3.

5   Meanwhile, for the lemon filling, zest two of the lemons into a saucepan. Squeeze all four lemons into the pan and add the water, the butter and sugar, and bring to the boil.

6   Add the slaked cornflour, bring up to the boil again and gently stir until thickened.

7   Beat the egg yolks together, then pour a little sauce on to them. Stir in and then pour back into the pan. Gently heat and stir – do not boil – for 2 minutes. Pour into the flan case.

8   Meanwhile, for the meringue topping, whisk the egg whites to peaks with the salt, then add 25g (1 oz) of sugar at a time, continually whisking, until all the sugar has been whisked in.

9   Spoon the meringue over the pie and use the back of the spoon to make random peaks. Sprinkle with a little icing sugar.

10   Bake the pie in the preheated oven for 25 minutes. Take out, sprinkle with more icing sugar and leave to cool. Eat cold.

■ Any citrus fruit will work – oranges, grapefruit, mandarins – but always check for the quantity of juice. I actually worry a little about giving fruit for juice in numbers: at certain times you might need ten fruit to get the same amount of juice as from four juicier ones at a different time.

■ If you want to be really posh, you could use a piping bag to put the meringue on.

Spotted Dick

SERVES 4–6

Perhaps the most infamous of British roly-poly puddings – and not just the cause of many a schoolboy snigger: recently an English health service board was forced to rescind its decision to re-christen the pudding 'Spotted Richard' on hospital menus, with a well-known supermarket chain following suit… It is also known as spotted dog (strictly speaking, when the dried fruit is mixed *with* the pastry instead of being encased in it) and plum bolster.

225g (8 oz) plain flour, plus extra
  for sprinkling
15g (½ oz) baking powder
a pinch of salt
115g (4 oz) finely chopped beef suet

150ml (5 fl oz) water
115g (4 oz) currants
55g (2 oz) raisins
finely grated zest of 1 lemon

1 To make the basic suet pastry, sift the flour, baking powder and salt together, then rub in the suet. Add the water and mix to a dough.

2 Roll out to a rectangle 25 x 15cm (10 x 6 in) and 1cm (½ in) thick. Sprinkle with the currants and raisins, leaving a border of 1cm (½ in) round all sides. Press the fruit in and sprinkle with the lemon zest. Paint the borders with water.

3 Turn the two short sides in and seal. Roll up from a long side carefully, to keep all the fruit in. Seal when rolled up.

4 Rinse a clean tea towel in boiling water. Sprinkle with flour and shake off the excess. Lay the roll on top of the cloth, fold the cloth over and fix at the ends with string. Steam the cloth-wrapped roll for 1½ hours. Or you could put the pud on a rack in a roasting tray full of water, then cover it with foil. Bring to

the boil then steam in the oven at 200°C/400°F/Gas 6 for about 2 hours. Top up the water occasionally. Or bake at the above oven temperature, but not in the cloth, brushed with egg wash, for about 1¼ hours.

5 Take out, unwrap while still hot (if necessary), cut into slices and serve with *Custard Sauce* (see page 220) or jam sauce.

Snowdon Pudding

SERVES 6

This Welsh suet pudding is made in the classic way, but with a few characteristic differences. The raisins and marmalade form a light coating around the rest of the pudding mix, and the white cream sauce, poured on at the end, looks like the snow that often lies on the top of Snowdon during winter.

25g (1 oz) unsalted butter

115g (4 oz) raisins

2 tbsp orange marmalade

115g (4 oz) chopped beef suet

175g (6 oz) fresh white breadcrumbs

1 tbsp ground rice

2 tbsp orange marmalade

finely grated zest of 1 orange

finely grated zest of 1 lemon

55g (2 oz) unrefined caster sugar

2 eggs

Sauce

85g (3 oz) unrefined caster sugar

juice of 1 lemon

150ml (5 fl oz) dry white wine

150ml (5 fl oz) double cream

1 Blitz the butter and raisins together in the blender, then push through a sieve. Brush the inside of a 1.2 litre (2 pint) pudding basin with this mixture, and then put the marmalade in the bottom of the pudding basin.

2 Mix all the other pudding ingredients together and put into the basin. Cover with greased greaseproof paper and a pudding cloth and tie tightly. Steam for 1½ hours.

3 Meanwhile, for the cream sauce, boil the sugar, lemon juice and white wine together to reduce by two-thirds. Add the double cream and boil to thicken.

4 To serve, turn the pudding out and pour the sauce over.

Sticky Toffee Pudding

SERVES 8

Dried fruit boiled in a suet pastry base in a cloth would once have been the most traditional British pudding. As ovens became more common, the pastry base became lighter, and here the fruit is mixed with a darkly sweet cake mixture. Francis Coulson and Brian Sack of the Sharrow Bay Hotel in Cumbria were responsible, I think, for reintroducing us to the joys of this pudding.

175g (6 oz) medjool dates

115g (4 oz) dried figs

55g (2 oz) sultanas

150ml (5 fl oz) boiling water

finely grated zest of 2 oranges

115g (4 oz) unsalted butter

175g (6 oz) unrefined demerara sugar

3 eggs, beaten

140g (5 oz) self-raising flour

55g (2 oz) ground almonds

55g (2 oz) pistachio nuts, chopped

Sauce

115g (4 oz) unsalted butter

175g (6 oz) unrefined demerara sugar

150ml (5 fl oz) double cream

1 Grease a baking tray about 20cm (8 in) square, or the same volume, and preheat the oven to 180°C/350°F/Gas 4.

2 Stone the dates and chop them finely with the figs and sultanas. Put them into a bowl and pour the boiling water over. Whisk to a pulp, then add the orange zest.

3 Cream the butter and sugar together, then add the egg. Beat together, then fold in the flour, ground almonds and fruit pulp.

4 Pour the mixture into the prepared baking tray and bake in the preheated oven for 30–40 minutes. To test if cooked, press with your hand: there will be some resistance. Take out when cooked and allow to cool slightly.

5 Cut the cooled cake into shapes. I like round ones, although this means wastage: use a round metal cutter (the leftover bits could possibly be used in one of the other puddings in the book). Squares mean you can use the whole thing!

6 Meanwhile, for the sauce, melt the butter, add the sugar and bring to the boil. Add the double cream and simmer for 5 minutes until lightly thickened.

7 Pour a little sauce over and around the pudding, sprinkle with the chopped pistachios and serve.

Rice Pudding

SERVES 8

A cereal 'pottage', a semi-liquid cooked dish, was everyday fare for rich and poor alike from the Middle Ages all over the country. In the north they would use oats (and 'porridge' is the dish still most similar to the medieval pottage), in the south, rye, barley and wheat. When rice was (expensively) introduced from Italy, it was mixed with milk and sweet spices and baked or boiled. Sometimes eggs were added for a richer result, and in Yorkshire, suet was often included as well. Our present-day rice puddings are not too different from these early originals. Whether they liked the skin then or not, I don't know…

55g (2 oz) Carolina short-grain rice
450ml (15 fl oz) milk
150ml (5 fl oz) double cream
55g (2 oz) unrefined caster sugar

1 vanilla pod
25g (1 oz) unsalted butter
freshly grated nutmeg

1 Put the rice, milk and cream into a thick-bottomed pan and bring to the boil, stirring all the time.

2 Add the sugar, the seeds from the vanilla pod and the pod itself. Simmer until cooked, stirring regularly, about 45–50 minutes. Remove the pod.

3 Add the butter and nutmeg to taste, then pour into a dish and colour the top under the preheated grill until golden brown.

4 Serve with freshly made, whole fruit *Strawberry Jam* (see page 206).

■ For a slightly fancier version, you could add a couple of eggs. When the rice is cooked, butter a pie dish. Beat 2 egg yolks into the rice. Whisk 2 egg whites and then fold them into the rice. Spoon into the pie dish and bake in the preheated oven at 160°C/325°F/Gas 3 for 15–20 minutes. Sprinkle with icing sugar and serve.

Apple and Pineapple Crumble

SERVES 6

Although we have long loved fruit pies using pastry, fruit with a crumble topping – basically sweet pastry ingredients without the water – is very much more recent. Some suggest it did not come into use until after World War Two, perhaps when sugar had stopped being rationed. And of course a crumble is much easier and quicker to make than a pastry! The idea may have come from the Austrian *'streusel'*, a cake topping which, because it contains less flour, bakes to a crisper texture than our distinctly crumbly crumble.

25g (1 oz) unsalted butter

350g (12 oz) eating apples

225g (8 oz) fresh peeled pineapple

85g (3 oz) unrefined caster sugar

Crumble topping

115g (4 oz) cold unsalted butter, diced

225g (8 oz) plain flour

115g (4 oz) unrefined demerara sugar

1 Preheat the oven to 180°C/350°F/Gas 4. Butter a pie dish generously.

2 Peel and core the apples and cut into 1cm (½ in) dice. Cut the fresh pineapple to the same size and mix with the apple. Put into the buttered pie dish and pat down. Sprinkle the caster sugar over to form a flat bed.

3 To make the crumble topping, rub the cold butter dice into the flour to form a breadcrumb-like mixture. Stir in the demerara sugar, then sprinkle some of this over the fruit. Pat down firmly, then sprinkle the rest on top.

4 Bake in the preheated oven for 15 minutes. Turn the oven temperature down to 160°C/325°F/Gas 3 and bake until well coloured, about another 25 minutes.

5 Serve with *Custard Sauce* (see page 220) or ice-cream.

- Apple and blackberry crumble is probably more familiar, but pineapple is a good foil for the apple. (And, although it is not very British, it has actually been enthusiastically grown in English hothouses since the seventeenth century. The pineapples which adorn iron railings and gates from that period are proof of its popularity and familiarity.)

Apple Charlotte

Although the pudding itself is a typical British combination of home-grown apples and bread (in this case fried), the name 'charlotte' has been the subject of some debate over the years. It is most likely that the pud was christened in honour of the wife of George III, Charlotte Sophia of Mecklenburg-Strelitz, in the late eighteenth century. This pudding is baked, but later the famous French chef, Carême, invented a cold version, the Charlotte Russe, when the mould was lined with sponge fingers instead of bread.

approx. 12 slices day-old bread

55g (2 oz) clarified butter (see page 49), melted

450g (1 lb) cooking apples

55g (2 oz) unsalted butter

115g (4 oz) unrefined caster sugar

1 cinnamon stick

finely grated zest of 1 lemon

juice of ½ lemon

55g (2 oz) fresh white breadcrumbs

icing sugar and clotted cream to serve

1 Take the crusts off the bread. Cut the bread out to line a 1.2 litre (2 pint) pie dish (or four individual ramekins).

2 Fry the bread quickly in the clarified butter, to brown only on one side. Lay the fried bread in the base and then round the sides of the dish, rather as you would for summer pudding, brown side down and outside.

3 Preheat the oven to 180°C/350°F/Gas 4.

4 Meanwhile, peel, core and quarter the apples. Put half of them into a pan with the butter, sugar, cinnamon, lemon zest and juice. Cook until the apples start to pulp, then add the rest. Cook for 5 more minutes, then add the breadcrumbs.

5 Pour this mixture into the pie dish and cover with more bread slices to seal the apples in. Bake in the preheated oven for 40–50 minutes.

6 Take out of the oven and leave to cool for 5 minutes only. Turn out, dredge with icing sugar and serve with clotted cream.

■ You could use brioche instead of bread, and pears instead of apples.

Summer Pudding

SERVES 4–6   The British pudding tradition is long established, but the word
'pudding' is most commonly associated with cooked and hot – suet
puds, baked batter, pastry and milk puds. Summer pudding, however,
is a later invention, and although the fruit is heated slightly to render
the juices, it is basically uncooked and it is served cold. The concept
of fruit encased in bread rather than pastry came into being in the
eighteenth century, created for patients not permitted the richness of
pastry. For some time it was actually known as hydropathic pudding,
after the sanatoria where the selfsame patients were being treated.

900g (2 lb) mixed summer fruits
   (blackberries, raspberries, bilberries,
   redcurrants, blackcurrants)
115g (4 oz) unrefined caster sugar

1 cinnamon stick
juice of 1 lemon
approx. 450g (1 lb) day-old, medium
   sliced bread

1 Clean the fruit and put into a pan. Add the sugar, cinnamon stick and lemon
   juice, bring up to the boil and simmer gently for 5 minutes.
2 Gently strain off the fruit – a colander works well – and keep the fruit to one
   side. Reduce the juices by half by boiling, then allow to cool.
3 Take the crusts off the bread and cut a circle from each slice to fit the bottom
   of four to six ramekin dishes. Cut the same number of circles for the tops as
   well. Cut the rest of the bread into wedges to fit the walls of the ramekins. It
   is important that there are no gaps in the bread: to overlap is better.
4 Dip the circles for the base into the reduced juices, and then put into the
   ramekins. Dip the bread for the sides into the juice and place around the
   sides. Fill the ramekins with the fruit, then lay the second circle on top. Put a
   piece of greaseproof paper on top and a light weight on top of that in turn
   to press it down. Refrigerate overnight.
5 Turn out and serve with clotted cream and a pool of the juice.

■ For an exciting alternative, use brioche loaf instead of ordinary bread.

Queen of Puddings

SERVES 6 This old-fashioned pudding combines two major strands of the British pudding tradition. The baked custard is one, and the use of bread is another. The jam is fairly characteristic too, but the meringue was a later, probably foreign addition (and which features in many other traditional sweets, such as *Lemon Meringue Pie*, see page 152).

However, having said all that, I've used cake crumbs here instead of breadcrumbs, which just refines the idea a little. In fact you could use any cake, really, even chocolate, as a good way of using up those last wedges that no-one wants. And, of course, instead of using a lattice meringue as in the photograph opposite you could always simply spread the meringue over the top with a palette knife.

300ml (10 fl oz) milk

300ml (10 fl oz) double cream

1 vanilla pod, split

4 eggs, separated

140g (5 oz) unrefined caster sugar

finely grated zest of 1 lemon

freshly grated nutmeg

55g (2 oz) unsalted butter

115g (4 oz) plain sponge cake crumbs

55g (2 oz) raspberry jam, warmed
  and strained

To decorate

glacé cherries

angelica

icing sugar

1 Put the milk and cream into a suitable saucepan, and scrape in the vanilla seeds. Add the pod and bring the mixture just to the boil.

2 Beat the egg yolks and 55g (2 oz) of the sugar together in a bowl. Pour the cream mixture over the eggs and sugar, then add the lemon zest and nutmeg to taste.

3 Grease a pie dish with the butter, and put the cake crumbs into it. Pour the sauce over and leave for 20 minutes. Remove the vanilla pod.

4 Meanwhile, preheat the oven to 180°C/350°F/Gas 4.

5 Bake the custard in the preheated oven until set, about 30 minutes. Take out and leave to set for 5 minutes, then spread the warmed raspberry jam over.

6 Warm the remaining sugar slightly in the oven, no more than 5 minutes. Take out when it feels just warm to the touch.

7 For the meringue topping, whisk the egg whites to firm, and then whisk in the warmed sugar. Put in a piping bag and pipe lattice style round and over the top.

8 Decorate (like a crown) with cherries and angelica, then dredge with icing sugar and put back in the oven to brown and set the meringue, about 10–15 minutes. Serve warm.

Slit your vanilla pod in half lengthways, and scrape out the seeds from both halves with the blade of a knife. The seeds hold the most intense flavour, but you should always use the pod as well.

Cabinet Pudding

SERVES 6

A relative of many other British custard puddings, this one can be either baked and served hot as here, or made to be served cold. It also varies in title, being known variously as cabinet, diplomat and chancellor's pudding. Why the political connection I don't know, but it's a good rib-sticking winter warmer.

55g (2 oz) unsalted butter

300ml (10 fl oz) milk

150ml (5 fl oz) double cream

1 vanilla pod

2 eggs plus 3 egg yolks

55g (2 oz) unrefined caster sugar

55g (2 oz) muscatel sultanas

25g (1 oz) glacé cherries

25g (1 oz) angelica

175g (6 oz) sponge cake, diced

finely grated zest of 2 lemons

150ml (5 fl oz) brandy

1 Using all the butter grease a medium-sized pie dish (or small moulds).

2 Put the milk and double cream on to a gentle heat. Scrape the vanilla seeds from the pod and put into the milk, along with the pod.

3 Beat the eggs and yolks well together with the sugar.

4 Chop the dried fruits finely, then sprinkle half of them on to the base of the pie dish. Mix the sponge cake with the rest of the fruit and the lemon zest, and pile into the pie dish. Pour the brandy over and leave for 5 minutes.

5 Pour the heated milk over the beaten eggs and sugar, and stir in well. Take the pod out and pour half of the custard over the cake. Leave for 15 minutes.

6 Meanwhile, preheat the oven to 180°C/350°F/Gas 4.

7 Pour the rest of the custard on top of the dish and bake in the preheated oven in a bain-marie of warm water for 20 minutes. Turn the temperature down to 160°C/325°F/Gas 3 and cook for another 20 minutes.

8 Take out of the oven and allow to stand for 5 minutes. Turn out and serve hot, with a jam sauce perhaps. Also good cold with ice-cream.

■ Instead of the sponge cake, you could use soaked sponge fingers, macaroons or ratafia biscuits.

Chocolate and Raspberry Trifle

SERVES 4

One of the most famous cold British desserts, the trifle has changed in nature over the years. Originally it consisted of wine-soaked almond biscuits, covered with custard, then topped with *Syllabub* (see opposite). When I was a child, trifle was made in a posh crystal bowl. The jelly was out of a packet, fruit out of a tin, sponge out of a packet, and custard out of a tin. If you were lucky, it was topped with cream out of a cow. When you put your spoon in, it made a noise that made Gran look askance… This is my version!

175g (6 oz) white chocolate

2 egg yolks

25g (1 oz) unrefined caster sugar

150ml (5 fl oz) milk

85ml (3 fl oz) double cream

2½ tbsp icing sugar

4 x 4cm (1½ in) slices Swiss roll

2 tbsp Kirsch liqueur

225g (8 oz) fresh raspberries

a few sprigs fresh mint

1 Put a 55g (2 oz) piece of the white chocolate in the fridge; this will make it easier to grate later. Break the remainder into small pieces.

2 Cream the egg yolks and sugar together in a large bowl. Whisk for about 2–3 minutes until the mixture is pale, thick, creamy and leaves a trail.

3 Pour the milk and cream into a small, heavy-based saucepan and bring to the boil. Pour on to the egg yolk mixture, whisking all the time. Pour back into the pan and place over a moderate heat. Stir the mixture with a wooden spoon until it starts to thicken and coats the back of the spoon. Add the broken-up pieces of chocolate and stir in until completely incorporated. Remove the pan from the heat and allow to cool slightly. Cover the custard with a little icing sugar and a piece of clingfilm to prevent a skin forming.

4 Place the Swiss roll slices in a large glass bowl and sprinkle with the Kirsch. Scatter with most of the fresh raspberries, reserving a few for decoration. Pour the white chocolate custard over the Swiss roll and leave to set in the fridge, preferably overnight.

5 To serve, decorate the trifle with the reserved raspberries. Take the piece of white chocolate from the fridge and finely grate over the trifle. Finally, dust with a little icing sugar and place the mint sprigs on top.

Syllabub

Syllabub is one of the great British milk puddings. Once it was made with milk squeezed straight from the cow on to a sweetened wine called 'sill' or 'sille' (from Champagne); this created a froth on top, and it was served as a drink. Sometimes the creamy milk was whipped, which led to the separation of curds and wine after sitting. Today it is made with cream and wine along with some spirit, which makes for a thicker mixture with a slight separation.

Incidentally, they say that a syllabub without brandy is like kissing a man without a moustache…

150ml (5 fl oz) white wine

1 tbsp dry sherry

1 tbsp brandy

finely grated zest of 1 lemon

juice of 2 lemons

freshly grated nutmeg

55g (2 oz) unrefined caster sugar

450ml (15 fl oz) double cream

150ml (5 fl oz) single cream

1 Mix the wine, sherry and brandy in a bowl with the lemon zest, and allow to stand for 2 hours.

2 Strain into a bowl, then add the lemon juice, nutmeg to taste and the sugar. Stir to dissolve the sugar.

3 Whip the double cream into peaks, then carefully stir in the single cream and then the wine mixture. Whisk back to stiffness, but do not over-whip.

4 Pour into chilled glasses and allow to stand overnight until a slight separation occurs in the glasses.

- Some syllabubs used to be made with cider, and many whisked raw egg white into it to make it lighter.
- Thinking about what I said above. Have you ever tried milking a cow straight into a glass? I should think it's impossible!

Burnt Cream

SERVES 6

There has been constant disagreement as to which came first, the French *crème brûlée* or the English burnt cream. The English version is usually accredited in cookbooks to an original served at Trinity College, Cambridge, dating from about the mid-nineteenth century. But recipes exist from earlier, and in one of 1769, a custard flavoured with orange-flower water is topped with sugar, and caramelised under a salamander. As custards have been part of the British tradition for so long, and sugar became such a passion, I think the British can have a good claim.

1 vanilla pod
600ml (1 pint) double cream

225g (8 oz) unrefined caster sugar
6 egg yolks

1 Preheat the oven to 140°C/275°F/Gas 1 and prepare a bain-marie (a deep roasting tray is fine).

2 Scrape the seeds from the vanilla pod into the cream, add the pod too, then bring up to the boil with 25g (1 oz) of the sugar.

3 Mix the egg yolks in a bowl with 55g (2 oz) of the sugar. Pour the hot cream over, stirring all the time. Put back on to the heat and slowly reheat until the cream starts to thicken.

4 Remove from the heat, and strain into individual ramekin dishes. Put into the bain-marie, pour in enough boiling water to come halfway up the dishes, and bake in the preheated oven for 30 minutes. Take out and cool.

5 Sprinkle the rest of the sugar over the top of each set custard, and put into a tray full of ice. (It may seem a bit of a fiddle, but the ice is really necessary. You don't want the custard to cook any more while the sugar is cooking, and the ice will keep it suitably cool. Brûlées are not meant to be warm…) Put under a well preheated grill until the sugar sizzles, melts and starts to turn colour.

6 Leave the dishes until the sugar sets, then serve very cold.

Brown Bread Ice-cream

SERVES 6–8   Milk- and cream-based ices are thought to have originated in Italy (an influence of the Arabs in Sicily, perhaps?), then spread through France (where they preferred, and still prefer, water ices) to other parts of Europe. Ice-creams were popular in England from the eighteenth century, and the cream base was often mixed with puréed fruit. Brown breadcrumbs were added then as well, another example of the widespread use of bread in British puddings. The ice-cream may seem to be modern in concept, but history has proved otherwise.

3 egg yolks

115g (4 oz) unrefined soft brown sugar

1 vanilla pod

300ml (10 fl oz) single cream

300ml (10 fl oz) double cream

140g (5 oz) brown breadcrumbs

2 tbsp brandy

1 Whisk the egg yolks and sugar together in a bowl to dissolve all the sugar.

2 Meanwhile, scrape the seeds from the vanilla pod and put them and the pod into a saucepan with the single cream. Bring to the boil.

3 Pour over the egg yolks, stir well, and put back into the pan on a gentle heat, stirring all the time. Allow to thicken slightly, then take off the heat. Take out the pod and leave the custard to cool. Cover with clingfilm to prevent a skin forming.

4 Whisk the double cream (not too much) and fold into the cold custard mixture.

5 Preheat the oven to 180°C/350°F/Gas 4.

6 Put the brown breadcrumbs on a tray and toast in the preheated oven for 5 or so minutes. Take out and cool. When the breadcrumbs are cold, mix into the ice-cream mixture with the brandy.

7 Put in a suitable tray, and place in the freezer. When the mixture starts to freeze, stir with a wooden spoon. As the whole tray starts to set, every now and then turn the ice-cream out into a bowl and whisk, then return to the tray and the freezer. Do this until completely set.

Chelsea Buns (see page 181)

The earliest breads would have been rather like oatcakes, ground cereal mixed with water or fat, and baked on heat – at first on hearthstones beside the fire. It wasn't until a form of aeration, or leaven, was discovered that lighter breads became possible. The Romans introduced basic forms of enclosed ovens, and many larger establishments would have had their own, but for many centuries thereafter, the poor still continued to bake bread at the hearth, or take their dough to be baked at a communal bakery.

Bread, Cakes and Baking

Plain breads – made from locally available grain – were gradually enriched by flavourings such as spices, and by dried fruits, much as were the pudding mixtures. Bara brith and barm brack are good examples of this, as are teabreads like gingerbread and parkin (both of which can, of course, be found in biscuit form). Small sweet breads were made too, raised by yeast or, later, by chemicals such as baking powder, and baked on the griddle or in an oven. Buns were a further and later development, a cross between an enriched yeast bread and a cake.

At first the dividing line between the two would have been hard to draw. It was only when it was realised that eggs could replace the previous bread yeasts and leavens that cake-making as we know it today properly developed, and cakes are now characterised by their high content of fat and eggs.

Baking seems very *British*, and of course we have two uniquely British institutions – afternoon tea and high tea – at which to enjoy many of its sweet results. High tea is rather more northern, perhaps one reason why the baking tradition has survived so much more successfully in the north of England, Scotland and Wales than it has in the south. There are numerous other theories, many of them quite plausible. And, although the north–south divide is sometimes referred to in disparaging terms, I'm really quite glad that it exists, in that it has ensured the survival of many wonderful breads, cakes and biscuits.

Irish Soda Bread

**MAKES 1
ROUND LOAF**

Ireland is famous for its simple baking. In the absence of sophisticated raising agents like yeast, and domestic ovens, other means of raising and cooking had to be utilised. At one time buttermilk and other leavens (including sourdough and fermented potato juice) would have raised breads. It was only after the introduction of baking chemicals such as bicarbonate of soda and cream of tartar in the early nineteenth century that the full range of Irish soda breads began to be baked. They are simple to make, but delicious to eat, with butter for breakfast, or as an accompaniment to stews.

Bread such as this would once have been baked on a girdle or griddle or in a frying pan. The bastible, an iron pot with its base in the fire, and hot coals on the lid, was an effective baking oven, still used until very recently in Ireland.

**450g (1 lb) flour, half plain white,
half wholemeal
salt to taste**

**½ tsp each of bicarbonate of soda and
cream of tartar (or 1 tsp baking powder)
300ml (10 fl oz) buttermilk**

1 Lightly grease a baking tray or cast-iron frying pan, and preheat the oven to 200°C/400°F/Gas 6.
2 Sift the flour, salt to taste, bicarb and cream of tartar into a bowl. Add the buttermilk and mix to a dough. Knead and stretch until smooth.
3 Shape into a round on a floured board, and roll flat, or use your knuckles, to 4cm (1½ in) thick.
4 Put on to the tray or into the frying pan, and cut lightly into quarters (or farls). Bake in the preheated oven for 25 minutes, then turn the oven down to 180°C/350°F/Gas 4, and cook for a further 20 minutes.
5 Take out and wrap in a cloth to keep soft. Eat quickly, as it does not keep well. In Ireland, it is made daily and eaten that day.

Bara Brith

MAKES 1 CAKE The Welsh bara brith, which means 'speckled bread', is very closely aligned to other British fruit loaves – especially the caraway-spiced barm brack of Ireland (the name of which means 'speckled cake'). Both the Welsh and Irish versions were associated with high days and holidays, particularly New Year, inviting comparison with black bun, the Scottish Hogmanay treat, although that is more like a huge 'fly cemetery' cake than a bread.

475g (1 lb 1 oz) plain flour

1 tsp salt

25g (1 oz) unrefined caster sugar

approx. 250ml (9 fl oz) warm milk

25g (1 oz) fresh yeast

1 egg, beaten

½ tsp ground mixed spice

½ tsp ground cinnamon

115g (4 oz) unsalted butter, melted,
   plus extra for greasing

115g (4 oz) currants

55g (2 oz) raisins

1 tbsp treacle

1 tsp caraway seeds

1 Sift 450g (1 lb) of the flour and the salt into a bowl. Make a well in the middle. Mix the sugar and milk together and warm to blood heat, then remove from the heat and crumble in the yeast. Stir to make sure it dissolves. Add to the flour and mix to make a dough. Leave in a warm place to prove until doubled in size, about 40 minutes.

2 Add the egg, spices and melted butter to the dough, then knead and knock back.

3 Cover the dried fruits in the remaining flour, and mix into the dough with the treacle and caraway seeds.

4 Butter a 20cm (8 in) round cake tin and preheat the oven to 180°C/350°F/Gas 4.

5 Split the dough in half, then split one of the halves into two-thirds and one-third pieces. Take the largest half piece, and roll it into a long snake-like shape. Lay this in the cake tin and coil around the inside edge. Do the same with the next largest piece, coiling it inside the first piece. Finally do the same with the smallest piece. Prove in a warm place for about 20 minutes.

6 Bake in the preheated oven for about 1 hour or until golden. Turn out of the tin and cool on a cake rack.

Saffron Bread

MAKES 2
LOAVES

Saffron, the most expensive of spices, consists of the orange-red stigmas of the saffron crocus. These have to be plucked by hand, which is the costly part. Although the spice seems very exotic – it comes mostly now from Spain, India and Iran – the crocuses used to be cultivated in Essex, causing one particular town to affix 'Saffron' to its original name of 'Walden'. Saffron became popular too in the West Country, and saffron cakes – enriched breads really – are still produced there. According to some, the original saffron bread was plain, coloured only by saffron water; the dried fruits were added later.

Eat as an afternoon teabread, sliced with butter. In Cornwall, buns made of this dough were once eaten with clotted cream on Good Friday. However, the best version I have ever had of saffron bread was baked by my friend Clive Davidson at the Champney Inn at Linlithgow, near Edinburgh. He wrapped the dough round black pudding and rolled it up like Chelsea buns.

a pinch of saffron strands

4 tbsp warm water

300ml (10 fl oz) milk

85g (3 oz) unrefined soft brown sugar

55g (2 oz) unsalted butter

25g (1 oz) fresh yeast

450g (1 lb) plain flour

a pinch of salt

½ tsp freshly grated nutmeg

115g (4 oz) lard, plus extra for greasing

1 egg, beaten

225g (8 oz) currants

115g (4 oz) mixed candied peel

1 tsp finely grated lemon peel

1 Put the saffron to soak in the warm water and leave overnight.
2 Warm the milk in a small pan very gently to blood temperature, then add a pinch of the sugar and the butter. Make sure it's the right temperature – that of a baby's bottle – then crumble in the yeast. Stir to dissolve.
3 Mix the flour, the salt, the rest of the sugar and the nutmeg in a bowl. Rub in the lard until the texture resembles breadcrumbs, then make a well in the centre. Pour in the yeast-milk mixture, saffron water and beaten egg, and mix to a dough.
4 Knead until the dough is smooth and elastic in consistency. Put to prove in a warm place, covered lightly (we use clingfilm), until doubled in size, about 1 hour. Meanwhile, use a little of the lard to grease 2 x 450g (1 lb) loaf tins.
5 Knock the dough back, then mix in the dried fruit and peel. Divide between the prepared loaf tins. Prove for a further 30 minutes until risen.
6 Meanwhile, preheat the oven to 200°C/400°F/Gas 6.
7 Bake the loaves in the preheated oven for 40–50 minutes. Remove from the heat, and leave to cool in the tin.

- You could use a mixture of equal parts of milk and caster sugar to brush over the top of the loaves as they come out of the oven. This gives a good shine.
- Saffron strands are better to use than powder (which can be adulterated). Don't strain the strands out from the coloured water after soaking, as they give exotic little pools of accentuated colour after baking. And never use turmeric as a cheaper alternative: the colour may be similar but the flavour is unpleasant.

Hot Cross Buns

MAKES 16

British buns are made from a sweet yeast dough enriched with butter and eggs, dried fruit and spices. The basic mixture for both these hot cross buns, *Chelsea Buns* (see page 181) and many other traditional sweet breads, is similar; the difference lies in what happens thereafter!

When I was a lad I worked during the school holidays, with Frank and Theo, in the Glendale bakery, which sold its product to market stalls. Our busiest time of the year was Maundy Thursday, preparing thousands of hot cross buns for Good Friday. We worked all night, moulding them all by hand (not much technology then…). Frank's late auntie was said to haunt the place, which gave me the willies, but my consolation was as many hot buns as I could eat, straight from the oven.

The cross on hot cross buns, traditionally associated with Easter, can be made simply by cutting into the dough, by piping in a dough mixture, by placing on a cross of separately made pastry, or lines of candied peel.

Basic bun dough

450g (1 lb) plain flour

a pinch of salt

approx. 300ml (10 fl oz) milk

115g (4 oz) unsalted butter

55g (2 oz) unrefined caster sugar

20g (¾ oz) fresh yeast

1 large egg, beaten

Filling

55g (2 oz) currants

55g (2 oz) sultanas

¼ tsp ground allspice

¼ tsp freshly grated nutmeg

Topping

55g (2 oz) plain flour

1–2 tbsp water

115g (4 oz) unrefined caster sugar

150ml (5 fl oz) water

1 To make the basic bun dough, sift the flour and salt into a bowl. Make a well in the centre.

2 Very gently warm the milk in a pan, with the butter and sugar, to blood temperature. Take off the heat, make sure it's the right temperature – as for a baby's bottle – then crumble in the yeast. Stir to make sure it dissolves.

3 Add to the well in the flour, along with the beaten egg, and mix to make a dough. Knead well, cover with a cloth, and put in a warm place to prove until doubled in size, usually anything from 20–50 minutes.

4 Knock the dough back and add the dried fruit, allspice and nutmeg. Form into sixteen even-sized balls, and flatten them slightly. Using a sharp knife carefully cut a cross on top of each bun.

5 Mix together the flour and water for the pastry cross. Put into a piping bag, and pipe into the crosses on top of the buns. Place the buns on a greased baking tray, cover and allow to prove until doubled in size, about 30 minutes.

6 Meanwhile, preheat the oven to 220°C/425°F/Gas 7.

7 Bake the buns in the preheated oven for 15–20 minutes. Meanwhile, boil the sugar and water together to make a syrup.

8 Take the buns out of the oven and, while still hot, brush with the syrup to glaze them, giving the buns their characteristic sticky sheen.

■ Perhaps the plainest of British buns is the well-known Sally Lunn from Bath. Apart from endless arguments about the origin of the name (is it the name of the baker herself, or derived from '*soleil et lune*'?), the basic dough as here is made up into a sweet bread or buns, occasionally enlivened with lemon zest.

■ You can add different spices and proportions of dried fruit etc. to the basic bun mixture, and you can also add different toppings. I love those buns with rock sugar on top – Bath buns – and at the Glendale we used to make up 'long buns' with an icing sugar mixture topping, and eat them split with slices of very cold butter.

■ It's said in the north of England that if you hang a hot cross bun up in your kitchen it will protect the house from fire for a whole year...

Chelsea Buns

MAKES 16

Made from the same dough as *Hot Cross Buns* (see page 178), Chelsea buns were the speciality of a bakery, The Chelsea Bun House, from the middle of the eighteenth century.

Basic bun dough (see page 178)

Filling and topping
55g (2 oz) unsalted butter, melted
55g (2 oz) unrefined caster sugar

½ tsp ground cinnamon
55g (2 oz) currants
115g (4 oz) sultanas
25g (1 oz) chopped candied peel
2 tbsp icing sugar

1 Make the basic bun dough as described in steps 1–3 of the recipe.
2 Knock the dough back and knead until it is firm, with no air in it. Roll out into a large square about 1cm (½ in) thick.
3 Brush the square with melted butter leaving a 1cm (½ in) margin all around. Sprinkle with the sugar and cinnamon, then the mixed dried fruits and peel, and carefully press these down.
4 Roll up like a Swiss roll and cut into sixteen 2.5cm (1 in) slices. Place these carefully on to a greased, deep-sided baking sheet about 5cm (2 in) apart. Cover with a clean cloth and allow to prove until doubled in size, about 30 minutes.
5 Meanwhile, preheat the oven to 220°C/425°F/Gas 7.
6 Bake the buns in the preheated oven for 15–20 minutes.
7 When taken out, brush immediately with a mixture of icing sugar and enough water to make a single cream consistency. This gives the buns their characteristic white sheen.

The coiled flat circles of fruity dough are placed together in a tin to bake, when they coalesce, creating the characteristic square shape.

Scotch Pancakes

SERVES 8

Pancakes – thin circles of cooked batter – exist all over Europe (think of the French crêpes), and the batter is very similar to that for Yorkshire pudding. In Scotland, though, what they call 'pancake' is actually a drop scone, made from a thicker batter, raised by baking powder, and cooked on a griddle to a fat circle rather like a crumpet or blini (although the last two are both yeast-raised).

Eat freshly made: they are not so good cold and old. Serve them with cream and jam, or maple syrup or golden syrup and butter.

225g (8 oz) plain flour

1 tsp baking powder

½ tsp salt

25g (1 oz) unrefined caster sugar

1 egg, beaten

1 tbsp golden syrup

approx. 150ml (5 fl oz) milk

25g (1 oz) unsalted butter, melted

vegetable oil for greasing

1 Sift the flour, baking powder, salt and sugar together into a bowl, and mix well. Add the beaten egg and golden syrup, along with some milk to make a stiff batter. Add the butter and enough of the rest of the milk to maintain a dropping consistency. Don't be frightened to add a little more milk if you think it needs it.

2 Heat a griddle or frying pan and brush with a little oil.

3 Using a tablespoon, 'drop' an amount on to the griddle and leave to set and colour. Turn over and cook the second side. Each pancake takes about 5 minutes to cook. Store the pancakes inside a tea towel while making the rest.

- A greased metal ring helps to keep the right shape and an even size.
- Although the pancakes are sweet, they go rather well with bacon, but make sure it is a sweet-cure bacon.
- In summer, these pancakes with marinated raspberries and strawberries, topped with clotted cream, make for a real treat.

Scone

Rather like soda bread (see page 174), a scone mixture would have been raised with buttermilk and cooked on the griddle until the advent of chemical leavens and domestic ovens in the nineteenth century. Varieties of scones are found all over Britain, but the name (pronounced to rhyme with 'gone' in Scotland, 'clone' elsewhere) and the basic concept are claimed as their own by the Scots.

In his café, my dad and his helper, Annie Denton, used to make large scones like this, divided into four farls. They were made to eat then and there, not to be kept.

115g (4 oz) cold butter, diced, plus extra
  for greasing
450g (1 lb) self-raising flour
a pinch of salt

115g (4 oz) unrefined caster sugar
300ml (10 fl oz) milk or buttermilk at room
  temperature, plus extra for brushing

1 Lightly butter a baking tray and preheat the oven to 200°C/400°F/Gas 6.
2 Sift the flour and salt into a bowl, and quickly rub in the cold butter. Make a well in the centre.
3 Dissolve the sugar in the milk or buttermilk and pour into the well. Gradually stir the flour into the liquid and mix to a dough. Do this as cleanly and quickly as you can. (Speed is of the essence when making scones.)
4 Shape into a large round, brush with milk, and cut a cross in the top.
5 Put on to the baking tray and bake in the preheated oven for 10–15 minutes.

- You can vary scones almost infinitely. The Welsh add 115g (4 oz) extra butter and 225g (8 oz) currants, and I remember Dad used to make date scones. You could also make savoury scones, adding 225g (8 oz) grated Cheddar to the above mixture instead of the sugar.
- In Yorkshire we used to roll out the mixture and cut small shapes out with a fluted cutter to make individual scones. These would take slightly less time to cook.

Parkin

SERVES
ABOUT 6–8

Gingerbread has been made in Britain for centuries, and parkin is basically the northern form of gingerbread, but made with the local cereal, oats. Like early gingerbreads, some parkins were made as biscuits, cooked until as hard as most gingerbread men, and on the griddle. Others were made into chemically raised soft sponges that could be baked in the oven, sliced and spread with butter. Different parkins are identified by county names, and this one, inevitably from Yorkshire, and one of the most famous, is traditionally eaten on 5 November. Guy Fawkes was a York man born and bred…

225g (8 oz) fine oatmeal

225g (8 oz) plain flour

1 tbsp ground ginger

½ tsp baking powder

115g (4 oz) unsalted butter

115g (4 oz) unrefined demerara sugar

1 egg, beaten

115g (4 oz) black treacle

115g (4 oz) golden syrup

2 tbsp milk (optional)

1 Line a 20cm (8 in) square baking tray with greaseproof paper and preheat the oven to 160°C/325°F/Gas 3.

2 Mix the oatmeal and flour with the ginger and baking powder, then rub in the butter to a crumb consistency. Add the sugar and beaten egg.

3 Warm the treacle and syrup gently to melt, and add to the mixture. Mix to a paste, using the milk if necessary to achieve a slightly sloppy consistency.

4 Pour the mixture into the prepared baking tray and bake for 1 hour plus. Press the top with the back of a spoon: if it springs back into shape immediately, it is cooked. Take out of the oven and leave to cool a little.

5 After 5 minutes cut into squares, and then leave to cool completely before taking out of the tin.

6 Store in an airtight container for about a week before eating. This is quite important, as the characteristics of the cake change. Eat as a cake.

Gingerbread

MAKES 1 LOAF Various types of ginger bread, biscuits and cakes exist through Europe – think of the French *pain d'épices* and the German *Lebküchen* – and this differentiation is actually found in Britain itself. The famous gingerbread from Grasmere is more like a shortbread, while *Parkin* (see page 185), the northern equivalent of gingerbread, can be biscuit-like or cake-like. Ginger nuts and gingerbread men are the most famous perhaps of the biscuit types (the latter often sold as 'fairings' and eaten on Guy Fawkes Night). Most other gingerbreads are either teabread-like in texture, for slicing and buttering, or richly cake-like as here. It is baked in a loaf tin as a teabread, but it is richer and moister, ideal as a pudding.

Serve cold with fresh fruit and ice-cream, or reheat in a little butter and serve as a pudding with a whisky sauce and perhaps some more diced preserved ginger – or some orange slices caramelised in butter, as in the photograph.

115g (4 oz) unsalted butter, plus extra
  for greasing
225g (8 oz) plain flour, plus extra
  for dusting
115g (4 oz) unrefined caster sugar
2 eggs, beaten

225g (8 oz) black treacle, lightly warmed
55g (2 oz) sultanas, finely chopped
85g (3 oz) preserved ginger, finely chopped
2 tsp ground ginger
2 tbsp double cream
½ tsp bicarbonate of soda

1 Butter and flour well a terrine mould or 900g (2 lb) loaf tin, and preheat the oven to 160°C/325°F/Gas 3.
2 Cream the butter and sugar together, then mix in the eggs, treacle, chopped sultanas and preserved ginger.
3 Sift the flour and ground ginger together, and stir into the mixture.
4 Warm the cream slightly, add the bicarb and stir into the mixture.
5 Pour into the prepared mould or tin and bake in the preheated oven for 1½–2 hours.
6 Leave to cool and 'set' in the tin, and then turn out on to a wire cake rack.

Victoria Sponge

MAKES
1 x 2-LAYER
CAKE

A true sponge is actually fatless – made from eggs, sugar and flour only – and is so light that it could never be used to hold any type of filling other than jam or some cream. The Victoria sponge, a 'creamed' cake, was created later, obviously named after the old Queen, and included butter 'creamed' with the sugar, and baking powder. (It's the butter that makes it rather crumbly.) I used to make these at school with Elsie Bibby, my teacher. We called them 'jam and cream' sponges, but would sometimes use a butter cream too (icing sugar and unsalted butter). A Victoria sandwich sponge cake is good for tea, along with other cakes and biscuits, but must be very fresh.

**115g (4 oz) unsalted butter, plus extra
  for greasing**

**115g (4 oz) plain flour, plus extra
  for dusting**

115g (4 oz) unrefined caster sugar

2 eggs, beaten

½ tsp baking powder

Filling and topping

about 4 tbsp jam

icing sugar

1 Butter and flour two 18cm (7 in) sponge tins and preheat the oven to 230°C/450°F/Gas 8.

2 Cream the measured butter and sugar together until soft and white. Gradually add the beaten eggs.

3 Sift the flour and baking powder together and lightly fold into the butter mixture.

4 Divide the mixture between the two tins and bake in the preheated oven for 10–15 minutes. Turn out on to a wire cake rack and cool.

5 Spread one sponge with jam and lay the other on top. Dust with icing sugar and serve.

Genoese Sponge

MAKES 1 CAKE This is actually one of the original types of sponge, being what we call a 'whisked' cake (when the eggs and sugar are first whisked lengthily to incorporate air). It is sturdier than the basic sponge or Victoria sandwich mixture, and less crumbly – it has less butter, but more egg – so I would say this is the cake to use as a vehicle for something else. It's good as a base for fruit and whipped cream, for instance, or in trifle. When I was at the Capital Hotel, we used to soak genoese sponges in sugar syrup flavoured with a liqueur (Kirsch, cherry brandy, Poire William), and then top the almost liquid sponge with fruit and cream. Very popular it was too.

55g (2 oz) unsalted butter, melted,
  plus extra for greasing
115g (4 oz) plain flour, plus extra
  for dusting

4 eggs
115g (4 oz) unrefined caster sugar

1 Butter and flour a 23cm (9 in) sponge tin and preheat the oven to 200°C/400°F/Gas 6.
2 Whisk the eggs and sugar together in a bowl over hot water until light, creamy and doubled in size. Take off the heat and whisk until cold.
3 Sift the flour, then carefully fold into the beaten mixture. Fold the melted butter in gently.
4 Pour into the prepared sponge tin and bake in the preheated oven for 25–35 minutes. To test if cooked, run your hand across the top of the cake: the indentations should disappear almost immediately.
5 Leave to cool in the tin, then turn out on to a wire rack.

■ There are a few danger signs with sponges:
  Too dense a crumb: too much flour, oven too low.
  Holes in the mixture: flour not sufficiently folded in.
  Sponge sinking or cracked uneven crust: tin filled unevenly, oven too hot.

Dundee Cake

MAKES

1 x 23cm
(9 in) CAKE

It is said that this rich and buttery sultana cake came into being through the Dundee marmalade industry. The Keiller family had started their first marmalade factory in 1797, having been inspired by imports of a Portuguese '*marmelo*' or quince paste several generations earlier. They used Seville oranges, which come into season at the end of January. After making the new preserve, the factory might stand unoccupied, so they decided to diversify, and make a cake. They would have established fairly close relationships with Spanish suppliers, so would have access to the almonds and sherry, and two of the cake's defining characteristics, the plump sultanas and candied orange peel, the latter possibly left over from the preserve manufacture. Some Dundee cakes include glacé cherries but, historically, this is a later addition.

225g (8 oz) unsalted butter

225g (8 oz) unrefined caster sugar

4 eggs, beaten

225g (8 oz) plain flour

1 tsp baking powder

85g (3 oz) ground almonds

2 tbsp dry sherry

350g (12 oz) sultanas

115g (4 oz) candied orange peel, chopped

55g (2 oz) blanched whole almonds

1 egg white

1 Grease or line with greaseproof paper a 23cm (9 in) round cake tin, and preheat the oven to 160°C/325°F/Gas 3.

2 Cream the butter and the sugar well together, and slowly beat in the eggs.

3 Sift the flour and baking powder together (keeping back 1 tbsp flour) and add to the mixture along with the ground almonds. Fold in carefully. Add the dry sherry. Mix the sultanas in the remaining 1 tbsp of flour and add to the mix with the orange peel.

4 Spoon into the prepared cake tin, smooth the top and decorate with the blanched almonds.

5 Beat the egg white and brush over the top of the cake. Bake in the preheated oven for 1 hour, then turn the oven down to 140°C/275°F/Gas 1. Bake for another hour plus until cooked through. To test, run a skewer all the way through the cake. If it comes out dry, the cake is ready.

Mince Pies

MAKES ABOUT
A DOZEN
INDIVIDUAL
PIES OR
1 LARGE PIE
TO SERVE 6

Apparently little pies with a filling of *Mincemeat* (see page 205) were associated with Christmas as long ago as the sixteenth century. They were known as 'minced' or 'shred' pies, referring to the actual meat they once contained. I make them now only for Christmas, but my dad served them throughout the year in his café, often making a single large tart.

They say you should eat a mince pie on each one of the twelve days of Christmas, preferably in a different house each time, to ensure twelve happy months in the year to come.

Individual Mince Pies

450g (1 lb) puff pastry
350g (12 oz) *Mincemeat* **(see page 205)**

milk and unrefined caster sugar to finish

1 Grease a Yorkshire pudding or muffin tray and preheat the oven to 220°C/425°F/Gas 7.

2 Roll out two-thirds of the pastry to 3mm (⅛ in) thick. Cut into small circles big enough to line the tins, both base and sides, usually about 13cm (5 in) in diameter. Fill the pastry-lined tins with mincemeat.

3 Roll out the rest of the pastry to 3mm (⅛ in) thick and cut smaller circles as lids, usually about two-thirds the size of the bases (so about 7.5cm/3 in).

4 Dampen the edges of the bases with water and press the lids on securely. Make two little holes in the middle to allow the steam to escape. Brush with milk and dredge with sugar.

5 Bake in the preheated oven for about 15 minutes. Serve hot with some brandy butter slotted in under the lid.

Large Mincemeat Pie

225g (8 oz) sweet pastry
(see *Bakewell Tart* on page 150)

225g (8 oz) *Mincemeat* (see page 205)
milk and unrefined caster sugar to finish

1 Grease a 20–25cm (8–10 in) ovenproof plate and preheat the oven to 220°C/425°F/Gas 7.

2 Take half of the pastry and mould it carefully and quickly into a ball. Roll out to a round of 3mm (⅛ in) thick and put on the greased plate. Prick the bottom with a fork, then put in the mincemeat.

3 Roll out the remaining pastry into the same circular shape. Moisten the edges of the pastry round the mincemeat and place the second pastry circle on top. Push down to seal and trim off excess pastry around the plate. Crimp the edges to decorate. Brush with milk and dredge with sugar.

4 Bake in the preheated oven for about 35–40 minutes. Serve hot, again with brandy butter if you like.

- You could use suet pastry to make a mincemeat roly-poly (see the *Spotted Dick* recipe on page 154). Mincemeat would be good in a cheesecake as well.
- Sweet or shortcrust pastry would work as well as puff in the small pies. No reason why not.

Sausage Rolls

MAKES
ABOUT 6

Given our British love for sausages and for pastry, it can be no surprise that the two came together. However, despite their continuing appearances on buffet tables, at cocktail and children's parties, and at picnics, I can find no history for them at all. They were a standby in my dad's café, and I remember learning how to make them at grammar school cookery classes, taught by Miss Elsie Bibby every third week.

225g (8 oz) puff pastry

1 garlic clove, peeled and crushed

1 tbsp chopped fresh parsley

450g (1 lb) sausagemeat

salt and freshly ground black pepper

1 egg, beaten with a little water

1 Grease a baking sheet and preheat the oven to 220°C/425°F/Gas 7.

2 Roll out the pastry to a long strip 3mm (⅛ in) thick and 10cm (4 in) wide.

3 Mix the crushed garlic and the parsley with the sausagemeat, and season with salt and pepper. Roll into a sausage shape of about 2.5cm (1 in) in diameter.

4 Lay this sausage on top of the pastry just off centre, closer to the front. Brush the edges of the pastry with water, then fold the pastry over and seal by pushing down carefully.

5 Brush the top with egg wash, then score the top with a fork and brush again with egg wash. Cut the sausage pastry shape into 7.5cm (3 in) lengths.

6 Put on to the greased baking sheet and bake in the preheated oven for about 20 minutes. Serve hot or cold.

- You could make these very much smaller, and serve them as canapés.
- You can vary them in infinite ways. Use shortcrust instead of puff pastry, or indeed filo pastry, which you could deep-fry as you might a spring roll. You can add diced tomato, chilli, cheese, herbs or other spices to the sausagemeat. I've already done that here – my mother would not have countenanced the garlic, for instance... Another idea is to chop up some black pudding with the sausagemeat.

Shortbread

Shortbread biscuits appear all over Britain (in Shrewsbury cakes and the Goosenargh cakes from Lancashire, for instance, both containing caraway seeds), but they are most associated with Scotland. They are 'short' because they contain no liquid, and may be made as 'fingers' or 'petticoat tails'. I've done the latter here, although I haven't cut out a circle from the middle in the traditional way (to prevent broken points to the wedges).

Through John Grant, whose family make Glenfarclas, my favourite whisky, I met James Walker of Aberlour, whose family make the best commercial shortbread. I have encountered him on the odd occasion since, at food exhibitions and the like, and always seem to get a box of shortbread shortly afterwards! Not that I'm complaining...

225g (8 oz) unsalted butter, plus extra
  for greasing
115g (4 oz) unrefined caster sugar,
  plus extra for dredging

225g (8 oz) plain flour
115g (4 oz) rice flour
a pinch of salt

1 Lightly butter a baking sheet and preheat the oven to 160°C/325°F/Gas 3.
2 Cream the measured butter and sugar together until light.
3 Sift the flour, rice flour and salt together, and fold carefully into the butter mixture.
4 Split the mixture in two and shape each half into balls. Flatten each with the hands and put on to the baking sheet. Crimp the edges, then cut across the top, not quite through, into eighths. Prick the centres with a fork.
5 Bake in the preheated oven for 20 minutes, then turn the oven down to 140°C/275°F/Gas 1 and bake for a further 20–30 minutes.
6 Leave to cool. The shortbread will be soft baked at this stage, but as it cools it will crisp up. Dredge with sugar before serving.

■ The secrets of shortbread are: use the best ingredients possible (there are so few) and handle the dough as briefly as possible.

Oatcakes

MAKES 2
ROUNDS,
ABOUT 16
PIECES

Oatcakes were made all over the country, particularly in the areas where oats flourished – upland Wales, Yorkshire and northwards, and in Scotland. Most were simple amalgams of oatmeal, fat and water as here, some were raised by baking powder, and a few from Derbyshire, Staffordshire and Yorkshire were raised by yeast, making them more like thin drop scones or pikelets than the crisp biscuits we mostly associate the name with.

Oatcakes such as these are delicious with cheese, or for breakfast, but were once the staple diet of many a Scot. In the eighteenth and nineteenth centuries, a Scottish university mid-term holiday was known as 'Meal Monday', allowing the student time to go home and stock up on oatmeal, the source of his porridge, brose and oatcakes while he was away.

115g (4 oz) fine oatmeal

½ tsp salt

1 tbsp melted lard

4 tbsp hot water

1 Mix the oatmeal and salt in a bowl. Add the fat and water and bind together.
2 Roll out to 3mm (⅛ in) thick, using extra oatmeal dusted on the work surface. Cut into 7.5cm (3 in) diameter circles.
3 Heat a heavy frying pan or griddle and cook the cakes, with no fat, for 2–3 minutes on one side. Turn over then take off the heat. The residual heat of the pan will finish the second side off.
4 Cool thoroughly, then store in an airtight tin.

Mint Sauce and Cumberland Sauce (see pages 215 and 218)

Before refrigeration, a culinary priority was finding a way of preserving ingredients for winter consumption, when fresh produce was unavailable. Meat and fish were salted, dried and smoked from very early on. Many of these techniques were said to have been learned from the invading Vikings although, oddly, we do not seem to have taken to the dried cod and stockfish that they introduced, to such long-lasting effect, in Iberia and the Mediterranean.

The flavours of these preserved meats and fish would have been rather strong, and

Preserves, Sauces and Accompaniments

indeed even fresh meat could probably have been rather high once it was eaten, leading to a generous addition of spices to mask any off tastes. Gluts of vegetables were not mild on the palate either, once preserved in salt and/or vinegar. This enforced familiarity with intensely sharp, salty and spicy flavours may explain why we British have invented and are so keen on all the pickles, ketchups, chutneys and sauces for which we have become renowned. You don't find bottled brown sauce on the Continent, or even the tanginess of mint or horseradish sauces. The famous commercial Worcestershire sauce – believed to be based on a recipe from the East – is another good example of the British penchant for the piquant.

Sweet preserves are a different kettle of fish (so to speak). Gluts of fruit needed to be preserved in much the same way as vegetables, but in a sweet preservative rather than salt or vinegar. Before sugar became more readily available in the eighteenth century, honey would have been used, and sweet quinces, cherries and plums, and sourer gooseberries, crab apples and rosehips, would have been put in containers to be enjoyed through the winter months. Jams, jellies and marmalade are all examples of this early British culinary thrift, as are what we call fruit 'curds', 'butters' and 'cheeses'.

Early British preserves were made to last, preferably throughout the winter, but today we don't need to bother with that. Try some of these simple recipes – it's good fun! – but eat them up quickly, as there are no E numbers here...

Pickled Onions

MAKES ABOUT
900g (2 lb)

Pickles have been around in Britain for much longer than ketchups or chutneys, and it was probably the taste for spicy, tangy, vinegary pickles that led to the introduction of the other two. Vegetables (and fruit) have been pickled since very early on, as they needed to be preserved for winter eating. The word 'pickle' comes from the German '*pekel*' which means 'brine', apt since most vegetables to be pickled in vinegar are brined first. This reduces the moisture content of the vegetable, ensuring a crisper texture.

Pickled onions are one of the country's favourite pickles, powerfully good with cold meats and with cheese (the proverbial ploughman's). At home we always had some on the table and ate them with fish and chips (you still see pickled onions, eggs and gherkins in chippies), and with meat pies. I think they're quite addictive…

900g (2 lb) small pickling onions
  (or shallots)
115g (4 oz) salt
850ml (1½ pints) water
450ml (15 fl oz) malt vinegar
450ml (15 fl oz) white malt vinegar

1 x 2.5cm (1 in) piece fresh root ginger,
  squashed
20 black peppercorns
1 tsp ground allspice
2 small fresh red chillies

1 Peel the onions and put them into a bowl.
2 Mix the salt and water together, pour over the onions, and leave to soak for 24 hours.
3 Rinse the onions in fresh water and put them into a sterilised glass jar. Bring the vinegars, ginger, peppercorns, allspice and chillies to the boil together, and pour over the onions.
4 Cool, then cover, and leave in a dark place for four to six weeks before opening and eating.

Tomato Ketchup

MAKES ABOUT
450ml
(15 fl oz)

Both tomatoes and the idea of 'ketchup' are fairly new in British culinary terms. The word 'ketchup', which comes from the Chinese name for a fermented fish sauce, did not enter the language until the seventeenth century and tomatoes, although known in Europe in the sixteenth century, did not become familiar (not necessarily *popular*) until well into the late eighteenth century.

Sharp sauces, pickled vegetables and other accompaniments, though, had always been popular, and many gradually acquired the name of 'ketchup', among them mushroom, anchovy, walnut and, eventually, the new-fangled tomato. America was first with its famous, commercially produced tomato 'catsup', and we in Britain have followed enthusiastically, even allying it with our much more traditional fish and chips.

175ml (6 fl oz) red wine vinegar
125g (4 oz) unrefined caster sugar
24 large ripe tomatoes

a couple of dashes each of Tabasco sauce
 and Worcestershire sauce

1 Bring the red wine vinegar and sugar to the boil together, stirring until the sugar has dissolved.
2 Meanwhile, skin the tomatoes, remove the seeds, then finely chop the flesh.
3 Add the tomato flesh to the vinegar and boil quickly until the tomatoes 'melt' and the sauce becomes smooth.
4 Remove from the heat and add the two seasoning sauces. Stir in and leave to cool.

■ Commercial ketchup is made very differently, but the simplicity of this recipe makes it very special in my book. Because it is so simple, it will not last long.

Fruit Chutney

MAKES ABOUT
1.8kg (4 lb)

Like 'ketchup', 'chutney' is an imported word, derived from the Hindi '*chatni*', meaning hot or spiced relish, and is a relic of the Raj. In India, the preserve would have been made with mangoes, limes or tamarind, but when the sahibs (or, more importantly, the memsahibs) retired to Britain, they quickly adapted the idea to use native fruit such as apples, pears, plums, gooseberries and green tomatoes.

just over 450g (1 lb) pears

just over 675g (1½ lb) apples

juice of 1 lemon

225g (8 oz) stoned dates

700ml (1¼ pints) malt vinegar

225g (8 oz) onions, peeled

1 fresh red chilli, seeded

1 tbsp salt

1 tbsp ground ginger

½ tsp dry mustard powder

225g (8 oz) unrefined soft brown sugar

1 Wash, peel and core the pears and apples. Make sure you have 1.1kg (2½ lb) in weight.

2 Dice 225g (8 oz) each of the pears and apples, and put to one side in a bowl of water acidulated with the lemon juice.

3 Put the rest of the apples and pears, plus the stoned dates, through the mincer.

4 Put into a pan with the vinegar, bring to the boil and simmer for 10 minutes.

5 Finely chop the onions and chilli and add to the pot along with the salt, ginger, mustard and sugar.

6 Drain and squeeze excess moisture from the diced pears and apples and add to the pan. Simmer for 20 minutes, then allow to cool.

7 Put into sterilised jars, cover with clingfilm and non-corrosive lids, and leave for at least 48 hours before eating, and for up to a month or so. As it ages it will become less acid.

■ This would go well with curry or cold meats, and I like it in toasted cheese (see page 38). At Turner's we served a chutney like this with a sweetbread terrine.

Banana Chutney

MAKES ABOUT 1.8kg (4 lb)

Bananas could very well have been included in the original Indian chutneys, for they are native to south-east Asia. As they did not travel well from their tropical homelands, they did not become common in Europe until the advent of steamships and refrigerated ships at about the end of the nineteenth and the beginning of the twentieth centuries. I still remember my astonishment at the look and taste of my first banana in the early 1950s, when shipments from the Caribbean started again after the war.

225g (8 oz) sultanas

850ml (1½ pints) malt vinegar

350g (12 oz) unrefined soft brown sugar

1 tsp turmeric

1 tsp curry powder

1 tsp salt

½ tsp ground ginger

225g (8 oz) stoned dates

450g (1 lb) onions, peeled

10 medium bananas, peeled

1 Chop the sultanas and then soak them in the vinegar overnight.

2 The next day, add the sugar, turmeric, curry powder, salt and ginger.

3 Finely chop the dates and onions and add to the other ingredients in a heavy-bottomed pot. Cut the bananas up roughly and add to the pot.

4 Bring up to the boil, then simmer gently until cooked, about 30 minutes. Pot in sterilised jars when cool, and you can eat it virtually straightaway.

■ Use as the fruit chutney opposite. It will be slightly sweeter.

Piccalilli

MAKES ABOUT
1.6–1.8kg
(3½–4 lb)

Nobody quite knows where this particular pickle got its name, but it must be related to the word 'pickle'. It probably originated later than other traditional British pickles, because it includes so many spices imported from India. The turmeric is used for both flavour and colour, and it is this and the generous use of the British-grown mustard that distinguishes piccalilli from its other relatives.

Our Sunday high tea table when I was a child would always have a jar of home-made piccalilli to go with the cold meats on offer.

450g (1 lb) small cauliflower florets

225g (8 oz) vegetable marrow or courgette, cut into 1cm (½ in) dice

225g (8 oz) small button onions, peeled

450g (1 lb) runner beans, cut into 5mm (¼ in) dice

225g (8 oz) cucumber, cut into 5mm (¼ in) dice

350g (12 oz) salt

1.2 litres (2 pints) white vinegar plus 1 tbsp

a pinch of curry powder

45g (1½ oz) dry English mustard powder

175g (6 oz) unrefined caster sugar

25g (1 oz) piece fresh root ginger, bruised

6 black peppercorns

1 fresh red chilli

25g (1 oz) plain flour

15g (½ oz) turmeric

1 Prepare the vegetables and spread on a deep tray. Sprinkle with the salt and 1.2 litres (2 pints) water, and leave for 24 hours. Rinse and drain.

2 Put the vegetables into a non-reactive pan with the bulk of the vinegar, the curry powder, mustard and sugar. Put the ginger, peppercorns and chilli in a muslin bag and add as well. Bring up to the boil and simmer for 20 minutes.

3 Blend the flour and turmeric with the remaining tbsp of vinegar, add to the mixture, and bring up to the boil. Cook for 3–5 minutes until thickened.

4 Leave to cool, then pot in sterilised jars. Cover with clingfilm and store in a cool dry place. It can be eaten virtually straight away.

■ Piccalilli does mature, though, and you'll often find it has a softer, rounder flavour if you leave it for at least three to four weeks.

Mincemeat

MAKES ABOUT
900g (2 lb)

In the Middle Ages, we British used to love sweet meat mixtures, and mincemeat is actually very medieval in flavour. It would once have contained meat – beef, lamb or offal – but the only remnant of that now is the beef suet. However, as late as the 1860s, Francatelli, chef to Queen Victoria, gave four recipes for mincemeat in his *A Plain Cookery Book for the Working Classes*. These were all price based: the cheapest, at 9d, was made with tripe. Hard to believe, but true. Could you imagine this today?

115g (4 oz) chopped beef suet

115g (4 oz) each of chopped mixed peel, currants, sultanas and raisins

2 apples, peeled, cored and finely diced

175g (6 oz) unrefined demerara sugar

finely grated zest and juice of 1 lemon

finely grated zest and juice of 1 orange

1 tsp ground mixed spice

½ tsp freshly grated nutmeg

75ml (2½ fl oz) each of rum and brandy

1 Make sure that all the chopped items are very finely chopped.

2 Mix all the ingredients together, then put into a bowl. Cover with clingfilm, pushing it on to the surfaces of the mincemeat – you don't want any air to get to it.

3 Allow to stand for 1 week in the fridge before using. It could last longer, but it's so delicious I don't think it'll get the chance.

■ Use this mincemeat in things like mincemeat roly-poly, mincemeat cheesecake, and *Mince Pies* (see page 193).

Strawberry Jam

MAKES ABOUT
1.3kg (3 lb)

Sweet preserves or jams are common and traditional all over Europe. Before sugar became more readily available, in the eighteenth century, honey would have been used to preserve fruits such as quinces, cherries, plums and raspberries. At one time jams would have been made with gluts of fruits, and they would last, hopefully, until the fruit season came round again. That's not so necessary nowadays, but it's still fun to make jam.

Although strawberries are the most difficult of the lot to turn into a jam – they lack the natural pectin vital for a good set – strawberry jam is somehow the one most revered. Lemon juice is used to supply the pectin, as is redcurrant juice, and this recipe, although very simple, is quite delicious.

1.1kg (2½ lb) strawberries

1.3kg (3 lb) unrefined granulated sugar

150ml (5 fl oz) redcurrant juice

juice of 1 lemon

15g (½ oz) unsalted butter

1 Put the strawberries into a large heavy-bottomed pan and heat gently.

2 As the juice starts to come out, add the sugar and stir until dissolved. Add the two juices.

3 Bring the mixture to the boil and remove any scum. Boil rapidly, testing for setting point every 15 minutes (see opposite). Take the pan off the heat to do this.

4 When setting point has been reached, add the butter. Allow the jam to cool slightly before putting into sterilised jars. Before doing this, give the jam a stir to move the fruit around.

5 Keep for a couple of days before eating, and eat within a couple of weeks.

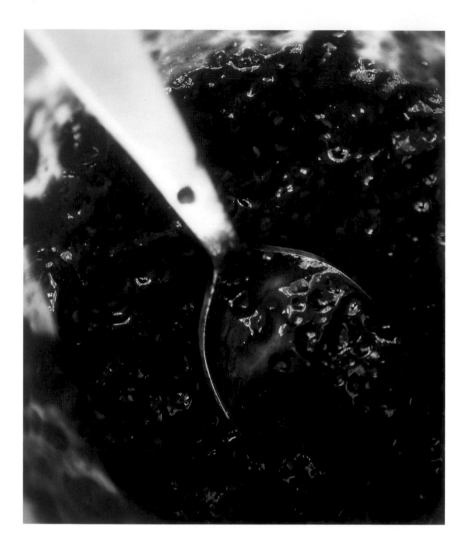

- Individual jams and jellies have individual setting points, which you can test with a sugar thermometer: dip it in hot water, then sink the bulb end into the jam. If the temperature is around 105°C/220°F, the jam has reached setting point.
- However, it is just as simple to keep several small saucers in the fridge. When you think the jam has reached setting point, take the pan off the heat and put a tsp of jam on the cold saucer. Let it cool for a few seconds – count to ten – then push the surface with your finger. If the surface wrinkles, the jam is ready. If the jam is 'loose', it needs to be boiled for a few minutes more and tested again.

Marmalade

MAKES ABOUT
1.3kg (3 lb)

Marmalade is thought of as very Scottish, but the idea is based on those solid and long-keeping confections popular on the Continent such as the Spanish 'dulce de membrillo' and the French 'coing' (in fact quite similar to our own fruit cheeses). The story goes that when Janet Keiller's husband bought some Seville oranges off a ship in their native Dundee at the turn of the eighteenth century, she made a preserve from them. This was based loosely on a recipe for 'marmelo', a Portuguese quince paste she had encountered previously. She altered the recipe though, making the preserve less solid, in order to fill more jars – she was a thrifty Scot, after all. (And the Keiller marmalade factory, which was founded thereafter, in 1797, was also where the Dundee Cake – see page 191 – is said to have originated.)

Most of Iberia's Seville orange crop in January is destined for the UK and marmalade manufacture. And, in case you didn't know, Dundee marmalade has shredded peel, while Oxford marmalade uses thick-cut peel…

900g (2 lb) oranges

1.4 litres (2½ pints) water

900g (2 lb) unrefined caster sugar

juice of 2 lemons

1 Wash the oranges well and put in a preserving pan with the water. Slowly boil in the water for around 1½–2 hours then take out and cool. Keep the water.

2 Carefully cut off the peel, leaving the pith behind. Mince or shred the peel – I prefer to mince it.

3 Peel the pith from the oranges with a sharp knife and discard. Take out the pips and wrap them in a muslin bag.

4 Cut the peeled oranges into halves and then slice thinly.

5 Put the orange slices into the orange water, then add the minced peel and the muslin bag of pips. Bring to the boil and simmer for 5 minutes.

6 Take off the heat, then add the sugar and lemon juice. Stir until the sugar has dissolved.

7 Put back on to the heat and bring up to the boil quickly. Test for setting after 15 minutes (see page 207).

8 If the marmalade is ready keep the pan off the heat and allow it to cool for 20 minutes. If not ready, put back on to the heat and bring back to the simmer. Check every 2 minutes.

9 When the marmalade has rested, stir and bottle in sterilised jars.

■ Most marmalades are made from Seville oranges, but this one, with less sugar, can be made from ordinary sweet oranges at any time of year.

Apple and Rowan Jelly

MAKES ABOUT
1.3–1.8kg
(3–4 lb)

Fruit jellies are wonderful preserves and have long been made by thrifty British housewives. They are a good way of using up gluts of fruit, fruit that is not perfect enough to eat, and a good way of supplying a tart-sweet accompaniment to many other dishes.

You can use redcurrants, quinces, crab apples, blackberries, plums or damsons, rosehips, gooseberries, grapes – and indeed herbs (with green cooking apples as the pectin source).

900g (2 lb) apples
1.3kg (3 lb) rowanberries

unrefined granulated sugar

1 Clean the fruit carefully and drain and dry. Cut the apples up roughly.
2 Put into a big pot with enough water just to cover, bring to the boil and simmer gently for 1 hour.
3 Carefully strain the juice through a jelly bag suspended above a bowl. Do not press, as the resultant juice will become cloudy. Be patient.
4 Measure the juice and put into a clean pot. For every 600ml (1 pint) juice, add 450g (1 lb) sugar.
5 Simmer and stir together until the sugar melts, then simmer gently until the jelly reaches setting point (see page 207). Test regularly.
6 Decant into sterilised jars, cool then cover with clingfilm. The jelly should last well for at least three weeks.

■ The principle is the same for most fruit jellies. So long as you have something with pectin in it (apples, lemons etc.), you should be successful. Try any of the fruits mentioned in the introduction above.

Lemon Curd

MAKES ABOUT 450g (1 lb)

The modern lemon curd is of fairly recent origins – the 1800s – and is a direct descendant of the flavoured curd fillings that had been used in pastry tarts since the Middle Ages. Curd, the lumpy protein and fat part of curdled milk (and the basis of most cheeses), was mixed with eggs and flavoured (the lemon only arrived in the late seventeenth century). Yorkshire boasts several curd tarts of this kind, and the famous Richmond Maids of Honour are basically small curd cakes.

Lemon curd was probably developed as a filling for tarts, although gradually it lost the curds, being made only with sugar, butter and eggs, and only very slowly would its other qualities have emerged – its spreadability on bread or on cake as a filling. You can make fruit curds with a variety of fruit.

My mother used to make lemon curd like this, but she called it 'lemon cheese', a prime example of the confusion there has always been in this area.

225g (8 oz) unrefined cube sugar
4 lemons, washed
115g (4 oz) unsalted butter

2 eggs
2 egg yolks

1 Rub the sugar lumps over three of the lemons to soak up the essential oils from the zest, and put into the top of a double saucepan or a bowl over simmering water.
2 Finely grate the rind of the fourth lemon into the pan, and then add the juice of all the lemons. Add the butter and gently melt these together.
3 Beat the eggs and yolks together lightly. Pour some of the hot mixture into the eggs, stirring continuously, then scrape back into the pan.
4 Heat gently, stirring continuously, until the mixture thickens enough to coat the back of a wooden spoon, about 30 minutes.
5 Leave to cool a little, then pot in small jars. Cover and seal when cold, then store in the fridge for no longer than two to four weeks (if you have the patience – I bet you haven't!).

Sage and Onion Stuffing

SERVES 4–6   A stuffing is hardly a preserve or a sauce, but it is almost as traditional an accompaniment to meats of all sorts as horseradish sauce or piccalilli. Birds and rolled pieces of meat have been stuffed with savoury fillings for centuries. Some of the most classic have got a seasonal nicety about them – the chestnuts with turkey for instance.

2 medium onions, peeled and finely chopped

55g (2 oz) pork dripping (lard will do)

1 tbsp chopped fresh sage

115g (4 oz) fresh white breadcrumbs

1 egg, beaten

salt and freshly ground black pepper

25g (1 oz) unsalted butter

1 Preheat the oven to 200°C/400°F/Gas 6.
2 Slowly fry the onion in the lard to soften, but do not colour. Take off the heat and add the sage, breadcrumbs, beaten egg and some salt and pepper.
3 Put in a small buttered ovenproof dish and bake in the preheated oven for 20–30 minutes until well coloured.

■ I am cooking the stuffing separately here, but you can of course stuff it into a bird, but remember to do so at the neck end, not in the cavity.
■ You could cook the stuffing rolled into individual balls, or you could roll it into a sausage inside foil and roast so that it could be sliced.
■ You could add chopped apple or bacon to the basic stuffing, or indeed some chopped dried apricots as in the photograph.

Apple Sauce

SERVES 8

It is said that traditional 'tracklements', or accompaniments, for animals should be made from ingredients on which the animals might have fed. Lamb could possibly have eaten wild mint or redcurrants, I suppose, but I find it hard to think of cattle enjoying horseradish! However, pigs being allowed to wander in apple orchards, eating up the windfalls, is a much more likely scenario, and apple sauce remains a wonderful accompaniment to pork, its sharpness cutting the sweetness and fattiness of the pork. (In Italy, the first food of some suckling pigs is windfall persimmons or sharon fruit, and their flesh is pink, tender and very sweet.)

450g (1 lb) cooking apples

75ml (2½ fl oz) dry cider

25g (1 oz) unrefined caster sugar

55g (2 oz) unsalted butter

a twist of freshly ground black pepper

1 Peel and core the apples. Chop them roughly and put into a non-reactive pan with the cider, sugar and butter. Put on a tight-fitting lid and cook slowly to a purée.

2 Season with black pepper, then pass through a sieve or blend in a liquidiser.

3 Reheat gently to serve.

■ If you use dessert apples, leave out the sugar. This is meant to be a tart, not sweet, sauce.

■ Try chopping some fresh marjoram into the sauce as you serve.

Mint Sauce

SERVES 4–6

In the Middle Ages, they used to love sweet and sour, herbal flavours in sauces, and this may be a relic of those tastes. Or it could be a reflection of the tradition, found all over Europe, of eating young lamb with bitter herbs (at Easter usually). It's the vinegar content of our mint sauce that the French object to, apparently, forgetting that there are many such sharp sauces in their own cuisine. The sweet redcurrant (or rowan) jelly often eaten with lamb as well (see page 210), can counter-balance the sharpness of the other.

We like mint a lot in this country, often putting a bunch in with the new potatoes or peas. In the north of England we actually eat mint sauce with peas, meat pies and a host of other foods. A famous northern chef was eating in Langan's Brasserie recently, and demanded some mint sauce to eat with his fish, chips and mushy peas. Nobody blinked…

3 tbsp chopped fresh mint leaves

1 tbsp unrefined caster sugar

freshly ground black pepper

150ml (5 fl oz) white malt vinegar

(or white wine vinegar)

1 Mix the mint with the sugar in a bowl, and give it a couple of good turns of the peppermill.

2 Stir in the vinegar and do a taste test. If it is too sharp, add a dash of water. Use within a couple of hours.

Horseradish Sauce

Horseradish was introduced to Europe from Asia, and to Britain from Germany apparently, where they use it a lot in sauces. Although we think its association with roast beef must be as old as the hills, it seems only to have been around since the beginning of the nineteenth century.

The flavour is incredibly pungent, but is the pain of peeling and grating worth it? The grated stuff in jars is fine, and is easy to find and use along with the other ingredients.

25g (1 oz) freshly grated horseradish

1 tbsp white wine vinegar

150ml (5 fl oz) double cream

salt and freshly ground black pepper

a squeeze of lemon juice

1 Mix the horseradish and vinegar together.

2 Lightly whip the cream, then season it with salt, pepper and lemon juice.

3 Mix the horseradish and cream mixtures together well. Use within a day or so.

Stand well back when you peel and grate fresh horseradish root, as the effect is ten times worse than peeling the strongest onion!

■ Use horseradish or horseradish sauce in various ways. It's particularly good with smoked meats or, perhaps surprisingly, smoked fish. It can also be added to mashed potatoes, and a horseradish mash can be made into a potato cake and fried like bubble and squeak.

Cumberland Sauce

SERVES 8

It was Elizabeth David who suggested that this sauce might have been named after Queen Victoria's uncle, the Duke of Cumberland. As the sauce is very German in feel, and he was the last independent ruler of Hanover, this could be correct. The recipe also first appeared in cookery books during Victoria's reign, and became a vital accompaniment to game dishes. We serve it with ham mostly now, but it's good with any cold meat. At The Capital we served scallop mousse with horseradish and Cumberland sauce.

Oxford sauce is very similar, but uses only the zest of the orange, not the juice.

1 orange
1 shallot, peeled and finely chopped
juice of ½ lemon

150ml (5 fl oz) port
a pinch of cayenne pepper
350g (12 oz) redcurrant jelly

1 Cut the zest from the orange, leaving behind any pith, and then cut it into fine julienne strips. Squeeze the juice from the denuded orange.
2 Put all the ingredients except the jelly into a pan and slowly simmer to reduce to one-third of its original volume. Pour into a bowl.
3 Whisk or liquidise the redcurrant jelly, then pour into the bowl. Mix well.

Wine Sauce

SERVES 4

There's nothing particularly British about this wine sauce, although we have been flavouring sauces with wines for centuries. In the Middle Ages it was verjuice, the juice of unripe grapes (all English grapes were good for, I should think).

This simple and straightforward sauce was taught to me by Eric Scamman, my mentor at The Savoy, and can add flavour and texture to many dishes. Make it with white wine, red wine, sherry, port or Madeira, or even with Cognac.

25g (1 oz) unsalted butter

2 shallots, peeled and finely chopped

300ml (10 fl oz) wine or spirit of choice

150ml (5 fl oz) white wine

600ml (1 pint) veal stock

115g (4 oz) butter, cold and chopped

salt and freshly ground black pepper

1 tsp fécule (potato flour), slaked in 1 tbsp white wine

1 Melt the unsalted butter in a pan, add the shallots, and sweat to soften, but do not colour.

2 Add your chosen wine or spirit, plus the white wine. Bring to the boil and reduce to nearly nothing, to what we call a syrup.

3 Add the veal stock to this intensely flavoured syrup, bring to the boil and reduce by one-third.

4 Shake in the chopped cold butter and check the seasoning.

5 Thicken slightly over a gentle heat, using the fécule and white wine.

6 Pass through a fine sieve and serve.

■ As to which sauce to serve with which meats, there are no real rules. A red wine sauce goes with the big red meats, beef and lamb. A white wine sauce is good with pork or chicken. A Madeira sauce is ideal with fillet of beef, or *Beef Wellington* (see page 82), and a port sauce accompanies kidneys, liver and game birds. Cognac is good with kidneys, chicken and beef, and sherry is delicious with offal, chicken and pork.

Custard Sauce

SERVES 4–6 Eggs and milk are basic ingredients in any cuisine, and most countries have several custard dishes. The English name comes from 'crustade', meaning a pastry case, in which custards were originally cooked (and Fullerton's in Morley High Street still sells custard tarts to die for). The sauce evolved from the baked puddings, and has become so indissolubly associated with Britain that the French call it '*crème anglaise*'. An accolade indeed!

This is a rich version, and although it is a little more difficult to make than simply opening a tin or carton, or mixing custard powder with milk (how times have changed!), it's well worth it.

450ml (15 fl oz) milk
300ml (10 fl oz) double cream
1 vanilla pod

6 egg yolks
4 tbsp unrefined caster sugar

1 Put the milk and double cream into a pan. Scrape the vanilla seeds from the pod into the pan, add the pod as well, and bring up to the boil. Pull to one side of the stove, off the heat.

2 Meanwhile, whisk the egg yolks, then add the sugar, and whisk until the sugar has dissolved.

3 Pour the warm milk over the egg yolks and stir well. Put back into the pan and, stirring continuously with a wooden spoon, bring back to heat, but do not boil. (A double boiler might be safer, if you have one.)

4 When the custard thickens sufficiently to coat the back of the wooden spoon, about 4–5 minutes, take off the heat and pour into an old-fashioned custard jug.

- If not using the sauce immediately, put a piece of buttered greaseproof on the top of it to prevent a skin forming. Or use a butter wrapper – waste not, want not!
- To re-use, either hot or cold, mix with some double cream. Even more luxurious!

Index

Acknowledgements

Thanks are due to a number of people, not least all those who have written about British food over the last few decades, and whose expertise was invaluable in my researches. I am hugely grateful to my editor, Susan Fleming, who pulled it all together and made it fun. Thanks also to my agent Laura Morris, to the Headline gang – particularly Heather Holden-Brown, Lorraine Jerram and Bryone Picton – and to those involved in the wonderful photography: William Shaw, Lisa Pettibone, Annabel Ford and Roisin Nield. A special mention too for the team at designsection, who have made the book look great. Finally a big thank you to Jon Jon Lucas, Gerard O'Sullivan and Paul Bates for their help in advising and testing recipes, to Louise Hewitt in the office and, last but not least, to my wife and sons.